FINANCIAL DECISION MAKING
UNDER UNCERTAINTY

FINANCIAL DECISION MAKING UNDER UNCERTAINTY

Edited by

Haim Levy   and   Marshall Sarnat

University of Florida
Gainesville, Florida
and
The Hebrew University
of Jerusalem
Israel

The Hebrew University
of Jerusalem
Israel

ACADEMIC PRESS   New York   San Francisco   London   1977
A Subsidiary of Harcourt Brace Jovanovich, Publishers

ACADEMIC PRESS, INC.
111 Fifth Avenue, New York, New York 10003

United Kingdom Edition published by
ACADEMIC PRESS, INC. (LONDON) LTD.
24/28 Oval Road, London NW1

Library of Congress Cataloging in Publication Data

Main entry under title:

Financial decision making under uncertainty.

    (Economic theory and mathematical economics)
    Includes bibliographies and index.
    1.   Finance—Mathematical models.   2.   Investments—
Mathematical models.   3.   Risk—Mathematical models.
I.   Levy, Haim.   II.   Sarnat, Marshall.
HG174.F48   658.1'5   77-4572
ISBN 0-12-445850-5

CONTENTS

PART II   INVESTMENT DECISIONS UNDER UNCERTAINTY

The Demand for Risky Assets: Some Extensions
Irwin Friend

Optimal Timing of Capital Expenditures
Myron J. Gordon

Leasing, Buying, and the Cost of Capital Services
Merton H. Miller and Charles W. Upton

PART III   PORTFOLIO ANALYSIS AND CAPITAL MARKET THEORY

The Capital Asset Pricing Model: A "Multi-Beta" Interpretation
William F. Sharpe

Portfolio Efficiency Analysis in Three Moments: The Multiperiod Case
Fred D. Arditti and Haim Levy

Equivalence among Alternative Portfolio Selection Criteria
D. Kira and W. T. Ziemba

PART IV   INFLATION AND FINANCIAL DECISIONS

The Superfund: Efficient Paths toward Efficient Capital Markets in Large and Small Countries
Nils H. Hakansson

PART V   APPLICATIONS OF RISK ANALYSIS

Default Risk and the Demand for Forward Exchange
Michael Adler and Bernard Dumas

Optimal Coupon Rate, Taxes, and Collusion between Borrower and Lender
Fred D. Arditti and Yoram C. Peles

An Optimal Screening Policy for R & D Projects
Arie Melnik and Moshe A. Pollatschek

Optimal Investment and Financing Patterns under Alternative Methods of Regulation
Edwin J. Elton and Martin J. Gruber

LIST OF CONTRIBUTORS

Numbers in parentheses indicate the pages on which the authors' contributions begin.

Michael Adler (205), Graduate School of Business, Columbia University, New York, New York

Fred D. Arditti (137, 237), School of Business Administration, University of Florida, Gainesville, Florida

Bernard Dumas (205), E.S.S.E.C., Cergy, France

Edwin J. Elton (265), Department of Finance, Graduate School of Business, New York University, New York, New York

Irwin Friend (65), Rodney L. White Center for Financial Research, The Wharton School, University of Pennsylvania, Philadelphia, Pennsylvania

Myron J. Gordon (83), Faculty of Management Studies, University of Toronto, Toronto, Ontario, Canada

Martin J. Gruber (265), Department of Finance, Graduate School of Business, New York University, New York, New York

Nils H. Hakansson (165), University of California, Berkeley, California

D. Kira (151), The University of British Columbia, Vancouver, British Columbia, Canada

Haim Levy (137), The Hebrew University, Jerusalem, Israel

Harry M. Markowitz (3), IBM Thomas J. Watson Research Center, Yorktown Heights, New York

Arie Melnik (251), Faculty of Industrial and Management Engineering, Technion—Israel Institute of Technology, Haifa, Israel

Merton H. Miller (95), Graduate School of Business, University of Chicago, Chicago, Illinois

Yoram C. Peles (237), The Hebrew University, Jerusalem, Israel

ix

Moshe A. Pollatschek (251), Faculty of Industrial and Management Engineering, Technion—Israel Institute of Technology, Haifa, Israel

Mark Rubinstein (11), Graduate School of Business Administration, University of California, Berkeley, California

William F. Sharpe (127), Graduate School of Business, Stanford University, Stanford, California

Charles W. Upton (95), Graduate School of Business, The University of Chicago, Chicago, Illinois

W. T. Ziemba (151), Faculty of Commerce and Business Administration, The University of British Columbia, Vancouver, British Columbia, Canada

PREFACE

The two and one-half decades that have elapsed since Harry Markowitz first applied the von Neumann–Morgenstern theory of expected utility to financial analysis have proved to be a period of great intellectual ferment. Accepted ideas and theories were critically examined, refined, extended, or, what is much more difficult, on occasion even discarded. But perhaps the salient feature of these years has been the ever increasing application of the new approach to financial decision making under uncertainty to a myriad of practical problems, many of which had hitherto escaped rigorous analysis.

Although one score and five is a relatively short period of time in which to assess the impact of any theory, it does seem adequate to support a "progress report" of sorts. This book brings together a number of papers that we feel can provide some fundamental insight into the current state of the art. As befits a young and dynamic subject, we try to achieve this goal, not through learned reviews of what already has been accomplished, but rather by presenting the reader with a representative cross section of papers by leading scholars dealing with a wide variety of actual problems. This reflects our own personal bias that the best way to learn any profession, e.g., carpentry, is to observe a master craftsman in action and then go out and try to emulate his work. Thus, this book should be considered as a first step in the two-stage process of "learning by doing," and as such is intended to serve as supplementary reading for a graduate course (or advanced undergraduate seminar) in financial theory.

Much of the responsibility for the book lies with a remarkable team of people in Jerusalem who organize the Israel Scientific Research Conferences for the National Council of Research and Development. In March 1975 an international group of scholars met at the invitation of the National Council at Ein Bokek on the shores of the Dead Sea to discuss the theory of financial decision making under uncertainty with special emphasis on its application in practice. Ein Bokek lies 400 meters below sea level, the lowest spot on earth, and has witnessed many dramas throughout history. To the south, a ruined Roman fortress was within walking distance, while 15 kilometers northward the participants could visit Herod's great stronghold of Massada, or go on to the beautiful nature reserve of Ein Gedi, the spot where David sought refuge from the anger of King Saul. The conference was designed to encourage the free exchange of ideas, and at times the animated discussion and debate almost seemed to recall the "wrath of Saul." This book provides a more tangible momento of what was, for us at least, a very memorable experience.

The publication of these papers also provides a very welcome opportunity to express, on behalf of all the participants, our gratitude to Dr. Schabtai Gairon, the Coordinator of ISRACON, and to Linda Cohen and Joy Lipson of his staff, as well as to Avraham Beja, Arie Melnik, and Meyer Ungar who served on the organizing committee. Finally, we wish to thank Marcia Don who very capably handled the not inconsiderable administrative task of seeing the manuscript through its publication.

Part I

UTILITY AND RISK ANALYSIS

AN ALGORITHM FOR FINDING UNDOMINATED PORTFOLIOS

Harry M. Markowitz

IBM Thomas J. Watson Research Center

I. Introduction

Let r_{it} be the return on the ith security in period t; $i = 1$ to N, $t = 1$ to T. "t" may represent a historical period or a sample from a complex model of joint returns (e.g., "complex" in the sense that the problem of finding undominated portfolios cannot be solved analytically). Let X_i be the amount invested in the ith security. The return on the portfolio as a whole in period t is

$$R_t = \sum_{i=1}^{N} X_i r_{it}, \qquad t = 1 \text{ to } T \tag{1}$$

While the matrix of returns (r_{it}) is in fact a sample—from history or from a model—we shall henceforth treat the columns of this matrix as the entire (finite) population of possible joint returns, each column having the same probability of occurrence. This paper presents an algorithm for finding port-

The author is indebted to Haim Levy for posing the problem presented here, for helping with its solution, and for comments on the first draft of this paper. Subsequent to the presentation of this paper, an alternate and perhaps superior algorithm has been designed and programmed by Bezalel Gavish of the Israel Scientific Center, IBM Israel Ltd., Haifa.

folios which are second-order stochastically undominated in the sense of Hadar and Russell [1], Hammond [2], and Hanoch and Levy [3].

Let

$$Z_1 = \text{Min } R_i, \qquad Z_2 = \underset{i \neq j}{\text{Min }} R_i + R_j$$

and, in general,

$$Z_K = \text{Min } R_{i_1} + R_{i_2} + \cdots + R_{i_K} \qquad \text{for} \quad K = 1 \text{ to } T \tag{2}$$

where the minimization is over sets of distinct indices $(i_1, i_2, \ldots, i_K)$ such that $i_j \neq i_k$ provided $j \neq k$. Writing $Z_0 = 0$, we define

$$V_t = Z_t - Z_{t-1} \qquad \text{for} \quad t = 1 \text{ to } T \tag{3a}$$

The inverse relationship is

$$Z_t = \sum_{i=1}^{t} V_i \qquad \text{for} \quad t = 1 \text{ to } T \tag{3b}$$

The cumulative probability distribution of returns provided by a portfolio is a step function $F(R)$ with steps at $V_1 \leq V_2 \leq V_3 \leq \cdots \leq V_T$. If all the V_t are distinct, then each step is of size $1/T$. If

$$V_{t-1} < V_t = V_{t+1} = \cdots = V_{t+n-1} < V_{t+n}$$

then $F(R)$ has a step of size n/T at $X = V_t = V_{t+1} = \cdots$.

A portfolio is undominated in the "first-order" sense if there is no other portfolio with

$$V_t^* > V_t \quad \text{for some } t \qquad \text{and} \qquad V_t^* \geq V_t \quad \text{for all } t$$

where the V_t^* define the cumulative distribution for "the other" portfolio. We show in the next section that a portfolio is undominated in the "second order" sense if there is no other portfolio with

$$Z_t^* > Z_t \quad \text{for some } t \qquad \text{and} \qquad Z_t^* \geq Z_t \quad \text{for all } t \tag{4a}$$

An investor who maximizes the expected value of a concave utility function will choose some second-order undominated portfolios. Such portfolios form a subset of the first-order undominated portfolios.

If

$$\beta_t > 0 \qquad \text{for} \quad t = 1 \text{ to } T$$

are given constants, then a portfolio which maximizes

$$\phi = \sum_{i=1}^{T} \beta_t Z_t \tag{4b}$$

must satisfy condition (4a) (else $Z^* = (Z_1^*, \ldots, Z_T^*)$ would have a greater value of ϕ), and hence must be undominated in the second-order sense. Thus, if we maximize (4b) with all $\beta_t > 0$, we obtain (if the maximum exists) a second-order undominated portfolio. A different undominated portfolio may result if we change the β's and maximize again.

We shall present below an economical algorithm for maximizing ϕ for any given positive β's, subject to (1), (2), and constraints of the form

$$\sum_{j=1}^{N} a_{ij} X_j = b_i , \qquad i = 1 \text{ to } M \tag{5}$$

$$X_j \geq 0, \qquad j = 1 \text{ to } N \tag{6}$$

Constraints of types (5) and (6) are those of the mean-variance portfolio analysis of Markowitz [4]. They may be used to include borrowing and/or lending, upper bounds on the amounts invested in industries or individual stocks, etc.

A major advantage of mean-variance analysis is that the set of (E, V) efficient portfolios may be drawn as a curve on a two-dimensional surface. In contrast, the set of undominated $(Z_1, Z_2, \ldots, Z_T)$ may be a $(T - 1)$-dimensional surface in a T-dimensional space. Thus if the conditions for using mean-variance are met (see Markowitz [4, Chapters 6 and 13]; Young and Trent [5]), then the latter is more convenient in practice than an analysis of undominated portfolios. If the aforementioned conditions are not met, however, an exploration of the space of undominated portfolios may be appropriate.

For a portfolio which maximizes ϕ, the given β's are essentially the economist's marginal rates of transformation among the Z's at a particular point on the efficient Z-surface, and imply marginal rates of transformation among the V's [by substitution of (3b) into (4b)]. The consumer of the analysis, upon being presented with the maximizing distribution, may find that he would like to trade some V_t's for other V_t's at the rates available; and hence may want to alter his β's. This process could proceed most conveniently if the algorithm described below were coded for an interactive computer system.

II. An Alternate Criterion for Dominance

We shall write

$$F_i(R), \quad V_{ti}, \quad Z_{ti}, \qquad i = 1, 2$$

for two distributions of the form described in the preceding section. We also define

$$H_i(X) = \int_{-\infty}^{X} dF_i(R) \tag{7}$$

The previously established criteria for determining that one cumulative distribution F_1 dominates another F_2 in the second-order sense may be written as

$$H_1(X) \leq H_2(X) \qquad \text{for all } X \tag{8a}$$

$$H_1(X_0) < H_2(X_0) \qquad \text{for some } X_0 \tag{8b}$$

We shall show in this section that (8a) and (8b) hold if and only if

$$Z_{t1} \geq Z_{t2} \qquad \text{for all } t \tag{9a}$$

$$Z_{t_0 1} > Z_{t_0 2} \qquad \text{for some } t_0 \tag{9b}$$

First, we note that

$$H_i(X) = 0 \qquad \text{for} \quad X \leq V_{1i} \tag{10a}$$

$$T \cdot H_i(X) = t \cdot (X - V_{ti}) + \sum_{j=1}^{t-1} j \cdot (V_{j+1, i} - V_{ji})$$

$$= tX - Z_{ti} \qquad \text{for} \quad V_{ti} \leq X \leq V_{t+1, i}, \quad 1 \leq t \leq T - 1 \tag{10b}$$

For example, for $V_{31} \leq X \leq V_{41}$,

$$T \cdot H_1(X) = 3(X - V_{31}) + 2(V_{31} - V_{21}) + 1 \cdot (V_{21} - V_{11}) = 3X - Z_{31}$$

(10b) follows directly from the definitions of H and Z. Note in particular that (10b) applies to the end points of the closed interval $[V_{ti}, V_{t+1, i}]$; and holds for all t from 1 to $T - 1$, even when $V_{ti} = V_{t+1, i}$ for one or more values of t. Finally,

$$T \cdot H_i(X) = T \cdot (X - V_{Ti}) + \sum_{j=1}^{T-1} j \cdot (V_{j+1, i} - V_{j, i})$$

$$= TX - Z_T \qquad \text{for} \quad X \geq V_T \tag{10c}$$

Lemma $H_1(X) = H_2(X)$ for all X if and only if

$$Z_{t1} = Z_{t2} \qquad \text{for all } t$$

Proof The nonsingular relationship between the V vector $(V_1, V_2, \ldots, V_T)$ and the Z vector $(Z_1, Z_2, \ldots, Z_T)$ implies that two distributions have the same Z vector if and only if they have the same V vector. The statement that identical V vectors implies identical $H(X)$ functions is trivial. The converse, that nonidentical V vectors imply nonidentical $H(X)$ functions, follows easily by considering any X in a small interval following $\min(V_{t1}, V_{t2})$ for the first t at which $V_{t1} \neq V_{t2}$.

A corollary of the lemma is that to prove that (8a) and (8b) hold if and only if (9a) and (9b) hold we need only prove that (8a) holds if and only if

(9a) holds. We begin by showing that (8a) implies (9a). For this purpose it will suffice to show that the negation of (9a) implies the negation of (8a).[1] Accordingly, we will show that the negation of (9a)—i.e., the existence of a t_0 such that $Z_{t_0 1} < Z_{t_0 2}$—implies the negation of (8a)—the existence of X_0 such that $H_1(X_0) > H_2(X_0)$.

Proof Let t_0 be the first value of t such that $Z_{t1} < Z_{t2}$. If $t_0 = 1$, then $Z_{11} < Z_{12}$; hence $V_{11} < V_{12}$; hence $H_1(X) > H_2(X)$ for $V_{11} < X \le V_{21}$. For $t > 1$ we distinguish two cases.

Case A $V_{t_0 1} \le V_{t_0 2}$. In this case, since $T \cdot F_1(X) \ge t_0$ for $X \ge V_{t_0 1}$, we have

$$T \cdot H_1(V_{t_0 2}) \ge TH_1(V_{t_0 1}) + t_0 \cdot (V_{t_0 2} - V_{t_0 1})$$

$$= t_0 \cdot V_{t_0 1} - Z_{t_0 1} + t_0 \cdot (V_{t_0 2} - V_{t_0 1})$$

$$= t_0 \cdot V_{t_0 2} - Z_{t_0 1}$$

$$> t_0 V_{t_0 2} - Z_{t_0 2} = T \cdot H_2(V_{t_0 2})$$

Case B $V_{t_0 1} > V_{t_0 2}$. $Z_{t_0 1} < Z_{t_0 2}$ and $V_{t_0 1} > V_{t_0 2}$ imply that $Z_{t_0 - 1, 1} < Z_{t_0 - 1, 2}$, contradicting the assumption that t_0 is the first t such that $Z_{t1} < Z_{t2}$. Thus, only Case A can occur, implying that $H_1(V_{t_0 2}) > H_2(V_{t_0 2})$ always for the first t at which $Z_{t1} < Z_{t2}$.

It remains to be shown that (9a) implies (8a), i.e., that $Z_{t1} \ge Z_{t2}$ for all t implies $H_1(X) - H_2(X) \le 0$ for all X. It follows from (10a)–(10c) that

$$H_1(X) - H_2(X) = 0 \qquad \text{for} \quad X \le V_{12}$$

$$H_1(X) - H_2(X) = Z_{T2} - Z_{T1} \le 0 \qquad \text{for} \quad X \ge \max(V_{T1}, V_{T2})$$

and, for all X, $H_1(X) - H_2(X)$ is continuous and piecewise linear. These considerations imply that in order to determine whether there is an X_0 such that

$$H_1(X_0) - H_2(X_0) > 0$$

we need only examine $H_1(X) - H_2(X)$ at points in a set S such that X_0 is in S if and only if

X_0 is the right-hand end of a linear segment in which

$$d[H_1(X) - H_2(X)]/dX = F_1(X) - F_2(X) > 0$$

and

the segment to the right of X_0 has

$$d[H_1(X) - H_2(X)]/dX \le 0$$

[1] Since (A implies B) means Not (A and Not B), whereas (Not B implies Not A) means Not (Not B and Not Not A), which is equivalent to Not (Not B and A).

for if there is a point with $H_1(X) - H_2(X) > 0$, S will include at least one such point [in fact, S will include one at which $H_1(X) - H_2(X)$ is a maximum].

Let X_0 be any point in S. (If S is empty, then $d[H_1(X) - H_2(X)]/dX \leq 0$ on every segment, and $H_1(X) - H_2(X) \leq 0$ for all X.) Let $t_0 = T \cdot F_1(X_0 - \varepsilon)$ which is unique for sufficiently small positive ε. Then $V_{t_0 1} < X_0$, $V_{t_0+1, 1} \geq X_0$, and $V_{t_0 2} = X_0$. (Other values of V_{t2} may also equal X_0, but this does not affect the argument.) Using (10b), we have

$$T \cdot [H_1(X_0) - H_2(X_0)] = (t_0 X_0 - Z_{t_0 1}) - (t_0 X_0 - Z_{t_0 2}) \leq 0$$

Since this is true for any X_0 in S, it follows that (9a) implies (8a), which completes the proof that (8a) and (8b) hold if and only if (9a) and (9b) hold.

III. The Algorithm

We shall show that the problem of maximizing (4b) subject to (1), (2), (5), and (6) may be formulated as a linear programming problem. Since it has more than 2^T variables and constraints, at first sight it may seem beyond the bounds of practical computation. But all but a few of the variables and constraints may always be "ignored," in a sense which will become clear later; thus, taking account of the special structure of the problem, a special code may be written which solves the "enormous problem" with only modest computer requirements.

To formulate the problem as a linear program, we replace (2) by

$$R_{i_1} + R_{i_2} + \cdots + R_{i_K} - e_{i_1 i_2 \cdots i_K} = Z_K \tag{2a}$$

$$e_{i_1, i_2, \ldots, i_K} \geq 0 \tag{2b}$$

for $K = 1, 2, \ldots, T$ and for each distinct combination of indices $(i_1, i_2, \ldots, i_K)$. The $e_{i_1, i_2, \ldots, i_K}$ are slack variables which assure that

$$R_{i_1} + R_{i_2} + \cdots + R_{i_K} \geq Z_K \tag{2c}$$

In any solution which maximizes ϕ for positive β's subject to (1), (2a), (2b), (5), and (6), each Z_K will equal Min $R_{i_1} + R_{i_2} + \cdots + R_{i_K}$; otherwise Z_K, and hence ϕ, could be increased without violating any constraint. Thus, in the optimal solution condition (2) is met, as well as conditions (2a) and (2b).

Equation (2a) introduces $2^T - 1$ equations with $2^T - 1$ slack variables. For $T = 20$, for example, we now have a system with over 1,000,000 equations and variables. Thus, even a modest size problem cannot be solved economically with a standard simplex code. Fortunately, most of the variables and constraints "take care of themselves" at each step in the simplex process.

To see this, let us first consider the problem of finding the shadow prices for a given basis. Writing

$$S = 2^T - 1 = \text{the number of equations in (2a)}$$

we note that the total number of equations including (1), (2a), and (5) is

$$T + S + M$$

This must equal the number of variables (R's, Z's, X's, and e's) which are " in " any basis. We may have the T R's and the T Z's always " in," since they are not constrained to be nonnegative; thus, writing (#IN X's) for the number of " in " X's, we have

$$T + S + M = (\#\,\text{IN } X\text{'s}) + (\#\,\text{IN } e\text{'s}) + 2T$$

$$S - (\#\,\text{IN } e\text{'s}) = (\#\,\text{IN } X\text{'s}) - M + T$$

$$(\#\text{OUT } e\text{'s}) \leq T + N - M$$

Thus, in every basis very few e's will be " out "; most will be " in."

The shadow price is zero for each Eq. (2a) whose slack variable, e, is in. The relatively few remaining shadow prices may be found by solving the dual of the system whose equations consist of (1) and (5), and those of (2a) whose slack variables are out. An efficient algorithm would make use of the fact that at most one such equation will be added or deleted at each step of the simplex algorithm.

We see then that the shadow prices may be found economically. Since relatively few variables are out of the basis, there is no problem in determining which " out " variable should be brought into the basis. The remaining problem is to determine which of the " in " variables is to go out as the new basis variable is brought in.

The problem here is the almost $2^T - 1$ e's which are in. It is clearly uneconomical to proceed in the usual way, expressing each as a linear combination of the incoming variable. We proceed in a different way.

The same submatrix whose dual version was used to solve economically for shadow prices, may (in its primal version) be used to solve economically for the X's and R's as linear functions of the incoming variables:

$$X_i = a_i + b_i\theta \qquad \text{for } \text{" in " } X\text{'s} \tag{11}$$

$$R_t = c_t + d_t\theta \qquad \text{for } t = 1 \text{ to } T \tag{12}$$

where θ is the value of the incoming new basis variable. We shall determine which e wants to go out first in terms of the R's as given in (12). [The X that wants to go out first is determined in the usual way from (11).]

We distinguish two cases in which an e in the basis goes out as the new variable is introduced:

Case 1 $e > 0$ before the new variable is introduced, and goes to zero as θ increases.

Case 2   Because of degeneracy, $e = 0$ even though e is in the basis.

We shall treat Case 1 first.

In order that

$$e_{i_1, i_2, ..., i_K} > 0$$

we must have

$$R_{i_1} + R_{i_2} + \cdots + R_{i_K} > \text{Min } R_{j_i} + R_{j_2} + \cdots + R_{j_K}$$

Or, to put it another way, the largest of the R_{i_K} must not be the Kth largest R (nor be tied for Kth largest R). In order that $e_{i_1, i_2, ..., i_K} = 0$ for $\theta = \theta_0$ we must have the largest R_{i_K} become tied for Kth largest R at $\theta = \theta_0$. In order to find the first such e to go from > 0 to $= 0$ as θ increases, we may order the R_t from smallest to largest (in the present case we may break ties arbitrarily) and solve at most $T - 1$ equations (one for each successive nontie) to determine which R_t first becomes tied with the next lower R_t.

Case 2 may occur when

$$R_{i_1} + R_{i_2} + \cdots + R_{i_K} = \text{Min } R_{j_i} + R_{j_2} + \cdots + R_{j_K}$$

but $e_{i_1, i_2, ..., i_K}$ is still in the basis though at a zero level. This can occur if there is a tie for Kth largest R. $e_{i_1, i_2, ..., i_K}$ must be dropped from the basis (or, more precisely, one such e or an X in at zero level must be dropped from the basis) if the increase in θ from 0 would make

$$R_{i_1} + R_{i_2} + \cdots + R_{i_K} < Z_K$$

i.e., if the largest R_{i_K} would become smaller than the largest R_{j_K} for the (one or more) $e_{j_1, j_2, ..., j_K}$ now out of the basis.

Since cycling is rare in linear programming, even in problems prone to degeneracy, no harm might come from breaking ties arbitrarily. Otherwise, an anticycling procedure can be used to select variables in ambiguous cases.

References

1. Hadar, J., and Russell, W. R., " Rules for Ordering Uncertain Prospects," *American Economic Review* **59** (March 1969), 25–34.
2. Hammond, J., "Towards Simplifying the Analysis of Decisions under Uncertainty Where Preference Is Nonlinear," Ph.D. thesis, Harvard Business School (1968).
3. Hanoch, G., and Levy, H., "The Efficiency Analysis of Choices Involving Risk," *Review of Economic Studies* **36** (July 1969), 335–346.
4. Markowitz, H. M., *Portfolio Selection: Efficient Diversification of Investments*. New York: Wiley, 1959.
5. Young, W. E., and Trent, R. M., " Geometric Mean Approximations of Individual Security and Portfolio Performance," *Journal of Financial and Quantitative Analysis* (June 1969).

THE STRONG CASE FOR THE GENERALIZED LOGARITHMIC UTILITY MODEL AS THE PREMIER MODEL OF FINANCIAL MARKETS

Mark Rubinstein

University of California, Berkeley

I. Introduction

In the microeconomic theory of finance, to develop detailed and/or empirically testable hypotheses recognizing uncertainty, it has become customary to follow the advice of James Tobin who, in summarizing almost two decades of research, wrote [53, p. 13][1]

> ... it is very difficult to derive propositions that are simultaneously *interesting* and *general*. ... To get propositions with significantly more content than the prescription that the investor should maximize ex-

Research for this paper was supported in part by a grant from the Dean Witter Foundation.

[1] Riskless arbitrage and welfare arguments constitute the chief exceptions to Tobin's statement. For example, see Modigliani and Miller [34], Stiglitz [51], Hakansson [18], Arrow [3], Leland [27], Hirshleifer [22], and Rubinstein [47]. Although, like Modigliani and Miller, Black and Scholes [8] also use an arbitrage argument to deduce the relationship of the values of associated securities, they impose strong (though possibly realistic) restrictions on the stochastic process of equity prices.

pected utility, it is necessary to place restrictions on this utility function or his subjective probability estimates . . . .

Theorists and empiricists, characteristically dividing in the United States along East–West lines, have developed both alternatives, resulting in the following model "types":

(I)   Restrictions on *beliefs*[2]
    (A)   discrete-time normality model
    (B)   continuous-time lognormality model
(II) Restrictions on *tastes*[3]
    (A)   generalized power utility model
    (B)   exponential utility model
    (C)   generalized logarithmic utility model

On the basis of the number of published papers, a head count of currently active researchers, or classroom acceptance, type I models would today be the overwhelming winners of a popularity contest. However, it is the thesis of this paper that type II models, and in particular the generalized logarithmic utility model (GLUM), are superior in the realism of their assumptions and the richness of their conclusions.

[2] Type I models are chiefly associated with the work of Markowitz [31], Sharpe [49], Lintner [28], Mossin [36], Fama and Miller [13], Jensen [24], Black [6], Scholes (1972), Merton [33], Long [30], and Gonedes [14].

[3] Type II models owe their etiology to Arrow [3], Debreu [12], and Hirshleifer [21] for their development of the complete markets economy, to the work of Arrow [4] for his concepts of absolute and proportional risk aversion, to the work of Wilson [55] for his aggregation and welfare analysis of HARA utility functions, to the work of Cass and Stiglitz [11] for their isolation of the significance of HARA utility functions for portfolio separation, and to the work of Hakansson [18] for his multiperiod portfolio analysis of constant proportional risk aversion under an arbitrary stochastic process of security prices. More recently, these strands have been tied together to model security market equilibrium in a single-period context by Rubinstein [45], Brennan and Kraus [10], and Grauer and Litzenberger [15], Grauer [17], and in a multiperiod context by Rubinstein [46] and Kraus and Litzenberger [26].

Type II models are distinguished from each other by the form of their assumed single-period utility of consumption functions. For

(A) $U(C_t) \sim b/(1 - b)(A + BC_t)^{1-b}$ $(B \neq 0, 1)$

(B) $U(C_t) \sim -Ae^{C_t/A}$ $(B = 0)$

(C) $U(C_t) \sim \ln(A + C_t)$ $(B = 1)$

where A and B are constants, $b \equiv B^{-1}$ and $\sim$ means "is equivalent up to an increasing linear transformation to." These utility functions belong to and exhaust the HARA or linear risk tolerance class of tastes and represent the solutions to the differential equation

$$-U'(C_t)/U''(C_t) = A + BC_t$$

for the given values of parameter (B).

Why, if this is true, are type I models so popular? While a complete answer[4] is difficult to provide, I believe a parallel can be drawn to many of the chief advances in the physical sciences. In the Aristotelian view, a body was naturally at rest so that once placed in motion it had to be accompanied by a mover at all times, or otherwise it would stop. This view of motion was the critical obstacle on the road to modern science; the continuous motion of the heavenly bodies seemed to require unseen hands, a sublime Intelligence exercising masterly control over the universe. The idea of natural rest was replaced with the Galilean–Newtonian idea of inertia, that a body once set in motion would naturally continue its motion at a constant velocity along a linear path until something intervened to accelerate or decelerate it. Aristotelian celestial mechanics, viewing the sun as rotating about the earth, after a long struggle, has given way to the modern Copernican view. The great barrier that for so long delayed the development of modern chemistry, the idea of phlogiston, a substance that was lost to a body in the process of burning, has now become a relic of history, displaced by the idea that a burning body takes in, and does not lose, a substance—oxygen. These great transpositions in the history of science, which we find so acceptable today, nonetheless defeated the greatest intellects for centuries. Men were not lacking in evidence, but inherited habits of thought, which often extended beyond science proper to a worldview, caused them to cling stubbornly to superannuated ideas.

A similar, although obviously not as philosophically significant, flexibility in thinking is required in the shift from models of type I to those of type II. In the former case, consumers directly choose actual securities and measure their desirability by their impact on the mean and variance of portfolio return. Like the old Aristotelian theories, consumer behavior is interpreted in its most natural terms. In the latter case, like the moden physical theories, an inversion (literally inversion of a matrix) of view is required: consumers are interpreted as indirectly choosing state-contingent securities (portfolios of which constitute actual securities) and measure their desirability by their impact on a more general set of risk parameters. Such an inversion of view is justified if it can (1) explain the same phenomena as the old view, (2) provide a more elegant explanation, and (3) explain other phenomena not capable of explanation under the old view. For example, it was not that the Aristotelian earth-centered view was false, but rather that the implications of the heliocentric view for the movements of other planets and stars commends it as superior. The remainder of this section will contrast type I and II models, and following sections will develop GLUM, since many of its properties are not well known.

---

[4] Hakansson [20] provided his own answer to this question in a recent paper.

A list of assumptions we hope would characterize a satisfactory micro-economic model of financial markets might include

Opportunities
   *(1)   perfect and competitive financial markets
   *(2)   choice and equilibrium over states
   *(3)   choice and equilibrium over dates
    (4)   discrete-time
Tastes
   *(5)   rationality, nonsatiation, risk aversion
    (6)   decreasing absolute risk aversion
    (7)   increasing, constant, or decreasing proportional risk aversion
Beliefs
    (8)   arbitrary contemporaneous stochastic process of security prices
    (9)   arbitrary intertemporal stochastic process of security prices
Heterogeneity
   *(10) wealth (composition and scale)
   *(11) risk-preference
   *(12) time-preference
   *(13) lifetime
    (14) beliefs

Starred assumptions are currently shared by both type I and II models; however, the other desiderata are only simultaneously met by the type IIC model—GLUM.

Assumption 3 is met by type II models without any unfortunate side effects; however, it is met for models of type I at the price of severe restrictions on the contemporaneous and intertemporal stochastic process of security prices. In particular, Fama and Miller [13, chapter 8] have argued that the discrete-time normality model applies in a multiperiod setting if the rates of return on *all* securities both are normally distributed at each date *and* follow a (possibly nonstationary) random walk. First, the inconsistency of the normality assumption with limited liability, unfortunate enough in a single-period model, is even more damaging in a multiperiod model. Now we are asked to tolerate the distinct prospect of trading securities at future dates with negative prices, with the vision of consumers bankrupted in the first period carrying forward negative "wealth" continuing to have their credit honored and, therefore, able to purchase a new portfolio and continue their participation in the securities market.[5] Second, if two- or more-period default-

----

[5] Hakansson [20] observes that approximation arguments are not convincing. Suppose we argue that the probability of negative second period consumption, $\varepsilon > 0$, is negligible. With a random walk, the probability of avoiding negative consumption over t periods becomes about $(1 - \varepsilon)^t$, which may not be negligible since $\lim_{t \to \infty} (1 - \varepsilon)^t = 0$.

free pure-discount bonds exist, all securities cannot follow a random walk. For example, such a two-period bond (with an uncertain price at the end of the first period) must have negative serial correlation of its period-by-period rate of return. Third, as Hakansson [20] observes, since the normal distribution does not reproduce itself multiplicatively, it cannot apply to returns on securities over two periods. However, by comparison, the chief virtue of the continuous-time lognormality model (IB) is that it escapes these objections.

Assumption 4 is met by all models except type IB, the continuous-time lognormality model. First, since the time interval between dates can be made arbitrarily small in discrete-time models, they are in this respect of greater generality. Second, if the limit of consumption and portfolio decisions as the time interval approaches zero were the same as the decisions made in continuous-time, then it could be argued that while less general, at least the continuous-time results are "close" to the discrete-time results for sufficiently small but finite time intervals. However, as Jim Ohlson and Barr Rosenberg have mentioned to me, the limit to the discrete-time decisions as the time interval approaches zero is not generally the continuous-time decisions. For example, with constant proportional risk aversion, in discrete-time a consumer never borrows on net at the risk-free rate, since to do so chances bankruptcy forcing expected utility to be negatively infinite; however, some borrowing is frequently optimal in continuous-time. Third, Rosenberg has also observed that the volume of trading required to continuously maintain the optimal portfolio in continuous-time may be infinite for any finite length of time. This obviates an analysis of the relative sources of trading volume.

Assumption 6 is only violated by model IIB; however, GLUM is the only model which is inconsistent with constant and increasing absolute risk aversion. While the issue of the realistic sign of absolute risk aversion seems to be settled, the direction of proportional risk aversion remains an open question. Therefore, a satisfactory model should be tolerant of differing attitudes of proportional risk aversion (assumption 7). However, the discrete-time normality model is internally inconsistent with constant proportional risk aversion, since in this case utility is undefined over negative levels of wealth. Yet such wealth levels are possible, since normal distributions, regardless of high positive means, attach a finite probability to any finite negative level of wealth. Moreover, since both type I models also attach a finite positive probability to any finite positive level of wealth, they are inconsistent with most commonly used utility functions which exhibit nonsatiation and risk aversion. For example, the HARA (linear risk tolerance) class, which contains all commonly used utility functions, is characterized by the differential equation $-U'(\cdot)/U''(\cdot) = A + B(\cdot)$, where U is a utility function and A and B are fixed parameters. The discrete-time normality model is inconsistent unless $B = 0$ (exponential utility) and the continuous-time lognormality model is inconsistent unless $B = 0$ (exponential utility), $B = 1$ (generalized logarithmic utility), or $A = 0$ (constant proportional risk aversion).

The most telling dividing line between the models is that between assumptions 8 and 9: type I models violate these requirements, while type II models do not. In an intertemporal equilibrium model, the stochastic process of security prices both across securities and over time is formally endogenous and should be derivable from the exogenous stochastic process of aggregate consumption or, with production, the exogenous stochastic process of parameters characterizing production functions. An intertemporal model, which takes significant features of the stochastic process of prices as given, should not be regarded as a complete model of equilibrium.[6] The discrete-time normality model adopts both the contemporaneous assumption of normality and the intertemporal assumption of a random walk. The continuous-time lognormality model, as developed by Merton [33], is somewhat more general since it permits some nonrandomness in period-by-period risk-free rates, but nonetheless exogenously ties the intertemporal stochastic process of all other securities to these risk-free rates. A second objection to the restrictions on the stochastic process of security prices imposed by type I models is its unrealism. Many securities, such as bonds near maturity, warrants, puts and calls, and insurance, have rates of return not even well approximated by normality or lognormality.

Assumption 14, heterogeneous beliefs, is met only by certain type II models—exponential utility model and GLUM. While Lintner [29] has developed a hybrid model joining discrete-time normality with exponential utility which encompasses heterogeneous beliefs, this has only been at the

---

[6] Indeed, the imposition of exogenous restrictions on the stochastic process of security prices may produce absurd conclusions. For example, both Rosenberg and Ohlson [43] and, independently, Goldman have shown that the joint properties of identically distributed security rates of return over time and portfolio separation at each date (which characterize the simpler version of Merton's [33] continuous-time lognormality model) force *all risky securities in equilibrium at any date to have the same rate of return!* In effect, all risky securities are identical from the point of view of an investor. As Bob Litzenberger has taught me, this degeneracy has a simple explanation. In the usual model, at each date the only state variables which affect portfolio choice are available wealth and rates of return on available securities. With portfolio separation, the composition of a consumer's portfolio of risky securities is only dependent on the joint distribution of security rates of return; but if this is identical at each date, then this composition must also be identical at each date. Therefore, if consumer i bought amounts S^i_{jt-1} and S^i_{kt-1} of risky securities j and k at date $t - 1$ such that $S^i_{jt-1}/S^i_{kt-1} = a_i$, then at date t he buys $S^i_{jt}/S^i_{kt} = a_i$. If all consumers hold portfolios of risky securities with the same composition at any given date, then they all purchase the market portfolio. Consequently, $a \equiv a_i$ the same for all i, and $S^M_{jt-1}/S^M_{kt-1} = S^M_{jt}/S^M_{kt} = a$, where $S^M_{jt} \equiv \sum_i S^i_{jt}$. Rates of return on the securities may be defined as $1 + r_{jt} \equiv S^M_{jt}/S^M_{jt-1}$ and $1 + r_{kt} \equiv S^M_{kt}/S^M_{kt-1}$. Therefore, it follows that whatever occurs, $r_{jt} = r_{kt}$.

cost of violating desideratum 6, decreasing absolute risk aversion. The chief drawback of the constant proportional risk aversion models (special cases of type IIA) is the absence of heterogeneity with respect to beliefs as well as risk-preference. GLUM is singular in its capacity to cope with heterogeneous beliefs while not imposing patently unreasonable restrictions on tastes.

In addition to the realism of assumptions, the models can also be compared on the basis of the richness of their conclusions. A list of conclusions which we hope would characterize a satisfactory microeconomic model of financial markets might include:

Choice
    (1)   complete specification of consumption/portfolio decision rules
    (2)   complete specification of consumption/portfolio sharing rules
Equilibrium
    (3)   solution of the aggregation problem
    (4)   complete specification of contemporaneous security price relationships
    (5)   complete specification of intertemporal security price relationships
    (6)   simplicity and empirical testability of security price relationships
Efficiency
   *(7)   Pareto-efficiency of exchange
   *(8)   Pareto-efficiency of production (by competitive value-maximizing firms)
    (9)   conditions for Pareto-efficiency of production and dissemination of information

Again starred conclusions are currently shared by both type I and II models; except for conclusion 6, the others are not deducible from type I models. Under type II models, the generalized power utility model (IIA) yields all but conclusions 6 and 9; the exponential utility model (IIB) yields all but conclusion 6; only GLUM (IIC) has sufficient fertility to yield them all.

Conclusions 1 and 2 are only partially reached by type I models through their separation properties, which imply that all consumers divide their wealth after consumption between the same two mutual funds, a risk-free security and the market portfolio. However, without forming a hybrid type I–II model,[7] this separation property has not been extended to infer whether

---

[7] Lintner's [29] discrete-time normality-exponential utility model is the chief example of a hybrid model. However, as shown in Rubinstein [45], he gains little in explanatory power not available in a pure exponential utility model. Moreover, adding the normality assumption unnecessarily complicates his derivations. Merton [32] also develops explicit consumption and portfolio decision rules combining the continuous-time lognormality model with HARA utility functions. Again as shown in Rubinstein [46], the lognormality assumption is unnecessary to the derivation of explicit multiperiod decision rules with HARA utility.

a given consumer is a borrower or a lender, let alone the magnitude of his borrowing or lending and as a result the amount of his consumption and his investment in the market portfolio. In contrast, to take the most successful type II model: With GLUM, a consumer's portfolio choice at each date can be broken down into 38 components, each of which expresses the extent to which his optimal portfolio differs from per capita holdings as a result of the deviation of his economic characteristics (wealth, risk-preference, time-preference, lifetime, and beliefs) from the average. Moreover, the portfolio separation property of GLUM, despite the permitted heterogeneity and the absence of restrictions on the intertemporal stochastic process of security prices, maintains the simplicity of the analogous results in type I models. In addition, the demand for bonds of various maturities can be inferred from GLUM, an issue which is closed to type I models due to their strong random walk restrictions on the intertemporal stochastic process of security rates of return. Likewise, demand for "options" with payoffs under various conditions can be inferred from GLUM, another issue closed to type I models due to their assumed homogeneity of beliefs.

Without creating a hybrid type I–II model or assuming all consumers are identical, it has yet to be shown if there are other conditions under which the aggregation problem (conclusion 3) can be solved.[8] Moreover, if restrictions on tastes required by type II models are adopted, the additional restrictions imposed on beliefs by type I models appear to be of no assistance in the solution of the aggregation problem. As a result of the ability of type II models to solve the aggregation problem under nontrivial homogeneity conditions, they provide a complete endogenous specification of both the contemporaneous and intertemporal relationships among security prices (conclusions 4 and 5). In contrast, while the type I models provide well-known contemporaneous linearity relationships between return and risk and precise measures of risk, neither the additive (risk-free rate) nor the multiplicative ("market price of risk") constants are determined from exogenous variables. Moreover, because of their strong exogenous restrictions on the intertemporal stochastic process of security prices, they are barred from developing nontrivial conditions for a random walk or unbiased term structure to be a natural outcome of equilibrium. In particular, the discrete-time normality model by assuming a random walk to start with, not only dodges the random walk question but also trivially forces an un-

---

[8] The aggregation problem is solvable in the *weak* form if it is possible to replace each heterogeneous economic characteristic with a homogeneous characteristic, such that social choices are determined as before and, for all characteristics denominated in wealth, the homogeneous characteristic is an unweighted arithmetic average of the corresponding heterogeneous characteristic. The problem is solved in the *strong* form if the homogeneous characteristics so defined are not themselves functions of private or social choices. See Rubinstein [45] and Section III of this chapter.

biased term structure.[9] Indeed, one of the great merits of type II models is their capacity to cope with these significant intertemporal pricing issues. However, among these models, only GLUM has relatively simple conditions for these two classic hypotheses of the intertemporal stochastic process of security rates of return.

Other than its failure to incorporate heterogeneous beliefs, the chief drawback of the generalized power utility model (IIA) is the difficulty of empirically testing its security price relationships. While permitting heterogeneous beliefs, the exponential utility model (IIB) has similar difficulties. Prospects are not entirely bleak, however. Their single-period forms can be tested and even used to infer social attitudes toward risk-preference and time-preference from the observed behavior of security prices (see Grauer [17]). However, when embedded in a multiperiod setting, testing the first-period valuation equation would appear to require either data on the rate of growth of aggregate consumption (currently only available at quarterly intervals in the United States) or exogenous restrictions on the intertemporal stochastic process of security prices, such as a random walk, which sufficiently insulate the first period valuation equation from consideration of future security rates of return (see Rubinstein [46]). But similar assumptions on type I models seem also required for their empirical testability. GLUM (model IIC) is the only intertemporal model, which does not exogenously restrict the intertemporal stochastic process of security prices, with a first-period valuation equation which can be tested without direct information on the rate of growth of aggregate consumption. Substituting in place of this is the rate of return on the market portfolio and the rate of return of a perpetual default-free annuity. Moreover, among type I and II models, GLUM yields the simplest multiperiod valuation formula for an uncertain income stream, which can be written as the discounted (at appropriate risk-free rates) sum of explicitly calculated certainty equivalents of the uncertain income at each date, even if this income is serially correlated over time. GLUM also offers empirically testable hypotheses concerning the intertemporal structure of security prices. As a final empirical advantage, at least with respect to the contemporaneous relationship among the rate of growth of aggregate consumption, the rate of return of the market portfolio, and the rate of return of a perpetual default-free annuity, GLUM avoids the ex post–ex ante problem of empirical work. To test this relationship, it is unnecessary to measure (*ex ante*) beliefs.

While all type I and II models are Pareto-efficient with respect to the variety of securities available (conclusion 7), certain popular generalizations of the discrete-time normality model are not. For example, in the absence of a risk-free security (Black [6]), consumers will generally find exchange ar-

---

[9] For example, for the period-by-period rates of return of a two-period default-free bond to follow a random walk, these rates of return must be certain; but in this case the term structure is trivially unbiased to avoid riskless arbitrage.

rangements Pareto-inefficient, since they would create a risk-free security if given the chance. Likewise, in the discrete-time normality model with exponential utility to accommodate heterogeneous beliefs, exchange arrangements are generally Pareto-inefficient unless a complete securities market exists (i.e., an uncountably infinite number of securities to correspond with the uncountably infinite number of states). Not only do type II models avoid these difficulties, but their very construction makes clear just what kinds of securities would need to exist to guarantee Pareto-efficiency. The mathematical development of these models begins with the assumption of a complete securities market which "automatically" assures Pareto-efficiency. The subsequent generation of sharing rules then reveals to what extent the securities market may be incomplete and yet remain Pareto-efficient. This indicates the types of securities which are apt to be in greatest demand.

As a result of the work of Hirshleifer [22] and Ng [38], we now know that in any pure exchange economy with Pareto-efficient exchange arrangements and homogeneous beliefs, the production of new information is Pareto-inefficient even if it is costless. However, the equally interesting question of the dissemination of existing information in an economy with heterogeneous beliefs (see Jaffe and Rubinstein [23]) can obviously only be examined by models permitting belief heterogeneity, and this leaves only the exponential utility model (IIB) and GLUM (IIC). Both models permit a comparative statics analysis of the effect on consumer choices and equilibrium prices of moving from one set of heterogeneous beliefs to another, or to homogeneous beliefs. To see how serious the effects of poor information dissemination are, it is also possible to measure precisely the nonspeculative (due to differences in wealth composition, wealth scale, risk-preference, time-preference, and lifetime) versus speculative (due to differences in beliefs) sources of trading volume. Finally, unlike the other models, IIB and IIC permit the explicit construction of consensus beliefs,[10] a function of the different beliefs of all consumers, which indicate what information is fully reflected in security prices. Here GLUM has a slight advantage over the exponential utility model, since its consensus beliefs, being arithmetic rather than geometric weighted averages of beliefs across consumers, have a more natural interpretation.

II. The Generalized Logarithmic Utility Model

For convenience in the development of the theory, we shall examine a three-date $(t = 0, 1, 2)$, complete markets economy; neither assumption is required. The state at date $t = 0$ is known with certainty; at date $t = 1$ any one of E $(e = 1, 2, ..., E)$ states can occur, and at date $t = 2$ any one of S

---

[10] Consensus beliefs are those beliefs which, if held by all consumers in an otherwise similar economy, would generate the same equilibrium prices as in the actual economy. See Rubinstein [47].

$(s = 1, 2, \ldots, S)$ states can occur. Each consumer, at date $t = 0$, allocates his positive present wealth W_0 among present consumption $C_0 > 0$ and E "state-contingent claims" to wealth $\{W_e\}$ at date $t = 1$. Since P_e denotes the date $t = 0$ present value of a unit of wealth received at date $t = 1$ if and only if state e occurs, then $W_0 \geq C_0 + \sum_e P_e W_e$. Similarly, at date $t = 1$, if state e occurs and a consumer is alive, he allocates his wealth W_e among consumption $C_e > 0$ at date $t = 1$ and S "state-contingent claims" to consumption $\{C_{s.e} > 0\}$ at date $t = 2$. Since it is conditional on the occurrence of state e, $P_{s.e}$ denotes the date $t = 1$ present value of a unit of consumption received at date $t = 2$ if and only if state s occurs; then $W_e \geq C_e + \sum_s P_{s.e} C_{s.e}$. On the other hand, if state e occurs and a consumer dies at date $t = 1$, then $W_e \geq C_e$ and he does not revise his portfolio. An exogenous counter λ will be used to denote whether a consumer is dead or alive at date $t = 1$; if he is dead $\lambda = 0$, and if he is alive $\lambda = 1$. If he is dead, his lifetime $T = 1$, and if he is alive, his lifetime $T = 2$.

To provide for the endogenous determination of security prices, we append closure conditions that effectively take aggregate production decisions across dates and states as given. The population of the economy at each date is denoted by I_t $(i = 1, 2, \ldots, I_t)$, where at date $t = 0$ all consumers (I) are alive, after consumption at date $t = 1$, $I_1 \equiv \sum_i \lambda_i$, and after consumption at date $t = 2$, $I_2 = 0$. Each consumer is endowed with resources $(\bar{C}_0^i, \{\bar{C}_e^i\}, \{\bar{C}_{s.e}^i\})$, so that, more fundamentally,

$$W_0^i \equiv \bar{C}_0^i + \sum_e P_e \bar{C}_e^i + \sum_e P_e \sum_s P_{s.e} \bar{C}_{s.e}^i$$

Closure conditions then become

$$\sum_i \bar{C}_0^i \equiv C_0^M = \sum_i C_0^i, \quad \sum_i \bar{C}_e^i \equiv C_e^M = \sum_i C_e^i, \quad \sum_i \bar{C}_{s.e}^i \equiv C_{s.e}^M = \sum_i C_{s.e}^i$$

for all e and s. Since the time–state distribution of resources across consumers is regarded as exogenous, the aggregate supply of resources across dates and states $(C_0^M, \{C_e^M\}, \{C_{s.e}^M\})$ is also exogenous.[11] As a result the

---

[11] Rather than start with a given time–start distribution of endowed consumption across consumers, production decisions can be introduced which are capable of shifting aggregate consumption across dates and states. In this case, we would denote $(\bar{X}_0^i, \{\bar{X}_e^i\}, \{\bar{X}_{s.e}^i\})$ as the endowed resources of consumer i. Each of J $(j = 1, 2, \ldots, J)$ producers can transform resources from earlier to later dates through a production function $f_j(X_0^j, \{X_e^j\}, \{X_{s.e}^j\}) = 0$ where, by convention, $X < 0$ represents an input and $X > 0$ an output. Although $X_0^j \leq 0$ and $X_{s.e}^j \geq 0$, X_e^j can have either sign. Consumer i is also endowed with shares η_{ij} of producer j such that $0 \leq \eta_{ij} \leq 1$ and $\sum_i \eta_{ij} = 1$. Therefore, given production decisions, his endowed consumption would then be

$$\bar{C}_0^i \equiv \bar{X}_0^i + \sum_j \eta_{ij} X_0^j, \qquad \bar{C}_e^i \equiv \bar{X}_e^i + \sum_j \eta_{ij} X_e^j, \qquad \bar{C}_{s.e}^i \equiv \bar{X}_{s.e}^i + \sum_j \eta_{ij} X_{s.e}^j$$

In this paper, although we take the decisions of producers as exogenous, its results would also apply if production decisions were endogenously determined.

period-by-period growth rates of aggregate consumption $1 + r_{C_e} \equiv C_e^M/C_0^M$ and $1 + r_{C_{s.e}} \equiv C_{s.e}^M/C_e^M$ are also exogenous. However, all wealth variables $(W_0^i, \{W_e^i\})$ are endogenous since they are, in part, functions of endogenously determined prices.

Since certain portfolios will play a significant role in the subsequent analysis, it is well to develop notation for them now. Aggregate wealth will be denoted by $W_0^M \equiv \sum_i W_0^i$ and $W_e^M = \sum_i W_e^i$ for all e, and the period-by-period rate of return on the market portfolio by $1 + r_{Me} \equiv W_e^M/(W_0^M - C_0^M)$ and $1 + r_{Ms.e} \equiv C_{s.e}^M/(W_e^M - C_e^M)$. In this context, $(C_0^M, \{C_e^M\}, \{C_{s.e}^M\})$ can be interpreted as net flows of cash from producers to consumers ("dividends"). A default-free first-period bond has a certain rate of return defined by $1 + r_F \equiv (\sum_e P_e)^{-1}$ and a default-free second-period bond has a rate of return conditional on state e of $1 + r_{Fe} \equiv (\sum_s P_{s.e})^{-1}$. A two-period default-free pure discount bond has the certain compound rate of return of $(1 + R_F)^2 \equiv (\sum_e P_e \sum_s P_{s.e})^{-1}$ and a rate of return in the first-period conditional on state e of $1 + R_{Fe} \equiv (1 + R_F)^2/(1 + r_{Fe})$. As a result, if the present value of a default-free annuity of one unit of wealth at date $t = 0, 1,$ and 2 is denoted by

$$\phi \equiv 1 + 1/(1 + r_F) + 1/(1 + R_F)^2$$

and a default-free annuity of one unit of wealth at dates $t = 1$ and $t = 2$ is denoted by

$$\phi_e \equiv 1 + 1/(1 + r_{Fe})$$

then the first-period rate of return of a default-free annuity purchased at date $t = 0$ and yielding one unit of wealth at dates $t = 1$ and $t = 2$ is

$$1 + r_{Ne} \equiv \phi_e/(\phi - 1)$$

We will also denote the present value of annuities maturing at a consumer's death by

$$\phi_\lambda \equiv 1 + 1/(1 + r_F) + \lambda/(1 + R_F)^2 \quad \text{and} \quad \phi_{\lambda e} \equiv 1 + \lambda/(1 + r_{Fe}).$$

Each consumer is assumed to obey the Savage (1954) Axioms of Rational Choice: He has beliefs and tastes representable by probabilities and a utility function over lifetime consumption. That is, each consumer is assumed to maximize

$$E[\bar{U}(C_0, C_1, C_2)] = \sum_e \pi_e \sum_s \pi_{s.e} \bar{U}(C_0, C_e, C_{s.e})$$

subject to his nonnegativity and budget constraints, where $\pi_e > 0$ denotes the consumer's subjective probability that state e will occur, and $\pi_{s.e} > 0$ denotes his state e conditional subjective probability that state s will occur.

Additionally, $\bar{U}$ is assumed to be strictly increasing in each of its arguments and strictly concave in the vector $(C_0, C_e, C_{s.e})$.

To this point (except for the finite number of states, the discreteness of time, and the nonnegativity of consumption) the structure of the generalized logarithmic utility model is shared by all type I and II models.[12] GLUM draws its distinctive explanatory power by adopting three special assumptions surrounding consumer tastes:

(1) *intertemporal risk neutrality:* $\partial \bar{U}(C_0, C_1, C_2)/\partial C_t = U_t'(C_t)$
(2) *separation of time- and risk-preference:* $U_t'(C)/U_{t-1}'(C) = \rho_t$ (all levels $C > 0$)
(3) *generalized logarithmic utility:* $U(C_t) = \ln(A + C_t)$.

Assumption (1) is common to the continuous-time lognormality model (IB) and all type II models; assumption (2) is common only to type II models; and assumption (3) distinguishes GLUM from other type II models.

Interpreting assumption (1) verbally, the marginal utility of consumption at any date is independent of consumption at all other dates. As· a consequence, a necessary and sufficient condition for assumption (1) is that there exist functions $\{U_t\}$ such that

$$\bar{U}(C_0, C_1, C_2) = U_0(C_0) + U_1(C_1) + U_2(C_2)$$

This implies two patterns of consumer behavior which if considered together may make this assumption reasonable. The first and most apparent is the independence of the utility of consumption at each date from consumption at other dates; for example, the utility added by consumption C_1 at date $t = 1$ is independent of the levels of consumption C_0 and C_2 at dates $t = 0$ and $t = 2$. Both habit formation and loss of enjoyment due to excessive past or excessive anticipated indulgence are not permitted. On the other hand, consider the following two lotteries over lifetime $T = 1$:

Lottery 1: $(\frac{1}{2}; C_0 = a, C_1 = b)$ versus $(\frac{1}{2}; C_0 = b, C_1 = a)$,
Lottery 2: $(\frac{1}{2}; C_0 = a, C_1 = a)$ versus $(\frac{1}{2}; C_0 = b, C_1 = b)$,

where $a < b$. A consumer who chooses the first lottery balances a poor year against a rich year regardless of which outcome occurs; a consumer who chooses the second lottery, either experiences a poor year every year or a rich year every year. The former consumer might aptly be termed "intertemporally risk averse" and the second consumer "intertemporally risk preferring." Richard [42] has shown that a consumer will be indifferent between the two lotteries if and only if his utility function satisfies assumption

[12] As previously observed, the completeness of the securities market is not crucial to the conclusions of types I or II models. Like the first stage of a moon rocket, it is very useful but will nonetheless be rejected once the payload has attained maximum thrust.

(1). GLUM consumers are therefore "intertemporally risk neutral." On the basis of causal empiricism, Richard argues that consumers tend to be "intertemporally risk averse": they prefer a little now and more later, or vice versa, to the all-or-nothing alternative. However, as Nils Hakansson has suggested to me, the "intertemporally risk preferring" consumer has the advantage of avoiding severe jolts in his lifetime consumption pattern. How uncomfortable it must be for consumers stuck with the first lottery to flip in the second outcome from a high standard of living early in life to a much lower standard of living later in life. Similarly, under the first outcome, a consumer with a low standard of living early in life may be both psychologically and educationally unprepared for a much higher standard of living in later years. Taking all the arguments in this paragraph into account, perhaps the neutral position of assumption (1) is not unreasonable.

Assumption (2) permits the formal separation of the psychological notions of risk-preference (risk aversion) and time-preference (patience). Taken together, a necessary and sufficient condition for assumptions (1) and (2) is that there exist positive constants $\{\rho_t\}$ and a function U such that

$$\bar{U}(C_0, C_1, C_2) = U(C_0) + \rho_1 U(C_1) + \rho_1 \rho_2 U(C_2).$$

These constants express the relative preference for consumption at different dates. For example, if $0 < \rho_1 < 1$, then the consumer prefers more consumption at date $t = 0$ than at date $t = 1$. In this instance, the consumer is characterized as "impatient" and if $\rho_1 > 1$ as "patient." Henceforth, (ρ_1, ρ_2) will be referred to as the measure of consumer *time-preference*. It will also be convenient to use the alternative notation $\delta_1 \equiv \rho_2(1 + \rho_2)^{-1}$ and $\delta \equiv \rho_1(1 + \rho_2)[1 + \rho_1(1 + \rho_2)]^{-1}$. Risk aversion prevents excessive concentration of consumption at a single date; that is, as a result of the nonsatiation and concavity properties of $\bar{U}$ it follows that $U' > 0$ and $U'' < 0$.[13]

Assumption (3), no doubt the most controversial of GLUM, requires that *all* consumers behave as if they have generalized logarithmic utility functions. This assumption is not as restrictive as it might at first seem. First, all consumers must have decreasing absolute risk aversion. Second, since the heterogeneity of the model permits consumers to have taste parameters A of different signs, it simultaneously tolerates quite diverse attitudes of proportional risk aversion:

A	Proportional risk aversion
positive	increasing
zero	constant
negative	decreasing

---

[13] Koopmans [25] provides an axiomatic justification of the distinction between time- and risk-preference.

Henceforth, A will be referred to as the measure of consumer *risk-preference;* the higher the A, the "more risk preferring" the consumer. The graph of $U(C_t) = \ln(A + C_t)$ (Fig. 1) shows an everywhere strictly increasing and strictly concave curve with no upper or lower bound, with an intercept along the horizontal axis at $-A + 1$, and with $\lim_{C_t\downarrow\,-A} \ln(A + C_t) = -\infty$.

Regardless of the size of A, as C_t increases, a consumer's behavior becomes closer to the behavior of a consumer with constant proportional risk aversion, since

$$\lim_{C_t \to \infty} [\ln(A + C_t) - \ln C_t] = 0$$

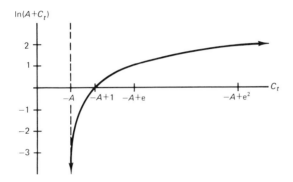

Fig. 1.

Moreover, when $A = 0$ (or when A is small relative to C_t), a consumer follows the famous Bernoulli–Laplace hypothesis about the marginal utility of income. Coincidentally, such a consumer also obeys the Weber–Fechner law of psychophysics, that the marginal impact of a stimulus is inversely proportional to the intensity of the stimulus. Observe that $dk \ln C_t/dC_t = kC_t^{-1}$ where k is a positive constant. More recently, Breiman [9] has shown that such a consumer

(1) maximizes the expected compound growth rate per dollar of investment;

(2) minimizes the probability of ruin in the long run;

(3) selects a portfolio strategy for which the probability that the compound growth rate per dollar of investment exceeds that generated by any other strategy approaches 1 as the number of periods goes to infinity;

(4) reaches any given target wealth (after given consumption) level in the shortest possible expected time.

When $A \leq 0$, the consumer will never take the chance that $C_t \leq -A$ since such low levels of consumption have infinite disutility. Consequently, when $A \leq 0$, $-A$ may be interpreted as subsistence-level consumption below which death occurs. When $A > 0$, the utility function by itself does not guard against zero or negative consumption, and additional conditions are required to prevent a consumer from taking risks that may result in negative consumption.[14]

A feeling for the implications of generalized logarithmic utility for portfolio choice may be obtained from a simple example. Suppose a consumer with generalized logarithmic utility has $\$W$ and he can choose what proportion $1 - \alpha$ of his money to leave in cash, and what proportion $0 \leq \alpha \leq 1$ to invest in a gamble yielding rate of return $r = 1$ with probability $0 < \pi < 1$, or rate of return $r = -1$ with probability $1 - \pi$. If the gamble is fair or unfavorable $(\pi \leq \frac{1}{2})$, he leaves all his money in cash $(\alpha = 0)$. If the gamble is favorable and a positive investment in it is sure to net the consumer more than $-A$, then he invests at least part of his money in the gamble $(\alpha > 0)$. Moreover, if $A \leq 0$, then he never invests all his money $(0 < \alpha < 1)$; but if $A > 0$ and the gamble is favorable enough, the consumer is tempted sufficiently to place all his funds at risk $(\alpha = 1)$. It is easy to show[15] that the following formula describes the optimal proportion α^* to invest in a favorable gamble:

$$\alpha^* = \begin{cases} 0 & \text{if} \quad \bar{\alpha} \leq 0 \\ \bar{\alpha} & \text{if} \quad 0 < \bar{\alpha} < 1 \\ 1 & \text{if} \quad \bar{\alpha} \geq 1 \end{cases} \qquad \text{where} \quad \bar{\alpha} \equiv (1 + A/W)(2\pi - 1)$$

Table I provides optimal proportions α^* for various levels of risk aversion A, wealth W, and belief π. Observe that, at the same level of wealth, consumers

---

[14] Irrespective of the sign of A, a consumer's endowed wealth must be assumed large enough so that he is not forced to chance levels of consumption $C_t \leq -A$ at any date t. A *necessary* condition for $C_t^i > -A_i$ for all i and t is $C_t^M > -\sum_i A_i$ for all t. For any consumer, a *sufficient* condition for $C_t > -A$ for all t is $\bar{C}_t > -A$ for all t. For any consumer, a *necessary and sufficient* condition for $C_t > -A$ for all t is $W_0 > -A\phi_\lambda$, where $-A\phi_\lambda$ is interpreted as the present value of $-A$ units of consumption at every date during the consumer's lifetime. Anyone for whom $W_0 \leq -A\phi_\lambda$ will not be able to bear the pain of life and will either have committed suicide or died at birth of natural causes.

With this innocuous condition, for any consumer with $A \leq 0$ his feasible and, therefore, his optimal consumption choices are always above his subsistence level. However, for $A > 0$, although positive consumption at every date is feasible, it will not always be optimal unless further conditions are added. These conditions can either (1) prevent any consumer from being too much of a nonconformist, or (2) reduce the differences in aggregate consumption among different dates and/or states. In an extreme case, if all consumers are identical, then even if $A > 0$, feasible positive consumption at every date for all consumers is also optimal. For examples of much less stringent conditions, see footnote 30. Henceforth, we will assume that such conditions apply.

with $A < 0$ are more conservative than consumers with $A > 0$; and in both cases, as their wealth increases, their choices approach those made if $A = 0$.

Summarizing this section, the programming problem of every consumer i in GLUM may be formally stated as

$$\max_{C_0^i, \{C_e^i\}, \{C_{s \cdot e}^i\}} \ln(A_i + C_0^i) + \rho_1^i \sum_e \pi_e^i \ln(A_i + C_e^i)$$

$$+ \rho_1^i \rho_2^i \sum_e \pi_e^i \sum_s \pi_{s \cdot e}^i \ln(A_i \lambda_i + C_{s \cdot e}^i)$$

subject to $C_t^i > 0$ for all t and

$$C_0^i + \sum_e P_e C_e^i + \sum_e P_e \sum_s P_{s \cdot e} C_{s \cdot e}^i \leq W_0^i \equiv \bar{C}_0^i + \sum_e P_e \bar{C}_e^i + \sum_e P_e \sum_s P_{s \cdot e} \bar{C}_{s \cdot e}^i$$

---

[15] For a quick solution to the problem; first solve for the optimal portfolio in terms of state-contingent securities and prices; second, determine the state-contingent prices from actual security prices; and third, convert the solution in terms of state-contingent securities to portfolio proportions of actual securities.

The programming problem is the Lagrangian expression

$$\max_{\{W_e\}} \sum_e \pi_e \ln(A + W_e) - \Lambda \left[\sum_e P_e W_e - W \right]$$

which yields the optimal decision rule: $W_e = (\pi_e / P_e)(A P_F + W) - A$, where $P_F \equiv \sum_e P_e$. In this example, there are two states and two actual securities; therefore, the state-contingent prices can be calculated from prices of actual securities by solving the simultaneous equations

$$1 = P_1 + P_2$$

$$1 = P_1(2) + P_2(0)$$

so that $P_1 = P_2 = \frac{1}{2}$. Substituting this into the optimal decision rule: $W_e = 2\pi_e(A + W) - A$ for $e = 1, 2$. Let α represent the proportion of initial wealth W allocated to the risky security; therefore

$$W_1 = (1 - \alpha)W + \alpha W(2) = (1 + \alpha)W \quad \text{and} \quad W_2 = (1 - \alpha)W + \alpha W(0) = (1 - \alpha)W$$

Selecting either state, say $e = 1$, and setting $2\pi(A + W) - A = (1 + \alpha)W$, it follows that $\alpha^* = [1 + (A/W)](2\pi - 1)$, whenever $0 < \alpha^* < 1$.

Whenever the number of different actual ("complex") securities available is equal to the number of assumed states, a procedure similar to the above may be used to determine portfolio choices of actual securities. In practice, it is necessary to form a coarse partition of the number of states to make them equal to the number of securities available. However, with about ten or more securities, considering the difficulties of estimation, this may be a reasonable approach. With large numbers of securities, a computer is only required first to determine the solution $\{P_e\}$ to the simultaneous equations $1 = \sum_e P_e(1 + r_{je})$ for all j, and second to determine the solution $\{\alpha_j\}$ to the simultaneous equations $W_e = W \sum_j \alpha_j(1 + r_{je})$ for all e, where j ($j = 1, 2, \ldots, J$) indexes available securities and r_{je} is the rate of return of security j associated with state e.

where $\lambda_i = 0$ or 1, and, if $\lambda_i = 0$, then $\rho_2^i = 0$; otherwise $\rho_t^i > 0$. Closure conditions require that

$$\sum_i C_0^i = C_0^M \equiv \sum_i \bar{C}_0^i , \quad \sum_i C_e^i = C_e^M \equiv \sum_i \bar{C}_e^i ,$$

$$\text{and} \quad \sum_i C_{s.e}^i = C_{s.e}^M \equiv \sum_i \bar{C}_{s.e}^i$$

for all e and s. The subscript or superscript i indicates that consumers may be different in every respect except that they all have generalized logarithmic

Table I

π	$A = -1$				$A = 0$	$A = +1$			
	W				All W	W			
	$\frac{1}{2}^a$	1	2	4		4	2	1	$\frac{1}{2}$
.5	0	0	0	0	0	0	0	0	0
.55	0	0	.05	.075	.1	.125	.15	.2	.3
.6	0	0	.1	.15	.2	.25	.3	.4	.6
.7	0	0	.2	.3	.4	.5	.6	.8	1.0
.8	0	0	.3	.45	.6	.725	.9	1.0	1.0
.9	0	0	.4	.6	.8	1.0	1.0	1.0	1.0
.95	0	0	.45	.675	.9	1.0	1.0	1.0	1.0

^{a} Utility undefined.

utility functions (but with different time- and risk-preference) and face the same prices, an implication of a competitive securities market. The problem confronting the theorist is to express the endogenous variables

$$choices: \quad \{C_0^i, \{C_e^i\}, \{C_{s.e}^i\}\} \quad \text{and} \quad prices: \quad \{\{P_e\}, \{P_{s.e}\}\}$$

in terms of the exogenous variables

$$resources: \quad \{\bar{C}_0^i, \{\bar{C}_e^i\}, \{\bar{C}_{s.e}^i\}\} \quad \text{and} \quad lifetime: \quad \{\lambda_i\}$$
$$risk\text{-}preference: \quad \{A_i\} \quad \text{and} \quad time\text{-}preference: \quad \{\rho_1^i, \rho_2^i\}$$
$$beliefs: \quad \{\{\pi_e^i\}, \{\pi_{s.e}^i\}\}.$$

III. Financial Choice

It is useful to view the consumer as solving a dynamic programming problem. That is, in place of solving the single-stage maximand of Section II, the consumer solves the following two-stage programming problem. First, at date $t = 1$, given state e and wealth W_e carried forward from the first period, the consumer

$$V_e(W_e) \equiv \max_{C_e, \{C_{s.e}\}} \ln(A + C_e) + \rho_2 \sum_s \pi_{s.e} \ln(A\lambda + C_{s.e})$$

$$- \Lambda_e \left(C_e + \sum_s P_{s.e} C_{s.e} - W_e \right)$$

where Λ_e is a state-dependent Lagrangian multiplier.[16] Second, at date $t = 0$, knowing $V_e(W_e)$, the consumer

$$V_0(W_0) \equiv \max_{C_0, \{W_e\}} \ln(A + C_0) + \rho_1 \sum_e \pi_e V_e(W_e) - \Lambda \left(C_0 + \sum_e P_e W_e - W_0 \right)$$

Following this pattern of analysis, the following optimal consumption and portfolio decision rules may be derived:

Theorem (*Decision Rules*) In the generalized logarithmic utility economy, the optimal consumption and portfolio decision rules at each date are linear to wealth at that date, and are otherwise independent of past decisions and the composition of wealth. Optimal consumption and portfolio decisions at any date also exhibit partial myopia in that they are dependent on security rates of return in future periods only through their dependence on future risk-free rates of return. In particular,[17]

$$C_0 = A[\phi_\lambda(1 - \delta) - 1] + (1 - \delta)W_0$$

$$W_e = A[(\pi_e/P_e)\phi_\lambda \, \delta - \phi_{\lambda e}] + (\pi_e/P_e) \delta W_0$$

The derived utility of wealth functions also imply partial myopia. In particular,

$$V_e(W_e) \approx (1 + \rho_2) \ln(A\phi_{\lambda e} + W_e)$$

$$V_0(W_0) \approx (1 + \rho_1 + \rho_1\rho_2) \ln(A\phi_\lambda + W_0)$$

where $\approx$ means "is equivalent up to an additive transformation to."

Proof Partially differentiating the first-stage maximand with respect to each choice variable, setting the derivatives equal to zero, and eliminating the Lagrangian multiplier,

$$P_{s.e}(A\lambda + C_{s.e}) = \pi_{s.e}\rho_2(A + C_e) \qquad \text{(all } s) \qquad (1)$$

---

[16] Recall from footnote 14 that we assume conditions on exogenous variables sufficient to insure $C_t > 0$ for all t.

[17] In terms of "normal" income, $C_0 = A[\phi_\lambda(1 - \delta) - 1] + (1 - \delta)\phi_y Y$, where Y is that constant income received over a consumer's lifetime which has the same present value as initial wealth (i.e., $W_0 = \phi Y$).

Summing over s, introducing the budget constraint and rearranging,

$$A\phi_{\lambda e} + W_e = (1 + \rho_2)(A + C_e) \tag{2}$$

or, alternatively stated,

$$C_e = A[\phi_{\lambda e}(1 - \delta_1) - 1] + (1 - \delta_1)W_e \tag{3}$$

Substituting this back into Eq. (1),

$$C_{s.e} = A[(\pi_{s.e}/P_{s.e})\phi_{\lambda e}\, \delta_1 - \lambda] + (\pi_{s.e}/P_{s.e})\,\delta_1\, W_e \qquad \text{(all } s) \tag{4}$$

Now, substituting these expressions for C_e and $\{C_{s.e}\}$ into

$$V_e(W_e) \equiv \ln(A + C_e) + \rho_2 \sum_s \pi_{s.e} \ln(A\lambda + C_{s.e})$$

and rearranging produces

$$V_e(W_e) = (1 + \rho_2)\ln[A\phi_{\lambda e} + W_e]$$

$$+ \left[\rho_2 \sum_s \pi_{s.e} \ln(\pi_{s.e}/P_{s.e}) + \rho_2 \ln \rho_2 - (1 + \rho_2)\ln(1 + \rho_2)\right]$$

Since the last bracketed expression depends only on exogenous variables, the derived utility of wealth function $V_e(W_e)$ is equivalent up to an additive transformation to the unbracketed term.[18] If the derived expression for $V_e(W_e)$ is itself substituted into the second-stage maximand, by partial differentiation it again follows that

$$P_e(A\phi_{\lambda e} + W_e) = \pi_e\rho_1(1 + \rho_2)(A + C_0) \qquad \text{(all } e) \tag{5}$$

or alternatively, in conjunction with Eq. (2),

$$P_e(A + C_e) = \pi_e\rho_1(A + C_0) \qquad \text{(all } e) \tag{1'}$$

A similar analysis to the above then shows that

$$A\phi_\lambda + W_0 = (1 + \rho_1 + \rho_1\rho_2)(A + C_0) \tag{2'}$$

$$C_0 = A[\phi_\lambda(1 - \delta) - 1] + (1 - \delta)W_0 \tag{3'}$$

$$W_e = A[(\pi_e/P_e)\phi_\lambda\, \delta - \phi_{\lambda e}] + (\pi_e/P_e)\,\delta W_0 \qquad \text{(all } e) \tag{4'}$$

$$V_0(W_0) = (1 + \rho_1 + \rho_1\rho_2)\ln(A\phi_\lambda + W_0)$$

$$+ \left\{\rho_1(1 + \rho_2) \sum_e \pi_e \ln(\pi_e/P_e) + \rho_1(1 + \rho_2)\ln[\rho_1(1 + \rho_2)]\right.$$

$$\left. - (1 + \rho_1 + \rho_1\rho_2)\ln(1 + \rho_1 + \rho_1\rho_2)\right\} \quad \text{Q.E.D.}$$

---

[18] For the purpose of determining optimal decision rules, it is unnecessary to know the exact form of the derived utility of wealth function $V_e(W_e)$ since, after differentiation to obtain optimal $(C_0, \{W_e\})$, additive constants have no effect on the first-order conditions. However, for the purpose of measuring a consumer's personal inflation index [45] or measuring the maximum price a consumer would pay for new information, the additive constant must be considered.

These decision rules yield immediate and sensible comparative statics results. The greater the initial wealth W_0, the greater the optimal consumption and portfolio holdings for each state, since by definition $0 < \delta < 1$. Since $\partial C_0/\partial \delta = -(A\phi_\lambda + W_0) < 0$ and $\partial W_e/\partial \delta = (\pi_e/P_e)(A\phi_\lambda + W_0) > 0$, the more patient the consumer, the less his initial consumption and the more his future consumption. Indeed, as a result of time-preference, he reduces his initial consumption by $\delta(A\phi_\lambda + W_0)$ and adds this to his initial investment. His initial consumption, even if δ is near one (extreme patience), has a greatest lower bound of $-A$; his initial investment, $\sum_e P_e W_e = A[\phi_\lambda(\delta - 1) + 1] + \delta W_0$, even if δ is near zero (extreme impatience), has a greatest lower bound of $-A(\phi_\lambda - 1)$. If $\phi_\lambda > (1 - \delta)^{-1} = 1 + \rho_1 + \rho_1\rho_2$, then as risk-preference increases (i.e., A increases), initial consumption rises and initial investment falls; and vice versa. $\phi_\lambda > 1 + \rho_1 + \rho_1\rho_2$ means that the securities market applies a higher series of discount rates to future consumption than that implied by a consumer's time-preference. In particular, if $1/(1 + r_F) + 1/(1 + R_F)^2 > \rho_1 + \rho_1\rho_2$, then with decreasing proportional risk aversion $(A < 0)$, a consumer reduces his consumption, but with increasing proportional risk aversion $(A > 0)$, he increases it. Finally, since $W_e = (\pi_e/P_e)\delta(A\phi_\lambda + W_0) - A\phi_{\lambda e}$, the consumer invests more in claims to states which he thinks more likely to occur or which have relatively cheap state-contingent claims.

Significantly, the derived utility of wealth functions are of the same "form" as the single-period utility function over consumption $U(\tilde{C}_t)$. To see this more clearly, consider a consumer who is alive at date $t = 1$ $(\lambda = 1)$ with a constant rate of time-preference $(\rho_1 = \rho_2 \equiv \rho < 1)$; for him

$$U(\tilde{C}_t) = \ln(A + \tilde{C}_t)$$

$$V_e(W_e) \approx (1 + \rho) \ln(A\phi_e + W_e)$$

$$\text{and} \qquad V_0(W_0) \approx (1 + \rho + \rho^2) \ln(A\phi + W_0)$$

This ensures that, even in an expanded setting with more than three dates, the sequence of single-period maximands is roughly similar. Indeed, if lifetime $T = \infty$, it is easy to extrapolate from the above to show that $V_0(W_0) = (1 - \rho)^{-1} \ln(A\phi + W_0)$, where ϕ now represents the present value of a perpetual annuity. If, additionally, at date $t = 0$, the period-by-period spot and forward risk-free rates were equal, then $\phi = (1 + r_F)/r_F$. Moreover, if future spot and forward risk-free rates were also equal to today's spot rate r_F, then for any date t, $V_t(\tilde{W}_t) = (1 - \rho)^{-1} \ln(A\phi + \tilde{W}_t)$; except for variations in wealth over time, the sequence of single-period maximands is *exactly* the same.[19] At this point, it is also worth noting that since $V_t' > 0$ and $V_t'' < 0$, then $-V_t'(\tilde{W}_t)/(V_t''(\tilde{W}_t)) = A\tilde{\phi}_{\lambda t} + \tilde{W}_t > 0$ for all dates t.

---

[19] Note also that under these conditions, $C_0 = (A/r_F)[1 - \rho(1 + r_F)] + (1 - \rho)W_0$.

The portfolio decision rules may be used to prove the following multi-period separation theorem.

Corollary (*Portfolio Separation*)   In the generalized logarithmic utility economy, portfolio choices satisfy the generalized separation property: at each date, the consumer divides his wealth after consumption between

(1)   a *default-free annuity* maturing at his death, and
(2)   a *risky portfolio*, the composition of which is independent of his wealth, time- and risk-preference, lifetime, and the returns of securities available at future dates.

In particular,

$$W_e = [1 + (1 - \lambda)r_F + \lambda r_{Ne}][(W_0 - C_0) - \delta(A\phi_\lambda + W_0)] + (1 + r_{Pe})$$
$$[\delta(A\phi_\lambda + W_0)]$$

for all e, where $1 + r_{Pe} \equiv \pi_e/P_e$.

Proof   Assume the conclusion and use Eq. (3′) to substitute for C_0. By canceling duplicating terms and rearranging, it is possible to derive the portfolio decision rule. This process can be repeated backwards.   Q.E.D.

This corollary generalizes the usual portfolio separation property to a nontrivial multiperiod setting[20] in which *none* of the following assumptions have been made:

(1)   all security rates of return follow a random walk,
(2)   tastes are logarithmic ($A = 0$),   and
(3)   lifetime is one period ($\lambda = 0$).

In any one of these special cases, the generalized separation property developed here collapses to more familiar single-period properties. With a random walk or a one-period lifetime, a consumer divides his wealth after consumption between a portfolio yielding the first-period risk-free rate and a risky portfolio, the composition of which is independent of his wealth. Similarly, with logarithmic utility, a consumer invests all his wealth after consumption in a single risky portfolio, the composition of which is independent of his wealth. In either case, default-free, long-term bonds have no *raison d'etre*; they are simply not needed by consumers to attain their optimal portfolio holdings. Therefore, since the default-free annuity can be regarded as an equally weighted portfolio of pure discount bonds of each possible maturity, one of the merits of the theory developed here is its ability to explain the demand for default-free bonds of varying maturities.

---

[20] Multiperiod separation results for the entire HARA class of utility functions may be found in Rubinstein [45].

One other somewhat surprising result is the independence of the composition of the bond portfolio from the time pattern of time-preference (ρ_1, ρ_2), provided $\lambda = 1$. In the extreme case, if a consumer dies at date $t = 1$, then he only demands short-term bonds. Similarly, it can be shown if a consumer's utility were defined only over consumption at dates $t = 0$ and $t = 2$, then he would only demand long-term bonds. However, for anything short of these two extremes $(\rho_1 > 0, \rho_2 > 0)$, a consumer balances his holdings of short- and long-term bonds equally. The "preferred habitat hypothesis" is therefore confirmed only for extreme forms of consumer tastes.[21]

The portfolio separation corollary will hold even for a generalized logarithmic utility consumer embedded in an economy in which other consumers do not have generalized logarithmic utility, but differ arbitrarily (provided they are risk averse) in their tastes for consumption. However, when all consumers, as in GLUM, have generalized logarithmic utility, the following stronger separation property may be demonstrated.

Corollary (*Universal Portfolio Separation*).   In the generalized logarithmic economy, if all consumers have the same beliefs, portfolio choices satisfy the generalized universal separation property: at each date, each consumer divides his wealth after consumption between

(1)   a *portfolio of default-free bonds* of mixed maturities, the composition of which depends upon his wealth, risk-preference, time-preference and lifetime; and

(2)   the *market portfolio*, containing all securities in proportion to their relative market values.

---

[21] However, in the exponential utility model (IIB), Rubinstein [46] shows that a consumer's bond portfolio is sensitive to the time pattern of his time-preference. In this model, other things equal, a consumer with a greater rate of time-preference ρ_2 toward consumption at date $t = 2$ than average will tend to slant his bond portfolio toward date $t = 2$ maturities.

This sensitivity (model IIB) or lack of sensitivity (model IIC) of the demand for short- versus long-term bonds to the time pattern of consumer time-preference differs from the results of Stiglitz [52]. Using a three-date model, he examines the relationship between the term structure and an individual's demand for short- versus long-term bonds. At date $t = 0$, individuals choose between short-, and long-term default-free pure discount bonds. At date $t = 1$, the previous short-term bonds mature and the previous long-terms now become the only existing short-term bonds. Consumers can revise their portfolios choosing between consumption and short-term bonds. At date $t = 2$, they consume their remaining wealth. Stiglitz introduces uncertainty by assuming the date $t = 1$ price of the long-term bonds is uncertain at date $t = 0$. His results differ because he admits no purely risky securities into his model. Had he done so, to the sources of demand for bonds he considers, he would have added their capacity as hedges against future shifts in the returns of risky securities. Moreover, without purely risky securities, if his model is carried to equilibrium by aggregating consumer demands for bonds, the equilibrium intermediate price of the long-term bonds becomes certain. Not only does this force the term structure to be unbiased to prevent riskless arbitrage, but also implies that consumers, irrespective of their tastes, will be indifferent between short- and long-term bonds.

If, additionally, all consumers have the same lifetime, then the portfolio of default-free bonds reduces to a default-free annuity maturing at their death.

Proof   Since Eq. (5) holds for all consumers in the economy and by assumption all consumers have the same beliefs

$$(\pi_e/P_e)\rho_1^i(1 + \rho_2^i)(A_i + C_0^i) = A_i[1 + \lambda_i(1 + r_{Fe})^{-1}] + W_e^i$$

for all i, where $\phi_{\lambda e} \equiv 1 + \lambda(1 + r_{Fe})^{-1}$. Summing this over all i,

$$(\pi_e/P_e)\sum_i [\rho_1^i(1 + \rho_2^i)(A_i + C_0^i)] = \left(\sum_i A_i\right) + (1 + r_{Fe})^{-1}\sum_i A_i\lambda_i + \sum_i W_e^i$$

By definition and closure, $W_e^M \equiv \sum_i W_e^i$, so that $(W_0^M - C_0^M) \times (1 + r_{Me}) = W_e^M$. Similarly, by definition, $1 + r_{Pe} \equiv \pi_e/P_e$, and $1 + R_{Fe} \equiv (1 + R_F)^2/(1 + r_{Fe})$. Letting $K^{-1} \equiv \sum_i [\rho_1^i(1 + \rho_2^i)(A_i + C_0^i)]$ and using these relationships to substitute into the previous equation,

$$(1 + r_{Pe}) = \left[K\left(\sum_i A_i\right)(1 + r_F)^{-1}\right](1 + r_F)$$

$$+ \left[K\left(\sum_i A_i\lambda_i\right)(1 + R_F)^{-2}\right](1 + R_{Fe}) + [K(W_0^M - C_0^M)](1 + r_{Me})$$

Therefore, there exist *constants a, b*, and *c* such that in equilibrium $(1 + r_{Pe}) = a(1 + r_F) + b(1 + R_{Fe}) + c(1 + r_{Me})$ so that the risky portfolio, which features in-the-portfolio separation property, may be replaced by holdings of short- and long-term default-free bonds and the market portfolio of all securities. This, added to the default-free annuity (i.e., short- and long-term default-free bonds) also held by each consumer, implies the universal portfolio separation property. It is also easy to see from the above equation that if all consumers have lifetime $T = 1$, then $b = 0$ and they only hold short-term bonds and the market portfolio. Likewise, if all consumers have lifetime $T = 2$, then $a(1 + r_{Fe}) + b(1 + R_{Fe}) = [K(\phi - 1)\sum_i A_i] \times (1 + r_{Ne})$ and they each hold a two-period default-free annuity and the market portfolio.   Q.E.D.

Under the conditions of the corollary, all consumers find it sufficient to hedge against all future shifts in portfolio opportunities by borrowing or lending default-free bonds of various maturities. This result generalizes to any number of dates. For example, if all consumers live forever $(T = \infty)$, then each either borrows or lends a perpetual default-free annuity in addition to a long-term[22] position in the market portfolio. Indeed, if the financial

---

[22] Holdings of the market portfolio must be long (not short) when all consumers have the same beliefs since, from risk aversion, in equilibrium, the market portfolio is a favorable gamble relative to holding the bond portfolio and all risk averters accept a positive fraction of favorable gamble (see Arrow [4]). In particular, from the portfolio separation corollaries, a consumer invests $\delta_i(A_i\phi_{\lambda i} + W_0^i)K(W_0^M - C_0^M)$ of his wealth after consumption in the market portfolio. Since $0 < \delta_i < 1$ and $-V_0^{i'}(W_0^i)/V_0^{i''}(W_0^i) = A_i\phi_{\lambda i} + W_0^i > 0$, this amount must be positive.

market is sufficiently rich in securities at date $t = 0$, then no consumer need ever revise his portfolio. In an extreme case, if a complete futures market existed at date $t = 0$, so that claims were not only available for each state e but also for each sequence of states e and s, then irrespective of consumer tastes, no consumer will ever need to revise his portfolio. However, in GLUM with homogeneous beliefs, a complete futures market is far from necessary. As long as at least default-free bonds exist of each maturity (the market portfolio exists trivially), then no portfolio revision will occur, consumers managing over time quite nicely off the interest income from the bonds and the dividend income from the market portfolio.

The behavior of consumers in GLUM can also be usefully characterized by comparing their choices with those made by an appropriately defined "average" consumer. In particular, portfolio choices can be broken down into components, each describing the demand for particular securities created by the deviation of a particular economic characteristic from average. The decomposition of the molecule of portfolio choice into its constituent atoms lays bare the comparative statics of financial choice.

Meaningful "average" economic characteristics (in this case, wealth composition and scale, risk-preference, time-preference, lifetime, and beliefs) should satisfy certain properties. Let the economic characteristics of consumer i be denoted by the set $\{x_c^i\}$, where subscript c indexes these characteristics. An "average" characteristic is denoted by x_c, and its relationship to the underlying characteristics of consumers is described by the explicit function $x_c - f_c(\{x_c^i\})$ for all i. A *consensus* (or social) characteristic x_c is said to exist if it satisfies the following properties:[23]

(i) *Homogeniety:* If x_c^i is homogeneous, then $x_c = x_c^i$;
(ii) *Commensurability:* If c is denominated in units of wealth, then $x_c = \sum_i x_c^i / I$;
(iii) *Agreement:* Social choices (e.g., prices) are determined as if $x_c^i = x_c$

---

[23] Other interesting properties include *nondictatorship* (no social choice depends solely on the characteristics of a group of consumers smaller than the population), *positive responsiveness* (an increase in a characteristic of any consumer affects social choices in the same direction as an increase in its corresponding consensus characteristic), and *anonymity* (any permutation of the same characteristic among consumers leaves social choices unchanged). Nondictatorship is satisfied by GLUM for all social choices ($\{P_e\}, \{P_{s,e}\}$). Even though a group of consumers die immediately after the first period, their demand for consumption at date $t = 1$ influences second-period prices. This, as well as their influence on first-period prices and, therefore, on the initial wealth of even long-lived consumers, also affects prices in the third period and beyond. However, even with endogenous production, their influence ebbs as they recede into the past. Indeed, with composite characteristics, they have no influence over prices after the second period. Positive responsiveness is satisfied by GLUM for all characteristics except lifetime. Anonymity is trivially satisfied by resources whenever the strong aggregation problem is solved; see Rubinstein [45] (p. 233). More generally, if $x_c = \sum_i x_c^i / I$ or $x_c = (\prod_i x_c^i)^1 / I$ and other characteristics are not a function of c, then social choices are anonymous with respect to c.

for all i. If a consensus characteristic is defined for all characteristics c, then we shall say the *weak aggregation problem* is solved. A *composite* characteristic x_c is said to exist if, in addition to properties (i)–(iii), it also satisfies;

(iv)   *Exogeneity:* x_c is not a function of private (e.g., consumption and portfolio) or social choices.

If a composite characteristic is defined for all characteristics c, we shall say the *strong aggregation problem* is solved.

We will use GLUM to construct consensus and composite characteristics. However, since this type of analysis may be unfamiliar, I will first provide a simple illustration. Suppose each consumer in the economy maximizes the expectation of a single-period logarithmic utility function of wealth

$$\max_{\{W_e^i\}} \sum_e \pi_e^i \ln W_e^i - \Lambda_i \left[\sum_e P_e W_e^i - W_0^i \right]$$

In this example, consumers are heterogeneous with respect to their resources ($W_0^i \equiv \sum_e P_e \overline{W}_e^i$) and beliefs $\{\pi_e^i\}$. Partially differentiating with respect to W_e^i, setting the derivative equal to zero, and eliminating the Lagrangian multiplier by introducing the budget constraint, produces the optimal decision rule: $W_e^i = (\pi_e^i/P_e)W_0^i$ for all e. Since this holds for all i, we can sum over all i and divide by I, so that $P_e(\sum_i W_e^i/I) = \sum_i \pi_e^i W_0^i/I$. By closure, since $\sum_i W_e^i = \sum_i \overline{W}_e^i$ we can define average resources $W_e \equiv \sum_i \overline{W}_e^i/I$, so that $P_e W_e = \sum_i \pi_e^i W_0^i/I$. Now define average beliefs π_e such that $P_e W_e = \pi_e \sum_i W_0^i/I$. Therefore, $\pi_e \equiv \sum_i (W_0^i/\sum_i W_0^i)\pi_e^i$. Finally, define average wealth $W_0 \equiv \sum_e P_e W_e = \sum_i W_0^i/I$ so that $P_e W_e = \pi_e W_0$. From their definitions it is easy to verify that these average variables satisfy properties (i) and (ii) of consensus characteristics. To see that they also satisfy (iii), observe that $P_e W_e = \pi_e W_0$ for all e together with $W_0 = \sum_e P_e W_e$ are the necessary and sufficient conditions for an optimum that would have been derived had there existed only consumers with the specified consensus characteristics. Therefore, prices are determined as if $\{\overline{W}_e^i = W_e\}$ and $\{\pi_e^i = \pi_e\}$ for all i.

However, composite beliefs do not exist, because π_e depends indirectly on prices through the dependence of initial wealth W_0^i on prices. To obtain composite beliefs, assume additionally that there exist constants $\mu_i \equiv \overline{W}_e^i/W_e$ for all e and i. μ_i can be interpreted as a measure of the scale of wealth of consumer i, *independent* of the price system. If $\mu_i > 1$, a consumer is unambiguously "rich," and if $\mu_i < 1$, a consumer is unambiguously "poor." The composite scale of wealth $\mu \equiv 1$ and $\sum_i \mu_i = I$. Clearly, since $W_0^i \equiv \sum_e P_e \overline{W}_e^i$ and $W_0 \equiv \sum_e P_e W_e$, then $W_0^i = \mu_i W_0$. With homogeneity of wealth composition, then composite beliefs $\pi_e = \sum_i \mu_i \pi_e^i/I$.

Permitting heterogeneity with respect to wealth composition and scale, lifetime, risk- and time-preference, and beliefs:

Theorem (*Weak Aggregation*) In the generalized logarithmic utility economy, consensus characteristics exist for all exogenous variables. In particular,

$$\text{resources:} \quad C_0 \equiv \sum_i \bar{C}_0^i/I, \quad C_e \equiv \sum_i \bar{C}_e^i/I, \quad C_{s.e} \equiv \sum_i \bar{C}_{s.e}^i/I$$

$$\text{(all } e \text{ and } s\text{)}$$

$$\text{risk-preference:} \quad A \equiv \sum_i A_i/I \quad \left(\sum_i A_i \neq 0\right), \quad A \equiv \sum_i (\lambda_i/\lambda I)A_i$$

$$\left(\sum_i A_i = 0\right) \quad \text{(all } e \text{ and } s\text{)}$$

$$\text{lifetime:} \quad \lambda \equiv \sum_i (A_i/AI)\lambda_i \quad \left(\sum_i A_i \neq 0\right), \quad \lambda \equiv \sum_i \lambda_i/I \quad \left(\sum_i A_i = 0\right)$$

$$\text{time-preference:} \quad \rho_1 \equiv \sum_i \left(\frac{A_i + C_0^i}{(A + C_0)I}\right)\rho_1^i, \quad \rho_2 \equiv \sum_i \left(\frac{\rho_1^i(A_i + C_0^i)}{\rho_1(A + C_0)I}\right)\rho_2^i$$

$$\text{beliefs:} \quad \pi_e \equiv \sum_i \left(\frac{\rho_1^i(A_i + C_0^i)}{\rho_1(A + C_0)I}\right)\pi_e^i \quad \text{(all } e\text{)}$$

$$\pi_{s.e} \equiv \sum_i \left(\frac{\pi_e^i\rho_2^i\rho_1^i(A_i + C_0^i)}{\pi_e\rho_2\rho_1(A + C_0)I}\right)\pi_{s.e}^i \quad \text{(all } e \text{ and } s\text{)}$$

Proof Summing Eq. (1′) over all i and dividing both sides by I,

$$P_e \sum_i (A_i + C_e^i)/I = \sum_i \pi_e^i\rho_1^i(A_i + C_0^i)/I$$

Define average resources $C_e \equiv \sum_i C_e^i/I$, average risk-preference $A \equiv \sum_i A_i/I$, and average beliefs π_e such that

$$P_e(A + C_e) = \pi_e \sum_i \rho_1^i(A_i + C_0^i)/I$$

Therefore, $\pi_e \equiv \sum_i [\rho_1^i(A_i + C_0)/\sum_i \rho_1^i(A_i + C_0^i)]\pi_e^i$. Define average time-preference ρ_1 such that

$$P_e(A + C_e) = \pi_e\rho_1 \sum_i (A_i + C_0^i)/I$$

Therefore, $\rho_1 \equiv \sum_i [A_i + C_0^i/\sum_i (A_i + C_0^i)]\rho_1^i$. Moreover, from the definition of A and defining average resources $C_0 \equiv \sum_i C_0^i/I$, it follows that

$$P_e(A + C_e) = \pi_e\rho_1(A + C_0) \tag{a}$$

in terms of the average variables. Combining (1), (2), and (5),

$$P_e P_{s.e}(A_i\lambda_i + C_{s.e}^i) = \pi_{s.e}^i\pi_e^i\rho_2^i\rho_1^i(A_i + C_0^i)$$

Summing over all i and dividing both sides by I,

$$P_e P_{s.e} \sum_i (A_i \lambda_i + C^i_{s.e})/I = \sum_i \pi^i_{s.e} \pi^i_e \rho^i_2 \rho^i_1 (A_i + C^i_0)/I$$

Define average resources $C^i_{s.e} \equiv \sum_i C^i_{s.e}/I$, average lifetime (provided $\sum_i A_i \neq 0$) $\lambda \equiv \sum_i (A_i/\sum_i A_i)\lambda_i$, and average beliefs $\pi_{s.e} \pi_e$ such that

$$P_e P_{s.e}(A\lambda + C_{s.e}) = \pi_{s.e} \pi_e \sum_i \rho^i_2 \rho^i_1 (A_i + C^i_0)/I$$

Therefore, $\pi_{s.e} \equiv \sum_i [\pi^i_e \rho^i_2 \rho^i_1 (A_i + C^i_0)/\pi_e \sum_i \rho^i_2 \rho^i_1 (A + C^i_0)]\pi^i_{s.e}$. Define average time-preference $\rho_2 \rho_1$ such that

$$P_e P_{s.e}(A\lambda + C_{s.e}) = \pi_{s.e} \pi_e \rho_2 \rho_1 \sum_i (A_i + C^i_0)I$$

Therefore, $\rho_2 \equiv \sum_i [\rho^i_1 (A_i + C^i_0)/\rho_1 \sum_i (A_i + C^i_0)]\rho^i_2$. Moreover, from the definitions of A and C_0, it follows that

$$P_e P_{s.e}(A\lambda + C_{s.e}) = \pi_{s.e} \pi_e \rho_2 \rho_1 (A + C_0)$$

Finally, combining this equation with Eq. (a),

$$P_{s.e}(A\lambda + C_{s.e}) = \pi_{s.e} \rho_2 (A + C_e) \tag{b}$$

From their definitions, it is easy to verify that these average variables satisfy properties (i) and (ii) of consensus characteristics. To see that they also satisfy property (iii), observe that Eqs. (a) and (b) are the necessary and sufficient conditions[24] for an optimum that would have been derived had there existed only consumers with the specified concensus characteristics. Therefore, prices $(\{P_e\}, \{P_{s.e}\})$ are determined as if $\bar{C}^i_0 = C_0$, $\{\bar{C}^i_e = C_e\}$, $\{\bar{C}^i_{s.e} = C_{s.e}\}$, $A_i = A$, $\lambda_i = \lambda$, $\rho^i_1 = \rho_1$, $\rho^i_2 = \rho_2$, $\{\pi^i_e = \pi_e\}$, and $\{\pi^i_{s.e} = \pi_{s.e}\}$ for all i. Q.E.D.

Corollary (*Strong Aggregation*) In the generalized logarithmic economy, composite characteristics exist for all exogenous variables if any one of the following homogeneity conditions holds:

(1) time-preference and beliefs are homogeneous;
(2) resources are homogeneous in composition (but not necessarily in scale), the ratio of risk-preference to scale of resources is homogeneous, and lifetime is homogeneous;
(3) resources are homogeneous in composition (but not necessarily in scale), and risk-preference is homogeneous and equal to zero.

---

[24] From the definition of consensus resource characteristics, the consensus budget constraint $W_0 = C_0 + \sum_e P_e C_e + \sum_e P_e \sum_s P_{s.e} C_{s.e}$ is trivially satisfied.

In particular, in each case

resources: $\quad C_0 \equiv \sum_i \bar{C}_0^i / I, \qquad C_e \equiv \sum_i \bar{C}_e^i / I, \qquad C_{s.e} \equiv \sum_i \bar{C}_{s.e}^i / I$

(all e and s)

risk-preference: $\quad A \equiv \sum_i A_i / I \quad \left(\sum_i A_i \neq 0 \right),$

$$A \equiv \sum_i (\lambda_i / \lambda I) A_i \quad \left(\sum_i A_i = 0 \right)$$

lifetime: $\quad \lambda \equiv \sum_i (A_i / AI) \lambda_i \quad \left(\sum_i A_i \neq 0 \right), \qquad \lambda \equiv \sum_i \lambda_i / I \quad \left(\sum_i A_i = 0 \right)$

and for case (1)

time-preference: $\quad \rho_1 \equiv \rho_1^i \qquad$ and $\qquad \rho_2 \equiv \rho_2^i \qquad$ (all i)

beliefs: $\quad \pi_e \equiv \pi_e^i \qquad$ and $\qquad \pi_{s.e} \equiv \pi_{s.e}^i \qquad$ (all e, s, and i)

and for cases (2) and (3)

time-preference: $\quad \rho_1 \equiv \sum_i \left(\dfrac{(1 - \delta_i)\mu_i}{(1 - \delta)I} \right) \rho_1^i, \qquad \rho_2 \equiv \sum_i \left(\dfrac{\rho_1^i (1 - \delta_i)\mu_i}{\rho_1 (1 - \delta)I} \right) \rho_2^i$

beliefs: $\quad \pi_e = \sum_i \left(\dfrac{\rho_1^i (1 - \delta_i)\mu_i}{\rho_1 (1 - \delta)I} \right) \pi_e^i \qquad$ (all e)

$$\pi_{s.e} = \sum_i \left(\frac{\pi_e^i \rho_2^i \rho_1^i (1 - \delta_i)\mu_i}{\pi_e \rho_2 \rho_1 (1 - \delta)I} \right) \pi_{s.e}^i \qquad \text{(all } e \text{ and } s)$$

where $1 - \delta \equiv (1 + \rho_1 + \rho_1 \rho_2)^{-1}$ and $\mu_i \equiv \bar{C}_0^i / C_0 = \bar{C}_e^i / C_e = \bar{C}_{s.e}^i / C_{s.e}$ for all e, s, and i.

Proof To see that composite characteristics can exist, observe immediately for case (1) that each consensus characteristic is defined only in terms of exogenous variables; they are not dependent on prices. For case (2), there exist constants $\mu_i \equiv \bar{C}_0^i / C_0 = \bar{C}_e^i / C_e = \bar{C}_{s.e}^i / C_{s.e}$ for all e, s, and i. Additionally, there also exists a constant k such that $A_i = k\mu_i$ for all i and $\lambda_i = \lambda$ for all i. Since Eq. (2′) holds for all i,

$$(A_i + C_0^i) = (1 - \delta_i)(A_i \phi_{\lambda_i} + W_0^i)$$

and making appropriate substitutions consistent with case (2),

$$(A_i + C_0^i) = (1 - \delta_i)\mu_i (k\phi_\lambda + W_0)$$

Using this relationship, a repetition of the above proof of the existence of consensus characteristics yields the composites defined in the theorem. For case (3), by following the same procedure, we derive similar composites, except that $A_i = A = 0$ for all i. Observe that in this case it is unnecessary to assume homogeneous lifetimes.   Q.E.D.

Since a complete set of consensus characteristics exists, we can meaningfully speak of a "consensus consumer" and imagine that prices are determined as if only consensus consumers existed. Since these consumers all make optimal choices according to Eqs. (a) and (b), then these equations can be used to determine the relationship among prices in equilibrium. As demonstrated in Section IV, these equations are especially useful for this purpose, since they facilitate relating the price system ($\{P_e\}$, $\{P_{s.e}\}$) to aggregate consumption variables ($C_0^M = IC_0$, $\{C_e^M = IC_e\}$, $\{C_{s.e}^M = IC_{s.e}\}$) by virtue of properties (ii) and (iii).

However, since the consensus taste and belief characteristics are themselves functions of prices [through their dependence on C_0^i and through its dependence on ϕ_{λ_i} and W_0^i by Eq. (2')], the price relationships derived with equations (a) and (b) will not be complete. For example, type I models contain similarly incomplete price relationships, since they fail to determine endogenously the risk-free rate and the "market price of risk."[25] However, composite characteristics, by virtue of their independence from the price system, enable us to write prices as explicit functions only of exogenous variables, providing a complete set of price relationships.[26] This will not be without the cost of imposing one of the set of strong homogeneity conditions described in the theorem. Fortunately, consensus statistics are sufficient to formulate most empirical hypotheses.

To highlight the comparative statics of the model, the consensus characteristics may be used to construct sharing rules which indicate how consumption or portfolio choices of a particular consumer deviate from the per capita choices of a consensus consumer. In contrast to type I models, where portfolio choices are broken down into two or at most three components,[27] GLUM achieves 38 components.

---

[25] Alternatively, since the "market price of risk" can be shown to be determined by the rate of return of the market portfolio and the risk-free rate, type I models have little to say about the relationship of these important portfolios, other than $E(r_M) > r_F$.

[26] The existence of composite characteristics also has important welfare implications, as developed in Section V.

[27] For example, in the discrete-time normality model, as a slight extension of Rubinstein (1973), for all i and e

$$W_e^i = \frac{(W_0^i - C_0^i)\theta_i - (W_0 - C_0)\theta}{\theta_i(\phi - 1)} + \frac{\theta}{\theta_i} W_e$$

where $\theta_i \equiv -E[V_i''(W_1^i)]/E[V_i'(W_1^i)]$, $\theta^{-1} \equiv \sum_i \theta_i^{-1}/I$, and $W_e \equiv \sum_i W_e^i/I$. Because of the random walk assumption, V_i is a state-independent derived utility of wealth function. This sharing rule implies that all consumers divide their wealth (after consumption) between a risk-free investment and the market portfolio. Note that θ_i is itself indirectly a function of prices.

Since this type of analysis may be unfamiliar, I will again first provide a simple illustration. Suppose each consumer in the economy maximizes the expectation of a single-period logarithmic utility function of wealth. Then, from the previous simple aggregation example, $P_e W_e^i = \pi_e^i W_0^i$ for all i and for the consensus consumer $P_e W_e = \pi_e W_0$. Dividing these equations into each other, $W_e^i = (\pi_e^i W_0^i / \pi_e W_0) W_e$. If to the right-hand side we subtract and add the same number $(\pi_e W_0^i / \pi_e W_0) W_e$, then $W_e^i = ((\pi_e^i - \pi_e)/\pi_e) \times (W_0^i / W_0) W_e + (W_0^i / W_0) W_e$. If again to the right-hand side we subtract and add $((\pi_e^i - \pi_e)/\pi_e)(W_0 / W_0) W_e$, then

$$W_e^i = ((\pi_e^i - \pi_e)/\pi_e)((W_0^i - W_0)/W_0) W_e + ((\pi_e^i - \pi_e)/\pi_e) W_e + (W_0^i / W_0) W_e$$

Finally, adding and subtracting (W_0 / W_0) to the right-hand side,

$$W_e^i = \left(\frac{\pi_e^i - \pi_e}{\pi_e}\right)\left(\frac{W_0^i - W_0}{W_0}\right) W_e + \left(\frac{\pi_e^i - \pi_e}{\pi_e}\right) W_e + \left(\frac{W_0^i - W_0}{W_0}\right) W_e + W_e$$

$$\langle BW \rangle \qquad\qquad \langle B \rangle \qquad\qquad \langle W \rangle \qquad\qquad \langle C \rangle$$

Here the portfolio sharing rule can be broken into four components: $\langle C \rangle$ is the (per capita) portfolio choice of the consensus consumer. $\langle W \rangle$ is the additional (to $\langle C \rangle$) portfolio position taken by consumers with the same beliefs but more wealth than average. Observe that

$$W_e \sum_i (W_0^i - W_0)/W_0 = 0$$

so that under state e for every dollar a *rich* ($W_0^i > W_0$) consumer receives more than the average, and a *poor* ($W_0^i < W_0$) consumer sacrifices. Similarly, $\langle B \rangle$ is the additional (to $\langle C \rangle$) portfolio position taken by consumers with the same wealth but with more optimistic beliefs than average. For *optimists* toward state e, $\pi_e^i > \pi_e$, and for *pessimists*, $\pi_e^i < \pi_e$. Moreover, if there is no correlation between the level of consumer wealth and consumer optimism (i.e., speaking loosely, if for every rich optimist there is also a rich pessimist), then from the definition of consensus beliefs, wealth effects cancel and $\pi_e = \sum_i \pi_e^i / I$. In this case, since $W_e \sum_i (\pi_e^i - \pi_e)/\pi_e = 0$, under state e every unit of wealth received by an optimist is lost by a pessimist. Optimists and pessimists can be interpretated as taking mutual and opposite *speculative side bets* (options) $\langle B \rangle$ in addition to their *state-dependent dividend* (market portfolio) $\langle C \rangle$. Finally, $\langle BW \rangle$ may be interpreted as the additional (to $\langle B \rangle$) speculative side bet taken by those consumers with both different beliefs and wealth than average. For example, as we would expect, rich optimists make larger speculative side bets than poor optimists.[28]

---

[28] One of the disadvantages of the exponential utility model (IIB), which also permits heterogeneous beliefs, is the insensitivity of speculative side bets to wealth. This property goes hand in hand with constant absolute risk aversion. See Rubinstein [46].

Permitting heterogeneity with respect to wealth composition and scale, lifetime, risk- and time-preference, and beliefs:

Theorem (*Sharing Rule*) In the generalized logarithmic utility economy, with respect to the consensus characteristics defined in the weak aggregation theorem, the optimal portfolio sharing rule for the first period may be written as the per capita return from the market portfolio plus the sum of 37 other components, each indicating the extent to which the portfolio of any consumer deviates from the consensus consumer. In particular, for any consumer i and for each state e, his portfolio choice W_e^i is equal to the sum of

1. $\langle C \rangle$ W_e
2. $\langle 1W \rangle$ $+ (W_0^i - W_0)[K]W_e$
3. $\langle 1R \rangle$ $+ (A_i - A)[\phi_\lambda K]W_e$
4. $\langle 1T \rangle$ $+ (\delta_i - \delta)[\delta^{-1}]W_e$
5. $\langle 1L \rangle$ $+ (\lambda_i - \lambda)[P_F K]AW_e$
6. $\langle 1WT \rangle$ $+ (W_0^i - W_0)(\delta_i - \delta)[\delta^{-1}K]W_e$
7. $\langle 1RT \rangle$ $+ (A_i - A)(\delta_i - \delta)[\phi_\lambda \, \delta^{-1}K]W_e$
8. $\langle 1RL \rangle$ $+ (A_i - A)(\lambda_i - \lambda)[P_F K]W_e$
9. $\langle 1TL \rangle$ $+ (\delta_i - \delta)(\lambda_i - \lambda)[\delta^{-1}P_F K]AW_e$
10. $\langle 1RTL \rangle$ $+ (A_i - A)(\delta_i - \delta)(\lambda_i - \lambda)[\delta^{-1}P_F K]W_e$
11. $\langle 2W \rangle$ $+ (W_0^i - W_0)[K]A$
12. $\langle 2R \rangle$ $- (A_i - A)[W_0 K]$
13. $\langle 2T \rangle$ $+ (\delta_i - \delta)[\delta^{-1}]A$
14. $\langle 2L \rangle$ $+ (\lambda_i - \lambda)[P_F KA^2]$
15. $\langle 2WT \rangle$ $+ (W_0^i - W_0)(\delta_i - \delta)[\delta^{-1}K]A$
16. $\langle 2RT \rangle$ $+ (A_i - A)(\delta_i - \delta)[\phi_\lambda \, \delta^{-1}K]A$
17. $\langle 2RL \rangle$ $+ (A_i - A)(\lambda_i - \lambda)[P_F K]A$
18. $\langle 2TL \rangle$ $+ (\delta_i - \delta)(\lambda_i - \lambda)[\delta^{-1}P_F KA^2]$
19. $\langle 2RTL \rangle$ $+ (A_i - A)(\delta_i - \delta)(\lambda_i - \lambda)[\delta^{-1}P_F K]A$
20. $\langle 3W \rangle$ $+ (W_0^i - W_0)[K\lambda]AP_{F.e}$
21. $\langle 3R \rangle$ $- (A_i - A)[W_0 K\lambda]P_{F.e}$
22. $\langle 3T \rangle$ $+ (\delta_i - \delta)[\delta^{-1}\lambda]AP_{F.e}$
23. $\langle 3L \rangle$ $- (\lambda_i - \lambda)[(A\phi_0 + W_0)K]AP_{F.e}$
24. $\langle 3WT \rangle$ $+ (W_0^i - W_0)(\delta_i - \delta)[\delta^{-1}K\lambda]AP_{F.e}$
25. $\langle 3RT \rangle$ $+ (A_i - A)(\delta_i - \delta)[\phi_\lambda \, \delta^{-1}K\lambda]AP_{F.e}$
26. $\langle 3RL \rangle$ $- (A_i - A)(\lambda_i - \lambda)[A\phi_0 + W_0)K]P_{F.e}$
27. $\langle 3TL \rangle$ $+ (\delta_i - \delta)(\lambda_i - \lambda)[\delta^{-1}P_F KA^2\lambda]P_{F.e}$
28. $\langle 3RTL \rangle$ $+ (A_i - A)(\delta_i - \delta)(\lambda_i - \lambda)[\delta^{-1}P_F K\lambda]AP_{F.e}$
29. $\langle B \rangle$ $+ (\pi_e^i - \pi_e)[\delta K^{-1}]P_e^{-1}$
30. $\langle BW \rangle$ $+ (\pi_e^i - \pi_e)(W_0^i - W_0)[\delta]P_e^{-1}$
31. $\langle BR \rangle$ $+ (\pi_e^i - \pi_e)(A_i - A)[\phi_\lambda \, \delta]P_e^{-1}$

32. $\langle BT \rangle$ $+ (\pi_e^i - \pi_e)(\delta_i - \delta)[K^{-1}]P_e^{-1}$
33. $\langle BL \rangle$ $+ (\pi_e^i - \pi_e)(\lambda_i - \lambda)[\delta P_F]AP_e^{-1}$
34. $\langle BWT \rangle$ $+ (\pi_e^i - \pi_e)(W_0^i - W_0)(\delta_i - \delta)P_e^{-1}$
35. $\langle BRT \rangle$ $+ (\pi_e^i - \pi_e)(A_i - A)(\delta_i - \delta)[\phi_\lambda]P_e^{-1}$
36. $\langle BRL \rangle$ $+ (\pi_e^i - \pi_e)(A_i - A)(\lambda_i - \lambda)[\delta P_F]P_e^{-1}$
37. $\langle BTL \rangle$ $+ (\pi_e^i - \pi_e)(\delta_i - \delta)(\lambda_i - \lambda)[P_F]AP_e^{-1}$
38. $\langle BRTL \rangle$ $+ (\pi_e^i - \pi_e)(A_i - A)(\delta_i - \delta)(\lambda_i - \lambda)[P_F]P_e^{-1}$

where the consensus absolute risk aversion of initial wealth $K \equiv (A\phi_\lambda + W_0)^{-1}$, $W_e \equiv C_e + \sum_s P_{s.e}C_{s.e}$, $P_F \equiv (1 + R_F)^{-2}$, and $P_{F.e} \equiv (1 + r_{Fe})^{-1}$.

Proof Rearranging the portfolio decision rule [Eq. (4′)], $P_e(A\phi_{\lambda e} + W_e) = \pi_e \delta(A\phi_\lambda + W_0)$. Since this holds for the consensus consumer as well as consumer i,

$$W_e^i = \frac{\pi_e^i \delta_i}{\pi_e \delta}(A_i\phi_{\lambda_i} + W_0^i)K(A\phi_{\lambda e} + W_e) - A_i\phi_{\lambda_i}e$$

$$\text{where} \quad K \equiv (A\phi_\lambda + W_0)^{-1}$$

The same method as in the example of adding and subtracting terms to the right-hand side of this equation will eventually produce the sharing rule. Since the algebra is very tedious, it will be left for the reader if he cares to verify the result.   Q.E.D.

The components of the sharing rule have been coded to reflect both the type of security purchased and the motivation for the purchase. $\langle C \rangle$ is again the portfolio choice of the concensus consumer. Components 2–10 coded with $\langle 1 \rangle$ are the additional holdings of the market portfolio of consumer i; components 11–19 coded with $\langle 2 \rangle$ are his position in short-term default-free bonds; components 20–28 coded with $\langle 3 \rangle$ are his position in long-term default-free bonds; and components 29–38 coded with $\langle B \rangle$ are his position in options. Components coded with $\langle W \rangle$ are nonzero due to above- or below-average wealth; components coded with $\langle R \rangle$ are nonzero due to above- or below-average risk-preference; and those with $\langle T \rangle$ are nonzero due to above or below average time-preference. All terms contained in brackets [·] are nonnegative (assuming $\lambda \geq 0$).

Focusing on the unadulterated components (2–5, 11–14, 20–24, 29–33) and including inferences from the optimal consumption sharing rule,[29] Table II summarizes the comparative statics of financial choice for the generalized logarithmic utility economy.

---

[29] The optimal consumption sharing rule is computed in a manner similar to the optimal portfolio sharing rule using the consumption decision rule (3′). It has been omitted to conserve space.

As one would expect, greater wealth permits more consumption, a larger investment in the market portfolio, and more extreme positions in options. However, greater wealth also leads to less investment in bonds of each maturity when the society exhibits decreasing proportional risk aversion in aggregate. Again this is to be expected since in the neutral case where all consumers have constant proportional risk aversion, there is no demand for default-free investments. As one would also expect, the more risk-preferring a consumer, the more he invests in the market portfolio, the less he invests in default-free bonds of each maturity, and the more extreme position he is

Table II[a]

Social risk-preference	Wealth (W_0)			Risk-preference (A)			Time-preference (δ)			Lifetime (λ)			Beliefs (π_e)		
	$(-)$	(0)	$(+)$	$(-)$	(0)	$(+)$	$(-)$	(0)	$(+)$	$(-)$	(0)	$(+)$	$(-)$	(0)	$(+)$
Consumption	+	+	+	?	?	?	−	−	−	−	0	+	0	0	0
Market portfolio	+	+	+	+	+	+	+	+	+	−	0	+	0	0	0
Short-term bonds	−	0	+	−	−	−	−	0	+	+	0	+	0	0	0
Long-term bonds	−	0	+	−	−	−	−	0	+	+	0	−	0	0	0
Options	+	+	+	+	+	+	+	+	+	−	0	+	+	+	+

[a] Social (consensus) risk-preference is measured by A, so that $A < 0$ is represented by $(-)$, $A = 0$ by (0), and $A > 0$ by $(+)$. Similarly, the other minuses (zeros, pluses) in the table indicate that given the social risk-preference indicated, less (same, more) of an item on the left margin of the table is held, if with respect to the corresponding characteristic on the top margin, a consumer is above the average (consensus) for the economy. The signs relating to options apply to an optimist; they are reversed for a pessimist. The implications of risk-preference for initial consumption cannot be inferred without knowing the time-state path of aggregate consumption. The signs in the table presume $\lambda > 0$.

willing to take in options. Likewise, the more patient a consumer, the less his consumption and the greater his investment in both the market portfolio and options. However, greater patience also leads to less investment in bonds of each maturity when the society exhibits decreasing proportional risk aversion. This also is to be expected since, in the neutral case where all consumers have constant proportional risk aversion, there is no demand for default-free investments. When society exhibits constant proportional risk aversion, lifetime has no separate effect on consumer behavior other than its impact on time-preference (recall that if $\lambda_i = 0$, then $\rho_2^i = 0$, and if $\lambda_i = 1$, then $\rho_2^i > 0$). Of course, from our definition of options, differences in beliefs do not create demand for the market portfolio or default-free bonds.

The sharing rule is also consistent with our portfolio separation corollary with respect to lifetime: if $\lambda_i = 0$ for all i, components 20–28 vanish and there is no demand for long-term bonds; likewise, if $\lambda_i = 1$ for all i, components 11–19 and 20–28 merge so that all consumers invest in an equally weighted portfolio of short- and long-term bonds (an annuity) in addition to the market portfolio and options. Finally, the magnitude as well as the sign of each component can be inferred from the strength of a consumer's nonconformist characteristics and the consensus variables in the brackets $[\cdot]$ of each component. For example, using components 3 and 4, other things equal, for the same percentage deviation in risk-preference as time-preference [i.e., $(A_i - A)/A = (\delta_i - \delta)/\delta$], in addition to the joint demand for the market portfolio (component 7), demand due purely to risk-preference is $A\phi_\lambda K$ times the demand due purely to time-preference. When $A > 0$, then $0 < A\phi_\lambda K < 1$ and time-preference is a more significant factor, influencing demand for the market portfolio.[30]

---

[30] Recall the previous analysis, which demonstrated that if $A_i \leq 0$ as long as $W_0^i > -A\phi_{\lambda_i}$, then positive consumption is assured at every date. However, this condition is not sufficient to guarantee positive consumption when $A_i > 0$. In this case, the sharing rule can be used to bound the heterogeneity of consumers for whom $A_i > 0$. To focus on the critical variables, suppose under certainty all consumers are identical except for their wealth and risk-preference and have lifetimes $\lambda_i = 0$. The sharing rules may then be simplified to

$$C_0^i = \frac{AW_0^i - A_i W_0}{A\phi + W_0} + \frac{A_i\phi + W_0^i}{A\phi + W_0} C_0 \quad \text{and} \quad C_1^i = \frac{AW_0^i - A_i W_0}{A\phi + W_0} + \frac{A_i\phi + W_0^i}{A\phi + W_0} C_1$$

for all i. Therefore, $C_0^i > 0$, and $C_1^i > 0$ if and only if $A_i(\phi C_0 - W_0) + W_0^i(A + C_0) > 0$ and $A_i(\phi C_1 - W_0) + W_0^i(A + C_1) > 0$. Since $\phi C_0 - W_0 = P_F(C_0 - C_1)$ and $\phi C_1 - W_0 = C_1 - C_0$, positive consumption is satisfied for $A_i > 0$ if and only if

$$\frac{W_0^i}{A_i} > \max\left[\frac{C_0 - C_1}{A + C_1}, \frac{P_F(C_1 - C_0)}{A + C_0}\right]$$

If aggregate consumption is equally spaced across time (i.e., $C_0 = C_1$), then positive consumption is always satisfied. With growing aggregate consumption (i.e., $C_1 > C_0$), we need only worry about the second term in the maximand. Since in equilibrium (see Section IV), $P_F = \rho(A + C_0)/(A + C_1)$, then we require

$$W_0^i/A_i > \rho(C_1 - C_0)/(A + C_1)$$

If the growth rate of aggregate consumption is denoted by r, so that $C_1 = C_0(1 + r)$ and time-preference is neutral so that $\rho = 1$, then this inequality is equivalent to

$$A_i < W_0^i[1 + (A + C_0)/rC_0]$$

This permits risk-preference A_i to exceed even W_0^i in absolute magnitude, even if most of the other consumers in the economy are highly decreasingly proportional risk averse (i.e., $A + C_0$ is near zero) and the growth rate of aggregate consumption is very high.

IV. Financial Equilibrium

With the weak aggregation problem solved, the chief obstacle blocking the analysis of security prices has been removed. We have only to use the first-order conditions for the consensus consumer, Eqs. (a) and (b), and his budget constraints. In short, we can act as if all consumers are identical.

In this section, we shall use GLUM to characterize three empirically oriented economic relationships:

(1)   the form of the aggregate consumption function,
(2)   the intertemporal stochastic relationships among returns on " basic " portfolios, and
(3)   the contemporaneous valuation formulas for arbitrary portfolios.

For some purposes, to simplify the nature of our empirical hypotheses, we shall assume *stationary social tastes*. That is, the consensus consumer will be assumed to be immortal $(T = \infty)$ and to have a constant rate of time-preference $(\rho_t = \rho < 1$ for all $t)$. This assumption for type II models stands in direct contrast to its popular corresponding counterpart, *stationary social beliefs*, of type I models. It is, of course, a matter of opinion which is apt to be closer to stationary tastes or beliefs. However, despite Galbraithian chastisement, economists have traditionally regarded taste formation as beyond their purview. Like Archimedes, who would have moved the earth but for a place to stand, economists have argued that tastes, at least in the short run, are relatively stationary compared to the macrovariables of prices and output.

With stationary social tastes, Eqs. (a) and (b) become

$$P_e(A + C_e) = \pi_e \rho(A + C_0) \qquad \text{for all } e \qquad (a')$$

$$P_{s.e}(A + C_{s.e}) = \pi_{s.e} \rho(A + C_e) \qquad \text{for all } s \text{ and } e \qquad (b')$$

and the consensus consumer's budget constraints, require

$$W_0 = C_0 + \sum_e P_e W_e \qquad \text{and} \qquad W_e = C_e + \sum_s P_{s.e} C_{s.e} \qquad \text{for all } e$$

Recall that private choices $(C_0, \{C_e\}, \{C_{s.e}\})$ are the per capita amounts and therefore exogenous to the economy; social choices $\{(P_e\}, \{P_{s.e}\})$ are the equilibrium prices in the economy with full heterogeneity; although social tastes represented by social time- and risk-preference (ρ, A) generally (if they are not composites) are not exogenous to the economy, nonetheless they are time–state independent constants; and social beliefs $(\{\pi_e\}, \{\pi_{s.e}\})$ are not only time–state dependent, but also are those homogeneous beliefs which lead to the same equilibrium prices as the actual heterogeneous beliefs of consumers.

Using Eqs. (a') and (b') and the consensus consumer's budget constraints.

Theorem (*Aggregate Consumption Function*) In the generalized logarithmic utility economy with stationary social tastes, at each date per capita consumption is linearly related to the present value of a perpetual default-free annuity and per capita wealth by time–state independent constants. In particular, for all dates and states

$$\tilde{C}_t = a + b\tilde{\phi}_t + c\tilde{W}_t$$

where $a(= -A)$ depends only on social risk-preference and has the opposite sign of social proportional risk aversion, $c(= 1 - \rho)$ depends only on social time-preference and is between zero and one, and $b = -ac$.

Proof Following an analysis identical to the construction of the optimal decision rules for arbitrary consumer i, for the consensus consumer at date $t = 0$,

$$C_0 = A[\phi(1 - \rho) - 1] + (1 - \rho)W_0 \qquad (c')$$

where, as a result of his immortality, $1 - \delta \equiv (1 + \rho + \rho^2 + \cdots)^{-1} = 1 - \rho$ and $\phi = 1 + 1/(1 + r_F) + 1/[(1 + R_F)^2] + \cdots$ is interpreted as the present value of a perpetual default-free annuity yielding one unit of wealth now and at every date in the future. Similarly, at date $t = 1$, if state e occurs

$$C_e = A[\phi_e(1 - \rho) - 1] + (1 - \rho)W_e \qquad (d')$$

where $\phi_e = 1 + 1/(1 + r_{Fe}) + \cdots$. More generally, for any date t,

$$\tilde{C}_t = A[\tilde{\phi}_t(1 - \rho) - 1] + (1 - \rho)\tilde{W}_t$$

where $\tilde{C}_t$, $\tilde{\phi}_t$, and $\tilde{W}_t$ are random variables depending on the state at date t. Therefore,

$$\tilde{C}_t = -A + A(1 - \rho)\tilde{\phi}_t + (1 - \rho)\tilde{W}_t \qquad \text{for all } t \quad \text{Q.E.D.}$$

Since the observable variables $(\tilde{C}_t, \tilde{\phi}_t, \tilde{W}_t)$ in the aggregate consumption function are related linearly by time–state independent constants (ρ, A), it can be used to formulate empirical hypotheses, even though the constants ρ and A are not directly observable. First, the equation predicts that realized (ex post) per capita consumption, the present value of a perpetual annuity, and the corresponding per capita wealth will have the same exact linear relationship over time. Alternatively, correlation coefficient $\kappa(C_t, A\phi_t + W_t) = 1$, both for *ex ante* social prediction at the same date and *ex post* realization over time. This is, in effect, a life-cycle version of the aggregate consumption function.[31] Second, regressing realized values of $\tilde{\phi}_t$

---

[31] As in Weber [54], the distinctive feature of this version of the life-cycle hypothesis is the inclusion of interest rates in the consumption function, more in the classical rather than the Keynesian tradition.

and $\tilde{W}_t$ against $\tilde{C}_t$ will determine constants a, b, and c, which may be used to determine social time- and risk-preference (ρ, A). Third, measuring the realized values of $\tilde{\phi}_t$ and $\tilde{C}_t$ to a close approximation may be relatively easy compared with measuring $\tilde{W}_t$. However, suppose a proportional proxy[32] $\tilde{W}'_t = k\tilde{W}_t$ for this variable can be obtained, where k is a time–state independent constant measuring the propensity of the proxy to underestimate the true W_t. In this case, there still exist time–state independent constants (a, b, c') such that $\tilde{C}_t = a + b\tilde{\phi}_t + c'\tilde{W}'_t$, where $A = -a$, $\rho = 1 + b/a$, and $k = -ac'/b$.

Unlike type I models, GLUM also predicts relationships between the rates of return of "basic" portfolios: risk-free rates of return and the market portfolio. From Eq. (a'), in equilibrium,

$$P_e = \rho(A + C_0)\pi_e(A + C_e)^{-1}$$

Summing this over e,

$$\frac{1}{1 + r_F} \equiv \sum_e P_e = \rho E\left(\frac{A + C_1}{A + C_0}\right)^{-1}$$

where E is an expectation operator. By Eqs. (c') and (d'),

$$A + C_0 = (1 - \rho)(A\phi + W_0) \quad \text{and} \quad A + C_e = (1 - \rho)(A\phi_e + W_e)$$

so that the above term in brackets $[\cdot]$ is equivalent to $[(A\phi_e + W_e)/(A\phi + W_0)]^{-1}$. Since $-V'_0(W_0)/V''_0(W_0) = A\phi + W_0$ and $-V'_e(W_e)/V''_e(W_e) = A\phi_e + W_e$, this term can be interpreted as one plus the rate of change in social absolute risk aversion (in terms of wealth). This important variable will be denoted by $(1 + r_{Ze})^{-1}$ and called the "Z factor," that is,[33]

$$1 + r_{Ze} \equiv (A\phi_e + W_e)/(A\phi + W_0)$$

---

[32] One plus the rate of return of the market portfolio, as estimated by Standard and Poors Composite Index of stocks or by the return on a joint stock and corporate bond portfolio such as constructed by Sharpe [50], are candidate proxies $\tilde{W}_t$. More traditional proxies can be found in the life-cycle consumption literature; see Ando and Modigliani [1].

[33] The chief empirical advantage of GLUM over all other type II models is the simple linear relationship between absolute risk aversion in terms of consumption and absolute risk aversion in terms of wealth at the same date. That is, for all type II models for all dates t,

$$-U''(C_t)/U'(C_t) = -(\partial C_t/\partial W_t)^{-1} V''_t(W_t)/V'_t(W_t)$$

This permits a direct translation from consumption variables to annuity and wealth variables. However, if the future marginal propensity to consume wealth $(\delta C_t/\delta W_t)$ is a random variable, this muddies this translation for empirical purposes. The generalized logarithmic utility model is the only type II model (in their multiperiod versions) for which $\partial C_t/\partial W_t = (1 + \rho_{t+1} + \rho_{t+1}\rho_{t+2} + \cdots)^{-1}$ is not random. Usually, the MPC is a function of all time–

Using this notation, $(1 + r_F)^{-1} = \rho E(1 + r_Z)^{-1}$. Extending this over many dates, for any date t,

$$1 + \tilde{r}_{Zt} \equiv (A\tilde{\phi}_r + \tilde{W}_t)/(A\tilde{\phi}_{t-1} + \tilde{W}_{t-1}),$$

$$(1 + \tilde{R}_{Zt})^t \equiv (1 + \tilde{r}_Z)(1 + \tilde{r}_{Z2}) \cdots (1 + \tilde{r}_{Zt})$$

Moreover, it is easy to show that in equilibrium the future riskless short-term rate given the state at date t is

$$(1 + \tilde{r}_{Ft})^{-1} = \rho E_{t-1}(1 + \tilde{r}_{Zt})^{-1}$$

where the subscript of the expectations operator means that expectations are taken with respect to social beliefs held at date $t - 1$. Finally, the present riskless long rate through date t is

$$(1 + R_{Ft})^{-t} = \rho^t E(1 + R_{Zt})^{-t}$$

These relationships can now be used to develop necessary and sufficient conditions for an unbiased term structure to emerge in equilibrium. The term structure of interest rates is said to be unbiased if *an investment in a sequence of default-free short-term bonds* (with proceeds at each date reinvested) *up to any date t is expected to yield the same inverse compound rate of return as a single investment in a default-free long-term bond maturing at date t.*[34] In a two-period economy, this implies and is implied by

$$\frac{1}{(1 + R_F)^2} = \frac{1}{1 + r_F} E\left(\frac{1}{1 + r_{F2}}\right)$$

From the definition of the first-period rate of return r_{Ne} on a two-period default-free annuity, it is easy to show that the above equation holds (i.e., the term structure is unbiased) if and only if $r_F = E(r_N)$. With many periods, the term structure is unbiased if and only if the expected first-period rates of return on default-free annuities of successive maturities are the same.

The following theorem provides necessary and sufficient conditions for an unbiased term structure.

---

state dependent prices and beliefs from date $t + 1$ into the future, as well as time-preference and parameter B. As a result, MPC itself is a random variable depending on the state at date t. Unless one cavalierly assumes MPC is not random (as would be the implication of assuming random walks for the rates of return on *all* securities) or confines himself to a single-period model, these other type II models are difficult to adapt to current empirical methodology. See Rubinstein [46].

[34] Rubinstein [46] compares this definition with other more popular definitions of an unbiased term structure.

Theorem (*Intertemporal Structure*)   In the generalized logarithmic utility economy,[35] the term structure is unbiased if and only if the Z factor is
serially uncorrelated. That is,

$$r_F = E(r_N) \qquad \text{if and only if} \qquad \kappa[(1 + r_Z)^{-1}, (1 + r_{Z2})^{-1}] = 0$$

Proof   From previous analysis,

$$\frac{1}{1 + r_F} = \rho E\left(\frac{1}{1 + r_Z}\right) \qquad \text{and} \qquad \frac{1}{1 + r_{Fe}} = \rho E_e\left(\frac{1}{1 + r_{Z2.e}}\right) \qquad \text{for all } e$$

Therefore,

$$\frac{1}{1 + r_F} E\left(\frac{1}{1 + r_{F2}}\right) = \rho^2 E\left(\frac{1}{1 + r_Z}\right) E\left(\frac{1}{1 + r_{Z2}}\right)$$

Moreover, from Eqs. (a') and (b'),

$$P_e P_{s.e} = \rho^2 \pi_e \pi_{s.e} 1/[(1 + r_Z)(1 + r_{Z2})] \qquad \text{for all } e \text{ and } s$$

Summing this over all e and s,

$$1/(1 + R_F)^2 = \rho^2 E1/[(1 + r_Z)(1 + r_{Z2})]$$

As a result,

$$\frac{1}{(1 + R_F)^2} = \frac{1}{1 + r_F} E\left[\frac{1}{1 + r_{F2}}\right]$$

if and only if

$$E\left[\frac{1}{(1 + r_Z)(1 + r_{Z2})}\right] = E\left(\frac{1}{1 + r_Z}\right) E\left(\frac{1}{1 + r_{Z2}}\right) \qquad \text{Q.E.D.}[36]$$

In the special case of socially constant proportional risk aversion (i.e.,
$A = 0$),[37] GLUM produces a surprisingly sharp portrait of the intertemporal
stochastic process of basic portfolios.

Corollary (*Logarithmic Intertemporal Structure*)   In the generalized logarithmic utility economy with zero social risk-preference (constant proportional risk aversion), any one of the following statements is true if and only if
the other statements are true.

(1)   The term structure is unbiased; that is,

$$r_F = E(r_N)$$

---

[35] To simplify presentation, this theorem has been developed with respect to the first two
periods only and under stationary social tastes; neither are crucial to the results.

[36] This makes use of the statistical property that two random variables are uncorrelated if
and only if the expectation of their product equals the product of their expectations.

[37] Note that $A = 0$ is consistent with heterogeneity with respect to risk-preference among
consumers, as long as $\sum_i (\lambda_i/\lambda I)A_i = 0$.

(2) The (inverse one plus) rate of return of the market portfolio is serially uncorrelated; that is,

$$\kappa[(1 + r_M)^{-1}, (1 + r_{M2})^{-1}] = 0$$

(3) The (inverse one plus) rate of growth of per capita consumption is serially uncorrelated; that is,

$$\kappa[(1 + r_C)^{-1}, (1 + r_{C2})^{-1}] = 0$$

Proof Since

$$1 + \tilde{r}_{Zt} \equiv (A\tilde{\phi}_t + \tilde{W}_t)/(A\tilde{\phi}_{t-1} + \tilde{W}_{t-1}) = (A + \tilde{C}_t)/(A + \tilde{C}_{t-1})$$

and $A = 0$, then $1 + \tilde{r}_{Zt} = \tilde{W}_t/\tilde{W}_{t-1} = \tilde{C}_t/\tilde{C}_{t-1}$. From the definition of the rate of growth of aggregate consumption, $1 + \tilde{r}_{Ct} \equiv \tilde{C}_t/\tilde{C}_{t-1}$, so that $\tilde{r}_{Zt} = \tilde{r}_{Ct}$. From the consumption decision rule, if $A = 0$, then $\tilde{C}_{t-1} = (1 - \rho)\tilde{W}_{t-1}$. Therefore, since $1 + \tilde{r}_{Mt} \equiv \tilde{W}_t/(\tilde{W}_{t-1} - \tilde{C}_{t-1})$, $1 + \tilde{r}_{Zt} = \rho(1 + \tilde{r}_{Mt})$. Q.E.D.

Whether or not (1) the term structure is unbiased or (2) the market portfolio follows a "random walk"[38] depends critically on (3) the stochastic process governing aggregate consumption over time. Indeed, with social logarithmic utility, only if this process is serially uncorrelated with the classical hypotheses be verified. The underlying real stochastic process of aggregate consumption carried directly over to the equilibrium financial stochastic process governing security prices. For example, it follows trivially from the theorem that if the (inverse one plus) growth rate of aggregate consumption is positively correlated over time, then the term structure will be biased with positive liquidity premiums. Moreover, although true of type II models generally, the logarithmic utility case provides a simple illustration of the inference of the probability law governing financial processes from the probability law governing real processes. For example, since $1 + r_{Ce} = \rho(1 + r_{Me})$, if $1 + r_{Ce}$ were normally or lognormally distributed, then $1 + r_{Me}$ would also be normally or lognormally distributed with greater mean and variance (since $\rho < 1$). Such an inference is the chief missing element from type I models.[39]

Like type I models, GLUM also produces an explicit and relatively simple formula for the valuation of arbitrary portfolios of state-contingent claims (i.e., actual securities and portfolios). In addition, unlike type I models, GLUM yields a convenient formula for discounting an uncertain stream of income.

[38] Strictly speaking, and as used in this paper, a random walk requires that the rate of return of the market portfolio be stochastically independent, not merely uncorrelated, over time.

[39] Rubinstein [46] carries the exogenous source of uncertainty back even further to exogenous stochastic parameters in production functions.

Suppose actual ("complex") security j yields a total return (initial price plus capital gain plus dividend) of $\bar{X}_{je}$ at date $t = 1$ if state e occurs. Then the present value P_j of security j will be determined like any other portfolio of state-contingent claims by discounting its future income by the corresponding state-contingent prices; that is, $P_j = \sum_e P_e \bar{X}_{je}$. Since, from Eq. (a'), $P_e = \rho\pi_e(1 + r_{Ze})^{-1}$, then $P_j = \rho E[\bar{X}_{j1}(1 + r_Z)^{-1}]$. Since the expectation of the product of two random variables equals the product of their expectations plus their covariance, and from the definition of correlation coefficient,

$$P_j = \rho E(\bar{X}_{j1})E(1 + r_Z)^{-1} + \rho\kappa(\bar{X}_{j1}, (1 + r_Z)^{-1})\,(\text{Std } \bar{X}_{j1})\,\text{Std}(1 + r_Z)^{-1}$$

By our previous analysis, $(1 + r_F)^{-1} = \rho E(1 + r_Z)^{-1}$, so that

$$P_j = \frac{E(\bar{X}_{j1}) - \gamma\kappa(\bar{X}_{j1}, -(1 + r_Z)^{-1})\,\text{Std } \bar{X}_{j1}}{1 + r_F}$$

where $\gamma \equiv \text{Std}(1 + r_Z)^{-1}/E(1 + r_Z)^{-1}$.

To extend this to valuation over two periods, suppose that $\bar{X}_{je}$ takes its value from a dividend X_{je} at date $t = 1$ and its value $\bar{X}_{js.e}$ at date $t = 2$. Then $\bar{X}_{je} = X_{je} + \sum_s P_{s.e} \bar{X}_{js.e}$, so that $P_j = \sum_e P_e X_{je} + \sum_e P_e \sum_s P_{s.e} \bar{X}_{js.e}$. Following a similar argument as in the single-period case, and then extending this to an infinite number of dates, leads to the following theorem.

Theorem (*Valuation*) In the generalized logarithmic utility economy with stationary social tastes,[40] the present price of any security (or portfolio of securities) equals the discounted sum at appropriate risk-free rates of its expected cash flows over time minus corresponding certainty equivalent factors reflecting risk aversion and uncertainty. In particular, for any security j,

$$P_j = \sum_{t=1}^{\infty} \frac{E(X_{jt}) - \gamma_t \kappa[X_{jt}, -(1 + R_{Zt})^{-1}]\,\text{Std } X_{jt}}{(1 + R_{Ft})^t}$$

where

$$1 + \tilde{r}_{Zt} \equiv (A\tilde{\phi}_t + \tilde{W}_t)/(A\tilde{\phi}_{t-1} + \tilde{W}_{t-1}) > 0$$

$$(1 + \tilde{R}_{Zt})^t \equiv (1 + \tilde{r}_Z)(1 + \tilde{r}_{Z2}) \cdots (1 + \tilde{r}_{Zt}) > 0$$

$$(1 + R_{Ft})^{-t} = \rho^t E[(1 + R_{Zt})^{-t}] > 0$$

$$\gamma_t \equiv \text{Std}[(1 + R_{Zt})^{-t}]/E[(1 + R_{Zt})^{-t}] > 0$$

In addition, in terms of total return for the first period,

$$E(r_j) = r_F + \gamma\kappa[r_j, -(1 + r_Z)^{-1}]\,\text{Std } r_j$$

where $1 + r_{je} \equiv \bar{X}_{je}/P_j$.

---

[40] Again, this theorem is little changed by nonstationary tastes.

In the special case of socially constant proportional risk aversions (i.e., $A = 0$), since $1 + \tilde{r}_{Zt} = \rho(1 + \tilde{r}_{Mt})$ the valuation equation takes a surprisingly simple form, considering that it allows us to value an uncertain and possibly serially correlated stream of income.

Corollary (*Logarithmic Valuation*) In the generalized logarithmic utility economy with zero social risk preference (constant proportional risk aversion), for any security (or portfolio of securities) j

$$P_j = \sum_{t=1}^{\infty} \frac{E(X_{jt}) - \gamma_t \kappa(X_{jt}, -(1 + R_{Mt})^{-t}) \text{ Std } X_{jt}}{(1 + R_{Ft})^t}$$

where

$$1 + \tilde{r}_{Mt} \equiv \tilde{W}_t / (\tilde{W}_{t-1} - \tilde{C}_{t-1})$$

$$(1 + \tilde{R}_{Mt})^t \equiv (1 + \tilde{r}_M)(1 + \tilde{r}_{M2}) \cdots (1 + \tilde{r}_{Mt})$$

$$(1 + R_{Ft})^{-t} \equiv E(1 + R_{Mt})^{-t}$$

$$\gamma_t \equiv \text{Std}(1 + R_{Mt})^{-t} / E(1 + R_{Mt})^{-t}$$

If, additionally, it is assumed that the rate of growth of aggregate consumption follows a stationary random walk, then

$$(1 + R_{Ft})^{-1} = (1 + r_F)^{-1} = E(1 + r_M)^{-1}, \qquad \gamma_t = [(\gamma^2 + 1)^t - 1]^{1/2}$$

for all dates t, where $\gamma \equiv \text{Std}(1 + r_M)^{-1} / E(1 + r_M)^{-1}$.

The prospects for empirically testing the first period valuation relationship depend on estimating $\tilde{r}_Z$. Much depends on whether we assume that the aggregate consumption function may be used to first obtain accurate estimates of social time- and risk-preference (ρ, A) as well as our propensity k to underestimate per capita wealth. Following this approach, the realized values of $\tilde{r}_Z$ over time can be calculated by then measuring $\tilde{\phi}_t$ and the proxy for W_t. Empirical tests of type I models also require a similar proxy for per capita wealth, such as the Standard and Poors Composite Index for the "true" market portfolio. However, GLUM goes a step further by showing how to correct this proxy to make it a better estimate of the true economic variable. As a second empirical advantage, GLUM contains endogenous predictions of the nonstationary tendencies of $\tilde{r}_Z$. Since $E(1 + r_Z)^{-1} = [\rho(1 + r_F)]^{-1}$, *ex ante* shifts in the mean of the Z factor can be anticipated by observing r_F at the beginning of each period. Furthermore, if it can be separately established that the term structure is unbiased, then $(1 + \tilde{r}_{Zt})^{-1}$ is predicted to be serially uncorrelated over time. We may then be justified in postulating a distribution of $(1 + \tilde{r}_{Zt})^{-1}$ with stationary shape and a shifting but predictable mean. On the other hand, if the term structure is positively biased, then $(1 + \tilde{r}_{Zt})^{-1}$ will be positively correlated over time. We may then be justified in postulating a distribution of $(1 + \tilde{r}_{Zt})^{-1}$ with a shifting variance predicted by the past observation of $(1 + \tilde{r}_{Zt-1})^{-1}$, as well as a shifting mean predicted by observing $\tilde{r}_{Ft}$.

On the other hand, if good estimates of ρ, A, and k are not obtainable from the aggregate consumption function, then we can adopt more traditional though less satisfactory means of testing the first-period valuation relationship. Type I models estimate the equivalent of γ by selecting a "basic" portfolio of securities and calculating γ in terms of it. If the basic portfolio is the market portfolio, then substituting $j = M$ in the type I valuation equation, $E(r_j) = r_F + \gamma\kappa(r_j, r_M)\,\text{Std}\,r_j$, $\gamma = [E(r_M) - r_F]/\text{Std}\,r_M$. According to the theory, any portfolio (even a single-security) could have been selected to obtain an estimate of γ; the market portfolio is selected to hope that the misspecifications in the equations of specific securities will cancel when they are aggregated to form this portfolio. The assumption of stationary social beliefs (relating to security rates of return) is then adopted to keep γ and the probability distribution of $\tilde{r}_M$ constant over time.[41] At this point, the empirical analysis runs roughshod over the theory, since, as shown in footnote 6, together with the separation property, this implies that rates of return of all risky securities at the same date will be the same. Finally, it is assumed the financial markets are efficient in digesting information, so that the social beliefs represent "unbiased" estimates of future realized rates of return. The joint effect of these assumptions is the validation of the procedure of aggregating *ex post* data to infer *ex ante* beliefs.

Frankly, as a theorist, I instinctively recoil at this brash methodology; however, this reaction may only spring from the natural proclivity of a theorist to exempt himself from matters of immediate practicality, in which a little dirt inevitably becomes lodged under one's fingernails. Brushing aside this propensity for the moment, and adopting similar assumptions, the *two* now unknown parameters γ and A may be inferred from the *two* basic portfolios, $j = M$ and $j = N$. Substituting $\tilde{r}_M$ and then $\tilde{r}_N$ in the first-period valuation relationship, it is easy to show that A is whatever value solves the equation

$$\text{Cov}[(E(r_M) - r_F)r_N - (E(r_N) - r_F)r_M, \quad (A\phi_1 + W_1)^{-1}] = 0$$

With A and, hence, the probability distribution of the Z factor $\tilde{r}_Z$ estimated, it is possible to estimate γ. Stating this in terms of rates of return,

$$A\phi_e + W_e = (W_0 - C_0)[\bar{A}(1 + r_{Ne}) + (1 + r_{Me})]$$

---

[41] In Rubinstein [44], the intertemporal behavior of γ in the discrete-time normality model is analyzed implicitly presuming that the single-period valuation equation can be applied successively over time. The analysis suggests that $\gamma = [E(r_M) - r_F]/\text{Std}\,r_M$ is unlikely to be an intertemporal constant. Other candidates in regression formulas, such as $E(r_M) - r_F$ or $[E(r_M) - r_F]/\text{Var}\,r_M$, are even less likely to be intertemporal constants.

where $\bar{A} \equiv A(\phi - 1)/(W_0 - C_0)$. Therefore, we can alternatively estimate $\bar{A}$ as the solution to

$$\text{Cov}\{[E(r_M) - r_F]r_N - [E(r_N) - r_F]r_M, \quad [\bar{A}(1 + r_N) + (1 + r_M)]^{-1}\} = 0$$

and then measure $1 + r_{Ze}$ by the proxy $\bar{A}(1 + r_{Ne}) + (1 + r_{Me})$, since the effect of $1 + r_{Ze}$ on the single-period valuation relationship remains the same under a positive multiplicative transformation.[42]

It is unlikely that GLUM can prove an inferior empirical model to type I models. These models, despite their strong assumptions governing the contemporaneous and intertemporal stochastic processes or prices and their assumption of homogeneous beliefs, yield surprisingly weak empirically testable conclusions. In essence, they only predict a linear relationship between expected return and risk (measured by covariance with the $\tilde{r}_M$) and predict the intercept and scope terms.[43] They do not offer any prediction concerning aggregate consumption, the intertemporal stochastic process of security prices, or even the contemporaneous relationship between r_F and $\tilde{r}_M$. Add to this, as Kraus and Litzenberger [26] have shown, that the logarithmic utility or "capital growth" model ($A = 0$), which is a special case of GLUM, is empirically indistinguishable from type I models with respect to the latter's linear risk-return relationship. This results from the high empirical correlation of the risk measures of the two models. In fact, the predictions of type I models are so weak, they are likely to be equally well supported by alternative single-period type II models.

V. Financial Efficiency

The efficiency or welfare properties of a financial market may be usefully categorized under

(1) *exchange:* consumers are not motivated to create exchange arrangements not already provided by the market;

(2) *production:* competitive value-maximizing producers make Pareto-efficient production decisions;

(3) *information:* the acquisition and dissemination of information are Pareto-efficient.

---

[42] Some simplification is possible when the term structure is unbiased. Then, $r_F = E(r_N)$ and the equation simplifies to

$$\text{Cov}\{r_N, [\bar{A}(1 + r_N) + (1 + r_M)]^{-1}\} = 0$$

Unfortunately, even this equation has no analytic solution, but may be solved, presuming a unique solution, numerically by computer.

[43] These comments do not strictly apply to Merton's[33] continuous-time generalization, where he allows nonrandomness in future risk-free rates.

A financial market can also be evaluated in terms of "ethical" efficiency criteria such as social rationality, nondictatorship, positive responsiveness, and anonymity (see footnote 23).

The complete market context in which GLUM has been developed is a powerful generator of financial theory and implies virtually no loss of generality relative to the current state of the art. For example, type I models are revealed, through their separation properties, as thinly disguised versions of a complete market. Despite limitations of the complete markets approach revealed by increasing generalization (see Radner [40]), it remains the most powerful theoretical tool in the microeconomic theory of finance capable of being shifted comfortably between individual and aggregate levels of analysis, between conditions of certainty and uncertainty, and between static and dynamic settings, with the fundamental theoretical elements exhibiting a continuity and a clarity otherwise unobtainable. Moreover, hopefully GLUM will forever dispel the undeserved bugaboo that complete markets are incapable of rendering refutable empirical hypotheses.

Not only does the complete markets[44] context of GLUM assure exchange-efficiency, but it reveals through its sharing rule the minimum number of complex securities required for efficiency. In particular, if beliefs are homogeneous, then only default-free bonds of each maturity and a mutual fund representing the market portfolio need be available to assure efficiency; beyond these, no other securities will be in demand. With heterogeneous beliefs, options only need to be created for those states toward which there is disagreement; from the sharing rule, it is immediate that if all consumers have the same beliefs for any state e, then no options are bought or sold with respect to that state. More generally, for any subset of states, if for any two states e and e' within the subset the ratio of probabilities $\pi^i_e/\pi^i_{e'}$ is the same for all consumers i, then one complex security can replace the underlying options for states in this subset.[45]

Since, in a complete market, every Pareto-efficient allocation can be reached by an appropriate redistribution of resources, the sharing rule

---

[44] Although a complete futures market has not been assumed, the opportunity to revise portfolios at future dates exactly compensates for the reduction in markets at any one date. See Arrow [3].

[45] Hakansson [19] has proposed an interesting organization of the options market. Under certain conditions, there will be a one-to-one correspondence between the state of the world and the level of aggregate future wealth. In this case, the options market could be efficiently organized by the creation of a "superfund" which would sell state-contingent securities with payoffs for each possible level of aggregate future wealth. In practice, a proxy would need to be used, such as a composite stock and bond index and securities would be issued with payoffs for discrete intervals of the index. For example, the superfund would market securities which would pay off if and only if the index were between 105 and 106 a year from the date of issue. Other securities would be issued covering other intervals.

reveals the necessary and sufficient conditions for exchange-efficiency even if a securities market were not utilized to effect exchanges. In particular, if a composite consumer existed, it is immediate that prices are insensitive to any redistribution of resources (which does not destroy the composite). Therefore, all components of the sharing rule are unchanged by a redistribution of resources except components 2, 6, 11, 15, 20, 24, 30, and 34 which can be shown to sum to $(W_0^i - W_0)\pi_e^i \delta_i P_e^{-1}$. If the sum of all the other components is represented by Q_e^i, a number independent of the distribution of resources, then the portfolio sharing rule collapses to

$$W_e^i = (W_0^i - W_0)\pi_e^i \delta_i P_e^{-1} + Q_e^i \qquad \text{for all } e \text{ and } i$$

All Pareto-efficient allocations can be spanned by varying W_0^i from zero to W_0^M in the first term.

Suppose a composite consumer exists and we try to answer the important social question of the optimal distribution of resources. Can we say that one distribution of resources $\{W_0^i\}$ is preferred over all others? Clearly, consumers will disagree, since any consumer i will vote for $W_0^i = W_0^M$. However, suppose we conceive of an "original situation"[46] where a consumer is asked to choose between alternative distributions of resources without knowing in advance what his initial wealth will be once the distribution has been chosen. In particular, let $\{W_0^k\}$ represent a feasible wealth distribution, so that $\sum_k W_0^k \le W_0^M$ and let π_k^i be the subjective probability of consumer i that he will receive initial wealth W_0^k. Therefore, judging among resources distributions, a consumer

$$\max_{\{W_0^k\}} \sum_k \pi_k^i V_0^i(W_0^k) - \Lambda_i\left(\sum_k W_0^k - W_0^M\right)$$

where V_0^i is his derived utility of initial wealth function such that $V_0^{i'} > 0$ and $V_0^{i''} < 0$. If a composite consumer can be constructed such that prices are independent of the distribution of resources (as in GLUM), then W_0^M is insensitive to the distribution of resources (i.e., $\partial W_0^M/\partial W_0^k = 0$).[47] In this case, from the point of view of consumer i, the optimum distribution of resources $\{W_0^k\}$ satisfies

$$\pi_k^i V_0^{i'}(W_0^k) = \Lambda_i \qquad \text{for all } k$$

If all consumers do not know in advance what their initial wealth will be once the distribution has been chosen, then $\pi_k^i = I^{-1}$ for all k and i, and $V_0^{i'}(W_0^k) = \Lambda_i I$, so that $W_0^k = W_0$ for all k and i.

---

[46] The phrase "original situation" is taken from Rawls [41]. However, Rawls defines it to mean a complete tabula rasa, where no participant knows who (resources, lifetime, tastes, beliefs) he will be. In my "original situation" participants know their lifetime, tastes, and beliefs, and are only uncertain as to their resources.

[47] If the distribution of wealth, by affecting incentives, could influence production, then this would be a poor assumption.

We can summarize our conclusions concerning the efficiency of exchange arrangements by the following theorem:

Theorem (*Exchange-Efficiency*) In the generalized logarithmic utility economy, financial markets are exchange-efficient, requiring only default-free bonds of each maturity and the market portfolio if beliefs are homogeneous. If a composite consumer exists,

(1) prices are insensitive to the distribution of resources;
(2) all Pareto-efficient allocations are spanned by varying W_0^i such that $0 \le W_0^i \le W_0^M$

$$W_e^i = (W_0^i - W_0)\pi_e^i \, \delta_i P_e^{-1} + Q_e^i \qquad \text{for all } e \text{ and } i$$

where Q_e^i is independent of the distribution of resources;

(3) in the "original situation" consumers will unanimously agree on an equal distribution of resources.

Not only does the complete markets context of GLUM assure exchange-efficiency, but it also assures production-efficiency.[48] Moreover, if a composite consumer exists, his expected utility is a social welfare function which satisfies all but one (unrestricted domain) of the conditions for Arrow's impossibility theorem [2], and satisfies the Savage Axioms of Rational Choice [48], in particular the independence of tastes and beliefs (postulate 4). As a result,

Theorem (*Production-Efficiency*) In the generalized logarithmic utility economy, financial markets are production-efficient. If a composite consumer exists, then competitive value-maximizing producers make the same production decisions as would have been chosen by using the social welfare function.

If now production decisions are regarded as exogenous, then it is well known that the social acquisition of new public information is Pareto-inefficient. However, if the effect on prices is ignored (or viewed as negligible), then from the exact derived utility of wealth functions (see the proof of the decision rules theorem), *information systems* will be ordered in preference by

$$\sum_z \pi_z \sum_e \pi_{e.z} \left[(1 + \rho_2^i) \ln(\pi_{e.z}/P_e) + \rho_2^i \sum_s \pi_{s.ez} \, \ln(\pi_{s.ez}/P_{s.e}) \right]$$

---

[48] The word "competitive" in the definition of production-efficiency must be carefully defined. See Rubinstein [45], for this definition as well as a proof of the next theorem. Following Radner [39], Rubinstein [46] develops closed-form production decision rules for logarithmic utility with Cobb-Douglas production functions containing random parameters.

where z is a possible signal, π_z the prior probability of that signal z being received, and $(\{\pi_{e.z}\}, \{\pi_{s.ez}\})$ the revised posterior beliefs that states e and s will occur. Consumers with lifetime $\lambda_i = 0$, so that $\rho_2^i = 0$, or more generally with the same ρ_2^i, will rank information systems $(\{\pi_z\}, \{\pi_{e.z}\}, \{\pi_{s.ez}\})$ in the same order.[49]

The dissemination of existing private information is always Pareto-efficient if prices are not affected (see Jaffe and Rubinstein [23]); in the extreme, homogeneous beliefs are formed and no speculative side bets are made. The lost demand by optimists is just offset by the lost supply by pessimists. This emphasizes that the options market is a zero sum game[50] that encourages consumers to slant their portfolio holdings away from perfect diversification. If prices are affected and a composite consumer exists, it is possible to identify who benefits and who loses from the publication of information. Even if the private information of an informed consumer is released without charge, he may still benefit if, for example, he is a borrower of short-term bonds and the information causes short-term interest rates to fall.[51]

The consensus beliefs reflect what information (i.e., beliefs) are reflected in security prices. If the full dissemination of private information were to leave the consensus beliefs unchanged (i.e., if optimistic private information were offset by pessimistic private information), then we would say that security prices fully reflect all available information.[52] Nonetheless, without the release of the information, specific consumers will be holding nonoptimal portfolios with respect to beliefs based on all information, public and private. These nonoptimal portfolio holdings will be his speculative side bets. The extent of failure of the financial market to disseminate available information can be measured by the ratio of the volume of *speculative* (due to differences in beliefs) to nonspeculative (due to differences in wealth composition and scale, lifetime, and time- and risk-preference) trading. The portfolio sharing rule can be used to compare speculative (components 29–38) with nonspeculative demand (components 1–28 plus $W_e - \overline{W}_e^i$).[53] If default-

---

[49] With logarithmic utility, Arrow [5] relates the expected gross value of perfect information to the Shannon entropy measure of the "amount of information," and Morris [35] determines the maximum amount a consumer would pay for an information system.

[50] However, if the existence of options provides an incentive for the private acquisition of information which affects production decisions, this will not be the case.

[51] Ng [38] has isolated similar effects of the social acquisition of good or bad news on the welfare of consumers.

[52] See Rubinstein [47]. By this same line of reasoning, we can also precisely define what we mean by a consumer's *subjective valuation* of a security, namely, the value the economy would assign to the security if all consumers shared his beliefs.

[53] Examples of calculations of the ratio of speculative to nonspeculative volume are contained in Rubinstein [46].

free bonds of each maturity and a mutual fund representing the market portfolio are available at date $t = 0$, then all trading volume at future dates is speculative. This results more generally from the relative ease with which standardized packages of securities can be created for nonspeculative purposes.

References

1. Ando, A., and Modigliani, F., "The 'Life-Cycle' Hypothesis of Saving: Aggregate Implications and Tests," *American Economic Review* (May 1963).
2. Arrow, K., *Social Choice and Individual Values*. New York: Wiley, 1951.
3. Arrow, K., "The Role of Securities in the Optimal Allocation of Risk-Bearing" (1953). Republished in English in K. Arrow, *Essays in the Theory of Risk-Bearing*, pp. 121–133. Chicago, Illinois: Markham, 1971.
4. Arrow, K., "The Theory of Risk Aversion" (1965). Republished with appendix in K. Arrow, *Essays in the Theory of Risk-Bearing*, pp. 90–120. Chicago, Illinois: Markham, 1971.
5. Arrow, K., "The Value and Demand for Information" (1971). Published in K. Arrow, *Essays in the Theory of Risk-Bearing*, pp. 267–278. Chicago, Illinois: Markham, 1971.
6. Black, F., "Capital Market Equilibrium with Restricted Borrowing," *Journal of Business* (July 1972).
7. Black, F., Jensen, M., and Scholes, M., "The Capital Asset Pricing Model: Some Empirical Tests," *Studies in the Theory of Capital Markets* (M. Jensen, ed.), pp. 79–121. New York: Praeger, 1972.
8. Black, F., and Scholes, M., "The Pricing of Options and Corporate Liabilities," *Journal of Political Economy* (May 1973).
9. Breiman, L., "Optimal Gambling Systems for Favorable Games," *Fourth Berkeley Symposium on Mathematical Statistics and Probability*, Berkeley (1961), pp. 65–78.
10. Brennan, M., and Kraus, A., "Necessary Conditions for Aggregation in Securities Markets," University of British Columbia: unpublished paper (1975).
11. Cass, D., and Stiglitz, J., "The Structure of Investor Preferences and Asset Returns and Separability in Portfolio Allocation: A Contribution to the Pure Theory of Mutual Funds," *Journal of Economic Theory* (June 1970).
12. Debreu, G., *Theory of Value: An Axiomatic Analysis of Economic Equilibrium*. New York: Wiley, 1959.
13 Fama, E., and Miller, M., *The Theory of Finance*. New York: Holt, 1972.
14. Gonedes, N., "Information-Production and Capital Market Equilibrium," *Journal of Finance* (1975) (forthcoming).
15. Grauer, R., and Litzenberger, R., "A State-Preference Model of the Valuation of Commodity Futures Contracts under Uncertain Commodity Prices," Stanford, California: Graduate School of Business, Working Paper #220 (1974).
16. Grauer, R., Litzenberger, R., and Stehle, R., "Valuation in an International Capital Market," *Journal of Financial Economics* (June 1976).
17. Grauer, R., "Risk Aversion and the Structure of Asset Prices: An Examination of Linear Risk Tolerance Capital Asset Pricing Models," Berkeley, California: unpublished (1975).
18. Hakansson, N., "Optimal Entrepreneurial Decisions in a Completely Stochastic Environment," *Management Science* (March 1971).
19. Hakansson, N., "The Superfund: Efficient Paths Toward a Complete Financial Market," Berkeley, California: Research Program in Finance, Working Paper #25 (1974).
20. Hakansson, N., "The Capital Asset Pricing Model: Some Open and Closed Ends," Published in I. Friend and J. Bicksler, *Risk and Return in Finance*. Cambridge, Massachusetts: Ballinger, 1975.

21. Hirshleifer, J., *Investment, Interest and Capital.* Englewood Cliffs, New Jersey: Prentice-Hall, 1970.
22. Hirshleifer, J., "The Private and Social Value of Information and the Reward to Inventive Activity," *American Economic Review* (September 1971).
23. Jaffe, J., and Rubinstein, M., "The Value of Information in Impersonal and Personal Markets," Berkeley, California: Research Program in Finance, Working Paper #23 (1975).
24. Jensen, M., "Capital Markets: Theory and Evidence," *Bell Journal of Economics and Management Science* (Autumn 1972).
25. Koopmans, T., "Stationary Ordinal Utility and Impatience," *Econometrica* (April 1960).
26. Kraus, A., and Litzenberger, R., "Market Equilibrium in a Multiperiod State-Preference Model with Logarithmic Utility," *Journal of Finance* (December 1975).
27. Leland, H., "Capital Asset Markets, Production, and Optimality: A Synthesis." Stanford, California: Institute for Mathematical Studies in the Social Sciences, Technical Report No. 115 (December 1973).
28. Lintner, J., "The Valuation of Risk Assets and the Selection of Risky Investments in Stock Portfolios and Capital Budgets," *Review of Economics and Statistics* (February 1965).
29. Lintner, J., "The Aggregation of Investor's Diverse Judgments and Preferences in Purely Competitive Security Markets," *Journal of Financial and Quantitative Analysis* (December 1969).
30. Long, J., "Stock Prices, Inflation and the Term Structure of Interest Rates," *Journal of Financial Economics* (July 1974).
31. Markowitz, H., *Portfolio Selection: Efficient Diversification of Investments* (1959). Republished by Yale, 1970.
32. Merton, R., "Optimal Consumption and Portfolio Rules in a Continuous-Time Model," *Journal of Economic Theory* (December 1971).
33. Merton R., "An Intertemporal Capital Asset Pricing Model," *Econometrica* (September 1973).
34. Modigliani, F., and Miller, M., "The Cost of Capital, Corporation Finance, and the Theory of Investment," *American Economic Review* (June 1958).
35. Morris, J., "The Logarithmic Investor's Decision to Acquire Costly Information," *Management Science* (December 1974).
36. Mossin, J., "Equilibrium in a Capital Asset Market," *Econometrica* (October 1966).
37. Mossin, J., "Security Pricing and Investment Criteria in Competitive Markets," *American Economic Review* (December 1969).
38. Ng, D., "Information Accuracy and Social Welfare under Homogeneous Beliefs," *Journal of Financial Economics* (March 1975).
39. Radner, R., "Optimal Growth in a Linear-Logarithmic Economy," *International Economic Review* (January 1966).
40. Radner, R., "Competitive Equilibrium under Uncertainty," *Econometrica* (January 1968).
41. Rawls, J., *A Theory of Justice.* Cambridge, Massachusetts: Harvard University Press, 1971.
42. Richard, S., "Multivariate Risk Aversion, Utility Independence and Separable Utility Functions," *Management Science* (September 1975).
43. Rosenberg, B., and Ohlson, J., "The Stationary Distribution of Returns and Portfolio Separation in Capital Markets: A Fundamental Contradiction." *Journal of Financial and Quantitative Analysis* (September 1976).
44. Rubinstein, M., "A Comparative Statics Analysis of Risk Premiums," *Journal of Business* (October 1973).
45. Rubinstein, M., "An Aggregation Theorem for Security Markets," *Journal of Financial Economics* (September 1974a).
46. Rubinstein, M., "A Discrete-Time Synthesis of Financial Theory: Part I. Optimal Decision and Sharing Rules; Part II. Valuation and Efficiency; Part III. Extensions and Prospec-

tive." Berkeley, California: Research Program in Finance: Working Papers #20, #21, and #26 (1974b).

47. Rubinstein, M., "Securities Market Efficiency in an Arrow-Debreu Economy," *American Economic Review* (December 1975).
48. Savage, L., *The Foundations of Statistics.* New York: Wiley (1954).
49. Sharpe, W., *Portfolio Theory and Capital Markets.* New York: McGraw-Hill (1972).
50. Sharpe, W., "Bonds versus Stocks: Some Lessons from Capital Market Theory," *Financial Analysts Journal* (November-December 1973).
51. Stiglitz, J., "A Re-Examination of the Modigliani-Miller Theorem," *American Economic Review* (December 1969).
52. Stiglitz, J., "A Consumption-Oriented Theory of the Demand for Financial Assets and the Term Structure of Interest Rates," *Review of Economic Studies* (July 1970).
53. Tobin, J., "Comment on Borch and Feldstein," *Review of Economic Studies* (January 1969).
54. Weber, W., "The Effect of Interest Rates of Aggregate Consumption," *American Economic Review* (September 1970).
55. Wilson, R., "The Theory of Syndicates," *Econometrica* (January 1968).

Part II

INVESTMENT DECISIONS UNDER UNCERTAINTY

THE DEMAND FOR RISKY ASSETS

Some Extensions

Irwin Friend

University of Pennsylvania

I. Introduction and Summary

Research on capital asset pricing has until very recently been devoted almost exclusively to the interrelationships of the risk premiums among different risky assets rather than to the determinants of the market price of risk.[1] Such research has also generally relied on theoretical preconceptions to determine the appropriate utility functions of individual investors upon which both the market price of risk and the pricing of individual risky assets depend.

In several recent papers, I have attempted together with a colleague to highlight and begin to fill in these gaps [1–4]. While the emphasis in these papers is to derive meaningful utility functions for individual households which can be combined to construct an aggregate demand function for risky assets, clearly these utility functions can be used for a variety of other significant uses, including derivation of the form of household saving func-

---

[1] The market price of risk is the difference between the expected rate of return on the market for risky assets as a whole and on a risk-free asset per unit of risk of the market portfolio. For purposes of this paper, the relevant measure of risk is the variance of returns.

tions, measurement of the impact of different government, fiscal or insurance measures on economic welfare, and assessment of the problems in extending single-period financial and economic investment decisions to a multiperiod world.

These earlier papers adapt and extend existing theory to obtain relationships between the composition of household wealth (both human and nonhuman) and household utility functions which are suitable for statistical analyses at both the micro and macro levels. They then proceed to derive the form of household utility functions by comprehensive analysis of detailed cross-sectional data on household asset holdings, and to estimate the market price of risk by analyzing *ex post* and *ex ante* market returns since the latter part of the nineteenth century. Most of this analysis assumes that investors have homogeneous expectations, but since new empirical evidence [5, 3] points fairly strongly to the pervasiveness of heterogeneous expectations, their implications have also been explored in a preliminary study.

Assuming homogeneous expectations, the main conclusions of this earlier work are: First, regardless of their wealth level, the coefficients of proportional risk aversion for households are on average well in excess of one and probably in excess of two. Thus, investors require a substantially larger premium to hold equities or other risky assets than they would if their attitudes towards risk were described by logarithmic utility functions.

Second, the assumption of constant proportional risk aversion for households is, as a first approximation, a fairly accurate description of the marketplace. These first two findings imply that the utility function of a representative investor is quite different from those that have been generally assumed in the literature. However, it should be pointed out that the conclusion of constant proportional risk aversion follows from the treatment of investment in housing. Other plausible treatments would imply either moderately increasing or moderately decreasing proportional risk aversion.

Third, under the assumption of constant proportional risk aversion, a simple form of the aggregate equilibrium relationship between the relative demand for risky assets and the market price of risk has been developed. To determine the actual values of the required rate of return on risky assets, the market price of risk, and the relative value of risky assets would of course entail the specification of supply conditions. For a constant physical supply of both risky and nonrisky assets, the aggregate relationship developed in this earlier work indicates how the required rate of return on risky assets as a whole is determined.

Finally, the substitution of the assumption of heterogeneous for homogeneous expectations does not change the first two of these conclusions, but does somewhat complicate the form of the aggregate equilibrium relationship between the demand for risky assets and the price of risk.

Since much of this earlier work has not yet been published, the present paper will discuss the highlights of the theoretical and empirical analysis leading to the conclusions cited above and will then use the same analytical framework to obtain new results on the effect of inflation on the market price of risk. It turns out that by using nominal values for returns, the market price of risk under inflation is increased by positive covariance between the rate of inflation and the market rate of return and decreased by negative covariance. Statistically, however, since the actual covariance has been very small since the latter part of the nineteenth century (at least in the USA), the measured market price of risk is not affected appreciably by the adjustment for inflation.

Two other extensions of this work on the demand for risky assets are now being carried out by Yoram Landskroner and myself and will not be discussed in this paper. The first is a more comprehensive analysis of the effect of inflation on the market price of risk and on the pricing of individual risky assets. The second is the investigation of aggregate time series data both to provide an independent test of the form of the utility functions derived from cross-sectional data and to determine whether there is any clear indication of historical changes in investors' attitudes toward risk.

II. Determinants of Market Price of Risk: Theoretical Background

Under the assumption of homogeneous expectations and frictionless capital markets, it has been shown (see [6–8]) for discrete planning periods that if investors' utility functions are quadratic, or if they are exponential or logarithmic and end-of-period wealth is normally distributed, the market price of all risky assets can be expressed as

$$\frac{E(r_m - r_f)}{\sigma^2(r_m)} = V_{m0}\left[\sum_k E\left(\frac{1}{R_k}\right)\right]^{-1} = \text{MPR} \tag{1}$$

where r_m is the return on the market portfolio of all risky assets, r_f the return on the risk-free asset, R_k is Pratt's measure of absolute risk aversion for the kth investor, and V_{m0} the market value of all risky assets at the beginning of the planning period. Stephen A. Ross has obtained a similar expression by using a continuous time model which assumes an infinitesimal planning horizon and no finite changes in value of any asset in an infinitesimal period

$$\frac{E(r_m - r_0)}{\sigma^2(r_m)} = \left[\sum_k \frac{\gamma_k}{W_k R_k}\right]^{-1} \tag{2}$$

where r_0 is the return on a minimum variance zero-beta asset, and γ_k the ratio of the kth investor's wealth W_k to aggregate wealth. It should be noted that neither (1) nor (2) is useful over time unless the distribution of wealth of individual investors is known.

Utilizing a continuous time model, assuming that all investment is either in risk-free assets or the market portfolio, and maximizing the expected utility of terminal wealth, it is easy to show that

$$\alpha_k = \frac{E(r_m - r_f)}{\sigma_m^2} \frac{1}{C_k} \tag{3}$$

where α_k is the proportion of the wealth of investor k placed in the portfolio of risky assets and $C_k \ (= W_k R_k)$ is the Pratt measure of relative risk aversion.

Introducing taxes for the first time,[2] where these are initially assumed proportional to income, it is obvious that (3) becomes

$$\alpha_k = \frac{E(r_m - r_f)}{\sigma_m^2} \frac{1}{(1 - t_k)C_k} \qquad \text{or} \qquad \alpha_k(1 - t_k)C_k = \frac{E(r_m - r_f)}{\sigma_m^2} \tag{4}$$

Allowing for a distinction between marketable and nonmarketable wealth[3] where nonmarketable wealth is likely to be mainly human wealth, all of which is considered risky, we obtain

$$\alpha_k = \frac{E(r_m - r_f)}{\sigma_m^2} \frac{1}{(1 - t_k)(1 - h_k)C_k} - \frac{h_k}{1 - h_k}\beta_{hk, m} \tag{5}$$

where h_k is the ratio of the value of human wealth of the kth investor to his total wealth (human and nonhuman) and $\beta_{hk, m}$ is the beta coefficient of the rate of return from human wealth on the rate of return from the kth investor's marketable risky assets. In the subsequent empirical application of (5), it is assumed that there is a high correlation between the return on the optimal portfolio of marketable risky assets for the kth investor and the return on the market portfolio of all marketable risky assets.

Now, aggregating (4) over all households leads to the equation

$$\sum \gamma_k \alpha_k = \alpha = \frac{E(r_m - r_f)}{\sigma_m^2} \sum \frac{\gamma_k}{(1 - t_k)C_k} \tag{6}$$

which can be greatly simplified if households are characterized by constant proportional risk aversion, so that γ_k and C_k are independent, with the result

$$E(r_m - r_f)/\sigma_m^2 = \alpha C(1 - t) \tag{7}$$

where C and $(1 - t)$ are, respectively, the simple and weighted harmonic means of C_k and $(1 - t_k)$.

Aggregating (5) instead of (4) and assuming that $E(\beta_{hk, m} | H_k) = \beta_{hm}$ is the

---

[2] The neglect of taxes in virtually all the earlier empirical literature seriously biases the results obtained. For a recent example, see Cohn *et al.* [9].

[3] This distinction was first made analytically by David Mayers who, however, used it for somewhat different purposes.

same for all households, we obtain

$$\frac{E(r_m - r_f)}{\sigma_m^2} = \frac{R}{W*} + \beta_{hm}\frac{H}{W*}C \tag{8}$$

where H is the value of human wealth, W is total wealth, R the total value of all risky marketable assets, L the total value of all marketable assets, and $W* = \sum W_k/(1 - t_k)$, or a tax adjusted sum of all wealth.[4]

Under the assumption of heterogeneous expectations, the microrelationship (4) is transformed into

$$(1 - t_k)\alpha_k(C_k) = E(r_k - r_f)/\sigma_k^2 \tag{9}$$

where $E(r_k)$ and σ_k^2 are the expected return and variance of the subjective distribution of returns attributed by investor k to his portfolio of risky assets.

Thus, the aggregate equilibrium relation under heterogeneous expectations which corresponds to (6) under homogeneous expectations can be written as

$$\sum \gamma_k\alpha_k\sigma_k = \sum \gamma_k[E(r_k - r_f)/\sigma_k](1 - t_k)^{-1}(C_k)^{-1} \tag{10}$$

In this instance, the simplification of (10) by the assumption of constant proportional risk aversion requires more heroic assumptions than the simplification of (6). However, if σ_k, $(C_k)^{-1}$, and $E(r_k - r_f)/\sigma_k$ are independent of γ_k and have expected values of σ_c, $(C)^{-1}$, and P_c, and if σ_h and α_k are also independent,[5] then we rewrite (10) in somewhat more tractable form as

$$(1 - t)\alpha C = (1/\sigma_c)P_c \tag{11}$$

Equation (11), as compared with (7), does permit us to draw qualitative but not quantitative conclusions about the effect of heterogeneous expectations on the relative demand for risky assets.

III. Determinants of Market Price of Risk: Statistical Tests

The conclusion that households are characterized by constant proportional risk aversion was obtained from data such as those presented in Tables I–III. Tables I and II indicate that if the household wealth relevant to

---

[4] Though (8) was developed under the restrictive assumption that the sole decision of the individual was how much of his marketable assets to place in the market portfolio of marketable risky assets, Landskroner [10] has shown that if r_0, the return on an asset uncorrelated with the return on the market portfolio of risky assets, is substituted for r_f and is also uncorrelated with the return on human capital, (8) holds in the more general case, where an investor's decision variables include not only how much to put into risky marketable assets, but also how much to place into each risky marketable asset.

[5] The assumption that σ_k is independent both of γ_k and α_k may be questioned and requires empirical verification.

Table I

Average Ratios of Assets and Selected Items to Household Net Worth Inclusive of Homes for Households Classified by Net Worth (December 31, 1962)[a]

Type of Item	Net worth ($000's)											
	1–10		10–100		100–200		200–500		500–1000		Over 1000	
Risk-free assets to net worth												
checking accounts	0.040		0.019		0.017		0.012		0.023		0.009	
other cash balances[b]	0.138		0.109		0.084		0.032		0.023		0.019	
savings bonds	0.029		0.025		0.020		0.020		0.009		0.003	
life insurance (cash value)	0.097		0.056		0.033		0.025		0.033		0.013	
other risk-free assets[c]	0.055	0.359	0.033	0.243	0.013	0.167	0.008	0.096	0.010	0.097	0.012	0.056
Mixed-risk assets to net worth												
state and local bonds	0.0		0.000		0.001		0.005		0.037		0.029	
other mixed-risk assets[d]	0.016	0.016	0.038	0.039	0.084	0.085	0.077	0.082	0.043	0.081	0.090	0.119
Risky assets to net worth												
market value of homes	1.539		0.657		0.216		0.098		0.112		0.046	
common and preferred stock	0.012		0.052		0.208		0.289		0.306		0.292	
equity in uninc. business	0.045		0.147		0.271		0.395		0.235		0.339	
other risky assets	0.035	1.631	0.101	0.957	0.108	0.803	0.084	0.866	0.213	0.866	0.216	0.892

Total assets to net worth	2.006	1.238	1.055	1.044	1.043	1.067
Liabilities to net worth	1.006	0.238	0.055	0.044	0.043	0.067
mortgage liabilities	0.924	0.204	0.041	0.016	0.008	0.003
other liabilities	0.083	0.034	0.014	0.028	0.035	0.064
Ancillary statistics						
$(1-t_k)z_k$ (equity in homes)^{f,g}	0.669	0.718	0.724	0.780	0.642	0.665
$(1-t_k)z_k$ (investment in homes)^{f,g}	1.495	0.897	0.758	0.793	0.648	0.667
number of households	459	731	94	103	76	108

[a] These averages are weighted by the inverse of the sampling probability for each household. These sampling probabilities have been adjusted for non-response and other factors. The net worth used in classifying households is defined in the same terms as the balance sheet.

[b] Includes checking and other commercial bank accounts, savings and loan savings accounts, credit union savings accounts, and mutual savings accounts.

[c] Includes US Treasury Bills, notes, and certificates, the withdrawal value of profit sharing and retirement plans, credit balances in brokerage accounts, and risk-free assets held in trust accounts. Risky assets held in trust accounts are included in the appropriate category of direct holdings, except that when they could not be classified in this manner, they were included in miscellaneous risky assets.

[d] Includes long-term corporate, state, local, and US Government bonds (other than savings bonds).

[e] Includes investment real estate assets and miscellaneous assets, such as patents, etc.

[f] The symbol α_k is defined as the ratio of the sum of the mixed-risk and risky assets to net worth for Investor k. The symbol t_k is the average federal tax rate for investor k as estimated by the procedure devised by the Survey of Financial Characteristics of Consumers. The only difference was that realized capital gain income or losses were included in adjusted gross income in this paper unlike the original procedure. The original survey ignored this type of income in calculating the tax rate.

[g] Includes automobiles.

investment decisions is assumed to exclude homes and human wealth, households would be characterized by decreasing proportional risk aversion [i.e., $(1 - t_k)\alpha_k$ rises with wealth]; if equity in homes is included, the data suggest constant proportional risk aversion; and if the gross investment in homes is substituted for equity in homes, the data point to increasing proportional risk aversion. The most appropriate of these three concepts of wealth for assessing the nature of household utility functions is probably the one which includes investment in housing measured at its equity value (see [4]). However, all three are deficient, since they make no allowance for the effect of human wealth on investment decisions.

Table II

Regressions of $(1 - t_k)\alpha_k$ on the Logarithm of Net Worth with and without Holding Constant Age, Education, and Occupation (December 31, 1962)

Net worth including homes	Housing[a] measured by	Simple regression			Regression with dummy variables for age, education, and occupation[b]		
		Coefficient on $\ln(NW)$			Coefficient on $\ln(NW)$		
		estimate	t-value	$\bar{R}^2$	estimate	t-value	$\bar{R}^2$
No		0.063	11.27	0.09	0.055	7.76	0.15
Yes	Equity	−0.006	−1.52	0.00	−0.001	−0.23	0.05
Yes	Full value	−0.185	−15.30	0.13	−0.155	−9.77	0.18

[a] Includes automobiles.

[b] The dummy variables, assuming the value of 1.0 if the characteristic is applicable to the head of the household and 0.0 otherwise, are for age (less than or equal to 25- and 5-year intervals from 25 to 65), for education (grade school or less, some high school, high school graduate, some college, and college graduate), and for occupation (self-employed, employed by others, retired, farm operator, not gainfully employed, and employer unknown).

The results in Table III incorporate human wealth by making use of the relationship developed in Eq. (5). Rearranging, and estimating the relationship for the *i*th wealth class, we obtain

$$(1 - h_k)(1 - t_k)\alpha_k = [E(r_m - r_f)/\sigma_m^2](1/C^i) - \beta_{hm}^i h_k(1 - t_k) + u_k \quad (12)$$

where C^i is the harmonic mean for the *i*th class and β_{hm}^i the human wealth beta coefficient for that class obtained under the assumption that $E(\beta_{hk,m}|H_k)$ is the same for all households in the class. Regressions were fitted for each of six wealth classes, where the unit of observation is an individual household. The entire left-hand term in Eq. (12) is the dependent

Table III

Estimated Coefficients and Other Statistics for Regressions of the Form[a]

$$(1 - h_k)(1 - t_k)\alpha_k = [E(r_m - r_f)/\sigma_m^2][1/C^i] - \beta_{hm}^i h_k(1 - t_k) + \eta_k$$

Net worth class ($000)	Estimates of		$\bar{R}^2$	Unweighted means				Number of households
	$[E(r_m - r_f)/\sigma_m^2](1/C^i)$	β_{hm}^i		$(1 - t_k)\alpha_k$	$(1 - h_k)(1 - t_k)\alpha_k$	$h_k(1 - t_k)$	$(1 - t_k)$	
A. Total sample[b]								
1–10	0.742 (0.035)	0.775 (0.069)	0.52	0.582	0.496	0.319	0.982	114
10–100	0.707 (0.009)	0.775 (0.014)	0.80	0.595	0.255	0.583	0.912	819
100–200	0.611 (0.010)	0.697 (0.013)	0.85	0.675	0.145	0.668	0.867	485
200–500	0.612 (0.016)	0.743 (0.029)	0.76	0.602	0.292	0.431	0.814	200
500–1000	0.529 (0.020)	0.613 (0.072)	0.44	0.584	0.412	0.192	0.705	90
over 1000	0.499 (0.021)	0.603 (0.146)	0.11	0.525	0.440	0.097	0.616	135
B. Households with income from salaries or wages								
1–10	0.759 (0.048)	0.796 (0.071)	0.66	0.466	0.314	0.559	0.976	65
10–100	0.650 (0.012)	0.704 (0.015)	0.76	0.564	0.153	0.706	0.908	676
100–200	0.595 (0.010)	0.676 (0.014)	0.83	0.678	0.113	0.712	0.869	455
200–500	0.565 (0.018)	0.671 (0.031)	0.73	0.590	0.227	0.504	0.815	171
500–1000	0.567 (0.022)	0.712 (0.070)	0.60	0.615	0.387	0.254	0.714	68
over 1000	0.515 (0.024)	0.676 (0.154)	0.13	0.536	0.441	0.110	0.522	119

[a] cf. footnotes for Table I.
[b] Numbers in parenthesis are standard errors.

variable, while the independent variable is $h_k(1 - t_k)$. The constant term in each of these regressions is equal to the market price of risk, a constant, times the reciprical of the Pratt measure of proportional risk aversion for that class. The slope coefficient of the independent variable is the human wealth beta coefficient.

The moderate decline in constant terms with higher wealth indicated in Table III suggests a moderate degree of increasing relative risk aversion (i.e., a declining C^i), with households possessing net worth in excess of $1 million having a C^i 33% less than that for households with net worth between $1000 and $10,000. However, virtually all the potentially significant biases in this result tend to bias it in this direction. These include the typically somewhat lower portfolio betas for lower than for higher income households unlike the assumption of a unitary beta for both; the understatement of the surrender value of life insurance, which is relatively more important in the lower than in the upper wealth classes, as a measure of the value of insurance for reducing risk; the transitory elements in net worth which are more likely to bias α_k upward for families of lower than for those of higher wealth; the omission of the value of relief payments;, and, probably most important of all, the omission of the value of social security or pension fund benefits.[6] Thus, when an approximate adjustment is made for the average value of social security or pension fund benefits accruing to households in each net worth class, the C^i of .742 for the $1000–$10,000 group is reduced to .609, with virtually no change in the over $1,000,000 group, so that now there is only an 18% difference in the estimated C^i between the lowest and highest net worth classes.[7]

As a result, while the partially adjusted results in Table III give some evidence of modestly increasing proportional risk aversion, the magnitude of the increase is not large, and corrections for the biases in our econometric model would tend to make the results closer to constant proportional risk aversion, and might even produce evidence of moderately decreasing proportional risk aversion. Thus the assumption of constant proportional risk aversion appears to be a good first approximation.[8]

Having established the empirical justification for the assumption of con-

[6] The assumption that the tax rates on income earned from the different types of assets are the same, when in fact they differ, results in an understatement of C_k which, however, does not appear to vary appreciably by wealth. (See Friend and Blume [4].)

[7] If housing is measured by market instead of equity value, the percentage decline in C^i is only moderately larger.

[8] This finding, it should be pointed out, not only greatly enhances the usefulness of the aggregate equilibrium demand relationship for risky assets but also potentially simplifies going from a single period to a multiperiod world (especially if the Pratt measure of proportional risk aversion is equal to one or if returns on risky assets are independently distributed over different time periods).

Table IV

Average Annual Arithmetic Rates of Return and Standard Deviations of Annual Returns (1872–1971)

| Period | New York Stock Exchange stocks[a] | | | | High grade corporate bonds[b] | | | | Calculated market price of risk | | |
| | Composite | | Industrial | | | | | | Stocks | | Bonds |
	Mean annual return	Standard deviation	Mean annual return	Standard deviation	Mean annual return	Standard deviation	Bond[c] beta	Risk-free[d] rate	Composite	Industrial	
1872–1881	0.0953	0.177	0.0820	0.129							
1882–1891	0.0429	0.130	0.0720	0.117							
1892–1901	0.0879	0.118	0.0773	0.163							
1902–1911	0.0794	0.218	0.1111	0.318	0.0436	0.0391	0.136	0.0409	0.808	0.692	1.712
1912–1921	0.0532	0.195	0.1128	0.296	0.0415	0.0545	0.179	0.0495	0.097	0.721	−2.718
1922–1931	0.1020	0.268	0.1108	0.289	0.0572	0.0369	0.061	0.0447	0.798	0.789	9.226
1932–1941	0.0866	0.282	0.1255	0.348	0.0672	0.0376	0.081	0.0138	0.925	0.915	37.782
1942–1951	0.1725	0.136	0.1697	0.105	0.0244	0.0289	0.044	0.0127	8.673	14.136	14.084
1952–1961	0.1804	0.189	0.1859	0.203	0.0177	0.0456	−0.055	0.0315	4.165	3.740	−6.623
1962–1971	0.0742	0.130	0.0779	0.136	0.0259	0.0596	0.131	0.0512	1.372	1.447	−7.125
1902–1961	0.1124	0.216	0.1360	0.263	0.0419	0.0431	0.072	0.0322	1.716	1.504	5.249
1902–1971	0.1069	0.206	0.1277	0.249	0.0396	0.0457	0.078	0.0349	1.702	1.501	2.276
1926–1971	0.1155	0.212	0.1256	0.234	0.0381	0.0420		0.0232	1.963	1.788	8.487
1872–1971	0.0974	0.188	0.1125	0.221							

[a] From 1926, the figures are estimated from the Standard & Poor's Stock Indexes. For earlier years, the data are from *Common-Stock Indexes* by the Cowles Commission for Research in Economics, 2nd edition (Bloomington, Indiana: Principia, 1939). The Cowles Index was converted to the Standard & Poor's base by adjusting overlapping figures.

The relative for the first quarter of the tth year was taken to be $i_1 = [P_1 + \frac{1}{4}(D_1/P_1)P_1]/P_0$ where P_1 and D_1/P_1 are stock price and annualized dividend yield, respectively, at end of quarter and the return for the year derived from the product of the four quarterly returns.

[b] Semiannual relatives were estimated as $(P + \frac{1}{2}C)/100$, where C is the coupon rate on a new 20-year bond sold at par and P is the price at the end of the six-months. The coupon rate C was estimated as the yield to maturity given by Standard & Poor's for High Grade Corporate Bonds. The price P was calculated using the coupon rate C and the yield to maturity given by Standard & Poor's at the end of the six months on the assumption that such a yield would be appropriate for a bond with 19 years and six months to maturity. Multiplying successive pairs of these relatives yields estimates of the annual returns.

[c] The βs are derived from semi-annual regressions of the form $r_b = \alpha + \beta r_m$, where r_b and r_m are annual rates of return on corporate grade bonds and corporate grade stocks, respectively.

[d] Prime Corporate Bonds 1-Year Maturity February Average from *The History of Interest Rates* by Sidney Homer (New Brunswick, New Jersey: Rutgers University Press, 1963), pp 336–367, updated by Salomon Brothers.

stant proportional risk aversion, it is still necessary to estimate the numerical value of the Pratt measure of proportional risk aversion before the form of investors' utility function can be satisfactorily specified [and before the macrorelationships provided by Eqs. (7) and (8) can be used for time-series analysis]. From the results presented in Tables IV and V using data from the

Table V

Expected Annual Rates of Return for Common Stocks and Bonds (1902–1971)

Period	High grade corporate bonds yields to maturity	New York Stock Exchange composite stocks		Calculated market price of risk for stocks using	
		Arithmetic estimate[a]	Geometric estimate[b]	Arithmetic estimate	Geometric estimate
1902–1911	0.0452	0.157	0.132	6.090	4.674
1912–1921	0.0519	0.132	0.097	1.988	1.120
1922–1931	0.0486	0.177	0.059	3.639	0.319
1932–1941	0.0363	0.064	0.011	0.518	−0.042
1942–1951	0.0270	0.160	0.126	3.829	3.075
1952–1961	0.0362	0.137	0.122	4.472	3.843
1962–1971	0.0562	0.086	0.080	1.228	1.047
1902–1961		0.138	0.091	3.423	2.165
1902–1971	0.0431	0.130	0.090	3.109	2.005

[a] The "arithmetic estimate" is the arithmetic mean of annual expected returns where the expected return for the tth year is taken to be $i_t = D_t/P_t + GE_t$, where GE_t = arithmetic mean of previous 10 years of earnings growth. Dividend yields were obtained and earnings growth rates calculated from Standard and Poor's Quarterly *Earnings, Dividends and Price Earnings Ratios.*

[b] The "geometric estimate" is the same, expect that GE_t is the geometric mean of the previous 10 years of earnings growth.

bond as well as stock markets, it would appear that the market price of risk is around 2.0 or more, which means that the coefficient of proportional risk aversion for households is likely to be in excess of 2.0. While statistical tests suggest that no great confidence can be placed on any specific value of this coefficient, the probability that it is in excess of 1.0, the value implied by the log utility function, is extremely high. For financial institutions, the only important group of investors in financial assets other than households, the coefficients of relative risk aversion would probably tend to be somewhat greater than for households.

So far in our empirical analysis, we have assumed homogeneous expectations. Data from the 1962 Survey of Consumer Finances and from a 1971 special sample of individual income tax returns [5, 3] indicate that this assumption is highly questionable. Thus, as indicated by Table VI (as well as other data on the diversification of all household asset holdings, as well as of their stock portfolios), investors do not generally hold well diversified portfolios. A detailed analysis suggests that the most likely reason for this result

Table VI

Distribution of 13 Diversification Measures for all Households Owning Stock as Estimated from 1962 Survey of Consumer Finances

Description of diversification measure[a]	Number of households	Fractiles[b]					Average
		0.05	0.20	0.50	0.80	0.95	
SD 1: Number of NYSE stocks held	641	0	0	1	2	7	1.72
SD 2: Number of holdings	641	1	1	2	4	11	3.41
SD 3: Values of largest NYSE holding to all NYSE holdings	447	0.29	0.54	0.98	1.00	1.00	0.79
SD 4: Value of largest holdings to all holdings	641	0.28	0.50	0.90	1.00	1.00	0.77
SD 5: Value of largest holding (except mutual funds) to all holdings	641	0.00	0.24	0.63	1.00	1.00	0.62
SD 6: Value of largest two NYSE holdings to all NYSE holdings[c]	447	0.44	0.83	1.00	1.00	1.00	0.91
SD 7: Value of largest two holdings to all holdings	641	0.46	0.76	1.00	1.00	1.00	0.89
SD 8: Value of largest two holdings (except mutual funds) to all holdings	641	0.00	0.36	0.97	1.00	1.00	0.72
SD 9: Value of largest NYSE holdings to all holdings	641	0.00	0.00	0.20	0.91	1.00	0.36
SD 10: Value of two largest NYSE holdings to all holdings	641	0.00	0.00	0.30	1.00	1.00	0.41
SD 11: Summation of squared portfolio weights (NYSE only)[c,d]	447	0.16	0.45	0.97	1.00	1.00	0.74
SD 12: Summation of squared portfolio weights (all holdings)	641	0.16	0.37	0.82	1.00	1.00	0.71
SD 13: Summation of squared portfolio weights (all holdings except mutual funds)[d]	586	0.17	0.40	0.86	1.00	1.00	0.72

[a] Stocks held in trust are not included.

[b] The fractiles and averages take into account the sampling probability associated with each household and thus are estimates of the population statistics.

[c] Only households with NYSE holdings are included.

[d] The proportions in each NYSE holding or in each nonmutual fund holding were rescaled so that their sum was 1.0 before the sum of squares was calculated.

is that investors generally hold heterogeneous expectations, though another plausible and, from the viewpoint of portfolio theory, even more troublesome explanation might be that investors do not properly aggregate risks of individual assets to measure the risk of an entire portfolio.

Fortunately, in reassessing the validity of the earlier findings based on the assumption of homogeneous expectations, we find that confining our analysis to households holding relatively diversified portfolios of stocks again provides evidence of approximately constant proportional risk aversion (Table VII). It is for these households that the underlying theoretical model developed earlier in this paper is most likely to hold.

IV. Market Price of Risk and Inflation

To assess the impact of uncertain inflation on the market price of risk, I shall again for simplicity assume homogeneous expectations, frictionless capital markets, and all wealth invested either in nominally risk-free assets or in the market portfolio. Also again using a continuous time model and now maximizing the expected utility of real terminal wealth, it is easy to show that in the presence of uncertain inflation Eq. (7) is replaced by

$$\frac{E(r_m - r_f) - \sigma_{pm}}{\sigma_m^2 - [\sigma_{pm}/\alpha(1 - t)]} = \alpha C(1 - t) = \text{New MPR} \tag{13}$$

where all variables are measured in nominal terms, $\sigma_{pm} = \text{cov}(r_p r_m)$, and r_p is the rate of general price inflation.

Thus, since $\alpha(1 - t)$ is positive (somewhat below one), and since—in view of the magnitude of $E(r_m - r_f)$ and $\sigma_m^2 - \sigma_{pm}$ is of much greater importance in the denominator than in the numerator of Eq. (13), the market price of risk in the presence of uncertain inflation is likely to be less than, equal to, or greater than the market price of risk as usually measured depending on whether $\sigma_{pm} \gtreqless 0$. Now, according to competitive economic theory, with rising prices the correlation between p and m should be strongly positive and, unless σ_p is negligible,[9] the value of σ_{pm} would be expected to be substantially greater than zero. In fact, the correlation between annual or quarterly rates of inflation and contemporaneous returns on New York Stock Exchange stocks as a whole, for any extensive period tested back to the latter part of the nineteenth century, is either statistically insignificantly different than zero or more commonly slightly (though significantly) negative.[10]

As a result, σ_{pm} in Eq. (13) is negligible in relation to σ_m^2 [and even more so in relation to $E(r_m - r_f)$], so that the usual measure of the market price of risk

[9] σ_m is known to be substantial.

[10] This does not mean of course that investment in stocks has not proved superior to investment in bonds as a hedge against inflation or that the market price of risk estimated from bond returns would be unaffected by adjustment for inflation. The correlation between quarterly rates of inflation and the contemporaneous returns on outstanding bonds has been -0.70 for the USA in the period after World War II.

is virtually unaffected by inflation.[11] It should be noted that this result largely reflects the effects of unanticipated changes in the inflation rate on stock returns and that inflation may be better anticipated in the future. In a forthcoming paper by Yoram Landskroner and myself, it will be shown that Eq. (13) is not affected by the substitution of n risky marketable assets for the market portfolio, and that so long as σ_{pm} is negligible the introduction of inflation does not change the market price of risk in Eq. (8), which integrates human wealth into the equilibrium demand relation for risky assets. When a zero-beta asset is substituted for the risk-free asset, the equilibrium demand relation becomes somewhat more complex, introducing the covariance of return on the zero-beta asset with the rate of inflation (as well as σ_{pm}). But it can be argued that in a single-period model expressed in nominal values, there is no rationale for a zero-beta as distinguished from a risk-free asset.

To conclude this discussion of the effect of inflation on the market price of risk, it should be pointed out that Chen and Boness [11], assuming a quadratic utility function, have obtained results for the expected rate of return on a risky asset under uncertain inflation, which implies a market price of risk analogous to that in Eq. (13).[12] However, their interpretation of their results is incorrect. They state that "the traditional capital asset pricing model *overstates* the market price of risk if an uncertain inflation is expected; and it *understates* the market price of risk if an uncertain deflation is expected." As indicated in Eq. (13), the reverse is true in theory, though, as noted above, the empirical results suggest that inflation does not appreciably affect the measured market price of risk.

The reason for the incorrect conclusion by Chen and Boness is that they assume in maximizing expected utility of terminal wealth that the coefficients of their quadratic utility function are the same regardless of whether wealth is measured in real or nominal terms. Thus, in their utility function with real wealth as the argument, $U_1(\tilde{Y}_k) = \tilde{Y}_k - C_1\tilde{Y}_k^2$, where Y is real wealth. They then assume that under "the traditional version of the capital asset pricing model which has not explicitly taken account of uncertain inflation" $U_2(\tilde{Z}_k) = \tilde{Z}_k - C_1\tilde{Z}_k^2$, where Z is nominal wealth. Since the market price of risk $(\text{MPR}_1) = [\sum_k (1/2C_{1k}) - \sum_k E_k(\tilde{Y}_k)]^{-1}$ with allowance for inflation and they state $\text{MPR}_2 = [\sum_k (1/2C_{1k}) - \sum_k E_k(\tilde{Z}_k)]^{-1}$ without such an allowance, they conclude $\text{MPR}_1 < \text{MPR}_2$ with positive inflation, since then $Z_k > Y_k$. In fact, $U_2(\tilde{Z}_k) = \tilde{Z}_k - C_2\tilde{Z}_k^2 = \tilde{R}_p\tilde{Y} - C_2\tilde{R}_p^2\tilde{Y}^2$, and it is no longer possible to draw their conclusion.

[11] Unpublished work by Marshall Blume and myself suggest that when past as well as current rates of inflation are allowed for, the overall correlations between inflation and return on stocks becomes positive, though weakly so, and stock risk in the longer run is slightly reduced by inflation.

[12] As a result of an approximation they use, Chen and Boness do not obtain the σ_{pm} term in the numerator of the left-hand side of Eq. (13).

Table VII

Regressions of $(1 - t_k)z_k$ on the Logarithms of Net Worth for Various Subsamples of the 1962 SCFF[a]

Net worth including homes	Housing measured by	Type of households	Simple Regression			Number	Regression with dummy variables for age, education, and occupation		
			Coefficient on ln(NW)	t-value	$\bar{R}^2$		Coefficient on ln(NW)	t-value	$\bar{R}^2$
No		All households	0.062	11.09	0.08	1320	0.054	7.64	0.16
		All stockholders	0.037	6.93	0.07	615	0.029	4.42	0.13
		Most diversified stockholders	0.007	0.86	0.00	220	0.000	0.04	0.02
		Most diversified stockholders adjusted for beta	0.008	0.76	0.00	205	0.001	0.10	0.11
Yes	Equity	All households	−0.007	−1.84	0.00	1550	−0.003	−0.58	0.06
		All stockholders	−0.002	−0.41	0.00	625	−0.002	−0.33	0.03
		Most diversified stockholders	−0.019	−2.64	0.03	221	−0.022	−2.85	0.05
		Most diversified stockholders adjusted for beta	−0.012	−1.14	0.00	205	−0.017	−1.52	0.02

Yes	Full value	All households	-0.187	-15.39	0.13	1550	-0.157	-9.89	0.19
		All stockholders	-0.102	-11.11	0.16	625	-0.071	-6.37	0.23
		Most diversified stockholders	-0.060	-5.89	0.13	221	-0.063	-5.78	0.14
		Most diversified stockholders adjusted for beta	-0.064	-4.23	0.08	205	-0.071	-4.35	0.09

^{a} The variable α_k includes mixed and risky assets as defined in Table I. Human wealth is excluded in the analyses of this table. The dummy variables, assuming the value of 1.0 if the characteristic is applicable to the head of the household and 0.0 otherwise, are for age (less than or equal to 25- and 5-year intervals from 25 to 65), for education (grade school or less, some high school, high school graduate, some college, and college graduate) and for occupation (self-employed, employed by others, retired, farm operator, not gainfully employed, and employer unknown). The beta coefficient for a household is calculated as a weighted average of the available beta coefficients of NYSE stocks, where the weights are proportional to the value of these stocks in the household's portfolio on December 31, 1962. The beta coefficients themselves were estimated with monthly data over the period 1958–1962 using the S & P Composite Index, providing there were at least 30 months of data.

81

It should be emphasized that while Eq. (13) demonstrates that the usual measure of the market price of risk understates the true value so long as $\sigma_{pm} > 0$, this does not mean that, with a positive covariance between the rate of inflation and the market rate of return, inflation increases the market price of risk. The nominal values appearing in Eq. (7) without inflation are not the same as those appearing in Eq. (13) with inflation.

References

1. Friend, I., "Mythodology in Finance," *Journal of Finance* (May 1973).
2. Friend, I., "Rates of Returns on Bonds and Stocks, the Market Price of Risk, and Implications for the Cost of Capital," Rodney L. White Center for Financial Research, Working Paper No. 23–73, University of Pennsylvania.
3. Blume, M. E., and Friend, I., "The Asset Structure of Individual Portfolios and Some Implications for Utility Functions," *Journal of Finance* (May 1975).
4. Friend, I., and Blume, M. E., "The Demand for Risky Assets," *American Economic Review* (December 1975).
5. Blume, M. E., Crockett, J., and Friend, I., "Stockownership in the United States: Characteristics and Trends," *Survey of Current Business* (November 1974).
6. Mossin, J., "Security Pricing and Investment Criteria in Competitive Markets," *American Economic Review* (December 1969).
7. Lintner, J., "The Market Price of Risk, Size of Market and Investor's Risk Aversion," *Review of Economic Statistics* (February 1970).
8. Budd, A. P., and Litzenberger, R. H., "The Market Price of Risk, Size of Market and Investor's Risk Aversion: A Comment," *Review of Economic Statistics* (May 1972).
9. Cohn, R. A., Lewellen, W. G., Lease, R. C., and Schlarbaum, G. G., "Individual Investor Risk Aversion and Investment Portfolio Composition," *Journal of Finance* (May 1975).
10. Landskroner, Yoram, "The Determinants of the Market Price of Risk," Doctoral Dissertation, University of Pennsylvania (1975) (unpublished).
11. Chen, A. H., and Boness, A. J., "Effects of Uncertain Inflation on the Investment and Financing Decisions of a firm," *Journal of Finance* (May 1975).

OPTIMAL TIMING OF CAPITAL EXPENDITURES

Myron J. Gordon

University of Toronto

Introduction

In deciding whether or not to make a capital expenditure, common practice is to use some variation on the following model[1]:

$$\text{NPV} = -C_0 + \sum_{t=1}^{n} R_t/(1+k)^t \tag{1}$$

In this expression, C_0 is the current expenditure, R_t the incremental cash flow in t due to the expenditure, n the life of the cash flows, and k the return the firm requires on the investment. The model indicates that the investment should be made if the net present value (NPV) of the cash flows is positive.

Implicit in this formulation of the capital expenditure problem is the assumption that the alternative to undertaking the investment at $t = 0$ is deferring it for n or more periods. Notice that R_t is the difference in cash flow between having the machine and not having it from $t = 1 \rightarrow n$. However, deferring the investment for n periods (or forever) is not the only alternative

The author has benefited from discussing the subject of this paper with David Fewings, David Quirin, and Suresh Sethi.

[1] The conclusions reached below hold for other variations on the model, such as the use of internal rate of return or payback as the decision criterion and the recognition of income taxes in the cash flows.

to undertaking it at $t = 0$. Rather, at $t = 0$ the firm has n mutually exclusive alternatives: buying a machine at $t = 0, 1, 2, \ldots$, or $n - 1$. The machine should be purchased now if doing so is more profitable than any of the $n - 1$ alternative courses of action.

This chapter presents a model for determining whether an investment expenditure should be made currently or deferred for one or more periods. The problem has already been recognized and solved. The work of Terborgh [6] in the postwar years constituted a massive attack on the problem. More recently, Smith [5], Masse [4], Bellman and Dreyfus [1]; and Marglin [3], among others, have recognized and solved the problem.

Unfortunately, this previous literature has had very little if any influence on business practice. The failure of business practice to use the models already developed cannot be explained on the grounds that the problem is of little importance. It will be seen that ignoring the alternative of deferring an expenditure one or more periods introduces significant error in capital expenditure decisions. Furthermore, with capital rationing a firm does not decide which of its profitable projects it should reject. Rather it decides which of the projects should be deferred. In practice, business firms frequently use qualitative judgements or crude rules of thumb to recognize the timing alternatives open to them.

A more reasonable explanation of business practice is that the models are difficult to understand and/or the data required to implement them are difficult to obtain with any reasonable degree of accuracy. Either state of affairs can result in worse decisions based on a formally accurate model than would take place with crude but familiar and roughly correct rules of thumb. The justification for presenting the model below is that it is significantly easier to understand and to obtain the data required to implement than is true of the previous solutions to the problem.

Section I presents the special case of the model for determining whether a machine replacement should be made currently or deferred for one period. Section II develops simplifications of the model which facilitate its use with data readily available to a firm. Section III considers the possible errors in failing to explicitly compare the alternatives of replacing two or more periods, hence with the alternatives of replacing currently or one period hence. Section IV illustrates the use of the model with numerical examples. Section V presents and discusses the formal generalization of the model to handle any type of investment, and Section VI concludes with a brief comparative review of the literature and some other observations.

I. The Replacement Model

In evaluating the desirability of a replacement expenditure, it is permissible to take the firm's revenue as given regardless of the equipment employed. Hence, the problem is cost minimization. If a machine currently employed is replaced at $t = 0$, the present value of all future outlays may be written

$$Q_0^0 = C_0 + \sum_{t=1}^{n} \frac{E_t^0}{(1 + k)^t} + \frac{Q_n}{(1 + k)^n} \tag{2}$$

In this expression, Q_0^0 is the present value, at $t = 0$, of all future outlays with a new machine purchased at $t = 0$, denoted by the superscript, and with an optimal replacement policy pursued thereafter; C_0 the cost of the machine purchased at $t = 0$; E_t^0 the production costs during t (more exactly, the period ending at t) when a new machine is acquired at $t = 0$, denoted by the superscript; n the optimal life of the machine acquired at $t = 0$; Q_n the value at $t = n$ of all costs subsequent to n with a new machine acquired at n; and k the return on investment the firm requires.

As indicated earlier, one alternative to replacing the existing machine at $t = 0$ is to do so one period later. The present value, at $t = 0$, of all future outlays associated with this decision is

$$Q_0^1 = \frac{C_1}{1 + k} + \frac{E_1^-}{1 + k} + \sum_{t=2}^{n+1} \frac{E_t^1}{(1 + k)^t} + \frac{Q_{n+1}}{(1 + k)^{n+1}} \tag{3}$$

on the assumption that the optimal life of a machine purchased at $t = 1$ is also n periods. In this expression, Q_0^1 is the present value at $t = 0$, of all future outlays with a new machine purchased at $t = 1$, and with an optimal replacement policy pursued thereafter; C_1 the estimate at $t = 0$ of the cost of the optimal machine that could be acquired at $t = 1$; E_1^- the production costs during $t = 1$ with the machine in use prior to $t = 0$; E_t^1 the production costs during t with the machine acquired at $t = 1$; and Q_{n+1} the value at $t = n + 1$ of all costs subsequent to $n + 1$ with a new machine acquired at $n + 1$.

Subtracting Eq. (3) from Eq. (2) provides an exact expression for the amount by which the present value of all future costs with replacement now exceeds the present value of all future costs with replacement one period hence. Carrying out the subtraction, with a slight rearrangement of terms and with C_0 both multiplied and divided by $1 + k$, results in

$$Q_0^0 - Q_0^1 = \frac{C_0 - C_1}{1 + k} + \frac{C_0 k}{1 + k} + \frac{E_1^0 - E_1^-}{1 + k} + \sum_{t=2}^{n} \frac{E_t^0 - E_t^1}{(1 + k)^t}$$

$$+ \frac{Q_n}{(1 + k)^n} - \frac{E_{n+1}^1 + Q_{n+1}}{(1 + k)^{n+1}} \tag{4}$$

If $Q_0^0 - Q_0^1 > 0$, deferring the replacement one period is more profitable, and if the expression is negative, it is more profitable to replace now. The interpretation of each term is presented below.

$C_0 - C_1$ is the amount by which the cost of a new machine now exceeds the cost of a new machine one period later. Technological progress will tend to make this term positive, inflation will tend to make it negative, and other factors such as tariff changes will work in either direction. Therefore, one cannot say a priori whether $C_0 - C_1$ will be positive or negative. The second term is the foregone return on the funds tied up for one period as a consequence of replacing now and not one period hence. $C_0 k$ will always be positive.

The third term is the chief and frequently the only reason for replacing now and not waiting. $E_1^0 - E_1^-$ will always be negative, since the production cost with the best currently available machine will be less than the cost with the machine in use, unless machines improve with age. Each element of the fourth term $E_t^0 - E_t^1$ is the excess production costs during t with the current replacement over the costs with next year's replacement. Two factors will tend to make this quantity positive in each period from $t = 2 \rightarrow n$: the superior technology with next year's machine, and the lower maintenance and repair costs with next year's machine, which is one year newer in each year from $2 \rightarrow n$.

Finally, the last two terms in Eq. (4) represent the present value at $t = 0$ of all costs subsequent to the end of the nth period, with replacement at $t = n$ minus the present value at $t = 0$ of all costs subsequent to the end of the nth period with replacement at $t = n + 1$. It will be shown shortly that this quantity is always positive. Hence, apart from the uncertain sign of $C_0 - C_1$, every term in Eq. (3) but the third is positive. The production cost advantage of a new machine over the old one currently in use *for one period* is the only reason for replacing a machine currently. The foregone return on the funds tied up, production costs from $t = 2 \rightarrow n$, and all costs subsequent to n favor the deferring of replacement.

II. Simplification of the Model

The usefulness of Eq. (4) for deciding whether a machine should be replaced immediately or the replacement should be deferred one or more periods in the future depends on its generality and ease of implementation. On the generality question, Eq. (4) explicitly considers only two among n possible replacement dates. What, if any, decision errors may result from the failure to explicitly consider the other possible replacement dates will be examined in the next section. Ease of implementation depends on the accuracy with which the variables can be measured and the ability of practitioners to understand the model.

With regard to measurement of the variables, current practice requires knowledge of the cost of a currently available machine C_0, its life n, the discount rate k, and R_t, the difference in operating costs between the machine in use and a currently available machine for $t = 1 \rightarrow n$. The practice in arriving at R_t is to estimate E_1^- and E_1^0 and to take R_t for $t = 1 \to n$ as equal to $E_1^- - E_1^0$. Hence, the variables in addition to those required by current practice to implement Eq. (4) are C_1, E_t^0, and E_t^1 for $t = 2 \to n$, and the variables in the last two terms of Eq. (4).

The estimation of C_1, the cost of the best machine available next year, is certainly not beyond the capacity of a firm's management. With regard to E_t^0 and E_t^1 for $t = 2 \to n$, we require only the difference between their values, and not the absolute value of each. A reasonable assumption is that $E_t^0 - E_t^1$ is independent of t. In that event, we only require $E_2^0 - E_2^1$. This, it will be recalled, is the excess in production costs during $t = 2$ with a currently purchased machine over next year's machine. The excess will be due to the technological superiority and superior physical condition of next year's machine over the current one.

Terborgh [6, p 261], Masse [4, pp 61–64], and others have shown that with constant technological progress the advantage of next year's machine over the current machine can be estimated from the estimated life of the machine, and vice versa. That is, letting $G = E_t^0 - E_t^1$, they have shown that

$$G = 2C_0/n^2 \tag{5}$$

Hence, under this assumption the knowledge of C_0 and n required by current practice provides a good estimate of $E_t^0 - E_t^1$ for $t = 2 \to n$. Conversely, if we know $E_2^0 - E_2^1$, Eq. (5) may be used to estimate n. However, Eq. (5) is not strictly accurate, and a somewhat longer calculation can be used to obtain an n that is more or less greater than $(2C_0/G)^{1/2}$.

The last two terms of Eq. (4) appear to be the most difficult to evaluate, since it is not clear how one would go about estimating E_{n+1}^1, Q_n, and Q_{n+1}. However, these two terms in the equation can be replaced by a simpler expression. B_0 and B_1 refer, respectively, to the buy now and buy next year decisions, and let the replacement at $n + 1$ for the B_1 decision be moved back to n. The last two terms of Eq. (4) become

$$\frac{Q_n}{(1 + k)^n} - \frac{Q_n}{(1 + k)^n} = 0 < \frac{Q_n}{(1 + k)^n} - \frac{E_{n+1}^1 + Q_{n+1}}{(1 + k)^{n+1}} \tag{6}$$

The "less than" sign holds for the following reason. Since $n + 1$ is the optimal replacement date for the B_1 machine, moving that replacement back to n must raise the present value of all costs subsequent to n. Hence, zero is the lower limit on the value of the last two terms of Eq. (4).

Let us now move the replacement of the B_0 machine forward in time from n to $n + 1$. This results in

$$\frac{E_{n+1}^0 + Q_{n+1}}{(1 + k)^{n+1}} - \frac{E_{n+1}^1 + Q_{n+1}}{(1 + k)^{n+1}} > \frac{Q_n}{(1 + k)^n} - \frac{E_{n+1} + Q_{n+1}}{(1 + k)^{n+1}} \tag{7}$$

The " greater than " sign holds because $Q_n/(1 + k)^n$ is the present value of all costs from $n \to \infty$ with the B_0 machine optimally replaced at $t = n$. Moving that replacement forward one period must raise the present value of all costs from $n \to \infty$.

Combining Eqs. (6) and (7) and simplifying slightly brackets the last two terms of Eq. (4) as follows:

$$\frac{E^0_{n+1} - E^1_{n+1}}{(1 + k)^{n+1}} > \frac{Q_n}{(1 + k)^n} - \frac{E^1_{n+1} + Q_{n+1}}{(1 + k)^{n+1}} > 0 \qquad (8)$$

Therefore, an approximation of the last two terms of Eq. (4) is

$$\lambda(E^0_{n+1} - E^1_{n+1})/(1 + k)^{n+1}$$

with $0 < \lambda < 1$, and with $E^0_{n+1} - E^1_{n+1}$ the excess operating costs in $n + 1$ with a currently available machine over next year's machine. If $n > 15$, this term can be ignored, and if $n < 15$, setting $\lambda = 0.5$ will provide adequate accuracy.

Finally, if the operating cost advantage of next year's machine over the current machine is taken to be equal to the Eq. (5) estimate, Eq. (4) reduces to the simple expression

$$Q^0_0 - Q^1_0 = \frac{C_0 - C_1}{1 + k} + \frac{C_0 k}{1 + k} - \frac{E^-_1 - E^0_1}{1 + k} + \sum_{t=2}^{n} \frac{G}{(1 + k)^t} + \frac{\lambda G}{(1 + k)^{n+1}} \qquad (9)$$

The interpretation of each term in this expression is straightforward, and the only implementation problem is the estimation of n, the life of the currently available machine. Alternatively, if G can be estimated directly, Eq. (5) can be used to obtain n.

III. Generality of the Replacement Model

Equation (9) compares replacement now with replacement one period hence. Can the failure to explicitly consider the alternatives of replacing two or more periods hence result in an incorrect decision? The answer is clearly no if Eq. (9) determines that deferring replacement one period is more profitable than replacement now. Assume that the most profitable replacement date is two periods hence. The finding that replacement one period hence is more profitable than current replacement defers the decision for at least one period. When the Eq. (9) calculation is repeated one period hence, we once again find that deferral is the most profitable course of action, but when it is repeated two periods hence, immediate replacement is then found to be the most profitable course of action.

It is sometimes though that if Eq. (9) indicates that replacement should be deferred, the recursive use of the equation will repeatedly produce the same conclusion. A more careful examination of the expression reveals the

contrary. $C_0 - C_1$ and $C_0 k$ should not change except for random distur-
bances as we move forward in time. With constant technological progress,
$G = E_t^0 - E_t^1$ will not change over time. However, technological progress
and wear will make $E_1^- - E_1^0$ increase and make replacement increasingly
attractive with the passage of time.

We have seen that if Eq. (9) signals defer replacement we have a correct
decision without explicitly considering the alternatives of replacement two
or more periods in the future. The decision not to replace now, however, is
all that is correct. We have not established that replacement should take
place one period hence. The problem is more difficult when Eq. (9) signals
replace now. Replacement at $t = 0$ may be less costly than replacement one
period later, but more costly than replacement two or more periods later. In
that event, replacement now forecloses on the less costly later replacement,
and it would be an incorrect decision. Such a situation cannot arise,
however, if technological progress is expected to take place at a constant rate
over time. If B_0, the buy decision, is less costly than the B_1 decision, it is
increasingly less costly than the B_2, B_3, ..., and B_n decisions.

An exact proof of this statement is difficult and will not be presented, but
its intuitive basis can be seen quite readily. Waiting two periods to replace
requires the high cost production with the machine currently in use for two
periods instead of one. If it is not profitable to defer the introduction of a
new machine for one period, it will be even less profitable to defer it for two
or more periods with the expectation of constant technological progress.

The messy problem arises when a technological breakthrough is expected
two or more periods in the future. In that event, we may have current
replacement more profitable than waiting one year, but waiting until the
radically improved machine is available may be the optimal course of action.
If a breakthrough is expected, say, three periods hence, it is necessary to
evaluate $Q_0^0 - Q_0^3$ if $Q_0^0 - Q_0^1$ in Eq. (9) is negative. In estimating $Q_0^0 - Q_0^3$, it
should be recognized that while n may be the life of a new machine available
in three years, that machine will shorten the life of a new machine purchased
at $t = 0$. Estimating $Q_0^0 - Q_0^t$ with $t > 1$ and reflecting a technological
breakthrough is possible, but it is more difficult than using Eq. (9).

The previous analysis leads to the following conclusion. Eq. (9) is an
accurate and adequate model for deciding whether or not to replace a machine, except for the special case where it signals replace now and a significant
technological breakthrough is expected two or more periods in the future. In
that case the logical extension of Eq. (4) to the problem must be used.

IV. Numerical Illustrations

A few numerical illustrations may help both to fix the ideas raised in the
previous pages and to demonstrate the empirical importance of recognizing
the alternative to current replacement of deferring it one or more periods.

Let the operating cost during $t = 1$ for a machine currently in use be $E_1^- = \$110{,}000$. For a new machine currently available at $t = 0$, let $C_0 = \$50{,}000$, $n = 10$, and $E_1^0 = \$100{,}000$. Current practice as reflected in Eq. (1) would produce $R_t = E_1^- - E_1^0 = \$10{,}000$ for $t = 1 \rightarrow n$, and with the discount rate $k = .10$, the net present value of the replacement expenditure is

$$\text{NPV} = -\$50{,}000 + \$10{,}000 \sum_{t=1}^{10} 1/(1.1)^t = \$11{,}446 \tag{10}$$

With $n = 10$, the implied estimate of $E_t^0 - E_t^1$ is

$$G = 2C_0/n^2 = \$1000 \tag{11}$$

Using this estimate in Eq. (9) with $C_1 = C_0$ results in

$$Q_0^0 - Q_0^1 = \frac{0}{1.1} + \frac{\$5000}{1.1} - \frac{\$10{,}000}{1.1} + \$1000 \sum_{t=2}^{10} \frac{1}{(1.1)^t} + \frac{\$500}{(1.1)^{11}} = \$865 \tag{12}$$

By comparison with the alternative of deferring the replacement for n periods, the firm makes \$11,146 by replacing now, but it loses \$865 by comparison with the alternative of waiting one year. In other words, the discounted to $t = 0$ value of all future costs are raised by \$11,146 if replacement is deferred n periods, but they are reduced by \$865 if replacement is deferred for one period.

Moving forward one period in time, with technological progress taking place as expected, will raise $E_1^- - E_1^0$ to \$11,000 and leave all the other terms of Eq. (12) unchanged. Hence, $Q_0^0 - Q_0^1$ is reduced to $-\$44$, and there is a slight gain in replacing now by comparison with the alternative of waiting one more year.

Raising the optimal life of a new machine increases the attractiveness of current replacement. In the limit, if $n = \infty$, NPV $= \$50{,}000$. If the currently available machine has an infinite life, future machines will not be any more productive and $E_t^0 - E_t^1 = G = 0$. The value of $Q_0^0 - Q_1^0 = -\$5000$. Note that the gain from immediate replacement is only \$5000 and not \$50,000 when it is recognized that the replacement can be made one year hence.

Reducing the value of n reduces the attractiveness of current replacement under both approaches. With $n = 5$, Eq. (10) NPV $= -\$12{,}092$, the implied estimate of $G = \$4000$, and $Q_0^0 - Q_0^1 = \$8112$. Current replacement raises the discounted value of future costs by \$12,092 over what they would be with replacement five years hence, but it is only \$8112 more costly than replacement one year hence. With each passing year and technology changing as expected, $E_1^- - E_1^0$ rises by \$4000. One year later, $E_1^- - E_1^0 = \$14{,}000$, and NPV $= \$3060$. However, with $E_t^0 - E_t^1 = \$4000$ and $n = 5$, we have

$Q_0^0 - Q_0^1 = \$4056$. Current replacement costs \$4056 more than replacement one period hence. Replacement becomes profitable in two more years.

In the previous examples, the firm knows the optimal life of a current machine, n, by one means or another, and we used the approximation for $E_t^0 - E_t^1$ provided by Eq. (5). Assume instead that the firm arrives at $E_t^0 - E_t^1 = \$1000$. Using the method described by Terborgh [6, p. 65], the accurate estimate of $n = 12$ years. With $n = 12$ and everything else unchanged, Eq. (10) becomes NPV $= \$18,137$. The Eq. (12) solution for $Q_0^0 - Q_0^1$ becomes \$1504. The discounted costs under buying now are \$18,137 less than waiting 12 years, but \$1504 more than waiting one year.

All of the previous illustrations have assumed that technological progress is expected to take place at a constant rate. That is, in any period t production costs with the machine available at the start of the period will be \$1000 less than with the machine available at the start of the previous period, and Q times \$1000 less than the costs with the machine available Q periods earlier.

Assume now that the new machine at the start of $t = 1$ is expected to incorporate a technological breakthrough. With everything else unchanged, $E_t^0 - E_t^1 = \$5000$ instead of \$1000. The solution to Eq. (12) becomes $Q_0^0 - Q_0^1 = \$22,508$. This overstates the cost of buying now, because the firm would find it profitable not to wait n periods before replacing the obsolete machine. However, the slightly lower true value of $Q_0^0 - Q_0^1$ is unlikely to reverse the conclusion that the firm should wait a year to replace the machine. By comparison, Eq. (10) is not changed by the presence of the great new machine on the horizon.

V. The General Model

The formal extension of the replacement model presented in Section II to deal with the optimal timing of all investment expenditures, for expansion and new products as well as replacements, is a simple task. A difficult task, it will be seen, is the substitution of empirically manageable quantities for the analog to the last two terms of Eq. (4).

Let a firm be considering the acquisition of a "machine" for any purpose whatsoever. The objective of the firm is to maximize the present value at $t = 0$ of all future revenues. If the machine is acquired at $t = 0$, the new present value of the incremental future cash flows is

$$V_0^0 = -C_0 + \sum_{t=1}^{n} R_t^0/(1 + k)^t + V_n^0/(1 + k)^n \tag{13}$$

where V_0^0 is the present value at $t = 0$ of all future cash inflow consequent on buying a machine at $t = 0$ and pursuing an optimal replacement policy thereafter; C_0 the cost of machine purchased at $t = 0$; R_t^0 the excess of cash inflow during t with a machine purchased at $t = 0$ over the inflow without the machine; n the expected life of the machine purchased at $t = 0$; and V_n^0 the value at $t = n$ of all subsequent cash flows with a new machine purchased at $t = 0$, denoted by superscript, and replaced at $t = n$. The reason why the last term in Eq. (13), V_n^0, has a superscript while the analogous term in Eq. (2), Q_n, does not, will be explained shortly.

Among the mutually exclusive alternatives at $t = 0$ to buying a machine at $t = 0$ is to buy it at $t = 1$. The net present value at $t = 0$ of all incremental future cash flows consequent upon this decision is

$$V_0^1 = -\frac{C_1}{1+k} + \sum_{t=2}^{n+1} \frac{R_t^1}{(1+k)^t} + \frac{V_{n+1}^1}{(1+k)^{n+1}} \tag{14}$$

The definition of each variable in Eq. (14) follows from the previous definitions. Note that R_1^1 does not appear in Eq. (14). For a replacement investment $R_1^0 = E_1^- - E_1^0$ and $R_1^1 = E_1^- - E_0^- = 0$. For a new product investment $R_1^1 = 0$, since the new product is not manufactured and sold during $t = 1$ if the new facilities are not acquired until the end of the period.

The investment should be made at $t = 0$ and not deferred one period if $V_0^0 > V_0^1$. Subtracting Eq. (14) from Eq. (13) results in

$$V_0^0 - V_0^1 = \frac{-C_0 + C_1}{1+k} - \frac{C_0 k}{1+k} + \frac{R_1^0}{1+k} + \sum_{t=2}^{n} \frac{R_t^0 - R_t^1}{(1+k)^t}$$

$$+ \frac{V_n^0}{(1+k)^n} - \frac{R_{n+1}^1 + V_{n+1}^1}{(1+k)^{n+1}} \tag{15}$$

In comparing Eqs. (15) and (4), it should be recalled that Q refers to costs and V refers to revenues. We defer if Eq. (4) is positive, but we buy now if Eq. (15) is positive.

The first three terms of Eq. (15) are identical to the corresponding terms of Eq. (4) with the sign changed. If waiting a year reduces the cost of the machine, then $C_1 < C_0$, and deferring is made more profitable. The foregone return on the funds tied up, $C_0 k$, is also a gain from deferring. $R_1^0 \geq 0$ and is a gain from not deferring.

For a replacement expenditure, $R_t^0 - R_t^1$ for $t = 2 \rightarrow n$ is always negative, as explained in Section II, but for a new product or an expansion expenditure this term can be negative or positive. It will be negative insofar as technology improves with time, and the technology of new products improves very rapidly with time. However, being the first to put a new product on the market can confer a market position. Also, improvement in technology can be associated with experience in manufacture. $R_t^0 - R_t^1$ will also be positive for a capacity expansion investment insofar as failure to meet demand during $t = 1$ reduces sales in subsequent periods.

The sum of the last two terms in Eq. (15) can be positive or negative. Furthermore, the simplification analogous to the derivation of Eq. (9) is not possible. In arriving at Eq. (9) it was correctly stated that if the B_1 machine replacement was moved back from $n + 1$ to n, all costs subsequent to n discounted to that date would become equal under the B_0 and B_1 decisions. However, $V_n^1 \neq V_n^0$ is possible. If the B_0 machine provides the firm with a stronger market position than the B_1 machine, $V_n^1 < V_n^0$ notwithstanding the fact both represent the acquisition of the same machine on the same date. Consequently, a simple expression such as $\lambda(R_{n+1}^0 - R_{n+1}^1)$ cannot be used to approximate the last two terms of Eq. (15).

There are conditions under which it is nonetheless possible to use Eq. (15) in deciding whether or not to defer a nonreplacement expenditure. First, if the market position to be gained by making the expenditure currently is not expected to last more than n periods, the last two terms can be replaced by $\lambda(R_{n+1}^0 - R_{n+1}^1)/(1 + k)^{n+1}$. If the market position is expected to last more than n periods, the firm may estimate its net value during $n + 1$ and derive its value for all future time by assigning a decay rate to this value and discounting the series.

VI. Concluding Observations

It was stated at the start of this chapter that the problem to which it is addressed has already been recognized and alternative models for solving the problem exist. It may therefore be of some value to present a brief comparative review of this literature.

For the most part, the replacement literature has been concerned with a related but different problem. From Lutz and Lutz [2], Masse [4], and others we learn how long a machine that will be acquired at $t = 0$ should be kept in operation before it is retired. This question must be answered to determine whether or not to acquire the machine as we saw earlier. However, a firm does not decide at $t = 0$ when it will retire a machine acquired at $t = 0$. The problem at this point in time is whether or not to acquire the machine.

Terborgh was, I believe, the first person to consider this problem. His work certainly represented the most significant attack on the problem up to that time. Under the assumption that technological progress is expected to take place at a constant rate, the replacement model presented here yields the same solution as the Terborgh model. Two advantages may be claimed for the present model. One is ease of interpretation and implementation. The other is some advance in dealing with situations where a technological breakthrough is expected one or more periods in the future.

Bellman and Dreyfus [1, pp. 114–24] have shown how dynamic programming provides a perfectly general solution to the optimal timing of capital expenditures. The expectation of uneven technological progress presents no problems in principle for this model. However, it does require complete knowledge of what the technology will be over the entire future time horizon. The horizon cannot be limited to the life of the currently available machine, while an infinite time horizon makes the problem completely insoluble. A finite horizon raises difficult problems with regard to when it can be terminated, and still leaves a massive data collection and information processing problem. In short, one cannot say a priori that, given the data available to a firm, the ability of operating personnel in a firm to relate it to a dynamic programming model, and the ability of dynamic programmers to make sense out of the data available to a firm, a dynamic programming solution to a timing problem will be superior to the solution obtained with the present model.

In conclusion, it is of some interest to note that the models presented here provide some explanation for otherwise strange rules of thumb employed by firms in their capital budgeting decisions. It has been my observation that many firms place an arbitrary upper limit on the funds that may be spent for replacement purposes and an arbitrary lower limit on the fraction of the budget to be spent on new products. Such an effort to overrule the results of profitability calculations for each project is justified if the calculations are biased in favor of replacement outlays and against new products. The previous pages have demonstrated that current practice systematically biases the profitability of replacement expenditures upward and at best fairly estimates the profitability of new product expenditures. An interesting aside is that the Terborgh model, like the one presented here, makes replacement less attractive than waiting. Perhaps he was able to advance his model under the sponsorship of the Machinery and Allied Products Institute, an organization of firms that sold capital equipment, because his replacement model, with a reasonable discount rate, could lead to more rapid replacement of equipment than the extremely short payoff requirements employed by firms at the time he wrote on the subject.

References

1. Bellman, R. E., and Dreyfus, S. E., *Applied Dynamic Programming.* Princeton, New Jersey: Princeton Univ. Press, 1962.
2. Lutz, F., and Lutz, V., *The Theory of Investment of the Firm.* Princeton, New Jersey: Princeton Univ. Press, 1951.
3. Marglin, S. A., "Approaches to Dynamic Investment Planning," *Contributions to Economic Analysis* **29** (1963).
4. Massé, P., *Optimal Investment Decisions.* Englewood Cliffs, New Jersey: Prentice-Hall, 1962.
5. Smith, V. L., *Investment and Production.* Cambridge, Massachusetts: Harvard Univ. Press, 1961.
6. Terborgh, G., *Dynamic Equipment Policy.* New York: McGraw-Hill, 1949.

LEASING, BUYING, AND THE COST OF CAPITAL SERVICES

Merton H. Miller and Charles W. Upton
The University of Chicago

I. Introduction

The contrast between the economist's and the accountant's approach to problems of corporate decision making is nowhere better illustrated than in the lease-or-buy decision. A neoclassical economist would take it for granted that the rental terms offered by lessors would reflect the inescapable financial costs of owning durable capital goods—interest and depreciation. The choice between renting or buying for any firm would depend on which method of acquiring the services of capital goods had the lower nonfinancial costs in the sense of the costs of acquisition, maintenance, and disposal. There would perhaps be some reason to believe that the balance of these nonfinancial costs would tend to favor leasing by user firms. Ownership and

Reprinted with permission from *The Journal of Finance* (June 1976).

An earlier version of this paper was presented at the Finance Workshop of the Graduate School of Business of the University of Chicago in February 1975; at the Conference on Financial Decision Making Under Uncertainty sponsored by Israel Scientific Research Conferences, Ein Bokek, Israel in March 1975; and at a Finance–Accounting Workshop at Georgia Institute of Technology in March 1975. We are grateful for the many helpful comments and suggestions received from the participants at these sessions. We are especially indebted to Fischer Black, Eugene Fama, Myron Scholes, and Roman Weil for helping us to clarify some of the issues involved in the treatment of tax subsidies.

use are distinct economic activities after all—a distinction implicit, for example, in the familiar neoclassical contrasts between profits and interest or between entrepreneurs and capitalists. Hence, specialization of these roles would presumably lead to greater efficiency. But the presumption in favor of leasing would certainly not be an overwhelming one, and it would be recognized that lower nonfinancial costs, particularly of maintenance and repair, might well be achieved in some cases by having the user assume the ownership. None of these considerations, however, would alter the fundamental point that the purely financial costs of the two methods are equivalent.

The accounting approach, on the other hand, takes the nonfinancial advantages as equal and makes the choice hinge on presumed *financial* advantages of one method over the other. Precisely what these advantages are and how they are to be incorporated into valuation formulas have been the subject of much controversy in recent years.[1] The discussions have focused on such issues as: (1) the nature of the risks of leasing versus those of ownership; (2) the appropriate risk and tax adjustments to apply to the rates used to discount the various relevant cash flows; and (3) the assumptions about financing that must be made to avoid biasing the decision in one direction or the other. Although the participants in these debates differ considerably in the ways they propose to resolve these issues, we feel that they (and, for that matter, virtually all textbooks in corporate finance or accounting) could certainly agree on the following proposition: The decision to lease or buy is neither a matter of indifference for the typical firm nor one for which any general presumption can be established a priori. Each case must be examined on its merits.[2]

It may seem hard to argue with the earnest advice to consider each case on its merits, but we shall try to do so. We shall argue that the accountants' look-at-both-sides approach ignores information about the relative financial advantages of the two modes that has been impounded in the rental rates being quoted. In a world with no taxes, or where every user of capital is subject to the same taxes, these quoted rates would adjust until the financial costs of leasing and buying were equivalent. This conclusion holds even when the standard neoclassical model is extended to deal explicitly with

---

[1] See, e.g., Johnson and Lewellen [11], Schall [18], Gordon [9], Bower *et al.* [4], Myers *et al.* [17].

[2] After completing an earlier draft of this paper, we received a copy of a paper entitled "Asset Leasing in Competitive Capital Markets" by Lewellen *et al.* [13]. It is the only paper dealing with the rent-or-buy decision that we have seen that gives a key role to the proposition that competition in the capital market can be expected to equalize the purely financial advantages of renting or buying. Since Lewellen *et al.* start from the same premise as we do, it is hardly surprising that they also reach many of the same conclusions. But there are enough differences in approach and emphasis to make their paper and ours complementary as well as competitive.

uncertainty and with the fact that owners of capital equipment may be permitted to deduct interest payments in computing taxes on profits. The neoclassical presumption of financial equivalence between buying and leasing breaks down, however, when allowance is made for the differences in rates, exemptions, and eligibility for subsidies under present tax laws. Nevertheless, it is still possible to establish some broad generalizations about lease-or-buy *policy*.

II. The Neoclassical Analysis for the Certainty Case

The term lease has come to be used in a variety of ways and with a variety of qualifying phrases—full-recourse leases, leveraged leases, operating leases, financial leases, net–net leases, and so on. From the economic point of view, the critical distinction is between what we shall call "short-term leases" and "long-term leases." A short-term lease is a commitment to acquire and pay for the services of a specific capital good for the shortest practical interval of time. Since we shall be working throughout in a discrete time context, we shall take this interval as a single time period. How much real time corresponds to this single time period will depend, of course, on the particular application. For renting an automobile it may be as short as a day; for a farm, the length of a single crop cycle; and for some kinds of specialized industrial equipment, perhaps several years. What matters, for analytical purposes, is simply that the terms of the commitment, once undertaken, cannot be altered within the period; and that at the end of the period both parties are free to recontract or not for the next and any subsequent periods.[3]

By a long-term lease we mean one in which the user has a commitment extending over more than a single period. The contract commitment itself will be assumed noncancellable over the agreed term of the lease. But the user firm has the right to sublet the property or to buy back the contract (or to pay penalties that are equivalent thereto). A limiting special case of a long-term lease is one we shall call a "life-of-the-property" lease, in which the residual value of the property at the end of the term of the lease is known to be zero.

In analyzing the firm's choice between buying and assuming either of these two types of lease commitments, we shall focus first in each of the assumed economic environments on the decision to acquire the capital ser-

---

[3] A contract in which the lessee has the right to renew for the next period at the same or some other stipulated rental (or to apply all or part of the rental towards the purchase of property at a stipulated price) would be a short-term lease plus an option. We shall assume throughout that the lease payments we are working with are net of any premium for such an option.

vices via the short-term lease. Then we take up whether to buy in preference to the short-term lease. And finally we check to see whether and how any of the conclusions would be altered by the existence of long-term rental contracts. This strategy of successive approximations and pairwise comparisons will make, alas, for some tedium; but it is the price we feel that must be paid to deal with the many unresolved issues in a clear and consistent way.

The neoclassical model under certainty is the natural place to begin because it permits us to introduce the basic notation and concepts with a minimum amount of distraction. Subsequent sections will then extend the results to allow for uncertainty and for various tax complications.

A. The Sell-or-Lease Decision

To emphasize that owning a capital good and using it in a production process are, in principle, two distinct economic activities, economists often make use of the convenient fiction that title to all capital goods must, by law, be vested in specialized leasing corporations. No generality is lost by this assumption; a manufacturer of capital goods may integrate forward and acquire a leasing subsidiary if economies could thereby be achieved; and, similarly, a user of capital equipment may acquire a leasing company and lease its equipment from that company if, for any reason, such an arrangement should prove more efficient than commercial leasing.

Suppose we accept this fiction, provisionally, and go on to ask how the management of such an independently operated, profit-making leasing company might set the rental on a particular type of capital equipment, say type i. To take the easy cases first, suppose further that the relevant technological, financial, and market conditions take the following forms.

(1)   The machines in question are produced by a perfectly competitive industry at a constant cost of π_{it} per unit. The same machines will be produced by the industry next period, again at a constant cost of $\pi_{i,t+1}$, not necessarily equal to π_{it}. Technological innovation, for example, may result in production costs declining over time. The deterioration of these machines is assumed to be of the "evaporation" type. That is, in period $t+1$ each machine produced in period t is equivalent in productive power to $1 - \delta_{it}$ new machines.

(2)   Maintenance and repair of the machines during use are obtained by purchase of a service policy from a competitive specialized service industry (with integration permissible). Let there initially be one and only one level of maintenance expenditures that is technologically feasible, and let the law be that this amount of maintenance must be purchased by the user firm whether it chooses to rent or buy.

(3)   Second-hand machines can be bought, sold, or sublet by leasing companies in unlimited quantities in perfect markets.

(4) Leasing companies can borrow or lend indefinitely in a perfect capital market at a known one-period rate of interest of r_t. Leasing, moreover, is a business that anyone is free to enter and requires the use of no real resources.

Given these simplifying assumptions, the equilibrium one-period rental L_{it}^* can easily be shown to be the familiar

$$L_{it}^* = \pi_{it}(r_t + d_{it}) = \pi_{it}\left[r_t + \frac{\pi_{i,t+1}}{\pi_{it}} \delta_{it} + \left(1 - \frac{\pi_{i,t+1}}{\pi_{it}} \right) \right] \qquad (1)$$

That is, the equilibrium rental is equal to the interest foregone on the capital invested in the machine, $\pi_{it} r_t$, plus the depreciation of the machine, $d_{it} \pi_{it}$. In this case, the depreciation consists of two parts: a "deterioration" or "operating inferiority" $\delta_{it} \pi_{i,t+1}$, and an "obsolescence" $[1 - (\pi_{i,t+1})/(\pi_{i,t})]\pi_{it}$, whenever the new machines of vintage $t + 1$ can be produced at a lower cost than those during t. No leasing firm need ever contract for a rental less than L_{it}^* because it always has the opportunity to sell the machine for π_{it} and invest the proceeds in the capital market to earn the rate r_t. And if the going rental rate were to rise to $L_{it}' > L_{it}^*$, leasing firms would earn a rate of return greater than r_t. New leasing companies would enter the industry, buying the equipment from the manufacturers at its cost of π_{it} per unit and cutting rentals until the market's quoted rental rate returned to L_{it}^*.

B. *The Decision from the User's Point of View*

Assumptions (1)–(4) are a good deal stronger than necessary to establish the existence of an equilibrium rental, but before discussing the ways in which they can be weakened, it is instructive to look at the decision problem as seen by the user on the other side of the transaction. The user actually faces two decision problems: (1) Given the market rental of L_{it}^*, how many units of machine i is it optimal to rent? (2) Given L_{it}^*, r_t, δ_{it}, π_{it} and $\pi_{i,t+1}$, does it pay to buy into the leasing business? These decisions, moreover, can clearly be taken separately under our assumptions. For even if the user decides to maintain a leasing subsidiary and rent to itself, the lease rate it should charge in its internal transfer pricing would be L_{it}^*, the rate that it could earn if it leased the same equipment to outsiders.

The first of the two decisions is the core of the neoclassical theory of production, and since the mechanics of the decision are described at length in most texts in price theory, we need not repeat the details here.[4] Suffice it at this point to say merely that the analysis leads to the decision rule: Keep adding to the amount of capital of type i used until the marginal revenue

---

[4] See, e.g., Ferguson and Gould [8]. See also Fama and Miller [7], especially Chapter 3, and Jorgenson [12].

product of capital is equal to the rental rate for equipment of that type, L_{it}^*. Following this good advice may not be easy in practice, of course. But, at least in principle, it is a computation that could be carried through with sufficient patience. And, more to the present point, it is a computation whose difficulty is in no way affected by whether the firm is renting the equipment from its own subsidiary or from an outside leasing company.

That decision, in turn, is already a solved problem under our assumptions. It is simply the entry decision in a slightly different disguise. We saw earlier that if the going market rental L_{it} should be above L_{it}^*, the leasing companies would be earning abnormal returns. New firms will enter the industry until these profits are competed away. Once equilibrium has been restored, therefore, a user firm currently renting would have no incentive, *on purely financial grounds*, to become an owner and rent equipment to itself or outsiders.

C. The Case of Long-Term Leases

The previous analysis and conclusions can readily be generalized to allow for leases extending over more than one period. The equilibrium n-period lease is found by first finding the present value of the n equilibrium one-period rentals plus the value of the machine at the start of period $t + n + 1$, viz,

$$V_{it}(n) = \sum_{j=t}^{t+n} \frac{L_{ij}^*(1-\delta)^{j-t}}{(1+r)^{j-t+1}} + \pi_{i,\,t+n+1}\left(\frac{1-\delta}{1+r}\right)^{n+1} \tag{2}$$

assuming, for simplicity, that the market rate of interest is constant over time. Any other pattern of rentals over the next n periods which had the same present value would be entirely equivalent, from the leasing company's point of view, to the sequence of n optimal one-period rentals L_{ij}^*. A common case, both in textbooks and in practice, is that of a uniform rental rate. This rate can be obtained by multiplying $V_{it}(n)$ by the appropriate capital recovery factor,

$$L_{it}(n) = V_{it}(n)r(1+r)^n/[(1+r)^n - 1] \tag{3}$$

It will be a property of the present-value calculations, of course, that the leasing company's rate of return on the machine will be exactly the same period by period as if it had engaged in the sequence of one-period rentals. In sum, the terms on short-term and long-term leases will adjust in such a way that user firms will find no purely financial advantages either in buying rather than renting or in choosing one form of rental contract over the other.

D. Some Extensions and Qualifications to the Basic Indifference Propositions

Further generality can be obtained, at least in principle, by relaxing the very severe restrictions imposed in assumption (1) on the conditions under which new machines are produced. Treating machine producers as a competitive constant-cost industry makes it possible to take the prices of machines now and in all subsequent periods as parameters in the valuation expressions, independent of the demand for the machines. The demand by users affects only the equilibrium stocks of machines of various types, not their prices.[5] If we were to permit the costs of production of the machines to vary with industry output, or if we were to consider a monopoly producer of machines, the scenario needed to describe the emergence of the equilibrium rental would have to be broadened to allow for the determination of the selling price for the machines as well as their rental terms. Such a scenario will clearly be a good deal more complicated, involving, as it does, the simultaneous solution of a very large number of equations. But when the dust has settled we must have exactly the same relation as before between the equilibrium rental rates and market prices of machines, whatever those market prices turn out to be. Otherwise, leasing firms would be able to exploit any departures from the relation to earn abnormal profits from renting out or subletting equipment.[6]

Though relaxing the assumptions about the production of machines leads to no change in the presumption that user firms will be indifferent between leasing or buying, some possible grounds for distinction emerge when we turn to other assumptions on the list. Assumption (2), it will be recalled, makes the convenient simplification that the maintenance required for any machine is given exogenously. Actually, of course, the level of maintenance is itself an economic decision, and one, moreover, in which the optimality criterion might be different under some conditions, depending on who happens to have the legal title to the machine.

The problem arises because the maintenance expenditures undertaken will affect the terminal value of the property and its efficiency in providing services during the period of the lease. A short-term lessee, after all, has an incentive to keep maintenance expenditures down to the level that minimizes the sum of his own production and maintenance costs, even though this may lead to a substantial drop in the resale value of the equipment. Leasing companies can protect themselves against such deterioration to a considerable extent by providing the maintenance services themselves. They can also bring suit for damages in cases of willful negligence. But going to

---

[5] However, to treat the value of a new machine as its cost of production, independent of current and future demands, we must rule out certain extreme cases. We cannot, for example, allow demand for the services of machines of type *i* in any future year to fall so far that the production of new machines falls to zero.

[6] It is sometimes argued that monopolists engage in leasing because it offers greater possibilities for price discrimination than an outright sale. Since our concern in this paper is primarily with the financial aspects of leasing, we shall not undertake to explore these and related issues of optimum price and marketing policy in any detail. Certain tax considerations bearing on the question are considered later.

court may be a sufficiently costly remedy that users will be forced to "internalize" the conflict of interest by assuming the burdens of ownership.

In the other direction, a nonfinancial advantage to leasing is a likely consequence of weakening our assumption (3)—that the purchase and rental markets for second-hand equipment are perfect. The twist is imparted not so much by the search costs, which, though they may well be substantial, are no different in principle whether one is searching for a buyer or a subtenant. The difference comes rather from the fact that it often costs considerably more in legal fees and taxes to transfer ownership in a property than to transfer a lease.[7] The transfer costs are particularly high, of course, where land is concerned.[8]

Finally, consider the consequences of weakening our assumption (4), that of perfect capital markets, to allow for one company having a lower effective borrowing rate than built into the rental rates. It is true that such a company, looking only at the conventional formulas, might find it profitable to buy rather than rent. But it would find it even more profitable, under those circumstances, to enter the leasing business! We can presume, therefore, that the leasing business will gravitate eventually to the firms whose efficiency in fund raising leads to the lowest cost of borrowing. They will be or will become "financial intermediaries." The fact that some (or even all) of these intermediaries may be subsidiaries of user firms does not alter the fundamental point that the typical user firm making its investment decisions can safely proceed on the assumption that renting will not be an option inferior to buying.

So much then for the standard neoclassical analysis of the rent-or-buy problem. We turn now to consider how that analysis must be modified when we marry it to the kind of standard framework in finance in which uncertainty is taken explicitly into account.

III. The Extension to Allow for Uncertainty

For some kinds of propositions in finance the introduction of uncertainty changes the picture a good deal. Such is the case, for example, with the problem of the optimal debt-equity mix, which really has no meaning except

---

[7] For example, Hertz could sell cars rather than rent them; the user's costs of searching for a buyer at the end of the day could presumably be avoided by including a repurchase agreement effective at the end of the day in the sales contract. But such a procedure would necessitate two filings of a title transfer. Another nonfinancial factor militating against the use of sales-cum-repurchase agreements is the cost of enforcement. Failing to return a rented car is a criminal offense, and the lessor has access to police powers to recover the car; failing to honor a repurchase agreement is a civil offense for which the only remedy available to Hertz would be an expensive civil suit.

[8] This discussion suggests the essential difference between what we have referred to as "financial" and "nonfinancial" costs. Differences in financial costs create arbitrage opportunities, whereas nonfinancial differences do not.

under conditions of uncertainty. For other problems such as, say, the problem of the optimal dividend policy, uncertainty complicates the proof but changes nothing fundamental. The rent-or-buy problem is in the latter category. The critical assumption leading to the indifference proposition is not that of certainty but that of competitive equilibrium in the leasing industry. If the rental terms offered by lessors did not reflect the opportunity costs of owning capital equipment, including the costs of bearing any uncertainties, leasing firms would be earning above or below normal returns. Quoted rates would adjust and leasing firms would enter or leave the business until the owners of leasing firms expected a return that was adequate, but no more than adequate, compensation for the risks assumed.

Thus, though we know that we can expect no major surprises by introducing uncertainty, there may nevertheless be some value in restating the equilibrium conditions in terms of an explicit model of valuation under uncertainty. Disagreements continue to exist over the appropriate discount rate to be used in leasing decisions as well as over such pieces of conventional wisdom as the proposition that the higher a firm's cost of capital, the greater the likely advantages of leasing over buying. Moreover, careful sorting out of the relevant risks at this point will enable us to avoid some otherwise unavoidable distractions in later sections dealing with the tax treatment of leases.

A. Equilibrium One-Period Leases in a CAPM Framework

The particular equilibrium framework we shall use in introducing uncertainty will be that of the Sharpe–Lintner capital asset pricing model. That model is admittedly a very special one, but it has the virtues of simplicity and familiarity.[9] We shall assume that all the simplifying assumptions stated above also hold, except that the rate of deterioration δ_{it} and the cost of production of next year's vintage of machines $\pi_{i,t+1}$ are now both to be taken as uncertain.

In a world conforming to the CAPM equilibrium, the expected rate of return on any asset j will be given by the familiar relation

$$E(R_j) = R_F + \beta_j[E(R_m) - R_F] \qquad (4)$$

where R_F is the riskless rate of interest, $E(R_m)$ is the expected rate of return on total wealth, and $\beta_j = \text{Cov } R_j R_m / \text{Var } R_m$ is a measure of the relative, nondiversifiable risk of asset j. From the standpoint of one of our hypothetical leasing companies, machine i is an asset like any other, and its (uncertain) rate of return is simply:

$$R_{it} = (L_{it}/\pi_{it}) - d_{it} \qquad (5)$$

[9] For the details of the model and its derivation see, e.g., Fama and Miller [7], especially Chapters 6 and 7.

We shall assume for the moment that the rental component L_{it} is a sure payment once the lease is signed. The depreciation component, however, remains uncertain, and can be expressed most revealingly for our purposes as

$$d_{it} = d'_{it} + \beta_{it} R_m + \varepsilon_{it} = E(d_{it}) + \beta_{it}[R_m - E(R_m)] + \varepsilon_{it} \qquad (6)$$

where $E(d_{it}) = d'_{it} + \beta_{it} E(R_m)$ is what we shall call the "normal" expected depreciation (in the sense of the depreciation to be expected even when the rate of return on total wealth does not differ from its expected value); $\beta_{it}[R_m - E(R_m)]$ is any depreciation above (or below) normal due to unexpected variations in the rate of return on total wealth; and ε_{it} is a catchall for all other (random) deviations from normal depreciation. Taking the expectations in Eqs. (5) and (6) and making use of equilibrium condition (4) (and remembering that we are stating the change in the value of the machine as a depreciation rather than an appreciation, so that the sign of β_{it} is the opposite of its usual interpretation), we have

$$E(R_{it}) = (L_{it}/\pi_{it}) - E(d_{it}) = R_F - \beta_{it}[E(R_m) - R_F] \qquad (7)$$

Hence, the equilibrium rental rate is

$$L^{**}_{it} = [E(R_{it}) + E(d_{it})]\pi_{it} = \{R_F - \beta_{it}[E(R_m) - R_F] + E(d_{it})\}\pi_{it} \qquad (8)$$

That is, the equilibrium one-period rental under uncertainty consists of the risk-free rate of interest on the capital invested, plus a risk adjustment which depends on the extent to which the depreciation varies with unexpected variations in the rate of return on total wealth, plus the normal depreciation.[10]

A point worth stressing is that the risk adjustment that is built into the equilibrium rental rate is based on the nondiversifiable risk of the machine itself (or, equivalently, of a specialized firm owning only that machine) and not on the risk of the eventual user firm. In fact, as we have developed the scenario so far, the equilibrium risk adjustment has been made even before the eventual user firms are known.

We lose this complete separation, of course, as soon as we allow for the possibility that the lease payment itself might be subject to some default risk.

---

[10] Note that if the depreciation is independent of the state of the economy, then $\beta_{it} = 0$ and the equilibrium rental will be the same as in the earlier certainty case. If, however, necessity is indeed the mother of invention and the pace of technological improvement steps up as the economy falls off, then $\beta_{it} < 0$, and rentals have to carry a premium over their certainty values to compensate the owners of the machines for the double dose of bad news, so to speak, when the return on total wealth is unexpectedly low. But if it is boom conditions in the economy that stimulate technological progress, as was often argued in the heyday of the growthmanship debates in the early 1960s, then we might perhaps find $\beta_{it} > 0$, in which case lease rentals under uncertainty would actually be *less* than in the certainty model.

Under those conditions, the expression for L_{it}^{**} in (8) must be interpreted not as the actual rental but as the equilibrium *expected* rental, which will still be independent of the identity of the user. The actual rental charged to any particular user will have to be larger than L_{it}^{**} by an amount that reflects the probability of default by that user (and which may or may not also reflect the user's β). Since details of this kind are not central at this point, we shall simply assume that leasing companies require user firms to place in escrow a sum equal to the discounted value of the rental.

B. The Investment Decision from the Point of View of the User Firm

Given an equilibrium rental of L_{it}^{**}, the user firm faces the same two decisions under uncertainty as in the certainty case: how many units to use and whether to buy rather than rent. As for the former—the investment decision—we saw that the optimality criterion under certainty calls for the firm to keep expanding the stock of capital of type i employed until the marginal revenue product of capital exactly equalled the rental rate. Under uncertainty, the marginal revenue product, being the sum of the marginal increase in the firm's cash flow plus the marginal change in its end-of-period value, is now a random variable whose exact outcome will not be known until the end of the period. But we can always compute its expected value $E(V_{it}')$ and then invoke the CAPM equilibrium conditions to test whether this expected marginal increase in value is sufficient, in the light of the risks involved, to justify the incurring of the rental charge.

In particular, note that if we let V_{0j} be the current value of asset j, V_{1j} its (uncertain) end-of-period value, M_0 the current value of total wealth, and M_1 its (uncertain) end-of-period value, then we can rewrite (4) as

$$E(V_{1j})/V_{0j} = 1 + R_F + \beta_j[E(R_m) - R_F]$$

$$= 1 + R_F + [E(R_m) - R_F] \frac{\mathrm{Cov}[(V_{1j}/V_{0j}) - 1][(M_1/M_0) - 1]}{(1/M_0)^2 \, \mathrm{Var} \, M_1}$$

$$= 1 + R_F + [E(R_m) - R_F]\beta_j'$$

where

$$\beta_j' = [\mathrm{Cov}(V_{1j}, M_1)/\mathrm{Var} \, M_1] \cdot M_0/V_{0j} \qquad (9)$$

Hence the current value of asset j can be expressed in terms of the expected end-of-period value of the asset and the asset's risk as

$$V_{0j} = \{E(V_{1j}) - [E(R_m) - R_F]\beta_j''\}/(1 + R_F) \qquad (10)$$

where $\beta_j'' = \beta_j' \cdot V_{0j}$.

Similarly, if $E(V'_{it})$ is the expected marginal product and β''_{it} is its relative risk, then the present value of that marginal product is

$$V_{0i} = \{E(V'_{it}) - [E(R_m) - R_F]\beta''_{it}\}/(1 + R_F) \tag{11}$$

Since the present value of the lease payment L^{**}_{it} is simply $L^{**}_{it}/(1 + R_F)$, the present wealth of the owners will increase or decrease depending on whether $E(V'_{it}) - [E(R_m) - R_F]\beta''_{it}$ exceeds or falls short of L^{**}_{it}. The optimal stock is thus found at the point where the expected marginal product, corrected for risk, is exactly equal to the rental rate.

Note that the risk factor β''_{it} is *not* the same as the risk of the machine itself—the β_{it} of Eq. (8). That risk was the risk of *ownership* that arises when the machine's depreciation varies systematically with the level of the economy. The risk β''_{it} is the risk in *use* and arises to the extent that the marginal values created by the machine in production vary systematically with the return on total wealth. Note also that here, as in capital budgeting problems generally, the risk in use is the risk of the particular machine and not necessarily that for the firm as a whole. For some kinds of "cost reducing" machines the relevant β''_{it} in some circumstances may be close to zero; for machines that pay off only when the firm is operating at very high capacity, the relevant β''_{it} may be substantially greater than that of the firm.

C. The Rent-or-Buy Decision from the Point of View of the User Firm

Given that the firm has somehow found the appropriate value for the risk-in-use and has determined the optimal stock of equipment of type i with which it proposes to operate, are there any circumstances in which the firm would find it more profitable to buy and own the machines (or equivalently, to buy a leasing company that specializes in these machines)? If we take a strict construction of the CAPM assumptions, including the assumption of homogeneous expectations, then the answer is no.

By buying, the firm will save the lease payment, L^{**}_{it}, but will incur the opportunity cost of the funds diverted from other business uses to purchase the machine plus the expected depreciation of the machine. In computing this opportunity cost, we must, of course, make sure that the results are not biased by any differences in return that reflect differences in the risk of the funds in the two uses. In particular, if the risk measure of the machine is $-\beta_{it}$ (recall our convention of working with depreciation rather than appreciation), then the equivalent-risk opportunity cost of the investment π_{it} in the machine is

$$\pi_{it} \cdot E(R_{it}) = \{R_F - \beta_{it}[E(R_m) - R_F]\} \cdot \pi_{it} \tag{12}$$

The normal expected rate of depreciation on the machine was defined earlier as $E(d_{it}) = d'_{it} + \beta_{it} E(R_m)$. Adding the two costs together gives a total cost of ownership of machine C_{it} of

$$C_{it} = [E(R_{it}) + E(d_{it})]\pi_{it} \tag{13}$$

which is, of course, precisely our earlier expression for the equilibrium one-period rental, L_{it}^{**}.

This same and, by this stage, hardly very surprising, result can also be obtained from the kind of present-value comparisons that dominate the standard discussions of the decision in the finance and accounting literature. If we let $V_L =$ the net present value of the lease option and $V_B =$ the net present value of the buy option, we have

$$V_L = \frac{E(V'_{it}) - [E(R_m) - R_F]\beta''_{it}}{1 + R_F} - \frac{L_{it}^{**}}{1 + R_F}$$

$$V_B = \frac{E(V'_{it}) - [E(R_m) - R_F]\beta''_{it}}{1 + R_F} - \frac{[E(R_{it}) + E(d_{it})]\pi_{it}}{1 + R_F} \tag{14}$$

so that $V_B > V_L$, and there is a financial advantage in buying if and only if $L_{it}^{**} > [E(R_{it}) + E(d_{it})]\pi_{it}$.[11,12]

Although this inequality would not hold under our full set of assumptions, it might do so if we were willing to allow for differences of opinion about some of the costs of ownership, say the cost of obsolescence. Even so, for buying to be a profitable strategy for a user firm, the firm would have to believe that the pace of technological improvement will be less than that implied in the consensus view already built into the market rental, L_{it}^{**}. And

[11] Stating the criterion in this form helps, among other things, to point out the element of truth in the conventional wisdom to the effect that the firm should first decide whether (and how much) to lease and, only then, whether to buy rather than lease. As we argued earlier, a finding by a user firm that buying was cheaper than leasing suggests that the firm should actually buy and lease to others at the market rental. If so, L_{it}^{**} would still be the relevant marginal cost of capital services and $E(V'_{it})$ would still be the expected marginal product.

[12] The presence of the riskless rate R_F in the denominators of V_L and V_B should not be interpreted as an endorsement of the view that the riskless rate is necessarily the appropriate rate to use in lease-or-buy calculations. This is a subject to which we shall return in greater detail below. At this stage, however, we would merely point out that the CAPM equilibrium condition (10) can be stated, in either of two equivalent forms, as

$$V_{0j} = \frac{E(V_{1j}) - \beta''_j[E(R_m) - R_F]}{1 + R_F} \quad \text{and} \quad V_{0j} = \frac{E(V_{1j})}{1 + R_F + \beta'_j[E(R_m) - R_F]}$$

The former is the "certainty equivalent" form and the latter the "risk-adjusted discount rate" form. Thus, the first terms in each of the options in Eq. (14) and the second term in the buy option are risky; they just happen to be stated in certainty–equivalent form, with the risk adjustment in the numerator rather than the denominator.

this in turn would require us to suppose that the user firm or its accountants had better insight into the future developments still on the drawing boards than the specialized firms producing the machinery (and who, of course, also have the option of entering the leasing business). The bones of the computer leasing companies that are littering Wall Street would suggest that there is little basis for such a belief and, more to the point, little need on these grounds to qualify the general neoclassical presumption that user firms are unlikely to find financial advantages in owning rather than leasing.

D. The Cost of Capital Services Under a Long-Term Lease

The rent-or-buy decision gets more complicated when we turn from single-period to multiperiod leases, both because we now have more types of risk to contend with and because there is no general theory of valuation of multiperiod uncertain streams that we can draw on to compare the various options available. With the help of some additional simplifying assumptions, however, we can at least treat some instructive special cases.

Suppose, for example, that the economic life of machine i were known with certainty to be precisely n years, at the end of which its salvage value, net of removal expenses, will be exactly zero. And suppose further that the riskless rate of interest R_F is also known with certainty to be constant over time. Then, assuming away any default risk on the rentals, the equilibrium n-period uniform rental rate of the machine, $L_{it}(n)$, is easily calculated; it is simply the current market value of the machine multiplied by the n-period capital recovery factor at the rate R_F, i.e.,

$$L_{it}(n) = \pi_{it}\left[\frac{R_F(1 + R_F)^n}{(1 + R_F)^n - 1}\right] \tag{15}$$

exactly as in the certainty case.

Consider now the investment decision as it appears to a user firm that plans to employ the equipment for one period only. Recall that in the previous one-period case, the optimal policy was seen to be to expand the capital stock until the present value of the risk-adjusted marginal product equals the present value of the one-period rental,

$$\frac{E(V'_{it}) - [E(R_m) - R_F]\beta''_{it}}{1 + R_F} = \frac{L_{it}^{**}}{1 + R_F} \tag{16}$$

Given a long-term lease payment $L_{it}(n)$, it is tempting but, of course, quite wrong simply to substitute $L_{it}(n)$ for L_{it}^{**} in (16). Both payments are certainties, it is true, and as such may legitimately be discounted by R_F. But when a long-term lease is assumed, the cash rental payment of the first year is only one part of the cost of the capital services acquired. At the end of the year, a new sublessee will have to be found to take over the remaining years of the lease. Thus, the cost of the capital services under a long-term lease is not only different in general from the lease payment but, like the cost under ownership, is an uncertain cost.

The expected, risk-adjusted cost of capital services during the first period under the long-term lease, $C_{it}(n)$, has two components: (1) the certain lease payment $L_{it}(n)$, and (2) the expected, risk-adjusted value of the compensation that will have to be paid to the sublessee. The sublessee must be paid an amount equal to the difference between the present value of the $n - 1$ lease payments remaining as of the start of the next period, $\sum_{\tau=1}^{n-1} L_{i,t}(n)/(1 + R_F)^\tau$, and the present value of the rental rates on one-period old machines, $\sum_{\tau=1}^{n-1} L_{i,t+1}(n - 1)/(1 + R_F)^\tau$. But equilibrium in the long-term rental market requires that the present value of leases on one-period old equipment next period be equal to the market price of such equipment, $\pi_{it}(1 - d_{it})$. The expected compensating payment is thus

$$\sum_{j=1}^{n-1} \frac{L_{i,t}(n)}{(1 + R_F)^j} - \pi_{it}[1 - E(d_{it})] \tag{17}$$

Making use of Eq. (10), the risk-adjusted present value of the compensating payment is

$$\frac{1}{1 + R_F} \left\{ \sum_{j=1}^{n-1} \frac{L_{i,t}(n)}{(1 + R_F)^j} - \pi_{it}[1 - E(d_{it}) + \beta_{it}(E(R_m) - R_F)] \right\} \tag{18}$$

Hence $C_{it}(n)$ is given by

$$C_{it}(n) = \left(\frac{1}{1 + R_F} \right) \left\{ L_{it}(n) + \sum_{j=1}^{n-1} \frac{L_{it}(n)}{(1 + R_F)^j} \right.$$
$$\left. - \pi_{it}[1 - E(d_{it}) - \beta_{it}(E(R_m) - R_F)] \right\} \tag{19}$$

Recall, however, that $L_{it}(n)$ has been set so that

$$\left(\frac{1}{1 + R_F} \right) \left[L_{it}(n) + \sum_{j=1}^{n-1} \frac{L_{it}(n)}{(1 + R_F)^j} \right] = \pi_{it} \tag{20}$$

and Eq. (19) can be thus rewritten as

$$C_{it}(n) = \left(\frac{1}{1 + R_F} \right) \{ R_F - \beta_{it}[E(R_m) - R_F] + E(d_{it}) \} \pi_{it} \tag{21}$$

The bracketed term in the right-hand side of Eq. (21) should by now be thoroughly familiar. It is precisely the same as the expression we derived earlier for the expected cost of ownership of the machine by the leasing company [Eq. (8)] and by a user firm [Eq. (13)]. Nor should this identification be in any way surprising. Under our assumption that the life of the lease is coterminal with the life of the asset, the risks assumed under ownership and under long-term leasing are also precisely the same.

Note that the critical assumption that makes the risk the same is the identity between the life of the lease and the life of the asset, and not our assumption that the user plans to employ the equipment for only one time period. A user firm, it is true, could avoid the physical act of having to find a sublessee by keeping the machine in use for the rest of its economic life. But it couldn't thereby avoid the changes in the market value of the owners' equity due to changes in the market value of its lease obligation any more than if it owned the machines outright. The only way to obtain the services of the machine without incurring the risks of ownership is by a short-term lease.[13]

When we break the assumption of coterminality and allow for leases of arbitrary length, we can no longer finesse the multiperiod nature of the problem. In principle, we could always turn to special multiperiod extensions of the CAPM by invoking additional regularizing assumptions along the lines of Bogue and Roll [5]. But rather than explore a host of additional special cases in detail, we shall simply make the blanket assumption that the standard "conservation" properties of economic systems continue to apply. In this context, the principle is that of the conservation of the total risk of ownership between the leasing company owner and the user firm renter. If the lease is short term, then the leasing company bears all the risk and the renter none. At the other extreme, the renter who assumes a life-of-the-property lease bears all the risk and the lessor none. In all cases in between, they share the risk. If, therefore, such intermediate term leases are to continue to be offered, their equilibrium rentals must compensate the leasing companies for such residual risks as remain to them (but for no more than that or there would be incentives to increase the supply of leases of that term). Hence it will continue to be true that there are no purely financial advantages in buying versus renting or in renting for one term relative to another.

IV. The Impact of Taxes on the Rent-or-Buy Decision

There are ample precedents in finance for indifference propositions that turn into corner solutions when tax considerations are introduced—the Modigliani–Miller capital structure propositions [15], [16] being the most

[13] A short-term rental is still riskless, in the strict sense in which we are here using the term, even though the rental at which the firm would be able to renew the lease is uncertain. The renewal rate may be uncertain, but it will be the same for all the firm's competitors and hence there will be no reason for the market to write the firm's value up or down as machine prices and rentals change. There is an obvious analogy here to the issue of short-term versus long-term borrowing by the firm.

obvious cases in point. It is natural to suspect that the same may be true in the present case as well. There is, after all, an asymmetry in the tax treatment of payments for capital services under the present corporate income tax—an asymmetry featured prominently in the advertisements of some leasing companies. Lease payments are deductible in full, whereas owners can deduct only the machine's depreciation plus that part of the capital costs represented by interest payments. Nevertheless, we shall argue that the deductibility provisions in the present law do not change the previous indifference results, at least insofar as fully taxable corporations are concerned. A bias in favor of renting by user firms is indeed imparted by the present tax structure, but it is of a different kind.

A. The Effect of Deductibility of Rental Payments: Short-Term Leases

To see that differences in deductibility do not, by themselves, bias the rent-or-buy decision, consider first the extreme case in which there is no corporate borrowing. All corporations, including leasing companies, must finance themselves entirely with equity capital, and thus none of the payments made to security holders are deductible from corporate income tax. The corporate tax rate itself, τ_c, is a constant independent of the level of profits and the same for all taxable corporations.

The equilibrium single-period rental will be that before-tax rental that leaves leasing companies just indifferent between renting their machines and selling them and investing the proceeds in assets of equivalent risk. Under the lease strategy, the leasing company's (uncertain) after-tax earnings y_{it} will be

$$y_{it} = L_{it}(1 - \tau_c) - d_{it}\pi_{it} + \tau_c \, d_{it}\pi_{it} \tag{22}$$

where, for the moment, we assume that the amount of depreciation allowed as a deduction for tax purposes is exactly the same as the decline in the market value of the machine. The leasing company's *expected* after-tax income under the lease option will be

$$E(y_{it}) = L_{it}(1 - \tau_c) - (1 - \tau_c)E(d_{it})\pi_{it} \tag{23}$$

Under the sell-out-and-reinvest option the expected earnings will depend, of course, on the level of risk assumed, and that level may, in principle, take any value. To make sure, however, that the results are in no way being biased by differences in risk, we shall again assume that the proceeds of the sale π_{it} are invested in financial assets with the same systematic risk $-\beta_{it}$ as that of the machine itself. The expected return to the leasing company under the sell option will then be

$$\pi_{it} E(R_{it}) = \pi_{it}\{R_F - \beta_{it}[E(R_m) - R_F]\} \tag{24}$$

Note that here and throughout we are interpreting rates of return such as $E(R_{it})$ as the expected rates of return to investors implied by CAPM equilibrium in the market for corporate securities. Hence the $E(R_{it})$ in Eq. (24) is to be taken as the return to the leasing company *after corporate taxes*. We call attention to the point here because distinctions between before-tax and after-tax discount rates are not always drawn as sharply as they should be in conventional treatments of the rent-or-buy problem, and not because there is anything peculiar about our interpretation. The present tax law does, after all, explicitly exempt from corporate tax virtually all dividends received from other taxable corporations; and the tax on even the small includable remainder can be avoided entirely if the acquiring firm has enough shares to qualify for filing a consolidated return.[14]

Equating Eqs. (23) and (24), we thus have as the equilibrium one-period rental

$$L_{it}^{***} = \{E(d_{it}) + [1/(1 - \tau_c)]E(R_{it})\}\pi_{it} \qquad (25)$$

which can be seen to differ from the corresponding value for the no-tax case, L_{it}^{**}, only in that the term representing the return on the capital invested must now be "grossed up" by the factor $1/(1 - \tau_c)$.

Given that the market sets the (before-tax) equilibrium rental at L_{it}^{***}, user firms that happen to have opted for a buy policy will have no purely financial incentive to switch. They will gain an after-tax return of $E(R_{it})\pi_{it}$ on the funds released, plus the expected depreciation avoided, $E(d_{it})\pi_{it}$, plus the tax shield on the lease, $\tau_c L_{it}^{***}$. But they will lose the tax shield on the depreciation, $\tau_c E(d_{it})\pi_{it}$, and incur the rental expense L_{it}^{***}. From (25), it is clear that these gains and losses must exactly balance.

B. The Effect of Deductibility of Rental Payments: Long-Term Leases

A similar equality obtains in the case of a lease for the life of the machine. The after-tax receipts of the leasing company in year j of the life of the lease will be

$$Y_{it}(j) = L_{it}(j)(1 - \tau_c) + D_{it}(j)\tau_c \qquad (26)$$

where $D_{it}(j)$ represents the amount of depreciation allowed for tax purposes and $L_{it}(j)$ is the lease payment for year j (not necessarily the same for all j). Since both the lease payments and the depreciation deductions are assumed

---

[14] The capital gain portion of the return would not be exempt from corporate income tax. But since the tax would have to be paid only upon sale or the equivalent, we shall assume that firms make this tax effectively zero either by not selling or by disposing of such assets in ways that are not considered to give rise to taxable corporate income (e.g., by allowing the corporation's shareholders to exchange some of their shares for the shares held by the corporation).

certain, the present value of these payments, computed by discounting at the risk-free interest rate R_F, is

$$\pi_{it}^{***} = \sum_{j=1}^{n} \frac{L_{it}(j)}{(1 + R_F)^j} - \tau_c \sum_{j=1}^{n} \frac{L_{it}(j) - D_{it}(j)}{(1 + R_F)^j} \tag{27}$$

Competition among leasing companies will force the lease payments to be set so that π_{it}^{***} is equal to π_{it}, the price of a new machine.

Given this equality, user firms will be indifferent between buying and renting. If they rent, the present value of the lease payments after taxes will be

$$\sum_{j=1}^{n} \frac{L_{it}(j)}{(1 + R_F)^j} (1 - \tau_c) = \pi_{it}^{***} - \tau_c \sum_{j=1}^{n} \frac{D_{it}(j)}{(1 + R_F)^j}$$

$$= \pi_{it} - \tau_c \sum_{j=1}^{n} \frac{D_{it}(j)}{(1 + R_F)^j} \tag{28}$$

which is, of course, the cost of buying a new machine, net of the present value of the tax deductions for depreciation allowed if the machine is bought.[15]

Note that this equality does not rest on the assumption that the lease payments follow some specific pattern, such as uniform payments over the life of the lease. It depends merely on lease payments being set so as to ensure competitive equilibrium in the leasing industry. It does require, however, that the tax deductions be the same whether the machine is owned by the "leasing" company or the using company, as they will be under our assumptions of a uniform tax rate and of depreciation deductions equal to the true economic depreciation.[16] We shall turn to these assumptions after we complete our discussion of deductibility by considering the deductibility of interest payments.

---

[15] Note that the discount rate in (27) and (28) is R_F and not $R_F(1 - \tau_c)$, even though it is an after-tax stream of rental payments that is being discounted. Remember that since we have not yet introduced deductible interest payments, our R_F is to be interpreted as the return on a riskless corporate stock; and returns on corporate stocks, under our assumptions, are exempt from corporate income tax. Equivalently, we can think of the leasing company's alternative to the riskless lease as being a return of the π_{it} of capital to its stockholders. The stockholders, in turn, can earn a riskless return of R_F.

[16] The assumption of a uniform tax rate also implies that renting and buying will be equivalent even in cases where the user firm does not intend to use the machine for its entire useful life. If, however, gains from sales of depreciable property were to be treated as capital gains subject to rates lower than the rate on other corporate income, then buying would be favored. Any gains on sale would get favored treatment, while losses could be recovered at full tax rates by leasing the machine out rather than selling it. Under present US tax law, there exist a few special cases, known as Section 1231 properties, for which asymmetry of this kind still exists.

C. The Effect of Deductibility of Interest Payments

With interest payments fully deductible from corporate income tax and with corporate rates in the neighborhood of 50%, corporations would appear to have powerful incentives to use debt financing to the maximum extent allowable. Yet the typical manufacturing corporation today has debt equal to only about a quarter of its book assets.[17] The current conventional wisdom in finance attributes this seeming disequilibrium to certain offsetting deadweight costs of debt financing. For example, the conflict of interest between lender and borrower creates a moral hazard that the lender can protect against only by incurring surveillance costs—costs that are normally passed on to the borrower in the form of stated interest rates higher than necessary to compensate for the systematic risk. Hence, the increasing burden of these costs as the debt ratio rises will eventually impose an upper limit on the amount of borrowing that any firm can profitably support.[18] Precisely where this limit is to be found in any particular case is something that, fortunately, we need not explore here in great detail. For the kind of rent-or-buy or rent-or-borrow comparisons that are our main concern at this point, it is sufficient to assume that if such limits do exist, they are lower the riskier is the underlying collateral.

In particular, let us suppose for concreteness that a firm owning an asset with systematic risk β_{it} finds it economic to borrow the fraction α of the purchase price of the asset at an expected interest rate of $E(R_\alpha)$ and pay $\alpha\pi_{it}$ out to its shareholders as a return of capital. If the firm is a leasing company, then its expected after-tax earnings $E(y_{it})$ from a one-period lease at the rate L_{it} will be

$$E(y_{it}) = L_{it}(1 - \tau_c) - E(d_{it})\pi_{it} - \alpha E(R_\alpha)\pi_{it}$$
$$+ \tau_c E(d_{it})\pi_{it} + \tau_c \alpha E(R_\alpha)\pi_{it}$$
$$= L_{it}(1 - \tau_c) - E(d_{it})\pi_{it}(1 - \tau_c) - \alpha E(R_\alpha)\pi_{it}(1 - \tau_c) \qquad (29)$$

That is, it will consist of (1) the after-tax return on the lease payment minus the expected depreciation and interest expense, plus (2) the tax shields on the depreciation and interest.

Instead of leasing the equipment, the firm could sell it for π_{it} and then invest the proceeds in financial assets of equivalent risk. To keep the degree of leverage constant, we will assume that the firm still borrows an amount $\alpha\pi_{it}$ which it distributes to its shareholders as a return of capital. Its books

[17] See the 1970 *Statistics of Income-Corporate Tax Returns.*
[18] The conflict of interest between stockholders and bondholders is discussed at some length in Fama and Miller [7]. Surveillance costs and their implications for quoted interest rates are considered in Black *et al.* [3]. See also Barro [2] and Jensen and Meckling [10].

then show financial assets of π_{it} and liabilities of $\alpha\pi_{it}$ for indebtedness plus $(1 - \alpha)\pi_{it}$ of stockholder's equity. The firm's expected after-tax income will now be

$$E(y'_{it}) = \pi_{it}[E(R_{it}) - \alpha E(R_\alpha)] \tag{30}$$

Note that we have assumed that the firm is neither taxed on the investment income nor allowed to deduct the interest payments involved in this transaction. The latter restriction is essential, since otherwise firms could eliminate their corporate tax payments (or perhaps even transform their corporate tax outflows into inflows) by the simple expedient of borrowing money to invest in corporate stock or other tax-exempt assets. We shall return to these and related issues in more detail in the next section in the course of our discussion of tax subsidies. At this stage of the argument, the important point to keep in mind is that firms will be allowed to deduct interest payments only on funds borrowed against *real* assets whose earnings are subject to corporate income tax.

Equating (29) and (30), the equilibrium value of a one-period lease L^α_{it} is

$$L^\alpha_{it} = \pi_{it}\left[E(R_{it})\frac{1}{1 - \tau_c} + E(d_{it}) - \frac{\tau_c}{1 - \tau_c}E(R_\alpha)\alpha\right] \tag{31}$$

It is an easy matter to show that the expected after-tax cost to a user company of owning the machine, assuming that it too borrows a fraction α of the purchase price, is equal to $(1 - \tau_c)L^\alpha_{it}$. Thus the deductibility of interest payments does not change the basic indifference proposition obtained earlier for taxable firms in the no-borrowing case.

D. The Long-Term Case and the "Lease-or-Borrow" Problem

We get these seemingly paradoxical results for the case of the one-period lease because the risk of the leasing company and the risk of a user–owner are exactly the same. But what if the lease were a multiperiod one? We showed earlier that the longer the term of the lease, the less the amount of the risk of ownership that is borne by the leasing company. The smaller the risk, the larger the borrowing power of the leasing company and the larger the tax shield on the interest paid; this will be reflected in lower lease rates.

Having made this point, it is important to emphasize immediately that the difference does *not* imply that user firms are thereby given an incentive to rent rather than buy. Consider, for example, the extreme case of a life-of-the-property lease in which the user firm has all the risks of ownership and the leasing company none. In principle, the lessor firm could then borrow 100% of the purchase price of the machine and this would certainly be a higher debt ratio than that of the user firm.

But what permits the lessor to borrow so much, of course, is the user company's implied guarantee of the lease payments that will flow through to the leasing company's bondholders. In fact, such guarantees of principal and interest to the lessor's bondholders have often been made explicit in long-term lease contracts in recent years just as they were in an earlier era, in railroad lease financing.[19] What gives these guarantees credibility in the eyes of the market can ultimately only be the equity cover of the user firm. If this equity cover is sufficient to render riskless the leasing firm's debt in the amount of the value of the property, then, in principle, it is equally sufficient to render riskless a loan of the same amount contracted by the user firm directly. Hence we are once again in a position of indifference between leasing and buying.

This way of looking at the problem makes it clear that the indifference proposition depends in no essential way on the assumption that the stream of lease payments is riskless. The critical point is simply that whatever value of debt and associated tax benefits that the equity cover of the user firm can support indirectly via a lease arrangement, it can support by borrowing directly (or through a wholly owned leasing subsidiary).[20] The only difference between the riskless and risky cases is that there is as yet no rigorously justified way of writing down an "exact" valuation for the risky case analogous to those for the riskless case in Eq. (27) or (28).[21]

Finally, the conclusion does not depend on the assumption of a life-of-the-property lease in which the user firm bears all the risk of changes in the value of the machine. This risk must be borne by someone, and if the leasing company bears more of it, the using company will bear less of it. Hence its own borrowing power and tax benefits will increase *pari passu* with the decrease of those of the leasing company, thereby maintaining the indifference between buying and renting (at least for leases of those lengths that will be permitted by the tax authorities).[22]

---

[19] In this connection, see Dewing [6], especially Chapter 31. For a more recent example involving airline leases of planes, see Altschul [1].

[20] We say "in no essential way" because there are differences in the legal status of lessors and secured creditors in the event of default (see Dewing [6]). Hence there may be differences in nonfinancial costs of the kind discussed earlier in footnote 7. It is by no means clear which arrangement leads to the lower total nonfinancial costs once the possibility that the specialized leasing company may also default is allowed. The primary nonfinancial cost under either arrangement is the cost of finding another user for the services of the machine.

[21] Equations (27) and (28) were derived before the deductibility of interest payments was introduced. The more general case is given later in Eqs. (36) and (37).

[22] The last qualification is needed because of the recent (May 1975) guidelines on leveraged leasing issued by the IRS in Revenue Procedures 75-21 and 75-28. Under these guidelines, lessors must, among other things, bear some of the risk of fluctuation in residual value; and, in particular, the estimated residual value of the property must be at least 20% of original cost. Thus, very long leases, and especially what we have been calling life-of-the-property leases, are effectively ruled out, though they may still have their use as expository devices.

V. The Impact of Tax Subsidies and Tax Exemptions

So far we have assumed that the depreciation deductions allowed for tax purposes equal the true economic depreciation. In practice, this is rarely the case. The investment tax credit and accelerated depreciation have been introduced precisely to make tax deductions larger than economic depreciation. We have argued elsewhere (Miller and Upton [14], especially pp. 158–159) that these devices are essentially means of reducing the effective tax on income from capital. For present purposes, however, it is more convenient to model them as tax subsidies rather than rate reductions, though this will in no way change the essential conclusions.

A. Tax Subsidies

Our use of the term tax subsidy, rather than simply subsidy, is intended as a reminder that the full benefit of tax subsidies cannot be obtained unless the affected firm has enough income from other sources to utilize the tax shields. A company contemplating a large capital expansion project could find the investment tax credit on that project exceeding the permissible deduction of 50% of gross tax liabilities. In that event, its effective tax subsidy would be lower than that of a leasing company, which presumably can take full advantage of the tax subsidy.[23]

To see the effects of tax subsidies, let s_L be the first-period flow-equivalent value of the tax subsidies to leasing companies. That is, assume that the leasing company has somehow computed the present value of all tax subsidies over the optimal period of ownership of the machine, and that it has allocated to its first year's income an amount that can appropriately be attributed to the first year's ownership.[24] The precise details of this calculation and allocation need not concern us at this point. And let s_B, which may or may not be equal to s_L, be the first-period flow-equivalent value of the subsidies to a using company that chooses to buy the equipment. Then it is a straightforward matter to show that the equilibrium, one-period rental rate will be

$$L_{it}^{\alpha}(s_L) = \left[E(R_{it}) \frac{1}{1 - \tau_L} + E(d_{it}) - \frac{\tau_L}{1 - \tau_L} E(R_{\alpha})\alpha - \frac{s_L}{1 - \tau_L} \right] \pi_{it} \quad (32)$$

---

[23] If the economic life of the equipment is n years, the leasing company can generate sufficient earnings to utilize the subsidies by holding n machines of different ages and replacing one each year. Earnings might be insufficient to utilize the credits during the start-up period, but the leasing company has other options. A common one has been to start up by consolidating the leasing operation with those of a parent company, or other third party, that can use the tax shields currently and then splitting off the leasing operation when it becomes self-sustaining.

[24] We have to define s_L in this somewhat convoluted way because, under present tax laws, some kinds of tax subsidies can be lost or recaptured if the property is sold after a short period of time.

and that the after-tax cost to a user–owner will be

$$C_{it}^\alpha(s_B) = [E(R_{it}) + (1 - \tau_B)\, E(d_{it}) - \tau_B E(R_\alpha)\alpha - s_B]\pi_{it} \qquad (33)$$

where τ_L and τ_B represent the tax rates of the leasing and buying companies, respectively. The difference between the after-tax cost of leasing and owning will be

$$(1 - \tau_B)L_{it}^\alpha(s_L) - C_{it}^\alpha(s_B)$$

$$\equiv \Delta = \left[\frac{\tau_L - \tau_B}{1 - \tau_L} E(R_{it}) - \frac{1 - \tau_B}{1 - \tau_L} s_L + s_B - \frac{\tau_L - \tau_B}{1 - \tau_L} E(R_\alpha)\alpha\right]\pi_{it} \qquad (34)$$

Thus, if the tax rate were the same for both parties (implying $\tau_L = \tau_B$), and if both had equal ability to utilize the tax subsidies (so that $s_L = s_B$), then the choice between renting or buying would remain a matter of indifference for the user firm. But where the user firm cannot take full advantage of the tax subsidy, it will pay to rent. That way, the firm can still get the indirect advantage of the congressional largesse that competition among leasing companies will build into rental rates.

Our tax laws in sum have created a new source of gains from specialization over and above those considered in the standard neoclassical analysis. Whether eliminating the waste of lost tax subsidies is a social gain is far from clear as indeed is the case for the subsidies themselves. But the private gains are substantial, as witness the explosive growth of the equipment leasing industry after the introduction of the investment tax credit in the early 1960s.

B. Rent-or-Buy Strategies for Tax-Exempt Organizations

The presumption in favor of renting is weakened, and in some circumstances even reversed, when the tax rate on income from the use of the property is smaller for the user than for the leasing company. Consider, for example, a university that is considering whether to buy a computer whose current one-period rental rate is the $L_{it}^\alpha(s_L)$ of Eq. (32). Since the university is tax exempt we have $\tau_B = 0$; and since s_B is a tax subsidy, we must also, therefore, have $s_B = 0$. Thus the difference in cost between leasing and buying becomes

$$\Delta = \left[\frac{\tau_L}{1 - \tau_L} E(R_{it}) - \frac{1}{1 - \tau_L} s_L - \frac{\tau_L}{1 - \tau_L} E(R_\alpha)\alpha\right]\pi_{it} \qquad (35)$$

Hence, as long as $\tau_L[E(R_{it}) - \alpha E(R_\alpha)] > s_L$, it will pay the university to buy rather than rent.

As a matter of arithmetic, of course, it is possible for s_L to exceed $\tau_L[E(R_{it}) - \alpha E(R_\alpha)]$. But this would imply that the subsidies collected by a leasing company, $s_L \pi_{it}$, would be greater than the taxes it paid on its rental income, given by

$$\tau_L L_{it}^a(s_L) - \tau_L E(d_{it})\pi_{it} - \tau_L \alpha E(R_a)\pi_{it}$$

$$= \pi_{it}\left(E(R_{it})\frac{\tau_L}{1-\tau_L} - \frac{\tau_L}{1-\tau_L} E(R_a)\alpha - \frac{\tau_L s_L}{1-\tau_L}\right) = \Delta$$

And this, in turn, would violate our premise that s_L and s_B are intended as tax subsidies. The word *intended* should be emphasized since ingenious tax-payers constantly search for (and sometimes find) new ways of expanding tax exemptions and subsidies. Our premise asserts only that such successful subversions of the intent of the law are transitory and will be eliminated by regulations or new legislation if they threaten to become widespread.[25]

The reason why a tax-exempt organization might gain from buying rather than leasing may also be seen by considering the extreme case of a life-of-the-property lease which would in principle permit the leasing company to finance the machine with full debt capital at the riskless rate R_F. Each period of the lease it makes a payment X_j to the bond holders, composed of X_{1j} in interest and X_{2j} as principal, and is allowed to take a tax deduction $D_{it}(j)$ in period j. The net cash flow to the leasing company in year j will be [cf. Eq. (26)]

$$L_{it}(j)(1-\tau_c) + \tau_c D_{it}(j) - X_{1j}(1-\tau_c) - X_{2j}$$

and the present value of the stream of such flows will be

$$\sum_{j=1}^{n} \frac{1}{(1+R_F)^j}[L_{it}(j)(1-\tau_c) + \tau_c D_{it}(j) - X_{1j}(1-\tau_c) - X_{2j}] \qquad (36)$$

and, in turn, competition will require the lease payments to be set so that the net present value of the cash flow is equal to zero. Rearranging terms, Eq. (36) then requires that

$$\sum_{j=1}^{n} \frac{L_{it}(j)}{(1+R_F)^j} = \sum_{j=1}^{n} \frac{X_{1j} + X_{2j}}{(1+R_F)^j} + \tau_c \sum_{j=1}^{n} \frac{L_{it}(j) - X_{1j} - D_{it}(j)}{(1+R_F)^j} \qquad (37)$$

and, since the present value of the payments to the bondholders equals π_{it},

$$\sum_{j=1}^{n} \frac{L_{it}(j)}{(1+R_F)^j} = \pi_{it} + \tau_c \sum_{j=1}^{n} \frac{L_{it}(j) - X_{1j} - D_{it}(j)}{(1+R_F)^j}$$

[25] The tax treatment of universities, in fact, provides some of the best illustrations of this catch-up process. Equation (35) implies that universities would find advantages in seeking out taxable corporations that own land or other capital assets and offer to share the tax savings via sale-and-leaseback arrangements. The spread of such arrangements was responsible, in part, for the imposition of the tax on "unrelated business income" of tax-exempt organizations. Note also in this connection that leasing companies are no longer permitted to claim the investment tax credit on any property they lease to a tax-exempt organization.

Note that $L_{it}(j) - X_{1j} - D_{it}(j)$ represents the taxable income to the leasing company in year j; thus, the final term in (37) represents the present value of the taxes paid by the leasing company. Assuming this to be nonnegative, the case for ownership by a university becomes clear: If it rents it must pay the leasing firm an amount equal in present value terms to the cost of buying the machine *plus* whatever taxes must be borne by the leasing firm in its role as an intermediary.[26,27]

C. Rent-or-Buy Strategies for Individuals

Another much-discussed case in which the tax on the user is smaller than that on the leasing company is that of owner-occupied housing. Under US law, the services provided by such housing (and other consumer durables, for that matter) are not considered part of taxable income. Nor are lease payments or depreciation allowed as deductions. Hence the τ_B of Eq. (33) is equal to zero, and the after-tax cost of home ownership becomes

$$C_H = E(R_{it})(1 - \tau_P) + [E(d_{it}) - s_B]\pi_{it} \qquad (38)$$

where τ_P is the rate of personal income tax on the expected investment income foregone if the house is purchased, and s_B is the (after-tax) value of any further specific tax subsidies to home ownership (such as the right to deduct local property taxes). The after-tax cost of leasing will be the $L_{it}^z(s_L)$ of Eq. (32), so that the excess of leasing cost over ownership cost will be

$$\Delta(H) = \left[E(R_{it}) \frac{\tau_P + \tau_L - \tau_P \tau_L}{1 - \tau_L} + - \frac{\tau_L \alpha}{1 - \tau_L} E(R_a) s_B - \frac{s_L}{1 - \tau_L} \right] \pi_{it} \qquad (39)$$

Note that as long as we continue to rule out cases of $s_L > \tau_L[E(R_{it}) - \alpha E(R_a)]$, $\Delta(H) > 0$ for any nonzero value of τ_L. Thus home-owning would be preferable to renting and the advantage would be greater the higher the personal tax rate of the owner.

These cases suggest that individuals and tax-exempt institutions would

---

[26] Note that even with straight-line depreciation, a lease contract calling for uniform annual payments would imply a negative present value of taxes for the leasing company if it could finance the asset with 100% debt. The algebraic *sum* of the taxes over the life of the property would be exactly zero, but the negative payments come first. We are indebted again to Fischer Black for calling our attention to this possibility. Such arrangements would, however, violate our premise against negative taxes. In this regard, it is interesting to note that the Revenue Proceedings referred to earlier prohibit levered leases unless the lessor demonstrates that it expects to receive a profit from the transaction apart from the value of the tax benefits.

[27] Note that the discount rate in (36) and (37) is still the same R_F as in (27) and (28), even though interest was assumed to be deductible in the derivation of (36) and (37) but not in (27) and (28). The reason is that in both cases, the leasing company's best alternative to taking on the riskless lease is to return the π_{it} of capital to its shareholders and let them earn the market riskless return of R_F directly.

find it financially advantageous to buy rather than lease. But care should be taken in drawing this conclusion, since both (35) and (39) were derived under the assumption that the implicit *before-tax* return to an individual or university from investing in a security with systematic risk β_{it} was the same whether that security was a bond or a stock. This equality need not hold; in particular, the before-tax returns on bonds may well be higher than those on stocks of equivalent risk. Such a differential in before-tax yields could arise because interest income is fully taxable, whereas the expected capital gain portion of the return on stocks is taxed at low rates (or not at all). To the extent that the market equalizes the after-tax returns on the two securities, bonds will be a better buy than stocks for a university or a taxpayer in a low tax bracket. And, more to the point, the opportunity cost of the investment income foregone will be larger than the $E(R_{it})$ built into the equilibrium rental, thereby narrowing (or perhaps even reversing) the advantages to individuals or universities in the buy strategy.[28]

D. The Effect of Tax Deferrals and Price Discrimination

Although we saw earlier that taxable user firms with sufficient earnings to be able to utilize any tax subsidies would have no grounds for preferring renting to buying or vice versa, there turns out to be another, more subtle tax effect that ultimately can be expected to tip the scales in favor of renting even for them. We refer to the fact that if the manufacturer of the equipment sells that equipment to a user firm or to an independent leasing company, then the manufacturer will incur an immediate tax liability on the profits from manufacture. If, on the other hand, the manufacturer should choose to lease the machine (or sell it under an installment plan) rather than sell it outright, then the tax on the manufacturing profits can be deferred. Competition among the manufacturers will push equilibrium rentals down to the point where *manufacturers* are indifferent between renting and selling. But by the same token *user* firms would find it profitable to rent, since if they buy, the price they pay for the equipment has to be enough higher than its rental equivalent to compensate the manufacturer for the loss of the tax deferral.

This presumption is not overturned if the manufacturer is a monopolist. In fact, we see some reinforcement. To the extent that tax-exempt organizations have an incentive to buy rather than rent, a monopolist manufacturer can engage in price discrimination by raising the selling price. He thereby recaptures some of the tax savings (vis-à-vis leasing) that would otherwise accrue to tax-exempt organizations. The higher sales price would give taxable firms a clear advantage in leasing from the manufacturer.

These points have a further implication: Independent leasing companies

---

[28] We are indebted to Fischer Black for helpful discussion on this point.

operate under a financial handicap when competing against manufacturers leasing their own products. The behavior of the stock prices of these independent leasing companies suggests that we are by no means alone in reaching this conclusion.

VI. Summary

Economists have largely taken for granted that rental rates for capital equipment would adjust until, in equilibrium, the purely financial advantages of the two arrangements were equal. The choice in any particular case would depend on which method had the lower nonfinancial costs of acquisition, maintenance, and disposal.

We have seen that this presumption of financial equivalence continues to hold when the neoclassical analysis of the lease-or-buy decision is extended to deal explicitly with uncertainty along lines that have become standard in the field of finance. The presumption of equivalence, however, often fails when we allow for the peculiarities of the present US tax laws. What tends to destroy the symmetry for ordinary corporations is not the way rentals and interest payments are treated for tax purposes, as has sometimes been suggested, but rather the fact that user firms may not always be able to take full advantage of some of the tax subsidies to hardware that Congress bestows. Leasing companies have thus tended to become entities specialized, among other things in the maximum utilization of these subsidies, which are in turn reflected in equilibrium rental rates. When the leasing company also happens to be owned by the company that manufactures the equipment, still another twist in favor of leasing is imparted by the deferral of taxes on the manufacturing profit that the manufacturer gains by leasing rather than selling. For nontaxable user firms, such as universities, however, and for the special case of consumer durables, there are tax-related financial benefits to ownership that must be considered.

References

1. Altschul, S., " New Ground Rules," *Barron's* (September 1, 1975).
2. Barro, R., "The Loan Market, Collateral and Rates of Return," Center for Math. Studies in Business and Economics, Univ. of Chicago, Rep. No. 7401 (January 1974).
3. Black, F., Miller, M. H., and Posner, R., "An Approach to the Regulation of Bank Holding Companies," Univ. of Chicago (January 1974). (Mimeographed.)
4. Bower, R., Herringer, F., and Williamson, P., " Lease Evaluation," *Accounting Review* (April 1966).
5. Bogue, M. C., and Roll, R., "Capital Budgeting of Risky Projects with ' Imperfect ' Markets for Physical Capital," *Journal of Finance* (May 1974).
6. Dewing, A. S., *The Financial Policy of Corporations*. New York: Ronald Press, 1953.
7. Fama, E., and Miller, M. H., *The Theory of Finance*. New York: Holt, 1972.
8. Ferguson, C., and Gould, J. P., *Microeconomic Theory*. Homewood, Illinois: Irwin, 1975.

9. Gordon, M., "A General Solution to the Buy or Lease Decision," *Journal of Finance* (September 1974).
10. Jensen, M. C., and Meckling, W. H., "Theory of the Firm: Managerial Behavior, Agency Costs and Capital Structure," Univ. of Rochester (February 1975). (Mimeographed.)
11. Johnson, R., and Lewellen, W., "Analysis of the Lease or Buy Decision," *Journal of Finance* (September 1972).
12. Jorgenson, D. W., "Capital Theory and Investment Behavior," *American Economic Review* (May 1963).
13. Lewellen, W., Long, M., and McConnell, J., "Asset Leasing in Competitive Capital Markets" (March 1975). (Mimeographed.)
14. Miller, M. H., and Upton, C. W., *Macroeconomics: A Neoclassical Introduction.* Homewood, Illinois: Irwin, 1974.
15. Modigliani, F., and Miller, M. H., "The Cost of Capital, Corporation Finance and the Theory of Investment," *American Economic Review* (June 1958).
16. Modigliani, F., and Miller, M. H., "Corporate Income Taxes and the Cost of Capital: A Correction," *American Economic Review* (June 1963).
17. Myers, S. C., Dill, D. A., and Bautista, A. J., "An Exact Solution to the Lease vs. Borrow Problem" (August 1975). (Mimeographed.)
18. Schall, L., "The Lease-or-Buy Asset Acquisition Decisions," *Journal of Finance* (September 1974).

Part III

PORTFOLIO ANALYSIS
AND CAPITAL MARKET THEORY

THE CAPITAL ASSET PRICING MODEL

A "Multi-Beta" Interpretation

William F. Sharpe

Stanford University

I. Introduction

In recent years, considerable attention has been accorded the Capital Asset Pricing Model of Sharpe [10], Lintner [4], and Mossin [7]. It suggests that in equilibrium the expected excess return on a security over and above the pure interest rate will equal some constant times its *ex ante* risk, measured by the security's so-called "beta coefficient." The latter equals the covariance of the security's return with that of the market portfolio (consisting of all assets, each in proportion to total value outstanding) divided by the variance of the return on the market portfolio, where all measures refer to *ex ante* probability distributions.

Many have used these ideas for practical investment policies. Moreover, a number of tests have been performed to determine the extent to which *ex post* results conform to the relationships predicted by the theory for *ex ante* values. In the light of empirical work to date, Black [1] has suggested a

I am indebted to Professor Marcus C. Bogue of Carnegie–Mellon University for a number of suggestions on this subject. Helpful comments were also provided by Professors Paul Cootner and Robert Litzenberger of Stanford University and Professor Alan Kraus of the University of British Columbia.

"zero-beta" model, while Blume and Friend [3] have argued in favor of an unspecified model of market segmentation.

Given this interest, it seems worthwhile to examine carefully the nature of the beta measure of risk. The following section shows that a security's beta relative to the market portfolio can be expressed as a weighted average of beta values relative to any desired number of portfolios, the collection of which equals the market portfolio. When the beta values are scaled appropriately, the applicable weights represent the relative contributions of the portfolios to the uncertainty of the market portfolio, and will sum to equal one. In the following section these results are reinterpreted in the context of a general multifactor model. Finally, some possible uses for the approach are suggested.

The model given here provides a general setting for the special cases discussed by Mayers [5], Roll [9], Pettit and Westerfield [8], Miller and Scholes [6], and Blume and Husic [2] in different contexts. Although many elements of this analysis can be found in these papers, the present version appears to be sufficiently general to provide new insights, as well as more complete proofs of earlier results.

II. The Multi-Beta Interpretation

To begin, assume that there are N securities, which constitute the market portfolio m. Let X_i be the proportion of total value of m invested in security i. The return on security i is $\tilde{r}_i$ (tildes are used to represent random variables). Let $\tilde{R}_m$ be the return on the market portfolio.

$$\tilde{R}_m = \sum_{i=1}^{N} X_i \tilde{r}_i$$

The beta value for security i relative to the market portfolio is defined as

$$\beta_{im} = \mathrm{cov}(\tilde{r}_i, \tilde{R}_m)/\mathrm{var}(\tilde{R}_m) \tag{1}$$

where "cov" is covariance and "var" is variance.

Now, assume that the market portfolio is used to form M portfolios, with x_{ij} representing the proportion of the total market value of m invested in security i in portfolio j. All securities are allocated to one or more of the M portfolios. Thus,

$$X_i = \sum_{j=1}^{M} x_{ij} \qquad \text{for} \quad i = 1, \ldots, N$$

Let the total proportion of market value invested in portfolio j be represented by w_j:

$$w_j = \sum_{i=1}^{N} x_{ij} \qquad \text{for} \quad j = 1, \ldots, M$$

The return on the jth portfolio will be

$$\tilde{R}_j = \sum_{i=1}^{N} \left(\frac{x_{ij}}{w_j}\right)\tilde{r}_i$$

and the return on the market portfolio can be viewed simply as a weighted average of the returns on the M portfolios:

$$\tilde{R}_m = \sum_{j=1}^{M} w_j \tilde{R}_j \tag{2}$$

Substituting (2) into (1), we obtain

$$\beta_{im} = \text{cov}\left(\tilde{r}_i, \sum_{j=1}^{M} w_j \tilde{R}_j\right) \bigg/ \text{var}(\tilde{R}_m)$$

Rearranging, we have

$$\beta_{im} = \sum_{j=1}^{M} w_j \, \text{cov}(\tilde{r}_i, \tilde{R}_j)/\text{var}(\tilde{R}_m) \tag{3}$$

Multiplying both numerator and denominator of (3) by $\text{cov}(\tilde{R}_m, \tilde{R}_j)$ gives

$$\beta_{im} = \sum_{j=1}^{M} \left[\frac{w_j \, \text{cov}(\tilde{R}_m, \tilde{R}_j)}{\text{var}(\tilde{R}_m)} \cdot \frac{\text{cov}(\tilde{r}_i, \tilde{R}_j)}{\text{cov}(\tilde{R}_m, \tilde{R}_j)}\right] \tag{4}$$

Note, however, that

$$\text{cov}(\tilde{R}_m, \tilde{R}_j) = \text{cov}\left(\sum_{k=1}^{M} w_k \tilde{R}_k, \tilde{R}_j\right) = \sum_{k=1}^{M} w_k \, \text{cov}(\tilde{R}_k, \tilde{R}_j) \tag{5}$$

Denote the first term in (4) by u_j. Substituting (5) in the numerator yields

$$u_j \equiv \frac{w_j \, \text{cov}(\tilde{R}_m, \tilde{R}_j)}{\text{var}(\tilde{R}_m)} = \frac{w_j \sum_{k=1}^{M} w_k \, \text{cov}(\tilde{R}_k, \tilde{R}_j)}{\text{var}(\tilde{R}_m)} \tag{6}$$

Note, however, that

$$\text{var}(\tilde{R}_m) = \text{cov}\left(\sum_{j=1}^{M} w_j \tilde{R}_j, \sum_{k=1}^{M} w_k \tilde{R}_k\right) = \sum_{j=1}^{M} \sum_{k=1}^{M} w_j w_k \, \text{cov}(\tilde{R}_j, \tilde{R}_k)$$

Thus, $\sum_{j=1}^{M} u_j = 1$. The value of u_j can be interpreted as the proportion of the total variance of $\tilde{R}_m$ attributed to portfolio j. It takes into account not only the portfolio's own variance, but also any covariance with the other $J - 1$ portfolios. It is, of course, an *ex ante* concept, as developed here. In other words, u_j is the relative *uncertainty* of portfolio j.

An alternative interpretation of u_j may prove more useful for subjective estimation. Note first that

$$\partial \, \text{var}(\tilde{R}_m)/\partial w_j = 2 \, \text{cov}(\tilde{R}_j, \tilde{R}_m)$$

Since $\sigma(\tilde{R}_m)$, the standard deviation of $\tilde{R}_m$, is the square root of $\mathrm{var}(\tilde{R}_m)$,

$$\partial\sigma(\tilde{R}_m)/\partial w_j = \mathrm{cov}(\tilde{R}_j, \tilde{R}_m)/\sigma(\tilde{R}_m)$$

It follows that

$$u_j = \frac{w_j\,\mathrm{cov}(\tilde{R}_j, \tilde{R}_m)}{\mathrm{var}(\tilde{R}_m)} = \frac{\partial\sigma(\tilde{R}_m)}{\partial w_j}\cdot\frac{w_j}{\sigma(\tilde{R}_m)} = \frac{\partial\sigma(\tilde{R}_m)/\sigma(\tilde{R}_m)}{\partial w_j/w_j} \tag{7}$$

The value of u_j may thus be interpreted as an *elasticity*, measuring the percentage change in the risk of the market portfolio per unit percentage change in w_j. Not surprisingly, the sum of such values must equal one, since under the assumed conditions an equal percentage change in all values of w_j will cause an equivalent percentage change in $\sigma(\tilde{R}_m)$.

Turning next to the second term of (4), we divide both numerator and denominator by $\mathrm{var}(\tilde{R}_j)$ to obtain[1]

$$\frac{\mathrm{cov}(\tilde{r}_i, \tilde{R}_j)/\mathrm{var}(\tilde{R}_j)}{\mathrm{cov}(\tilde{R}_m, \tilde{R}_j)/\mathrm{var}(\tilde{R}_j)} \tag{8}$$

These may be defined as the beta values of the security and the market, respectively, relative to portfolio j:

$$\beta_{ij} \equiv \mathrm{cov}(\tilde{r}_i, \tilde{R}_j)/\mathrm{var}(\tilde{R}_j), \qquad \beta_{mj} \equiv \mathrm{cov}(\tilde{R}_m, \tilde{R}_j)/\mathrm{var}(\tilde{R}_j) \tag{9}$$

Thus, (8) may be written as

$$\beta_{ij}/\beta_{mj} \tag{10}$$

Combining (4), (6), and (10) gives the important relationship

$$\beta_{im} = \sum_{j=1}^{M} u_j \frac{\beta_{ij}}{\beta_{mj}} \tag{11}$$

That is, a security's beta relative to the market will be a weighted average of its betas relative to the M portfolios, where the weights represent the relative degrees of uncertainty associated with the portfolios, and the beta values are scaled relative to corresponding values for the market as a whole.[2]

The values of beta used in (11) are, of course, those defined in Eqs. (9). They correspond to the slope coefficients in a *simple* regression. In other words, β_{ij} captures the entire sensitivity of $\tilde{r}_i$ to variations in $\tilde{R}_j$, including any arising through induced effects on the variations of other portfolios.

Another form that may prove useful for subjective estimation can be

---

[1] This operation can only be performed when the return on portfolio j is uncertain (i.e., $\mathrm{var}(\tilde{R}_j) \neq 0$).

[2] The scaling can be considered to apply to the value of β_{im} as well, since $\beta_{mm} = 1$.

obtained by multiplying each term on the right-hand side of (3) by $\text{var}(\tilde{R}_j)/\text{var}(\tilde{R}_j)$:

$$\beta_{im} = \sum_{j=1}^{M} \frac{w_j \, \text{cov}(\tilde{r}_i, \tilde{R}_j)}{\text{var}(\tilde{R}_m)} \cdot \frac{\text{var}(\tilde{R}_j)}{\text{var}(\tilde{R}_j)} \tag{12}$$

then substituting the definition of β_{ij} to obtain

$$\beta_{im} = \sum_{j=1}^{M} \frac{w_j \, \text{var}(\tilde{R}_j)}{\text{var}(\tilde{R}_m)} \beta_{ij} \tag{13}$$

In this version, β_{im} is seen to be a weighted average of the β_{ij}'s, with the weight for β_{ij} dependent on the contribution of $\tilde{R}_j$ to $\tilde{R}_m$ (i.e., w_j) and the uncertainty concerning the value of $\tilde{R}_j$ [i.e., $\text{var}(\tilde{R}_j)$].

III. A Multifactor Model

Assume that f key factors, $\tilde{F}_1$ through $\tilde{F}_f$, influencing security returns have been identified, and that the return on the market portfolio can be expressed as

$$\tilde{R}_m = \sum_{k=1}^{f} b_{mk}\tilde{F}_k + \tilde{c}_m \tag{14}$$

where $\tilde{c}_m$ represents the (random) difference between $\tilde{R}_m$ and the proportion of $\tilde{R}_m$ attributable to the factors.

Denote the proportion of the market return determined by the factors by $\tilde{M}$:

$$\tilde{M} = \sum_{k=1}^{f} b_{mk}\tilde{F}_k \tag{15}$$

Now assume that the chosen factors "explain" a large proportion of the uncertainty about $\tilde{R}_m$, that is,

$$\text{var}(\tilde{R}_m) \approx \text{var}(\tilde{M}) \tag{16}$$

A special case arises when $\text{var}(\tilde{c}_m)$ is zero. This can be obtained by the choice of n factors, each of which corresponds to the return on one of the securities. It can also be obtained with one factor, defined as $\tilde{R}_m$. However, neither of these cases is particularly instructive for present purposes. Nor is one in which factor-analytic techniques are applied to the full covariance matrix to determine a few factors with high explanatory power. Far more important are cases in which the factors represent anticipations about important economic variables affecting more than one firm. If enough appropriate factors of this type are chosen, (16) will hold only approximately, but can be employed for most practical purposes.

While variations in $\tilde{M}$ may serve as an adequate explanation of variations in $\tilde{R}_m$, they need not, of course, explain a large part of the variation in the return on any single security. However, variations in $\tilde{M}$ should prove adequate for explaining the covariance of a security's return with that of $\tilde{R}_m$, since

$$\text{cov}(\tilde{r}_i, \tilde{R}_m) = \text{cov}(\tilde{r}_i, \tilde{M} + \tilde{c}_m) = \text{cov}(\tilde{r}_i, \tilde{M}) + \text{cov}(\tilde{r}_i, \tilde{c}_m)$$

$$= [\text{var}(\tilde{r}_i)]^{1/2} \{\text{corr}(\tilde{r}_i, \tilde{M})[\text{var}(\tilde{M})]^{1/2}$$

$$+ \text{corr}(\tilde{r}_i, \tilde{c}_m)[\text{var}(\tilde{c}_m)]^{1/2}\} \tag{17}$$

where "corr" denotes correlation coefficient. Under the assumed conditions, $\text{var}(\tilde{c}_m)$ is small, allowing the approximation

$$\text{cov}(\tilde{r}_i, \tilde{R}_m) \approx \text{cov}(\tilde{r}_i, \tilde{M}) \tag{18}$$

The results obtained earlier can now be applied. In (2), interpret $\tilde{R}_j$ as the value of factor j and w_j as the sensitivity of $\tilde{R}_m$ to a change in factor j [e.g., as b_{mj} in (15)]. In (11), u_j then represents the percentage change in the uncertainty of the market portfolio per unit percentage change in the sensitivity of $\tilde{R}_m$ to factor j; the value of β_{ij} equals the covariance of $\tilde{r}_i$ with factor j, divided by the variance of the factor; and β_{mj} equals the covariance of $\tilde{R}_m$ with factor j divided by the variance of the factor. Of course, each beta value captures the entire sensitivity of a return to changes in a factor, including any arising through induced effects on the variations of other factors.

A similar interpretation can be given formula (13). Again, β_{im} is a weighted average of the β_{ij}'s, with the weight for β_{ij} dependent on the sensitivity of $\tilde{R}_m$ to a change in factor j (i.e., w_j) and the uncertainty about the factor [i.e., $\text{var}(\tilde{R}_j)$].

IV. A Discrete-State Model

A particularly simple version of the result obtained earlier can be derived if possible future values are assumed to depend entirely on the occurrence of mutually exclusive and exhaustive states of the world.

Let there be S such states; denote the return on the market portfolio and security i in state s by R_{ms} and R_{is}, respectively. Let π_s be the probability that state s will occur. Expected returns will be

$$\bar{R}_m = \sum_{s=1}^{S} \pi_s R_{ms}, \qquad \bar{R}_i = \sum_{s=1}^{S} \pi_s R_{is} \tag{19}$$

If state s occurs, security i's return will diverge from its expected value by the amount $(R_{is} - \bar{R}_i)$, while the market portfolio's return diverges from its expectation by $(R_{ms} - \bar{R}_m)$. The ratio of the former to the latter can be defined as the security's beta if state i occurs:[3]

$$\beta_{is} = (R_{is} - \bar{R}_i)/(R_{ms} - \bar{R}_m) \qquad (20)$$

The overall beta value of the security will, of course, be

$$\beta_i = \sum_{s=1}^{S} \pi_s(R_{is} - \bar{R}_i)(R_{ms} - \bar{R}_m) / \sum_{s=1}^{S} \pi_s(R_{ms} - \bar{R}_m)^2 \qquad (21)$$

Rearranging,

$$\beta_i = \sum_{s=1}^{S} \left[\frac{\pi_s(R_{ms} - \bar{R}_m)^2}{\sum_{s=1}^{S} \pi_s(R_{ms} - \bar{R}_m)^2} \cdot \frac{R_{is} - \bar{R}_i}{R_{ms} - \bar{R}_m} \right] \qquad (22)$$

or

$$\beta_i = \sum_{s=1}^{S} u_s \beta_{is} \qquad (23)$$

where

$$u_s = \pi_s(R_{ms} - \bar{R}_m)^2 / \sum_{s=1}^{S} \pi_s(R_{ms} - \bar{R}_m)^2 \qquad (24)$$

Clearly, u_s is the relative contribution of state s to the overall uncertainty of the market portfolio; and all the u_s values sum to equal one.

V. Expected Returns

Thus far, no use has been made of equilibrium relationships between expected return and risk. We now introduce the standard result obtained from the Capital Asset Pricing Model of Sharpe, Lintner, and Mossin, with homogeneous expectations and equal borrowing and lending rates. In this model, prices adjust until the expected excess return of any security or portfolio, over and above the pure interest rate, will equal the expected excess return on the market portfolio, times the security's beta relative to the market. Since the one-period pure interest rate is known with certainty *ex ante*, we can simply assume all returns are stated as excess returns. Letting $E(\bar{R}_m)$ denote the expected excess return on the market portfolio, and $E(\bar{r}_i)$ the expected excess return on security or portfolio i,

$$E(\bar{r}_i) = E(\tilde{R}_m)\beta_{im} \qquad (25)$$

---

[3] If $R_{ms} = \bar{R}_m$, this value is undefined; for purposes of formula (23), to follow, any value may be used.

Substituting (11),

$$E(\tilde{r}_i) = E(\tilde{R}_m) \sum_{j=1}^{M} \left(u_j \frac{\beta_{ij}}{\beta_{mj}} \right) \tag{26}$$

Now consider a security or portfolio with $\beta_{ij} = \beta_{mj}$ for one j, say j', and $\beta_{ij} = 0$ for all other j's. Then,

$$E(\tilde{r}_i) = E(\tilde{R}_m) u_{j'} \tag{27}$$

This is the expected return associated with the markets' average sensitivity to $\tilde{R}_j$. Since (25) holds for any security or combination of securities, it holds for the market portfolio as well. Thus,

$$E(\tilde{R}_m) = \sum_{j=1}^{M} [u_j E(\tilde{R}_m)] \tag{28}$$

That is, each portfolio or factor j contributes to the market's expected excess return in proportion to the market's overall risk.

VI. Historic Betas, *Ex Ante* Betas, and Actual Returns

As shown previously, the key *ex ante* measure of a security's risk, β_{im}, depends on current *ex ante* estimates of the security's sensitivity to various factors (its β_{ij} values) and the current relative uncertainties associated with those factors (the u_j values). Historic betas, measured via regression analysis using data from previous periods, can be decomposed in precisely the same manner, but the relevant values will be the security's historic sensitivities to the factors and the relative degrees of variation in anticipations about the major economic variables measured by those factors during the period studied. Historic betas may thus be poor surrogates for *ex ante* betas. This is most likely to occur when current relative uncertainties about major factors differ considerably from relative variations in anticipations about those factors in the historic period. Subjective estimates of appropriate u_j values, even if combined with historic β_{ij} values, may, under such circumstances, produce superior *ex ante* estimates of risk and thus expected return. To estimate the u_j's, one need not predict the level of each factor, only its current relative contribution to uncertainty—a difficult, but not necessarily impossible, task.

VII. Measurement of Factors

It should be emphasized that the relevant factors for the approach described here measure *anticipations* about key economic variables. Thus measures of, say, $\text{cov}(\tilde{r}_i, \tilde{R}_j)$, and hence the associated β_{ij} value, must be obtained by measuring a change in the factor with the simultaneous effect on the security. For example, a security's sensitivity to inflation might be measured by determining a company's accounting return's sensitivity to actual inflation, or by measuring the sensitivity of the stock's market return to some measure of change in anticipated inflation. Attempts to regress market return on actual inflation (with or without arbitrarily chosen lags) are likely to result in poor or meaningless estimates of the relevant sensitivity.

This emphasizes the need to try to measure anticipations. A fruitful line of inquiry involves the use of surrogates for initial estimates of the beta values for various securities (e.g., net debtor/creditor status for sensitivity to changes in anticipated inflation). Given such surrogates, one might construct a large portfolio (with both long and short positions of various stocks, if needed), attempting to maximize the portfolio's sensitivity to one factor while making it virtually insensitive to every other factor. The return on such a portfolio could then serve as a surrogate for changes in anticipations about the factor in question. By constructing similar portfolios for other factors, a multifactor model could be implemented using the more general multi-beta approach.

References

1. Black, F., "Capital Market Equilibrium with Restricted Borrowing," *Journal of Business* (July 1972).
2. Blume, M., and Husic, F. J., "Risk and Return on the American Stock Exchange," paper presented at the Rodney L. White seminar (February 19, 1971).
3. Blume, M., and Friend, I., "A New Look at the Capital Asset Pricing Model," *Journal of Finance* (March 1973).
4. Lintner, J., "The Valuation of Risk Assets and the Selection of Risky Investments in Stock Portfolios and Capital Budgets," *Review of Economics and Statistics* (February 1965).
5. Mayers, D., "Nonmarketable Assets and Capital Market Equilibrium," in *Studies in the Theory of Capital Markets* (M. C. Jensen, ed.). New York: Praeger, 1972.
6. Miller, M. H., and Scholes, M., "Rates of Return in Relation to Risk: A Re-Examination of Some Recent Findings," in *Studies in the Theory of Capital Markets* (M. C. Jensen, ed.). New York: Praeger, 1972.
7. Mossin, J., "Equilibrium in a Capital Asset Market," *Econometrica* (October 1966).
8. Pettit, R. R., and Westerfield, R., "A Model of Capital Asset Risk," *Journal of Financial and Quantitative Analysis* (March 1972).
9. Roll, R., "Bias in Fitting the Sharpe Model to Time Series Data," *Journal of Financial and Quantitative Analysis* (September 1969).
10. Sharpe, W. F., "Capital Asset Prices: A Theory of Market Equilibrium under Conditions of Risk," *Journal of Finance* (September 1964).

PORTFOLIO EFFICIENCY ANALYSIS
IN THREE MOMENTS
The Multiperiod Case

Fred D. Arditti

Haim Levy

University of Florida
and
The Hebrew University

The Hebrew University

I.

The notion of two-moment efficiency analysis and the subsequent deriva-tion of security market equilibrium conditions in terms of the first two moments of return distributions has been introduced, extended, and dis-cussed by Markowitz [14], Tobin [19], Sharpe [17], Lintner [12], Mossin [16], Fama [4], and others. While concentration on the first two moments permits the achievement of far reaching results, these results are obtained at the cost of restricting the analysis to quadratic utility or normal return distributions (see [19] and [9]). If one believes that these assumptions regarding the utility function or rate of return distribution are unreasonable,

Reprinted with permission from *The Journal of Finance* **30**, No. 3 (June 1975).

We are indebted to Harry Markowitz for his observation and explanation to us of how a numerical solution to the formal problem presented in Section III, Eqs. (18a) and (18b), can be obtained by application of the Markowitz Critical Line Algorithm. The paper benefited from all of his comments.

the alternative is to work with an unrestricted utility function, which in turn implies that the decision process (efficiency analysis) must consider higher distribution moments.

While the economic importance of the *first three moments* is recognized— the role of skewness in purchasing a lottery ticket [7] and in the pricing of stocks [1] seems clear—there is no complete agreement about the importance of the role played by the higher moments (kurtosis, etc.)—neither among statisticians [10] nor among stock market investors [11]. The purpose of this paper is to shed some light on three-moment efficiency analysis by first studying the relationship of the first three moments of an asset's single-period return to the first three moments of its multiperiod returns. In the process, we provide a theoretical explanation that reconciles the seemingly contradictory empirical evidence presented by Blume [3] and Friend and Blume [8], indicating that when monthly returns are used the third moment of a portfolio's rate of return is not significantly different from zero, to that given by Arditti [2], Levy and Sarnat [11], and Miller and Scholes [15], indicating that the estimate of the third moment based on annual returns is often positive. All of this is covered in Section II.

In Section III, we confront the question of multiperiod efficiency in terms of the parameters of single-period feasible portfolios. Assuming the single period to be one month, and thus making use of the empirical finding that the third moment of portfolio returns for this period is zero, the relevant single-period parameters are mean and variance. We then provide a method that can be used to determine the three-moment multiperiod efficient frontier.

II.

Let us denote the ith "one-period" return on a given portfolio by $1 + x_i$, where x_i denotes the *rate* of return for this period. The first three moments of the distribution of the one-period returns are given by

$$E(1 + x_i) = 1 + \mu_i$$
$$E[(1 + x_i) - (1 + \mu_i)]^2 = \sigma_i^2$$
$$E[(1 + x_i) - (1 + \mu_i)]^3 = \mu_{3i}$$

The n-period return is given by $\prod_{i=1}^{n} (1 + x_i)$, and assuming independence over time of the returns,[1] the first three moments of this return, denoted by

---

[1] This assumption follows the empirical evidence supporting the random walk theory of stock price changes, cf. [5].

$(1 + E)$, V, and M, respectively, are[2]

$$1 + E = \prod_{i=1}^{n} (1 + \mu_i) \tag{1}$$

$$V = \prod_{i=1}^{n} [(1 + \mu_i)^2 + \sigma_i^2] - \prod_{i=1}^{n} (1 + \mu_i)^2 \tag{2}$$

$$M = E\left[\prod_{i=1}^{n} (1 + x_i) - \prod_{i=1}^{n} (1 + \mu_i)\right]^3 \tag{3}$$

The next step is to express multiperiod skewness M in terms of the single-period moments. Expanding (3), we obtain

$$M = E\left[\prod_{i=1}^{n} (1 + x_i)\right]^3 - 3E\left[\prod_{i=1}^{n} (1 + x_i)^2\right]\left[\prod_{i=1}^{n} (1 + \mu_i)\right]$$

$$+ 3E\left[\prod_{i=1}^{n} (1 + x_i)\right]\left[\prod_{i=1}^{n} (1 + \mu_i)\right]^2 - \left[\prod_{i=1}^{n} (1 + \mu_i)\right]^3 \tag{4}$$

Simplifying (4), we get

$$M = E\left[\prod_{i=1}^{n} (1 + x_i)^3\right] - 3\left[\prod_{i=1}^{n} (1 + \mu_i)\right]$$

$$\times E\left[\prod_{i=1}^{n} (1 + x_i)\right]^2 + 2\left[\prod_{i=1}^{n} (1 + \mu_i)\right]^3 \tag{4'}$$

Using the independence assumption the first term on the right side of (4') can be rewritten as

$$E\left[\prod_{i=1}^{n} (1 + x_i)^3\right] = \prod_{i=1}^{n}\left[E(1 + x_i)^3\right]$$

$$= \prod_{i=1}^{n} [1 + 3\mu_i + 3\mu_i^2 + 3\sigma_i^2 + E(x_i)^3] \tag{5}$$

However, since

$$E(x_i^3) = \mu_{3i} + \mu_i(3\sigma_i^2 + \mu_i^2)$$

Eq. (5) can be rewritten as

$$E\left[\prod_{i=1}^{n} (1 + x_i)^3\right] = \prod_{i=1}^{n} [1 + 3\mu_i + 3\mu_i^2 + 3\sigma_i^2 + \mu_{3i} + \mu_i(3\sigma_i^2 + \mu_i^2)]$$

$$= \prod_{i=1}^{n} [(1 + \mu_i)^3 + 3(1 + \mu_i)\sigma_i^2 + \mu_{3i}] \tag{5'}$$

[2] For the derivation of V, see Tobin [20].

Similarly, expanding the $E[\prod_{i=1}^{n}(1 + x_i)^2]$ term on the right side of (4′) yields

$$E\left[\prod_{i=1}^{n}(1 + x_i)^2\right] = \prod_{i=1}^{n}[(1 + \mu_i)^2 + \sigma_i^2] \tag{6}$$

And substituting the results of (5′) and (6) in (4′) yields

$$M = \prod_{i=1}^{n}[(1 + \mu_i)^3 + 3(1 + \mu_i)\sigma_i^2 + \mu_{3i}]$$

$$- 3\prod_{i=1}^{n}(1 + \mu_i)\left\{\prod_{i=1}^{n}[(1 + \mu_i)^2 + \sigma_i^2]\right\} + 2\prod_{i=1}^{n}(1 + \mu_i)^3 \tag{7}$$

Accepting the empirical findings which claim that for short periods skewness is equal to zero, i.e., $\mu_{3i} = 0$ for each period i, we get

$$M = \prod_{i=1}^{n}[(1 + \mu_i)^3 + 3(1 + \mu_i)\sigma_i^2]$$

$$- 3\prod_{i=1}^{n}(1 + \mu_i)\left\{\prod_{i=1}^{n}[(1 + \mu_i)^2 + \sigma_i^2]\right\} + 2\prod_{i=1}^{n}(1 + \mu_i)^3 \tag{8}$$

Obviously, there is no reason why the multiperiod skewness given by Eq. (8) will be equal to zero, even though the one-period skewness μ_{3i} is indeed equal to zero for all values $i = 1, \ldots, n$. Equation (8) and the assumption that $\mu_{3i} = 0$ explains the conflicting results in the empirical works of Blume ([3], p. 164, footnote 31) and Friend and Blume ([8], p. 562, footnote 3), who found symmetric monthly return distributions for the portfolios in their sample, while Arditti [2] and Levy and Sarnat [11] found the distributions of annual portfolio returns to be positively skewed. The practical implication of Eq. (8) is that skewness is clearly a function of the investment horizon, which is, in turn, determined by investors' behavior. For those investors with short investment horizons, skewness of portfolio returns can be ignored, since existing empirical evidence indicates that these distributions are symmetric; however, for investors with longer horizons, the distribution's skewness may be significant, and therefore becomes a relevant variable in investment decision-making.

In order to analyze how multiperiod skewness M varies with the investment horizon n, and the single-period mean and variance parameters μ_i and σ_i^2, we assume stationarity of the single-period return distribution, i.e., $\mu_i = \mu$, $\sigma_i^2 = \sigma^2$ and $\mu_{3i} = 0$ for $i = 1, 2, \ldots, n$. In this case, Eq. (8) reduces to

$$M = [(1 + \mu)^3 + 3(1 + \mu)\sigma^2]^n - 3(1 + \mu)^n[(1 + \mu)^2 + \sigma^2]^n + 2(1 + \mu)^{3n} \tag{9}$$

or

$$M = (1 + \mu)^n\{[(1 + \mu)^2 + 3\sigma^2]^n - 3[(1 + \mu)^2 + \sigma^2]^n\} + 2(1 + \mu)^{3n} \tag{9′}$$

Suppose now that one increases the investment horizon n. What is the impact of that change on M? To facilitate the mathematical analysis, we assume discrete changes in the investment horizon. That is, if the shortest investment period is, say, one month, we examine the changes in M by moving to investment horizons of two months, three months, etc.

Using the binomial expansion, Eq. (9′) becomes

$$M = (1 + \mu)^n \left\{ \sum_{r=0}^{n} \binom{n}{r} [(1 + \mu)^2]^{n-r} [3\sigma^2]^r \right.$$

$$\left. - 3 \sum_{r=0}^{n} \binom{n}{r} [(1 + \mu)^2]^{n-r} (\sigma^2)^r \right\} + 2(1 + \mu)^{3n} \qquad (10)$$

or

$$M = (1 + \mu)^n \left\{ \sum_{r=1}^{n} \binom{n}{r} [(1 + \mu)^2]^{n-r} [\sigma^2]^r [3^r - 3] \right\}$$

$$+ (1 + \mu)^n (1 + \mu)^{2n} (-2) + 2(1 + \mu)^{3n} \qquad (11)$$

Since the last two terms cancel out, (11) becomes

$$M = (1 + \mu)^n \left\{ \sum_{r=1}^{n} \binom{n}{r} [(1 + \mu)^2]^{n-r} [\sigma^2]^r (3^r - 3) \right\} \qquad (12)$$

Now, for $r = 1$, $3^r - 3 = 0$; and for $r > 1$, $3^r - 3 > 0$. Given that $\mu > 0$, it is clear that M is an increasing function of n; that is, $M(n + 1) > M(n)$ for all $n = 1, 2, \ldots$. This is clearly true for $\sigma^2 \geq 1$, but holds even for cases when σ^2 is a fraction, since by increasing the number of periods we add positive terms to the existing series, on the one hand, and also increase the magnitude of the existing terms on the other hand.[3] Another result obtained from (12) is that since all terms in the series are positive, increasing either μ or σ^2 leads to an increase in M, i.e., $\partial M / \partial \mu > 0$ and $\partial M / \partial \sigma^2 > 0$.

[3] To show this, let $a \equiv (1 + \mu)^2$ and $b \equiv \sigma^2$. Then it is sufficient to prove that for each such r term in an n term series as

$$\binom{n}{r} [(1 + \mu)^2]^{n-r} [\sigma^2]^r = \binom{n}{r} a^{n-r} b^r$$

we can find a corresponding r term in an $n + 1$ series that is larger than the above term. The typical r term in the $n + 1$ series is

$$\binom{n+1}{r} a^{n-r+1} b^r = a \left[\binom{n+1}{r} a^{n-r} b^r \right]$$

But since $a > 1$ and $\binom{n+1}{r}$ is greater than $\binom{n}{r}$, we see that

$$\binom{n}{r} a^{n-r} b^r < a \left[\binom{n+1}{r} a^{n-r} b^r \right]$$

The $n + 1$ series will, of course, possess one more term than the n series, but this term is positive, namely b^{n+1}.

Table I gives the values of M to four significant digits, as a function of the number of investment periods, for selected values of μ and σ. In constructing the table's figures, Eq. (9) has been employed; thus symmetric and stationary single-period distributions are assumed. Table I indicates that even if a stock has a symmetric single-period rate of return distribution, its multiperiod rate of return distribution may be highly skewed. For example, a speculative stock with a monthly expected rate of return of 3% and a standard deviation of 10% will have a positive third moment equal to 0.751 for its 20-month rate of return distribution.

Table I

The Multiperiod Skewness M as a Function of the Investment Horizon N

Number of periods n	Multiperiod skewness (M) for selected values of (μ, σ)		
	$\mu = 0.02$ $\sigma = 0.05$	$\mu = 0.02$ $\sigma = 0.10$	$\mu = 0.03$ $\sigma = 0.10$
1	0.0000	0.0000	0.0000
2	0.0000	0.0006	0.0006
3	0.0005	0.0056	0.0086
10	0.0029	0.0501	0.0644
20	0.0229	0.4365	0.7510

III.

In the absence of a riskless asset, the mean-variance one-period efficient portfolio set is given by the curve *cd* of Fig. 1, with the feasible set of one-period portfolios denoted by the shaded area. If one restricts the analysis to our single period or "short investment period," then *cd* also represents the three-moment efficient set for this *short period*, since by assumption single-period skewness is equal to zero. But how is the *multiperiod* three-moment efficient set related to the one-period portfolios portrayed in Fig. 1, given that an individual believes that the portfolio selected today will be kept for n periods?[4]

Assuming that individuals with preference function U are risk averse and like positive skewness, then

$$\frac{\partial U}{\partial (1 + E)} > 0, \qquad \frac{\partial U}{\partial V} < 0, \qquad \frac{\partial U}{\partial M} > 0$$

[4] Though stationarity over time of investment or diversification strategies is not always optimal (see Stevens [18]), it is a legitimate strategy and in some cases provides an optimal rule [18]. Moreover, there is no known multiperiod strategy that is generally optimal.

and recalling that in Section II we proved that $\partial M/\partial \mu > 0$ and $\partial M/\partial \sigma^2 > 0$, we can begin to study the relationship between the multiperiod, three-moment efficient set and the one-period portfolio set depicted in Fig. 1. For example, compare portfolios e, f, and g in Fig. 2. By moving from portfolio e

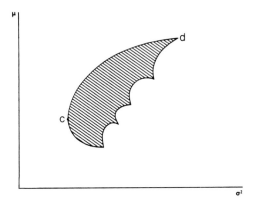

Fig. 1. The single-period portfolio set.

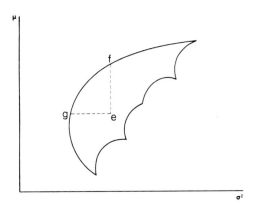

Fig. 2. A comparison of multiperiod portfolios in terms of single-period parameters.

to f we increase μ and hence $1 + E$, but V is also increased, since $\partial V/\partial \mu > 0$ (see Tobin [20] for this result) and so is M, since $\partial M/\partial \mu > 0$. Consequently, while portfolio f carries higher E and M than portfolio e, it also has larger V, and thus f does not dominate e in a three-moment, multiperiod efficiency analysis. A similar comparison demonstrates that neither g nor e dominates the other, since g has lower V and lower M than e; this follows because $\partial V/\partial \sigma^2 > 0$ and $\partial M/\partial \sigma^2 > 0$.

By this simple comparison, one might be tempted to believe that all feasible one-period portfolios are multiperiod efficient. However, a more careful analysis shows that this is not necessarily true, and that the three-moment efficient set may be a subset of portfolios portrayed in Fig. 2. To demonstrate this, we reconsider the portfolios g, e, and f, but now label them with their multiperiod values (see Fig. 3).

The labeling of the multiperiod portfolio parameter designates its value relative to the corresponding value for that parameter of the e portfolio; for example, the symbol V_- at point e indicates that the g portfolio has lower multiperiod variance than the e portfolio, while the symbol M_+ at f means that point f has higher multiperiod skewness than point e, and so on.

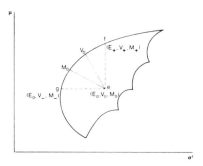

Fig. 3. A comparison of multiperiod portfolios in terms of multiperiod parameters.

Recalling the reasoning that lies behind this labeling ($\partial E/\partial\mu > 0$, $\partial V/\partial\mu > 0$, $\partial V/\partial\sigma^2 > 0$, $\partial M/\partial\mu > 0$, $\partial M/\partial\sigma^2 > 0$), one immediately sees that no portfolio on the horizontal dotted line, eg dominates any other portfolio on that line and no portfolio on the dotted vertical line ef dominates any other on that line. Thus, by moving along horizontal or vertical lines not a single portfolio can be eliminated from the feasible set; but such limited movements ignore many other comparisons. For example, moving along the arc gf in a clockwise direction means that we pass to higher E, V, and M portfolios. Since this transition takes us from the (E_0, V_-, M_-) point to the (E_+, V_+, M_+) point in a continuous manner, we must pass through a portfolio on this arc with a multiperiod variance equal to V_0 and a (another) portfolio with an M_0 value. If in our passage we reach the M_0 portfolio prior to the V_0 portfolio (as drawn in Fig. 3), then the M_0 portfolio dominates portfolio e, since both have the same M but the former has higher E and lower V than the latter. On the other hand, if the V_0 portfolio appears prior to the M_0 portfolio as we move clockwise along the gf arc, then portfolio e cannot be eliminated. Clearly, what is needed is a general procedure for eliminating inefficient points. To this we now turn.

We begin by studying the feasible set of multiperiod mean-variance, E–V, points for a given value of multiperiod skewness, say $M = M_1$. In particular, we are interested in the slope of the curve (iso-M curve) that describes this set of points in E–V space.

We can write M as a function of E and V by using Eq. (9) and recognizing that in the case of stationarity of single-period probability distributions Eq. (2) gives

$$\sigma^2 = [V + (1 + E)^2]^{1/n} - (1 + E)^{2/n}$$

Then

$$M = (1 + E)[+3[V + (1 + E)^2]^{1/n} - 2(1 + E)^{2/n}]^n$$
$$- 3(1 + E)[V + (1 + E)^2] + 2(1 + E)^3 \tag{13}$$

In other words M can be written as

$$M = f[E(\mu), V(\mu, \sigma^2)] \tag{14}$$

But then

$$dM = (\partial M/\partial E)\, dE + (\partial M/\partial V)\, dV \tag{15}$$

And along any iso-M curve $dM = 0$, so that (15) becomes

$$(\partial M/\partial E)\, dE + (\partial M/\partial V)\, dV = 0 \tag{15a}$$

The iso-M slope is then

$$\frac{dE}{dV} = -\frac{\partial M/\partial V}{\partial M/\partial E} \tag{16}$$

In the original version of this paper, we believed that

$$\frac{\partial M}{\partial E} = \frac{\partial M}{\partial \mu}\frac{\partial \mu}{\partial E} \tag{17a}$$

$$\frac{\partial M}{\partial V} = \frac{\partial M}{\partial \mu}\frac{\partial \mu}{\partial V} + \frac{\partial M}{\partial \sigma^2}\frac{\partial \sigma^2}{\partial V} \tag{17b}$$

but M. Granito and P. Walsh in "Comment on Portfolio Efficiency in Three Moments: The Multiperiod Case" (unpublished manuscript) prove that we were mistaken and that the correct version of these expressions are

$$\frac{\partial M}{\partial E} = \frac{\partial M}{\partial \mu}\frac{\partial \mu}{\partial E} + \frac{\partial M}{\partial \sigma^2}\frac{\partial \sigma^2}{\partial E} \tag{17a'}$$

and

$$\frac{\partial M}{\partial V} = \frac{\partial M}{\partial \sigma^2}\frac{\partial \sigma^2}{\partial V} \tag{17b'}$$

Since from Section II we know that

$$\frac{\partial M}{\partial \mu} > 0, \quad \frac{\partial M}{\partial \sigma^2} > 0$$

and from Tobin [19]

$$\frac{\partial \mu}{\partial E} > 0, \quad \frac{\partial \mu}{\partial V} > 0, \quad \text{and} \quad \frac{\partial \sigma^2}{\partial V} > 0$$

then our Eqs. (17a) and (17b) indicated that $\partial M/\partial V$ and $\partial M/\partial E$ were positive. We thus concluded that the iso-M curves must be negatively sloped. However, when the correct expressions (17a') and (17b') are considered, we can no longer make this claim, for as Granito and Walsh point out: while $\partial M/\partial V$ remains positive and the signs of $\partial M/\partial \mu$, $\partial \mu/\partial E$, $\partial M/\partial \sigma^2$ are as given above, $\partial \sigma^2/\partial E$ is negative, and therefore $\partial M/\partial E$ may be negative. If, in fact, $\partial M/\partial E$ is negative, then the iso-M lines may have positively sloped segments or may be positively sloped everywhere. In the former case, the technique that we shall present can be used to significantly reduce the size of the efficient set. However, in the latter case, all (E, V) points are (E, V, M) efficient; consequently, all (μ, σ) points are (E, V, M) efficient.

In order to investigate whether the iso-M lines are negatively or positively sloped, one must study the formula for $\partial M/\partial E$. Given that

$$\frac{\partial M}{\partial \mu} = n(1 + \mu)^{n-1} \sum_{r=1}^{n} a(r) \left[3 - \frac{2r}{n} \right]$$

$$\frac{\partial \mu}{\partial E} = \frac{1}{n}(1 + \mu)^{1-n}; \quad \frac{\partial M}{\partial \sigma^2} = \frac{(1 + \mu)^n}{\sigma^2} \sum_{r=1}^{n} ra(r)$$

$$\frac{\partial \sigma^2}{\partial E} = \frac{2}{n} \left\{ \frac{(1 + \mu)^n}{[(1 + \mu)^2 + \sigma^2]^{n-1}} - \frac{1}{(1 + \mu)^{n-2}} \right\}$$

then defining,

$$a(r) \equiv \binom{n}{r} [(1 + \mu)^2]^{n-r} (\sigma^2)^r (3^r - 3)$$

we obtain

$$\frac{\partial M}{\partial E} = \sum_{r=1}^{n} a(r) \left[3 - \frac{2r}{n} \right] + \frac{2(1 + \mu)^2}{\sigma^2} \sum_{r=1}^{n} \binom{r}{n} a(r)$$

$$\times \left[\frac{(1 + \mu)^{2n-2}}{[(1 + \mu)^2 + \sigma^2]^{n-1}} - 1 \right]$$

Since all $a(r) \geq 0$ and $r \leq n$, the first term on the right-hand side is positive; on the other hand, the second term is negative. To be able to use the technique that follows for determining the efficient set in (E, V, M), one must have advance knowledge that $\partial M/\partial E$ is positive at all (μ, σ) points. Thus, the above equation must be tested in a manner that will reveal whether this is true for the data describing the feasible (μ, σ) set. One approach would be to develop an algorithm for finding the minimum of the $\partial M/\partial E$ function over the (μ, σ) set. If the minimum value is positive, then we know that all $\partial M/\partial E$ values are positive and the iso-M curves have negative slope in E–V space. A curve that has this characteristic is depicted in Fig. 4

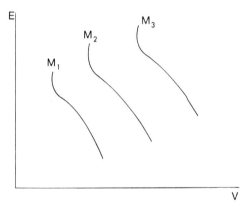

Fig. 4. Iso-M curves.

and labeled M_1. For another choice of M, say $M = M_2 > M_1$, we obtain another iso-M curve that must be to the right of the M_1 curve, since for given E (which implies given μ) to achieve higher M we need higher σ^2, but this means that we end up with higher V.

Now consider any iso-M curve. The extreme northern point on that curve dominates all others because it has higher E and lower V than any other point on that iso-M curve. A similar conclusion applies for every other iso-M curve, since they all have negative slope. Therefore, a procedure for isolating the efficient points in E–V–M space is to fix M at some value[5] and maximize $(1 + E)$. Formally,

$$\max(1 + E) \tag{18a}$$

subject to

$$M = \text{constant} \tag{18b}$$

---

[5] One must of course check to see that the chosen M value corresponds to a feasible (μ, σ^2) point in the one-period set.

This yields the best point on an iso-M line.[6] Repeat the procedure for different values of M to get the locus of all such points.[7] For the iso-M curves of Fig. 4, a locus of such points, rs, is drawn in Fig. 5.

Are we done? That is, will this procedure eliminate all inefficient points? If the locus of points generated looks like rs, or $r's'$, i.e., E is a single-valued function of V, then we are left with only efficient points and we are done. But if the locus looks like tux, where E is not a single-valued function of V (see Fig. 5), then there are still points that remain to be eliminated, namely, all points between t and u.

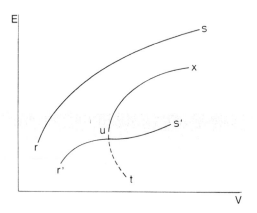

Fig. 5. Loci of best points.

Exactly how can we numerically generate this set of points in the $E-V$ plane? An answer, generously provided to us by Harry Markowitz, follows. Consider the set of attainable (E, V) combinations as pictured in Fig. 6. According to the prior results of this paper, this set may be divided into negatively sloped iso-M lines as illustrated in Fig. 6. Clearly all portfolios

---

[6] The best point on the iso-M curve will correspond to a unique (μ, σ^2) point since there is one-to-one correspondence between (E, V) and (μ, σ^2) points. Fix E, and μ is determined. Now V can be written as

$$V = \sum_{r=1}^{n} \binom{n}{r} [(1 + \mu)^2]^{n-r} (\sigma^2)^r$$

Since V is fixed and so is μ (by virtue of fixing E), the above equation becomes a polynomial in σ^2 with all positive coefficients; thus it has only one positive real σ^2 root.

[7] The precise statistical definition of a distribution's skewness, γ, is $\gamma \equiv M/V^{3/2}$. The distribution's γ is preferred as a measure of the distribution's "shape," since it is not altered by a change of scale, whereas the third moment is altered by such a change. However, the reader should note that portfolios which are (E, V, M) efficient include the portfolios which are (E, V, γ) efficient, since with $E = E_0$ and $V = V_0$, maximizing γ is equivalent to maximize M.

along the *ab* arc are efficient, since each portfolio on that arc represents the extreme northern point of an iso-*M* line in the feasible set. Furthermore, a point such as *d* (where the slope of the *abc* arc is negative) is inefficient in (*E*, *V*, *M*), since *d* is dominated by point *e*, for *e* represents a portfolio with the same *V* but higher *E* and higher *M*; however, *e* has already been proven

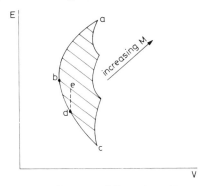

Fig. 6. The efficient portfolio set in *E*–*V* space.

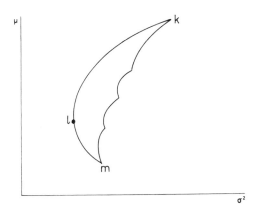

Fig. 7. Feasible one-period portfolio set.

to be inferior to *b*. Thus any point on the *bc* arc can be shown to be dominated by a point on the *ab* arc. Consequently, the *ab* arc, *which represents the set of efficient* (*E*, *V*) *portfolios*, contains the set of efficient (*E*, *V*, *M*) portfolios.

Now to find the set of efficient (*E*, *V*) portfolios. Given our stationarity assumption of the single period return distribution, Eqs. (1) and (2) imply that to minimize *n*-period *V* for given *n*-period *E*, we must minimize one-period σ^2 for given one-period μ. Therefore, we must be somewhere on the *klm* arc of Fig. 7. The Markowitz Critical Line Algorithm may be used to find the set of portfolios which give all (μ, σ^2) combinations on the *klm* arc, and the corresponding *E*, *V*, and *M* values for each of these portfolios are easily calculated and plotted. The portion of the plotted (E, V) curve that is not (E, V, M) efficient (cf. the *tux* curve in Fig. 5) can be discarded. The remainder of the curve and its corresponding portfolios represent the (E, V, M) efficient set.

References

 1. Arditti, F., " Risk and the Required Return on Equity," *Journal of Finance* (March 1967), 19–36.
 2. Arditti, F., "Another Look at Mutual Fund Performance," *Journal of Financial and Quantitative Analysis* (June 1971), 1–4.
 3. Blume, M., " Portfolio Theory: A Step Toward Its Practical Application," *Journal of Business* (April 1970), 152–173.
 4. Fama, E., " Risk, Return, and Equilibrium: Some Clarifying Comments," *Journal of Finance* (March 1968), 29–40.
 5. Fama, E., " Efficient Capital Markets: A Review of Theory and Empirical Work," *Journal of Finance* (May 1970), 383–417.
 6. Fogler, H. R., and Radcliffe, R. "A Note on Measurement of Skewness," *Journal of Financial and Quantitative Analysis* (June, 1974), 485–489.
 7. Friedman, M., and Savage, L., " The Utility Analysis of Choices Involving Risk," *Journal of Political Economy* (August 1948), 279–304.
 8. Friend, I., and Blume, M., " Measurement of Portfolio Performance under Uncertainty," *American Economic Review* (September 1970), 561–575.
 9. Hanoch, G., and Levy, H., " The Efficiency Analysis of Choices Involving Risk," *Review of Economic Studies* (July 1969), 335–345.
10. Kaplansky, I., "A Common Error Concerning Kurtosis," *American Statistical Association Journal* (June 1945), 259.
11. Levy, H., and Sarnat, M., *Investment and Portfolio Analysis*. New York: Wiley, 1972.
12. Lintner, J., " The Valuation of Risk Assets and the Selection of Risky Investments in Stock Portfolios and Capital Budgets," *Review of Economics and Statistics* (February 1965), 13–31.
13. Linter, J., " Security Prices, Risk, and Maximal Gains From Diversification," *Journal of Finance* (December 1965), 587–616.
14. Markowitz, H., *Portfolio Selection: Efficient Diversification of Investments*. New York: Wiley, 1959.
15. Miller, M., and Scholes, M., " Rates of Return in Relation to Risk: A Re-examination of Some Recent Findings," *Studies in the Theory of Capital Markets*, (C. Jensen, ed.). New York: Praeger, 1972.
16. Mossin, J., "Equilibrium in A Capital Asset Market," *Econometrica* (October 1966), 768–783.
17. Sharpe, W., "Capital Asset Prices: A Theory of Market Equilibrium Under Conditions of Risk," *Journal of Finance* (September 1964), 425–442.
18. Stevens, G., "On Tobin's Multiperiod Portfolio Theorem," *Review of Economic Studies* (October 1972), 461–468.
19. Tobin, J., "Liquidity Preference as Behaviour Towards Risk," *Review of Economic Studies* (February 1958), 65–86.
20. Tobin, J., " The Theory of Portfolio Selection," in *The Theory of Interest Rates* (F. H. Hahn and F. P. R. Brechling, eds.). New York: Macmillan, 1965.

EQUIVALENCE AMONG ALTERNATIVE PORTFOLIO SELECTION CRITERIA

D. Kira and W. T. Ziemba

The University of British Columbia

I. Introduction

In decision making under uncertainty, one is interested in selecting the best combination of alternatives. The set of indifferent alternatives or efficient set depends upon the given selection criteria. In choosing among alternatives, one is concerned with the risk and return of given alternatives. Portfolio analysts have suggested various criteria to quantify the return and the risk explicitly. Returns are generally measured in expected returns. However, there is no such general agreement on the risk measure, and authors have suggested numerous alternatives.

In Markowitz's mean-variance rule [28] the risk is measured in terms of the variance. Baumol [3] extends the mean-variance criteria to the mean-lower confidence rule, where the difference between the mean and a constant multiple of the standard deviation is considered as a risk measure. The use of the semivariance as a risk measure is explored and developed by Mao [27] and Hogan–Warren [18].

This research was partially supported by the National Research Council of Canada under grant 67-7147.

Assuming that the investor is principally concerned with avoiding possible disaster, Roy [37] suggests that the risk should be measured by the probability of occurrence of such a disaster. The mean-entropy rule was recently proposed by Philippatos and Wilson [33], where higher entropy implies higher risk.

From the expected-utility theoretic point of view, the most general concept is the stochastic dominance criteria. Alternative A is said to dominate stochastically alternative B if the expected utility of A is not exceeded by the expected utility of B for all possible utility functions within a specified class. If the inequality is replaced by the strict inequality, then the dominance is strict.

Conditions are known that imply equality of the efficient sets corresponding to different criteria. Philippatos and Gressis [32] show that the mean-variance, the second-degree dominance, and the mean-entropy efficient sets are equal when the random variables have uniform or normal distributions. If the random variables are restricted to distributions having two parameters that are independent increasing functions of mean and variance, then Hanoch–Levy [16] show that the SSD efficient set is equivalent to the mean-variance efficient set. The equivalence between the mean-semivariance and the stochastic dominance criteria has been investigated by Porter [34] and Jean [20]. Porter shows that the second-degree dominance implies semivariance preference under reasonably general conditions. Jean shows that under certain extremely restrictive conditions,[1] third-degree dominance implies mean-semivariance preference. The definitions of these criteria are given in the next section. A general theorem which demonstrates the equivalence of the various efficient sets is given under the assumptions that the distribution functions of the random variables cross precisely once and are members of two independent parameter family with the scale parameter as an increasing monotone function of the variance.

II. Mathematical Definitions and Comprehensive Theorem

Let X and Y be random variables with right continuous cumulative distribution functions F and G having finite means μ_F, μ_G and finite nonzero variances σ_F^2 and σ_G^2, respectively. Then the following definitions can be stated.

---

[1] Let $F_1(x) = \int_a^x F(t)\,dt$, $G_1(x) = \int_a^x G(t)\,dt$, $F_k(x) = \int_a^x F_{k-1}(t)\,dt$, and $G_k(x) = \int_a^x G_{k-1}(t)\,dt$ for $k = 2, 3, \ldots$; then $F_1(b) = G_1(b)$, $F_2(\mu_F) = G_2(\mu_G)$, $F_2(x) < G_2(x)$ for some $x \neq \mu_F, \mu_G$, $F_2(x) = G_2(x)$ for all other x implies F is preferred to G in mean-semivariance.

Mean-Variance $(E - \sigma^2)$ X is preferred to Y in $(E - \sigma^2)$ iff

(i) $\mu_F \geq \mu_G$, and
(ii) $\sigma_F^2 \leq \sigma_G^2$

with strict inequality holding for at least one inequality. As a selection rule, this criterion has serious drawbacks [4, 10, 13, 16, 32, 36, 40]. In practice, however, it is a very popular and useful rule because of its simplicity.

Mean-Lower Confidence $(E - L)$ Baumol [3] introduced this rule in order to eliminate some shortcomings in the $E - \sigma^2$ rule. Let $L_F = \mu_F - \alpha\sigma_F$ and $L_G = \mu_G - \alpha\sigma_G$, where $\alpha > 0$ is a given constant. Then X is said to be preferred to Y in $E - L$ iff

(i) $\mu_F \geq \mu_G$
(ii) $L_F \geq L_G$

with strict inequality holding for at least one inequality.

Moeseke [29] independently proposed this criterion and called it the truncated minimax criterion. For a recent statement of theory of this method and an algorithm for calculating the efficient frontier, see Moeseke [30]. A more efficient algorithm appears in Hohenbalken [19]. Hanoch and Levy [16] give a critique of this rule based on the fact that available information for the choice of an optimal α is not utilized. In addition, $E - L$ is not entirely an efficient criterion, since it depends on individual tastes through the choice of α.

Mean-Semivariance $[E - SV(h)]$ Let $SV_F(h) \equiv \int_{-\infty}^{h} (x - h)^2 \, dF(x)$ and $SV_G(h) \equiv \int_{-\infty}^{h} (X - h)^2 \, dG(x)$ be the semivariance of F and G. Then X is preferred to Y in $E - SV(h)$ iff

(i) $\mu_F \geq \mu_G$,
(ii) $SV_F(h) \leq SV_G(h)$,

where one inequality is strict.

Markowitz [28] considered the semivariance as a risk measure, but because of computational difficulties he rejected it as a risk measure. Mao [27] applied this rule to a capital budgeting problem. An efficient algorithm to compute the efficient frontier in mean semivariance space appears in Hogan–Warren [18].

Mean-Aspiration $[E - F(s)]$ Let s be the individual's aspiration or target level. Then X is said to be preferred to Y in $E - F(s)$ iff

(i) $\mu_F \geq \mu_G$,
(ii) $F(s) \leq G(s)$,

where one inequality is strict.

This criterion is similar in spirit to the chance constrained rules, where

(1) X is preferred to Y iff $F(s) < G(s)$,
(2) X is preferred to Y iff $s_F > s_G$ (s_K denotes the aspiration level associated with distribution function K) and $F(s_F)$, $G(s_G) \leq \alpha$, where α is an acceptable probability level, or
(3) X is preferred to Y iff $\mu_F > \mu_G$ and $F(s)$, $G(s) \leq \alpha$.

Pyle and Turnovsky [35], Roy [37], Levy and Sarnat [25], and Telser [44] relate (1), (2), and (3) to the mean-variance rule.

If X and Y are normally distributed, then deterministic nonlinear models are equivalent to these models. (See, e.g., [48, pp. 358–360].) Several efficient algorithms are available to compute the efficient set. (See, e.g., Geoffrion [12], Sengupta and Portillo-Campbell[2] [43], Sengupta [42], and Kataoka [21].)

Mean-Entropy $(E - H)$ Let $H_F \equiv -\int_{-\infty}^{\infty} \ln[f(x)]\, dF(x)$ and $H_G \equiv -\int_{-\infty}^{\infty} \ln[g(x)]\, dG(x)$ be the entropies of X and Y, respectively. Then X is preferred to Y in $E - H$ iff

(i) $\mu_F \geq \mu_G$,
(ii) $H_F \leq H_G$,

with strict inequality holding for at least one inequality.

In general, H is large whenever the distributions are nearly completely random, i.e., distributions are uniform or with the equal mass. This rule was proposed by Philippatos and Wilson [33].

Stochastic Dominance   This concept has been studied by Quirk and Saposnik [36], Fishburn [11], Hammond [14], Hanoch and Levy [16], Hadar and Russell [13], Rothschild and Stiglitz [38], Whitmore [46], Vickson [45], and others. Stochastic dominance rules order uncertain prospects in a manner consistent with expected utility theory. We assume throughout that expected utility is finite. Let

$$F_1(x) = \int_{-\infty}^{x} F(t)\, dt, \qquad G_1(x) = \int_{-\infty}^{x} G(t)\, dt$$

$$F_2(x) = \int_{-\infty}^{x} \int_{-\infty}^{y} F(t)\, dt\, dy, \qquad G_2(x) = \int_{-\infty}^{x} \int_{-\infty}^{y} G(t)\, dt\, dy$$

---

[2] Sengupta and Portillo-Campbell claim that the fractile model gives a less risky solution than the mean-variance model. This, however, is criticized by Hazell [12]. The criticism is essentially based on the fact that for $\alpha > .5$, the fractile programming model is closely related to Baumol's $E - L$ model. The difficulty in S-P's statement is that the choice of α-level in the fractile programming implicitly defines the individual's preference toward the risk and the trade-off curve between α, and the target level s is not defined explicitly.

then X is said to dominate Y in

(a) (FSD) iff $F(x) \le G(x)$ for all $x \in R$ and $F(x_0) < G(x_0)$ for some $x_0 \in R$,

(b) (SSD) iff $F_1(x) \le G_1(x)$ for all $x \in R$ and $F_1(x_0) < G_1(x_0)$ for some $x_0 \in R$, and

(c) (TSD) iff $F_2(x) \le G_2(x)$ for all $x \in R$ and $\mu_F \ge \mu_G$ with strict inequality holding for at least one inequality.

Thus FSD, SSD, and TSD indicate that $E_F u \ge E_G u$ for all u (and $>$ for some u) that are nondecreasing, nondecreasing and concave, and nondecreasing, concave with nonnegative third derivative, respectively.

Theorems which relate the above rules to expected utility theory can be found in the papers quoted above. Necessary and sufficient conditions for the class of decreasing absolute risk-aversion utility function can be found in Vickson [45]. An extension to nth-order stochastic dominance appears in Ziemba and Vickson [48]. Ali [1] and Bawa [4] provide simple stochastic dominance rules in terms of specific parameters of the distributions for a number of common distributions such as the β, γ, t, and the location-scale families of distributions for various utility function classes. A different type of generalization is considered by Diamond and Stiglitz [6], in which Rothschild and Stiglitz's work in mean preserving risk spreading is extended to expected utility preserving risk. Examples of this type of risk are considered by Diamond and Yaari [7].

Theorem 1 Let X and Y be random variables with distributions F and G, respectively. Suppose

(1) F intersects G only at y_0,[3]

(2) F and G belong to the same family of distributions, with two parameters that are independent increasing functions of mean and variance, and

(3) the aspiration and semivariance levels s and h are less than y_0.

Then the arrangement shown in Fig. 1 results, where the solid arrows denote general implications and the dashed ones the uniform and normal cases.

Proof (1) see Hanoch and Levy [16].

(2) Let F SSD G, then $G_1(x) - F_1(x) \ge 0$ for all $x \in R$. Hence by integration by parts $SV_F(h) - SV_G(h) = -2 \int_{-\infty}^{h} [G_1(x) - F_1(x)] \, dx \le 0$, i.e., $SV_F(h) \le SV_G(h)$. Thus X dominates Y in $E - SV(h)$. Now suppose X dominates Y in $E - SV(h)$, then $\int_{-\infty}^{h} [G_1(x) - F_1(x)] \, dx \ge 0$ and $\int_{-\infty}^{\infty} [G(t) - F(t)] \, dt \ge 0$. Let $H(t) = G(t) - F(t)$. There are two possibilities: either

---

[3] A table for single crossing distributions can be found in Hammond [14].

$H(t) > 0$ and changes to $H(t) < 0$ or $H(t) < 0$ and changes to $H(t) > 0$. It is impossible for $H(t)$'s initial sign to be negative and $\int_{-\infty}^{h} \int_{-\infty}^{x} H(t) \, dt \, dx \geq 0$, since $h < y_0$. If $H(t)$'s initial sign is positive, then $\int_{-\infty}^{x} H(t) \, dt \geq 0$ for all $x \in R$, since $\int_{-\infty}^{\infty} H(t) \, dt \geq 0$ and only one sign change is possible for $\int_{-\infty}^{x} H(t) \, dt$.

(3) Follows from (1) and (2).

(4) Suppose X SSD Y; then $\mu_F \geq \mu_G$ and $F(x) \leq G(x)$ for all $x \leq y_0$. Thus $F(s) < G(s)$, since $s < y_0$. If $\mu_F \geq \mu_G$ and $F(s) \leq G(s)$, then F (SSD) G. This follows from Hanoch and Levy [16; Theorem 3].

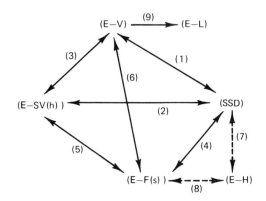

Fig. 1.

(5) Follows from (2) and (4).
(6) Follows from (1) and (4).
(7) See Philippatos and Gressis [32].
(8) Follows from (4) and (7).
(9) Since $L_F - L_G = (\mu_F - \alpha\sigma_F) - (\mu_F - \alpha\sigma_G) = (\mu_F - \mu_G) + \alpha(\sigma_G - \sigma_F)$.

Let the sets of efficient portfolios under $E - V$, $E - L$, SSD, $E - F(s)$, $E - SV(h)$, and $E - H$ be $e(E - V)$, $e(E - L)$, $e(\text{SSD})$, $e[E - F(s)]$, $e[E - SV(h)]$ and $e(E - H)$, respectively, then

$$e(\text{SSD}) = e(E - V) = e[E - F(s)] = e[E - SV(h)] \subset e(E - L)$$

$$e(\text{SSD}) = e(E - H) = e[E - F(s)]$$

Atkinson [2] gives an interesting characterization of the SSD rule in terms of the Lorenz curve. It is shown that if the distribution means are equal, then the SSD criterion is equivalent to the nonintersection property of the Lorenz curve. Rothschild and Stiglitz [39] extend this and show that three partial orderings of income distributions are equivalent.

III. Comments and Additional Results

The mean-variance criterion is consistent with expected utility theory if the random variables are Gaussian. Hanoch and Levy show that the $E - V$ rule is equivalent to the SSD rule, for convergent utilities, if X and Y are members of a two-parameter family, where the two parameters are independent increasing functions of mean and variance.

For a distribution with two dependent parameters, Philippatos and Gressis [32] claim that "in the case of the uniform distribution parameters a and b, their space of positive probabilities is not a product space and, therefore, a and b are dependent. Thus, we have shown that the equivalence holds for the uniform distribution where the two parameters are dependent." However, in general, two parameters considered in statistics are the location $(a + b)/2$ and the scale $b\text{-}a$ parameters rather than a and b [22]. These parameters are independent. To clarify this, we restate the following result, which is the first implication in Theorem 1.

Theorem 2 Let $F(x)$ and $G(y)$ be two distributions with finite means μ_F and μ_G and scale parameters $0 < s_F < \infty$ and $0 < s_G < \infty$, respectively, such that $F(x) = G(y)$ for all x and y satisfying $(x - \mu_F)/s_F = (y - \mu_G)/s_G$. Let $\mu_F \geq \mu_G$ and $F(x_1) < G(x_1)$ for some $x_1 \in R$. Then X SSD Y if and only if $s_F \leq s_G$.

If the scale parameters are related to the variances by a monotone transformation, then the ordering is preserved with respect to the variance.

Thus, if X and Y are uniformly distributed with parameters $((a_F + b_F)/2, b_F - a_F)$ and $((a_G + b_G)/2, b_G - a_G)$, then $(a_F + b_F)/2 \geq (a_G + b_G)/2$ and $b_F - a_F \leq b_G - a_G$ iff X SSD Y is equivalent to $\mu_F \geq \mu_G$ and $\sigma_F^2 \leq \sigma_G^2$ iff X (SSD) Y, since $\mu = (a + b)/2$, $\sigma^2 = (b - a)^2/12 = [(b - a)/12]s$ for any uniform distribution.

In studies of the diversification analysis, rates of returns on common stocks are often assumed to be normally distributed. Recent empirical studies, however, have shown that the returns are often better described by lognormal (see Lintner [26] and references therein) or stable distributions [8, 9].

Let X and Y be lognormal; then Philippatos and Gressis [32] show correctly that $X(E - V)Y$ implies X SSD Y, but their proof of $X(\text{SSD})Y$ not implying $X(E - V)Y$ has an error. This follows from their fallacious claim that $E(\ln X) \geq E(\ln Y)$ and $V(\ln X) \leq V(\ln Y)$ implies X SSD Y. Correct results of this nature appear in Levy [24]. Ohlson [31] gives an asymptotic justification of the mean-variance rule for lognormal variates. This result is important since Samuelson's [41] "compactness" result does not hold for lognormal distributions.

If X and Y have symmetric stable distributions with $|\mu_k| < \infty$,

$0 < s_k < \infty$, common characteristic exponent α, $1 < \alpha \leq 2$, $\mu_F \geq \mu_G$, and $F(x) < G(x)$ for some $x \in R$, then Ziemba [47] shows that $E_F u \geq E_G u$ for all convergent concave nondecreasing u if and only if $s_1^{1/\alpha} \leq s_2^{1/\alpha}$. This result is used to derive the efficient frontier in mean-α dispersion space, a generalization of Tobin's separation theorem, and an algorithm for computing approximately optimal portfolio allocations.

Let $F(\mu, s, \beta, \alpha)$ be a cumulative distribution of a stable random variable, where parameters μ, s, β, and α are location, scale, skewness, and characteristic exponent, respectively. Then the following additional result can be obtained.

Theorem 3   Suppose $F(x) \sim F(0, 1, 0, \alpha_F)$ and $G(x) \sim G(0, 1, 0, \alpha_G)$. Then $E_F u \geq E_G u$ for all convergent concave nondecreasing differentiable utility functions if and only if $\alpha_F \geq \alpha_G$.

Proof:

$$\Delta u = E_F u - E_G u = \int_{-\infty}^{\infty} u(x) \, d(F - G) = -\int_{-\infty}^{\infty} (F - G) u'(x) \, dx$$

$$= \int_{-\infty}^{\infty} (G - F) u'(x) \, dx = \int_{-\infty}^{0} (G - F) u'(x) \, dx + \int_{0}^{\infty} (G - F) u'(x) \, dx$$

Suppose $\Delta u \geq 0$ and $\alpha_F < \alpha_G$; then $F(x) > G(x)$ on $(-\infty, 0)$. Then, from symmetry, $(\beta = 0)$, $G(x) \geq F(x)$ on $(0, \infty)$. Thus $\int_{-\infty}^{0} (G - F) u'(x) \, dx < 0$ and $\int_{0}^{\infty} (G - F) u'(x) \, dx > 0$. But then $\Delta u < 0$, since $u'(x)$ decreasing implies $\left| \int_{-\infty}^{0} (G - F) u'(x) \, dx \right| > \int_{0}^{\infty} (G - F) u'(x) \, dx$, a contradiction. Therefore $\alpha_F \geq \alpha_G$ is a necessary condition. If $\alpha_F \geq \alpha_G$, then we have the opposite situation, thus $\Delta u \geq 0$.

This result is similar to that of La Cava [23]. La Cava gives a necessary and sufficient condition for FSD and SSD in terms of the location and the scale parameters. He also shows that in order to relate the SSD rule to the scale parameter, it is necessary to assume that the distributions are symmetric.

Since any symmetric stable distribution can be written as a linear transformation of the standard symmetric stable distribution, $F(0, 1, 0, \alpha)$, it is of interest to find conditions on a and b such that the following proposition holds.

Let X and Y be the random variables such that X SSD Y, then $a_F + b_F X$ (SSD) $a_G + b_G Y$.

Clearly, we need to show

$$\int_{-\infty}^{(t - a_F)/b_F} F(y) \, dy \leq \int_{-\infty}^{(t - a_G)/b_G} \frac{b_G}{b_F} G(y) \, dy, \quad t \in R \text{ for some subset of } a\text{-}b \text{ space}$$

Jean [14] attempts to show the following TSD and $E - SV(h)$ relation.

If $F_1(b) < G_1(b)$, $R = [a, b]$, $F_2(x) = G_2(x)$ for all $x \in R$, then $\mu_F > \mu_G$ and $SV(\mu_F) \le SV(\mu_G)$.

However, the above result *cannot* hold, since $2F_2(\mu_F) = SV(\mu_F)$, $2G_2(\mu_G) = SV(\mu_G)$ and, for some F and G, $F_2(\mu_F) > F_2(\mu_G) = G_2(\mu_G)$. Thus $SV(\mu_F) > SV(\mu_G)$. The above problem stems from the fact that the distributions X and Y do not have a common h point. If X and Y have a single intersection property, then the SSD efficient set is equal to the TSD efficient set. Hence $e(\text{TSD}) = e[E - SV(h)]$ from Theorem 1.

References

1. Ali, M. M., " Stochastic Dominance and Portfolio Analysis," *Journal of Financial Economics* **2** (1975), 205–229.
2. Atkinson, A. B., " On the Measurement of Inequality," *Journal of Economic Theory* **2** (1970), 244–263.
3. Baumol, W. J.. "An Expected Gain-Confidence Limit Criterion for Portfolio Selection," *Management Science* **10** (1963), 174–181.
4. Bawa, V. S., "Optimal Rules for Ordering Uncertain Prospects," *Journal of Financial Economics* **2** (1975), 95–121.
5. Borch, K., "A Note on Uncertainty and Indifference Curves," *Review of Economic Studies* **36** (1969), 1–4.
6. Diamond, P. A., and Stiglitz, J. E., "Increasing Risk and Risk Aversion," *Journal of Economic Theory* **8** (1974), 337–360.
7. Diamond, P. A., and Yaari, M., "Implications of the Theory of Rationing for Consumer Choice under Uncertainty," *American Economic Review* **62** (1972), 333–343.
8. Fama, E., "Portfolio Analysis in a Stable Paretian Market," *Management Science* **11** (1965), 404–419.
9. Fama, E., "The Behavior of Stock Market Price," *Journal of Business* **38** (1965), 34–105.
10. Feldstein, M. S., "Mean Variance Analysis in the Theory of Liquidity Preference and Portfolio Selection," *Review of Economic Studies* **47** (1969), 5–12.
11. Fishburn, P., *Decision and Value Theory*. New York: Wiley, 1964.
12. Geofferion, A. M., "Stochastic Programming with Aspiration or Fractile Criteria," *Management Science* **13** (1967), 672–679.
13. Hadar, J., and Russell, W. R., " Rules for Ordering Uncertain Prospects," *American Economic Review* **59** (1969), 25–34.
14. Hammond, J. S., "Simplifying the Choice Between Uncertain Prospects where Preference is Nonlinear," *Management Science* **20** (1974), 1047–1072.
15. Hanoch, G., and Levy, H., " Efficient Portfolio Selection with Quadratic and Cubic Utility," *Journal of Business* **43** (1971), 181–189.
16. Hanoch, G., and Levy, H., " The Efficiency Analysis of Choices Involving Risk," *Review of Economic Studies* **36** (1969), 335–346.
17. Hazell, P., " Comment of the Fractile Approach to Linear Programming Under Risk," *Management Science* **18** (1970), 236–237.
18. Hogan, W., and Warren, J., " Computation of the Efficient Boundary in the E-S Portfolio Selection Model," *Journal of Financial and Quantitative Analysis* **7** (1972), 1881–1896.
19. Hohenbalken, V. B., "A Finite Algorithm for Maximizing Certain Pseudo-Concave Functions on Polytopes," *Mathematical Programming* **9** (1975), 189–206.
20. Jean, W. H., "Comparison of Moment and Stochastic Dominance Ranking Methods," *Journal of Financial and Quantitative Analysis* **10** (1975), 151–161.

21. Kataoka, S., "A Stochastic Programming Model," *Econometrica* **31** (1963), 181–196.
22. Kendall, M. G., and Stuart, A., *The Advanced Theory of Statistics.* London: Griffin, 1969.
23. La Cava, C. J., "Improving the Mean-Variance Criterion Using Stochastic Dominance," Georgia State University, 1971.
24. Levy, H., "Stochastic Dominance Among Lognormal Prospects," *International Economic Review* **14** (1973), 601–614.
25. Levy, H., and Sarnat, M., "Safety First—An Expected Utility Principle," *Journal of Financial and Quantitative Analysis* **7** (1972), 1829–1834.
26. Lintner, J., "Equilibrium in a Random Walk and Lognormal Securities Market," Discussion Paper Number 235, Harvard Institute of Economic Research, Cambridge, Massachusetts (July 1972).
27. Mao, J. C. T., "Models of Capital Budgeting, $E - V$ vs $E - S$," *Journal of Financial and Quantitative Analysis* **4** (1970), 657–675.
28. Markowitz, H., *Portfolio Selection: Efficient Diversification of Investments.* New York: Wiley, 1959.
29. Moeseke, P. V., "Minimax-Maximax Solution to Linear Programming Under Risk," *Econometrica* **31**, (1963), 749–750.
30. Moeseke, P. V., and Hohenbalken, V. B., "Efficient and Optimal Portfolios by Homogeneous Programming," *Zeitschrift fur Operations Research* **18** (1974), 205–214.
31. Ohlson, J. A., "The Asymptotic Validity of Quadratic Utility as the Period-Spacing Approaches Zero," *Stochastic Optimization Models in Finance* (W. T. Ziemba and R. G. Vickson, eds.), pp. 221–234. NewYork: Academic Press, 1975.
32. Philippatos, G. C., and Gressis, N., "Conditions of Equivalence Among $E - V$, SSD and $E - H$ Portfolio Selection Criteria: The Case for Uniform, Normal and·Lognormal Distributions," *Management Science* **21** (1975), 617–625.
33. Philippatos, G. C., and Wilson, C. J., "Entropy, Market Risk, and the Selection of Efficiency Portfolios," *Applied Economics* **4** (1972), 209–220.
34. Porter, R. B., "Semivariance and Stochastic Dominance: A Comparison," *American Economic Review* **64** (1974), 200–204.
35. Pyle, D. H., and Turnovsky, S. J., "Safety-first and Expected Utility Maximization in Mean-Standard Deviation Portfolio Analysis," *Review of Economics and Statistics,* **52** (1970), 75–81.
36. Quirk, J. P., and Saposnik, R., "Admissibility and Measurable Utility Functions," *Review of Economic Studies* **29** (1962), 140–146.
37. Roy, A. D., "Safety-First and the Holding of Assets," *Econometrica* **20** (1952), 431–449.
38. Rothschild, M., and Stiglitz, J. E., "Increasing Risk: I, A Definition," *Journal of Economic Theory* **2** (1970), 225–243.
39. Rothschild, M., and Stiglitz, J. E., "Some Further Results on the Measurement of Inequality," *Journal of Economic Theory* **6** (1973), 188–204.
40. Samuelson, P. A., "General Proof that Diversification Pays," *Journal of Financial and Quantitative Analysis* **2** (1967), 1–13.
41. Samuelson, P. A., "The Fundamental Approximation Theorem of Portfolio Analysis in Terms of Mean, Variance, and Higher Moments," *Review of Economic Studies* **37** (1970), 537–542.
42. Sengupta, J. K., "A System Reliability Approach to Linear Programming," *Unternehmensforschung* **15** (1971), 112–130.
43. Sengupta, J. K., and Portillo-Campbell, J. H., "A Fractile Approach to Linear Programming Under Risk," *Management Science* **16** (1970), 298–308.
44. Telser, L. G., "Safety First and Hedging," *Review of Economic Studies* **23** (1955–56), 1–16.
45. Vickson, R. G., "Stochastic Dominance Tests for Decreasing Absolute Risk-Aversion:

General Random Variables," *Management Science* **23** (1977), 478–489.

46. Whitmore, G. A., "Third-Degree Stochastic Dominance," *American Economic Review* **60** (1970), 457–459.
47. Ziemba, W. T., "Choosing Investment Portfolios When The Returns Have Stable Distributions," *Mathematical Programming in Theory and Practice* (P. L. Hammer and G. Zoutendijk, eds.), pp. 443–482. Amsterdam: North-Holland Publishing Company, 1975.
48. Ziemba, W. T., and Vickson, R. G. (eds.), *Stochastic Optimization Models in Finance*. New York: Academic Press, 1975.

Part IV

INFLATION AND FINANCIAL DECISIONS

THE SUPERFUND: EFFICIENT PATHS TOWARD EFFICIENT CAPITAL MARKETS IN LARGE AND SMALL COUNTRIES

Nils H. Hakansson

University of California, Berkeley

I. Introduction and Summary

A financial market is complete when investors can, in effect, trade in Arrow–Debreu [1, 5] certificates; this would be the case when the number of linearly independent real-world securities is the same as the number of visualized states of the world and short sales are unrestricted. But the benefits of a complete market can also, under specialized conditions, be attained by trade in as few as a single instrument (issued by a mutual fund holding all "regular" securities). The case when two instruments, one riskless and one risky, are sufficient to achieve the benefits of a complete market has received particular attention in the literature; essentially, it holds under any one of the following conditions:

This research was supported by Grant No. GS-35700 from the National Science Foundation. The author would like to thank Michael Jensen, Hayne Leland, Michael Rothschild, Mark Rubinstein, William Sharpe, and Joseph Stiglitz for helpful comments on an earlier draft. He also benefited from stimulating discussions with the participants at the Conference on Decision-Making Under Uncertainty, Ein Bokek, Israel, March 9–14, 1975, where the paper was presented.

   (i) homogeneous probability beliefs and utility belonging to the HARA-class,[1] with the exponent the same for all investors (unless utility is negative exponential);

   (ii) homogeneous beliefs, normally distributed returns, and utility functions (at a minimum) defined on the whole line; or

   (iii) homogeneous probability beliefs, continuous-time decision making by investors, and a stochastic process of the Itô variety.

The reason is that in these cases all investors mix risky assets the same way.[2] Extensions incorporating two or more riskless assets of differing maturities have recently been made by Merton [17] and by Rubinstein [21].

   The real world apparently lies somewhere between the highly restrictive conditions (i)–(iii) and a market which is sufficiently rich to be " complete " in the presence of significant diversity. But when investor preferences and beliefs exhibit substantial heterogeneity, incomplete markets are distinctly inferior, in a welfare sense, to " more complete" markets (Hakansson [10]). Thus, the strongest argument in favor of a complete financial market rests on the unique ability of such a market to achieve a Pareto-efficient allocation of resources among investors under heterogeneous preferences and beliefs. Despite this decided virtue, there are at least four important reasons why complete markets have not come into existence, giving rise to the view that the Arrow–Debreu model is ". . . in the nature of a magnificent *tour de force*, enriching our insight, but with a somewhat strained relation to reality" (Koopmans [14, p. 327]). The first obstacle is the difficulty of reaching agreement (a priori) on a set of acceptable time-states. The second problem has to do with the subsequent determination of which state actually occurred, by no means a trivial task. The third obstacle haunting any implementation of a complete market has aptly been dubbed "the moral hazard": the temptation, not unknown in the insurance industry, to bring about by illicit means a particularly fortuitous state. The final major problem has to do with the enormity of the number of states, and consequently the number of securities, that, by most calculations, must be available for such a market to function properly.

   This paper examines the implications surrounding the establishment of a new type of financial intermediary, which, for want of a better name, will be

---

   [1] The HARA-class (hyperbolic absolute risk aversion) consists of the following utility functions of wealth with the properties $u'(w) > 0$, $u''(w) < 0$ (the first over at least a finite range of positive wealth):

$$u(w) = \begin{cases} (1/\gamma)(w + a)^{\gamma}, & \gamma < 1 & \text{(decreasing absolute risk aversion)} \\ -\exp(\gamma w), & \gamma < 0 & \text{(constant absolute risk aversion)} \\ -(a - w)^{\gamma}, & \gamma > 1, a \text{ large} & \text{(increasing absolute risk aversion).} \end{cases}$$

   [2] See, e.g., Cass and Stiglitz [4] and Merton [16].

called the "superfund." In essence, the superfund owns a portion of the "market portfolio" and periodically issues fixed-term securities, each of which pays off if and only if a prespecified "superstate" occurs. Under weak assumptions about investor preferences and probability beliefs and apparently innocuous assumptions with respect to investor willingness to process predecision information in great detail, this chapter shows that the superfund is, in principle, able to bring about a complete financial market (in the Arrow–Debreu sense) by issuing surprisingly few "supersecurities." As a practical matter, it should have little difficulty in providing all the "advantages" of a complete financial market for a majority of investors, particularly "small" investors. These advantages include "greater" economic welfare (by incorporating into the market, in a particularly efficient manner, all or the major profitable side-bet opportunities which are unresolvable within the regular markets), the ability to investors in effect to borrow and lend at the same "riskless" rate and to make (implicit) pure short sales (without actually having to engage in borrowing or short-sale transactions), and possibly a reduction in transaction costs for those who revise their portfolios fairly infrequently. Another noteworthy peculiarity of the superfund is its special ability to apparently overcome or circumvent the four obstacles stated in the previous paragraph with ease.

The paper proceeds as follows. The bulk of the theoretical framework is developed in Section II, with the basic model specified in Section II.A. Section II.B identifies and characterizes the equilibrium conditions when all securities are of the regular type and Section II.C when they are of the Arrow–Debreu variety. Section II.D defines the notion of equivalent markets and compares the two market structures via the Fundamental Implicit Price Theorem. The superfund is introduced in Section II.E; in its ultimate (single-period) form, its presence is shown to result in a market structure which is equivalent to a complete financial market, and when it holds a sufficiently large fraction of the market portfolio, all short selling (and borrowing) can be avoided (Theorem 2). Section II.G considers superfunds issuing less than a full array of Arrow–Debreu securities; the Basic Market Structure Dominance Criterion (Section II.F) is shown to give a partial ordering of all possible superfunds. Finally, the conditions applicable to the present model under which Arrow–Debreu certificates can be consolidated are given in Section II.H.

The ability to expand the opportunities of investors is the property of the superfund that is essentially responsible for its power to improve economic welfare. But welfare improvements are also available via security proliferation by firms and the expansion of option markets. Section III argues that, as a practical matter, these alternatives are not only limited in what they can ultimately accomplish, but are much more inefficient in reaching any given "level" of improvement. The superfund's relationship to regular mutual funds is also analyzed.

Section IV imposes two assumptions which essentially state that the amount of (probability) detail an investor is willing to process before making his decision is limited. These assumptions may be viewed as an attempt to implicitly ". . . add to our usual economic calculations an appropriate measure of the costs of information gathering and transmission" (Arrow [2, p. 5]). The implications of these premises are a drastic reduction in the number of "states" that need to be distinguished and virtual elimination of problems bearing on which states are relevant, on which state occurred *ex post*, and on the "moral hazard." An illustration is also included. Section V then turns to some of the pragmatic issues concerning return patterns, short sales, borrowing, probability estimation, transaction costs, administration, and the implications for the firm and for monetary policy. The fact that the "supersecurities" can be made payable in terms of deflated aggregate wealth (returns) just as easily as on a nominal basis is noted in Section VI. Section VII identifies the conditions under which the basic model considered can be embedded in an intertemporal setting without effect on the theorems presented. Finally, Section VIII contains some concluding remarks.

II. Theoretical Foundations

A. Basic Assumptions and Notation

We consider an ongoing economy in which productive activities are carried out by firms and perhaps government agencies; the capital necessary to undertake these productive activities is obtained by sale of financial instruments to investors. Instruments issued by productive units will be called regular securities to distinguish them from instruments created by financial intermediaries or investors themselves. All securities are traded in financial markets, in which investors make decisions at the same (fixed) decision points. Our focus will be on an arbitrarily chosen single period over which, in the interest of simplicity, consumption and production decisions are viewed as fixed. In line with the usual assumptions in this context, we postulate that investors see themselves as price-takers and that all investment opportunities are perfectly divisible and can be sold short without restriction; transaction costs and taxes are ignored. The following basic notation will be used:

s a basic state of the world at the end of the period

n the number of basic states s

S the set of basic states s (i.e., $S = \{s_1, \ldots, s_n\}$)

W_s total wealth available for allocation if state s occurs

I the number of investors i

y_i the resources of investor i available for investment (endogenous)

w_i end-of-period wealth of investor i (random variable)

d_{is} value assumed by w_i if state s occurs (investor i's allocation if state s occurs, or his demand for state s Arrow–Debreu securities when only such securities are available)

π_{is} the probability assessment of investor i that state s will occur

$u_i(w_i)$ the utility function of investor i

J the number of regular investment vehicles j (stocks, bonds, warrants, etc.) available in the market for the coming period

J^0 the number of continuing regular securities already present in investor portfolios ($J^\circ \le J$) as a result of previous decisions

a_{js} proceeds per share of security j if state s occurs ($a_{js} \ge 0$, all s, $a_{js} > 0$, some s, all j)

$\bar{J}$ rank of matrix $[a_{js}]$

Z_j number of shares of security j outstanding in current period ($Z_j > 0$)

P_j price per share of regular security j

z_{ij} number of shares of security j demanded by investor i at beginning of period

z_{ij}^0 number of shares of security j owned by investor i at end of previous period

r_i amount of investor i's resources not in form of regular security holdings (withdrawals, additions)

x_{is} number of state s Arrow–Debreu securities, if available in conjunction with other securities, demanded by investor i at beginning of period

p_s price per share of the state s Arrow–Debreu security (if available) at beginning of period

M a market structure (the set of investment vehicles available in the market)

The investors' probability assessments are postulated to satisfy

$$\pi_{is} > 0, \quad s = 1, \ldots, n, \quad \sum_{s=1}^{n} \pi_{is} = 1, \quad \text{all } i \qquad (1)$$

Thus, while we permit probability assessments to differ among investors, none assigns probability 0 to any of the identified states[3] $1, \ldots, n$. The set of

---

[3] Two complications are circumvented by assuming strong rather than weak inequalities in (1). First, our expressions become less complex, with little qualitative change in the results. Second, we avoid confronting the possibility that state s actually occurred, even though some individuals assessed π_{is} to be 0—which, in turn, raises issues beyond the scope of this paper.

states S is assumed to be specified in sufficient detail for each a_{js}, which is exogenous, to be a number (as opposed to a random variable). Each investor is also assumed to be rational in the von Neumann–Morgenstern sense, with preferences that differentiate only with respect to his own end-of-period wealth;[4] the utility functions $u_i(w_i)$ are assumed to have the following properties (where b_i is a parameter):[5]

$$u_i'(w_i) > 0, \qquad u_i''(w_i) < 0$$

$$\text{for} \quad w_i \geq b_i \geq 0, \qquad u'(b_i) = \infty, \qquad i = 1, \dots, I \qquad (2)$$

We assume that total wealth W_s is positive and bounded in each state, satisfying

$$\sum_{i=1}^{I} b_i < W_s \leq W, \qquad \text{all } s \qquad (3)$$

for some W, and, for simplicity, that it is composed entirely of securities in positive supply, i.e.,

$$Z_j > 0, \qquad \text{all } j \qquad (4)$$

some of which may be riskless.[6] Thus, if all securities are of the regular variety, we obtain

$$W_s = \sum_{j=1}^{J} a_{js} Z_j = \sum_{i=1}^{I} d_{is}, \qquad \text{all } s \qquad (5)$$

while if they are all of the Arrow–Debreu type,[7] we have

$$W_s = \sum_{i=1}^{I} d_{is}, \qquad \text{all } s \qquad (6)$$

note that the number of distinct values of W_s will in general be substantially smaller than the number of states n. The rank $\bar{J}$ of the $J \times n$ matrix $[a_{js}]$ (i.e., the number of linearly independent regular securities) clearly satisfies

$$\bar{J} \leq \min\{J, n\} \qquad (7)$$

---

[4] A richer preference framework is considered in Section VI.

[5] The first and second properties (more wealth preferred to less, nonsaturation, and risk aversion) require no comment. The third assumption (infinite marginal utility of wealth at some nonnegative level), while not difficult to defend on empirical grounds, also keeps the technicalities of our analysis to a minimum.

[6] A riskless asset is one for which $a_{js} = a_j$ for all s. While it is common to assume that the riskless asset, when it exists, is created by the investors themselves, i.e., that $Z_j = 0$, there is no loss of generality in assuming that some quantity has already been issued by, for example, a government agency.

[7] An Arrow–Debreu security may be viewed as a special case of a regular security, that is, one for which $a_{js} = 1$ for one s, and $a_{js} = 0$ for all other s.

Summing the components of initial wealth to be invested, we obtain

$$y_i = \sum_{j=1}^{J^0} P_j z_{ij}^0 + r_i, \qquad i = 1, \ldots, I \tag{8}$$

The numbers r_i, which represent net new investment by individual i and are exogenous in the present model, are assumed to be consistent with positive prices in the budget constraint [see (13); when $J = J^0$, for example, this requires $\sum_{i=1}^{I} r_i = 0$], and with[8]

$$y_i > 0, \qquad \text{all } i \tag{9}$$

The r_i thus capture consumption-induced changes in the amount to be reinvested, the proceeds from liquidated firms, "new" capital going into new firms, and the expansion of existing firms without formally modeling the underlying process. Little is lost by this short-cut, since our analysis is essentially one of comparative statics and the main result also obtains when consumption is formally introduced, as noted in Section VII. End-of-period wealth w_i, in the case of regular securities only, is given by

$$w_i(s) = \sum_{j=1}^{J} a_{js} z_{ij}, \qquad s = 1, \ldots, n, \quad i = 1, \ldots, I \tag{10}$$

while in an Arrow–Debreu world we obtain

$$w_i(s) = d_{is}, \qquad s = 1, \ldots, n, \quad i = 1, \ldots, I \tag{11}$$

B. Market Structure M1: Regular Securities

In the remainder of this section we shall examine the welfare implications of various market structures, also referred to simply as markets, market situations, and market arrangements. For our purpose, the focal point of a given market arrangement in these comparisons will be the set of instruments available for investment. Thus, even though in a larger sense the totality of the participants is an integral part of a complete description of a market arrangement M, it is generally sufficient to think of the distinctive feature of M as simply the set of securities available for purchase.

When only regular securities are available, the resulting market situation may be described as

M1

$$\max_{\{z_{ij}\}} \sum_{s=1}^{n} \pi_{is} u_i \left(\sum_{j=1}^{J} a_{js} z_{ij} \right), \qquad i = 1, \ldots, I \tag{12}$$

[8] Since last period's w_i equals this period's $y_i - r_i$, and since $Pr\{w_i > 0\} = 1$ in (the previous) equilibrium (see, e.g., Eq. (16)), this assumption is rather mild.

subject to the budget constraints

$$\sum_{j=1}^{J} P_j z_{ij} = \sum_{j=1}^{J^0} P_j z_{ij}^0 + r_i, \qquad i = 1, \ldots, I \qquad (13)$$

where the prices $P_1, \ldots, P_J$ are such that the optimal portfolios satisfy the market clearing conditions

$$\sum_{i=1}^{I} z_{ij} = Z_j, \qquad j = 1, \ldots, J \qquad (14)$$

The equilibrium conditions for this case (EC1) consist of the following $I \times J + I + J$ equations in the $(I \times J + I + J)$ unknowns z_{ij}, λ_i, P_j (where the λ_i are Lagrange multipliers)

EC1

$$\sum_{s=1}^{n} \pi_{is} u_i' \left(\sum_{j=1}^{J} a_{js} z_{ij} \right) a_{js} = \lambda_i P_j, \qquad j = 1, \ldots, J, \quad i = 1, \ldots, I \qquad (15)$$

$$\sum_{j=1}^{J} P_j z_{ij} = \sum_{j=1}^{J^0} P_j z_{ij}^0 + r_i, \qquad i = 1, \ldots, I \qquad (13)$$

$$\sum_{i=1}^{I} z_{ij} = Z_j, \qquad\qquad j = 1, \ldots, J \qquad (14)$$

in view of assumptions (1)–(4) and (9). The assumptions also guarantee that a solution to EC1 exists (Hart [11]), but need not be unique,[9] and that the equilibrium holdings z_{ij}', multipliers λ_i', and prices P_j' satisfy[10]

$$d_{is}' \equiv \sum_{j=1}^{J} a_{js} z_{ij}' > b_i \geq 0, \qquad s = 1, \ldots, n, \quad i = 1, \ldots, I \qquad (16)$$

$$\lambda_i' > 0, \qquad i = 1, \ldots, I \qquad (17)$$

$$P_j' > 0, \qquad j = 1, \ldots, J \qquad (18)$$

i.e., each investor's wealth in each state is positive, as are the Lagrange multipliers and the equilibrium prices. However, in spite of (16), some of the z_{ij}' will generally be negative, i.e., in the absence of strong investor homogeneity, the equilibrium solution generally requires some investors to take short positions in some securities.

---

[9] Even though, for *given* prices P_j, (15) and (13) have a unique solution for each i if all securities are linearly independent (e.g., Hakansson [8]).

[10] Due to the presence of the r_i terms, the equilibrium prices will be expressed in absolute terms, not just relative terms.

C. Market Arrangement M2: Arrow–Debreu Securities

When only Arrow–Debreu securities are available in the current period, the market situation can be described as

M2

$$\max_{\{d_{is}\}} \sum_{s=1}^{n} \pi_{is} u_i(d_{is}), \qquad i = 1, \ldots, I \tag{19}$$

subject to the budget constraints

$$\sum_{s=1}^{n} p_s d_{is} = \sum_{s=1}^{n} p_s \sum_{j=1}^{J^0} a_{js} z_{ij}^0 + r_i, \qquad i = 1, \ldots, I \tag{20}$$

where the prices $p_1, \ldots, p_n$ are such that the optimal portfolios satisfy the market clearing conditions

$$\sum_{i=1}^{I} d_{is} = W_s, \qquad s = 1, \ldots, n \tag{21}$$

The equilibrium conditions for this case (EC2) reduce the following $I \times n + I + n$ equations in the variables d_{is}, λ_i, and p_s.

EC2

$$\pi_{is} u_i'(d_{is}) = \lambda_i p_s, \qquad s = 1, \ldots, n, \qquad i = 1, \ldots, I \tag{22}$$

$$\sum_{s=1}^{n} p_s d_{is} = \sum_{s=1}^{n} p_s \sum_{j=1}^{J^0} a_{js} z_{ij}^0 + r_i, \qquad i = 1, \ldots, I \tag{20}$$

$$\sum_{i=1}^{I} d_{is} = W_s, \qquad s = 1, \ldots, n \tag{21}$$

Again, assumptions (1)–(3) and (9) insure that a solution, not necessarily unique, to EC2 exists (e.g., Arrow [1]) and that the equilibrium holdings d_{is}'', multipliers λ_i'', and prices p_s'' satisfy

$$d_{is}'' > b_i \geq 0, \qquad s = 1, \ldots, n, \quad i = 1, \ldots, I \tag{23}$$

$$\lambda_i'' > 0, \qquad i = 1, \ldots, I \tag{24}$$

$$p_s'' > 0, \qquad s = 1, \ldots, n \tag{25}$$

Note that (23) implies that short positions need no longer be taken by investors. But the most important property of *M2*, in fact the very reason for examining complete markets (the Arrow–Debreu model of markets) in the first place, is that the allocations d_{is}'' are Pareto-efficient " in the ultimate sense," i.e., not only are there no additional *market* trades that investors wish to engage in, but, in addition, there are no mutually beneficial *nonmarket* trades that investors desire with each other,[11] a point we shall return to shortly.

D. Equivalent Markets

In attempting to develop an ordering over market structures, we begin by establishing a notion of equivalent markets. A more complete analysis of equivalent markets is given by Hakansson [10].

Definition 1 Market structure M' is (strongly) equivalent to market structure M'' $(M' \sim M'')$ if, for all collections[12] $[\pi_{is}, u_i(w_i)]$ satisfying (1) and (2), every equilibrium final allocation under M' is also an equilibrium final allocation under M'', and conversely.

Remark 1 $M \sim M$.

Assume for a moment that $M1$ has full rank $(\bar{J} = J)$ and hence contains no securities issued by mutual funds or other pure holding companies with less than 100% ownership in each instrument held, and that $M1'$ differs from $M1$ only by the presence of such securities. Then the opportunities for choice of final allocations d_{is} in $M1'$ are clearly the same as in $M1$ and, given that the shares of holding companies do not sell at premiums or discounts, we obtain

Remark 2 $M1' \sim M1$.

By our definition, it is not sufficient for two market arrangements to have the same equilibrium for only a narrow class of preferences and probability assessments but not for other classes. To be (strongly) equivalent, the two market arrangements must yield identical final allocations for *any* combination of preferences and probability assessments held by investors which satisfy the rather broad assumptions (1) and (2). Thus, even though $M1$ and $M2$ yield the same final allocations in special cases when $J = 1$ or 2, say, and n is large (Rubinstein [21]), $M1$ (with $J = 1$ or 2) and $M2$ (with n large) are easily shown not to yield the same sets of equilibria in all cases and are therefore not equivalent.

The question that arises, then, is under what conditions, if any, $M1$ and $M2$ are equivalent. We first observe that $M1$ and $M2$ yield the same solution

---

[11] The term "constrained Pareto-efficiency" is sometimes used to denote allocations which are efficient relative to a given (constrained) set of allocation possibilities (such as that in $M1$) (see, e.g., Stiglitz [25, p. 26]).

[12] By a collection $[\pi_{is}, u_i(w_i)]$ we mean the set of preferences and beliefs possessed by the collection of investors in the market $(i = 1, \ldots, I)$.

if and only if [see (16) and (23)]

$$\sum_{j=1}^{J} a_{js} z'_{ij} = d''_{is}, \qquad s = 1, \ldots, n, \quad i = 1, \ldots, I \tag{26}$$

in this case we also get for all i and j

$$\lambda'_i = \lambda''_i \tag{27}$$

and

$$P'_j = \sum_{s=1}^{n} p''_s a_{js} \tag{28}$$

In view (7), (26)–(28) always hold (for certain equilibrium pairs) if $\bar{J} = n$ (see also Cass and Stiglitz [4], pp. 149–152), i.e., if the number of (linearly independent) instruments traded in the market is equal to the number of states. That is, when $\bar{J} = n$, every equilibrium final allocation under $M2$ is also an equilibrium final allocation under $M1$; conversely, $\bar{J} = n$ implies that $\pi_{is} u'_i(d'_{is})/\lambda_i$, $s = 1, \ldots, n$, in (15) must be the same for all i for each equilibrium price structure $\{P'_j\}$ so that every equilibrium final allocation under $M1$ is also an equilibrium under $M2$. But if $\bar{J} < n$, there are (collections $[u_i(w_i), \pi_{is}]$ satisfying (1) and (2), which produce) equilibrium allocations d''_{is} which are simply not attainable [see (26)] under $M1$. Thus:

Remark 3 $M1 \sim M2$ if and only if $\bar{J} = n$.

The relationship between $M1$ and $M2$ may also be studied by reference to (15) and (22), which, in turn, provide a simple and revealing means for proving that $M1$ does not tend to a Pareto-efficient allocation unless (22) is satisfied for some p_s at $d_{is} = d'_{is}$, $i = 1, \ldots, I$. To this end, let (by reference to EC1)

$$P'_{ijs} \equiv \pi_{is} u'_i(d'_{is}) a_{js}/\lambda'_i, \qquad s = 1, \ldots, n, \quad j = 1, \ldots, J, \quad i = 1, \ldots, I \tag{29}$$

which gives

$$P'_{is} \equiv P'_{i1s}/a_{1s} = \cdots = P'_{iJs}/a_{Js} \qquad \text{all } i, s \tag{30}$$

By (15), we obtain

$$\sum_{s=1}^{n} P'_{ijs} = P'_j, \qquad i = 1, \ldots, I, \quad j = 1, \ldots, J \tag{31}$$

and, rewriting Eq. (29),

$$\pi_{is} u'_i(d'_{is}) a_{js} = \lambda'_i P'_{ijs}, \qquad s = 1, \ldots, n, \quad j = 1, \ldots, J, \quad i = 1, \ldots, I$$

P'_{ijs} may be viewed as that part of the total equilibrium price P'_j of instrument j which is attributed to state s by individual i. Similarly, P'_{is} is the marginal value to investor i of a small increment to his state s wealth d'_{is}. We can now state

Theorem 1 (*The Fundamental Implicit Price Theorem*) $M1$ results in a Pareto-efficient allocation if and only if the shadow prices P'_{is} given by (30) satisfy

$$P'_{is} = P'_{1s}, \qquad s = 1, \dots, n, \quad i = 2, \dots, I \tag{32}$$

The proof may be sketched as follows. Suppose (32) does not hold for two investors, i_1 and i_2, e.g., that we have for some state s,

$$P'_{i_1 s_1} > P'_{i_2 s_1}$$

In view of (30) and (31), there is then also some state s_2 such that

$$P'_{i_1 s_2} < P'_{i_2 s_2}$$

But since the marginal utility of wealth in each state is diminishing, this means that investor i_1 can improve his welfare by agreeing to acquire $k\Delta_1$ additional units of wealth in state s_1 at a price $P_1 < P'_{i_1 s_1}$ in an (even) exchange for $k\Delta_2$ units of his wealth in state s_2 at a price $P_2 > P'_{i_1 s_2}$, where $k\Delta_1 P_1 = k\Delta_2 P_2$. As long as $P_1 > P'_{i_2 s_1}$ and $P_2 < P'_{i_2 s_2}$ investor i_2 will benefit by taking the opposite action for some $k > 0$. Only when (32) does not hold can mutually beneficial nonmarket trades among investors be constructed; when (32) does hold no such opportunities exist.

The following corollary is immediate.

Corollary 1 (32) holds if and only if (26)–(28) hold, i.e., if and only if $M1$ and $M2$ have the same solution(s), which is guaranteed for all collections $[\pi_{is}, u_i(w_i)]$ satisfying (1) and (2) only if $\bar{J} = n$.

Since (32) generally does not hold in $M1$, it is apparent that in some sense $M1$ is inferior to $M2$. Before turning our attention to the problem of ordering market structures in more detail, we shall examine the notion of a "mixture" of $M1$ and $M2$.

E. Market Structure M3: Combining M1 and M2

Suppose a fraction δ $(0 < \delta < 1)$ of all ordinary shares were owned by a fund, which in turn issues Arrow–Debreu securities. To distinguish it from the usual mutual fund, such a fund will be called a superfund. Thus, the number of shares traded in the market would be $J + n$; the supply of ordinary shares j would be $(1 - \delta)Z_j$, and that of the state s Arrow–Debreu security δW_s, since the market value of the fund in state s would be δW_s. The resulting market situation can now be described as

M3

$$\max_{\{z_{ij}, \, x_{is}\}} \sum_{s=1}^{n} \pi_i u_i \left(\sum_{j=1}^{J} a_{js} z_{ij} + x_{is} \right), \qquad i = 1, \ldots, I \qquad (33)$$

subject to the budget constraints

$$\sum_{j=1}^{J} P_j z_{ij} + \sum_{s=1}^{n} p_s x_{is} = \sum_{j=1}^{J^0} P_j z_{ij}^0 + r_i, \qquad i = 1, \ldots, I \qquad (34)$$

where the prices $P_1, \ldots, P_j, p_1, \ldots, p_n$ are such that the optimal portfolios satisfy the market clearing conditions

$$\sum_{i=1}^{I} z_{ij} = (1 - \delta) Z_j, \qquad j = 1, \ldots, J \qquad (35)$$

$$\sum_{i=1}^{I} x_{is} = \delta W_s, \qquad s = 1, \ldots, n \qquad (36)$$

The equilibrium conditions for this case (EC3) reduce to the following $I \times (J + S) + I + J + S$ equations in the variables z_{ij}, x_{is}, λ_i, P_j, and p_s.

EC3

$$\sum_{s=1}^{n} \pi_{is} u_i' \left(\sum_{j=1}^{J} a_{js} z_{ij} + x_{is} \right) a_{js} = \lambda_i P_j, \qquad j = 1, \ldots, J, \quad i = 1, \ldots, I \qquad (37)$$

$$\pi_{is} u_i' \left(\sum_{j=1}^{J} a_{js} z_{ij} + x_{is} \right) = \lambda_i p_s, \qquad s = 1, \ldots, n, \quad i = 1, \ldots, I \qquad (38)$$

$$\sum_{j=1}^{J} P_j z_{ij} + \sum_{s=1}^{n} p_s x_{is} = \sum_{j=1}^{J^0} P_j z_{ij}^0 + r_i, \qquad i = 1, \ldots, I \qquad (34)$$

$$\sum_{i=1}^{I} z_{ij} = (1 - \delta) Z_j, \qquad j = 1, \ldots, J \qquad (35)$$

$$\sum_{i=1}^{I} x_{is} = \delta W_s, \qquad s = 1, \ldots, n \qquad (36)$$

As before, assumptions (1)–(4) and (9) ensure that a solution, not necessarily unique, to EC3 exists, and that the equilibrium holdings d_{is}''', multipliers λ_i''', and prices P_j''', p_s''' satisfy

$$d_{is}''' > b_i \geq 0, \qquad s = 1, \ldots, n, \quad i = 1, \ldots, I \qquad (39)$$

$$\lambda_i''' > 0, \qquad i = 1, \ldots, I \qquad (40)$$

$$P_j''' > 0, \qquad j = 1, \ldots, J \qquad (41)$$

$$p_s''' > 0, \qquad s = 1, \ldots, n \qquad (42)$$

But, by (29) and (38), $P'''_{ijs} = a_{js} p''_s$, $i = 1, \ldots, I$, so that by Corollary 1, every solution to EC2 is also a solution to EC3 and conversely, i.e.,

$$d'''_{is} \equiv \sum_{j=1}^{J} a_{js} z'''_{ij} + x'''_{is} = d''_{is} \tag{43}$$

$$\lambda'''_i = \lambda''_i \tag{44}$$

$$p'''_s = p''_s \tag{45}$$

$$P'''_j = \sum_{s=1}^{n} p''_s a_{js} \tag{46}$$

Formally, this gives

Remark 4 $M3 \sim M2$.

As in $M1$, however, it is entirely possible that $z'''_{ij} < 0$ and $x'''_{is} < 0$ for some i, j, and s, i.e., that for each optimal solution, short selling is necessary for some individuals. We now show that short selling can be avoided by all investors, no matter how heterogeneous [within the limits of (1) and (2)], by choosing δ sufficiently large.

Theorem 2   If $\delta < 1$ is sufficiently large in $M3$, there exist solutions $(\sum_{j=1}^{J} a_{js} z'''_{ij} + x'''_{is} = d'''_{is})$ to EC3 such that

$$z'''_{ij} \geq 0, \, x'''_{is} \geq 0, \qquad s = 1, \ldots, n, \quad j = 1, \ldots, J, \quad i = 1, \ldots, I \tag{47}$$

In particular, (47) always holds if $\delta \geq 1 - K$, where $K > 0$ is given by

$$K \equiv \min_{i,s} \frac{d'''_{is} / \sum_{s=1}^{n} d'''_{is}}{W_s / \sum_{s=1}^{n} W_s} \tag{48}$$

Proof   Recall that d'''_{is} is independent of δ [see (43)] and let

$$v_s \equiv W_s / \sum_{s=1}^{n} W_s, \quad s = 1, \ldots, n; \qquad D'''_i \equiv \sum_{s=1}^{n} d'''_{is}, \quad i = 1, \ldots, I \tag{49}$$

and let K be defined as in (48). By (39) and (3)

$$0 < K \leq 1 \tag{50}$$

and, using (48),

$$K D'''_i v_s \leq d'''_{is}, \qquad s = 1, \ldots, n, \quad i = 1, \ldots, I \tag{51}$$

Now set

$$z'''_{ij} = K \left(D'''_i / \sum_{s=1}^{n} W_s \right) Z_j, \qquad j = 1, \ldots, J, \quad i = 1, \ldots, I \tag{52}$$

which gives, by (4),

$$z_{ij}''' > 0, \qquad j = 1, \ldots, J, \quad i = 1, \ldots, I \tag{53}$$

and total demand of

$$\sum_{i=1}^{I} z_{ij}''' = K Z_j, \qquad j = 1, \ldots, J \tag{54}$$

By definition,

$$x_{ij}'''' = d_{is}'''' - \sum_{j=1}^{n} a_{js} z_{ij}''' = d_{is}'''' - K D_i''' v_s \geq 0$$

using (52), (5), (49), and (51). By (54), we set $\delta = 1 - K$, which completes the proof.

Note that the less heterogeneous investors are, the smaller the δ that can be chosen. The reader will also recognize that (52) calls for purchasing the "market portfolio," which establishes

Corollary 2 The optimal allocation d_{is}''' is obtainable even if all complex securities not held by the Arrow–Debreu fund were owned by a regular mutual fund. That is, a Pareto-efficient allocation in which all holdings are nonnegative is obtainable via ownership in two funds, each holding a fraction of all instruments, one issuing regular pro rata shares and the other issuing Arrow–Debreu securities.

On the basis of (53), the following may be separately noted.

Remark 5 If there is a riskless security in $M3$, a Pareto-efficient allocation of investment resources can be achieved without borrowing by any investor whenever δ is sufficiently large.

F. Ordering Market Structures

Via Theorem 1 and Corollary 1, we observed that when $\bar{J} < n$, market structure $M1$ is generally distinctly inferior to $M2$, and hence, by Remark 4, to $M3$, in that at least some investors under $M1$ can make themselves better off, without causing anyone to become worse off, by engaging in exchanges not provided for by the market. Even if we did not wish to move all the way from $M1$ to $M3$, we might be interested in adding some new instruments to $M1$, on the presumption that this would improve the general welfare. Clearly, the possibilities for new securities are staggering; at the same time, the welfare effects of different proliferation patterns may well be quite diverse. Before considering specific suggestions for new instruments, therefore, some criterion for choosing among them appears most desirable. One such criterion was formulated by Hakansson [10].

The weak basic market structure dominance criterion (*WBMSDC*).[13] Market structure M' is weakly dominated by market structure M'' (M'' dom M') if, in moving from every equilibrium under M' to every (different) equilibrium under M'', the change in expected utility of investor i, Δu_i, is such that

$$\Delta u_i > 0 \qquad \text{for some } i, \text{ for every collection } [\pi_{is}, u_i(w_i)] \qquad (55)$$
$$\text{satisfying (1) and (2)}$$

$$\Delta u_i > 0 \qquad \text{for all } i, \text{ for some collections } [\pi_{is}, u_i(w_i)] \qquad (56)$$
$$\text{satisfying (1) and (2)}$$

Paraphrased, the criterion says that if we compare equilibrium under M' with equilibrium under M'', then M'' dom M' if, under every conceivable situation consistent with our basic assumptions, at least some investors, and sometimes all investors, are better off under M''.

We observe that if M'' dom M', then we cannot also have M' dom M'' [because (55) would then be violated for some collection $\{\pi_{is}, u_i(w_i)\}$]. Neither can we have M dom M.

G. Market Structure M4: Partitioning S

In the amplification of Theorem 1, the kind of nonmarket exchange which investors engaged in to improve their lot involved private exchange of Arrow–Debreu securities. Of course, mutually beneficial side bets could also have been employed which involve more complex securities. In this section, we consider a special class of such securities, namely, securities which pay off only if one of several states occurs, in proportion to the quantity W_s for the states in question.

More specifically, let $\bar{S} = \{\bar{s}_1, \ldots, \bar{s}_K\}$ be a partition[14] of S. Now consider a "different" kind of superfund, one which owns proportion δ of all regular securities and which issues one security for each *subset* of states, $\bar{s}_k$, $k = 1, \ldots, K$. Let the supply of supersecurities be $\delta W_{\min} \equiv \delta \min_s W_s > 0$, i.e.,

$$\bar{Z}_j = \delta W_{\min}, \qquad j = J + 1, \ldots, J + K \qquad (57)$$

---

[13] WBMSDC is the "relevant" criterion in comparing two market structures unless the endowment allocation under one market structure (say M'') is an equilibrium under the alternative market structure (say M')—in this case the relevant ("strong") criterion is equivalent to the Pareto-criterion.

[14] $\bar{S} = \{\bar{s}_1, \ldots, \bar{s}_K\}$ is a partition of $S = [s_1, \ldots, s_n]$ if $\bar{s}_k \subset S$, $k = 1, \ldots, K$, $\bar{s}_j \cap \bar{s}_k = \phi$ if $j \neq k$, and $\bigcup_{k=1}^{K} \bar{s}_k = S$.

This gives

$$a_{js} = \begin{cases} W_s/W_{\min}, & s \in \bar{s}_k, \quad j = J + k, \quad k = 1, \ldots, K \\ 0 & \text{otherwise} \end{cases} \tag{58}$$

The resulting market situation can be described as follows.

M4

$$\max_{\{z_{ij}, \bar{z}_{ij}\}} \sum_{s=1}^{n} \pi_i u_i \left(\sum_{j=1}^{J} a_{js} z_{ij} + \sum_{j=J+1}^{J+K} a_{js} \bar{z}_{ij} \right), \quad i = 1, \ldots, I \tag{59}$$

subject to the budget constraints

$$\sum_{j=1}^{J} P_j z_{ij} + \sum_{j=J+1}^{J+K} \bar{P}_j \bar{z}_{ij} = \sum_{j=1}^{J^0} P_j z_{ij}^0 + r_i, \quad i = 1, \ldots, I \tag{60}$$

where the prices $P_1, \ldots, P_J, \bar{P}_{J+1}, \ldots, \bar{P}_{J+K}$ are such that the optimal portfolios satisfy the market clearing conditions

$$\sum_{i=1}^{I} z_{ij} = (1 - \delta) Z_j, \quad j = 1, \ldots, J \tag{61}$$

$$\sum_{i=1}^{I} \bar{z}_{ij} = \delta W_{\min}, \quad j = J + 1, \ldots, J + K \tag{62}$$

The equilibrium conditions for this case (EC4) reduce to the following $I \times (J + K) + I + J + K$ equations in the variables z_{ij}, $\bar{z}_{ij}$, λ_i, P_j, and $\bar{P}_j$.

EC4

$$\sum_{s=1}^{n} \pi_{is} u_1' \left(\sum_{j=1}^{J} a_{js} z_{ij} + \sum_{j=J+1}^{J+K} a_{js} \bar{z}_{ij} \right) a_{js} = \lambda_i P_j,$$

$$j = 1, \ldots, J \quad i = 1, \ldots, I \tag{63}$$

$$\sum_{s=1}^{n} \pi_{is} u_i' \left(\sum_{j=1}^{J} a_{js} z_{ij} + \sum_{j=J+1}^{J+K} a_{js} \bar{z}_{ij} \right) a_{js} = \lambda_i \bar{P}_j,$$

$$j = J + 1, \ldots, J + K, \quad i = i, \ldots, I \tag{64}$$

$$\sum_{j=1}^{J} P_j z_{ij} + \sum_{j=J+1}^{J+K} \bar{P}_j \bar{z}_{ij} = \sum_{j=1}^{J^0} P_j z_{ij}^0 + r_i, \quad i = 1, \ldots, I \tag{60}$$

$$\sum_{i=1}^{I} z_{ij} = (1 - \delta) Z_j, \quad j = 1, \ldots, J \tag{61}$$

$$\sum_{i=1}^{I} \bar{z}_{ij} = \delta W_{\min}, \quad j = J + 1, \ldots, J + K \tag{62}$$

Assumptions (1)–(4) and (9) again ensure that a (nonunique) solution to EC4 exists and that the equilibrium holdings $\bar{d}_{is}$, multipliers $\bar{\lambda}_i$, and prices $\bar{P}_j$, $\bar{\bar{P}}_j$ satisfy

$$\bar{d}_{is} > b_i \geq 0, \qquad s = 1, \ldots, n, \quad i = 1, \ldots, I \qquad (65)$$

$$\bar{\lambda}_i > 0, \qquad i = 1, \ldots, I \qquad (66)$$

$$\bar{P}_j > 0, \qquad j = 1, \ldots, J \qquad (67)$$

$$\bar{\bar{P}}_j > 0, \qquad j = J + 1, \ldots, J + K \qquad (68)$$

It is readily verified that when $K = 1$, any solution to EC4 also satisfies EC1 and conversely, and that when $K = n$, any solution to EC4 satisfies EC3 and conversely. This gives

Remark 6   When $K = 1$ in M4, M4 $\sim$ M1.

Remark 7   When $K = n$ in M4, M4 $\sim$ M3 $\sim$ M2.

In contrast to M1, M2, and M3, M4 is actually a *set* of market structures with a very large number of members. In comparing the members of M4 we will require the following definition.

Definition 2   Let $\bar{S}' = \{\bar{s}'_1, \ldots, \bar{s}'_{K'}\}$ and $\bar{S}''$ be partitions of S. Then $\bar{S}''$ is strictly finer than $\bar{S}'$ ($\bar{S}''$ sf $\bar{S}'$), if for each $\bar{s}'' \in \bar{S}''$ there is an $\bar{s}' \in \bar{S}'$ such that $\bar{s}'' \subseteq \bar{s}'$ and $K'' > K'$.

Our dominance criterion now makes possible the following partial ordering of the market structures $M \in$ M4.

Theorem 3   Let M', $M'' \in$ M4, where M', with rank R', is based on partition $\bar{S}'$ of S, and M'', with rank R'', is based on partition $\bar{S}''$. Then M'' dom M' if and only if $\bar{S}''$ sf $\bar{S}'$ and $R'' > R'$.

(Since Theorem 3 is a special case of Theorem 2 in Hakansson [10], the proof is omitted.)

Remark 8   M2 dom M1 if and only if $\bar{J} < n$.

Remark 9   If M'' dom M' and M''' dom M'', then M''' dom M'.

Remark 10   If $\bar{S}''$ sf $\bar{S}'$ and $R'' = R'$, then $M'' \sim M'$.

Remark 11   Let $M \in$ M4 and have rank $R = \bar{J}$ (the rank of M1). Then $M \sim$ M1.

Remark 12   Let $M \in$ M4 and have rank $R > \bar{J}$ (the rank of M1). Then M dom M1.

Remark 13   Let $M \in$ M4 and have rank $R < n$. Then M3 dom M.

Remark 14   Let $M \in M4$ and have rank $R = n$. Then $M \sim M3 \sim M2$.

The essence of Theorem 3 is twofold. First, to improve on market structure $M = M1$ or $M \in M4$, we need only find a strictly finer partition of S such that the rank of M is increased. Second, if neither M'' sf M' nor M' sf M'', then regardless of the respective ranks of M'' and M', there exist collections $[\pi_{is}, u_i(w_i)]$ satisfying (1) and (2) such that everyone is better off under M'', and other collections such that everyone is better off under M'—unless, of course, $M' \sim M''$.

Remark 8 reminds us that in moving from an incomplete to a complete or a "more complete" market some investors may become worse off. But *all* investors cannot become worse off, whereas *all* investors may become better off. This, then, is what we shall refer to as a weak improvement in economic welfare.

H. Security Consolidation

Finally, we state the following result.

Theorem 4   In $M2$, let N be the number of distinct values assumed by W_s, $s = 1, \ldots, n$. Then the Arrow–Debreu certificates can, for every equilibrium price vector $p''_1, \ldots, p''_n$, be consolidated into m trading instruments attached to superstates t_k, $k = 1, \ldots, m$, where

$$N \le m \le n, \qquad \bigcup_{k=1}^{m} t_k = S, \qquad \bigcap_{k=1}^{m} t_k = \varnothing$$

which yield the same allocation as before, i.e., the optimal allocation satisfies

$$d''_{is_1} = d''_{is_2}, \qquad \text{all } s_1, s_2 \in t_k, \quad \text{all } k, \quad \text{all } i \tag{69}$$

for *all* utility functions $u_i(w_i)$ satisfying (2) if and only if

$$W_{s_1} = W_{s_2}, \qquad \text{all } \ s_1, s_2 \in t_k, \quad k = 1, \ldots, m \tag{70}$$

and

$$\pi_{is_1}/\pi_{is_2} = \pi_{1s_1}/\pi_{1s_2}, \qquad \text{all } \ s_1, s_2 \in t_k, \quad k = 1, \ldots, m, \quad i = 2, \ldots, I \tag{71}$$

Proof   In view of (1), (2), and (22)–(25), we obtain

$$d''_{is_1} \gtreqless d''_{is_2} \quad \text{if and only if} \quad \pi_{is_1}/\pi_{is_2} \gtreqless p_{s_1}/p_{s_2} \tag{72}$$

Since, in equilibrium,

$$\sum_{i=1}^{I} d''_{is} = W_s, \qquad s = 1, \ldots, n$$

$W_{s_1} = W_{s_2}$ implies that

$$\sum_{i=1}^{I} d''_{is_1} = \sum_{i=1}^{I} d''_{is_2} \tag{73}$$

(71)–(73) now imply

$$d''_{is_1} = d''_{is_2}, \quad \text{all } s_1, s_2 \in t_k; \quad k = 1, \ldots, m; \quad \text{all } i$$

i.e., that in equilibrium each investor holds an equal number of Arrow–Debreu certificates for each state belonging to superstate t. The necessity of (70) in achieving (69) is immediate; the necessity of (71) follows from (72).

Remark 15   When $\pi_{is} = \pi_s, s = 1, \ldots, n, i = 1, \ldots, I$, i.e., all investors have the same probability beliefs, then $m = N$.

Remark 16 $p_t = \sum_{s \in t} p_s$.

Remark 17 $p_{s_1}/p_{s_2} = \pi_{is_1}/\pi_{is_2}, s_1, s_2 \in t_k, k = 1, \ldots, m$, all i.

What Theorem 4 says is that a group of basic states s can be combined into a superstate t, and a single superstate security substituted for all of the basic state securities in the group, if the following three conditions hold:

(i)   the supply of basic securities in the group is the same for each state,
(ii)   the conditional probabilities of each s given t, denoted $\pi_{is|t}$, are the same for all investors, and
(iii)   preferences depend only on wealth.

It is important to note that the preceding permits fully heterogeneous preferences as well as nonhomogeneous probability assessments for all states (and, in particular, for the superstates). From another vantage point the theorem also says that two states cannot be consolidated into one simply because the total allocation W_s is the same for the two states—unless the probability assignments are homogeneous (Remark 15) or satisfy (71). Thus, even when all investors are concerned only about ending wealth, a larger number of states must be distinguished, and trading in a larger number of instruments is required, when probability assessments are nonhomogeneous than when they are homogeneous.

III. Pragmatics: Some Basic Considerations

A. Introduction

As a financial intermediary, the superfund differs from the usual mutual fund in two respects. First, in contrast to a mutual fund, a superfund (generally) owns the so-called market portfolio, i.e., it purchases the same percentage, e.g., 25%, of all the shares that are traded in the market.[15]

---

[15] As a technical matter it is not necessary that the superfund purchase the "market portfolio," only that it own a substantial portion of the "wealth" in each state. But this requirement is most readily satisfied via ownership of the "market portfolio" and, as we will see, there are many pragmatic reasons for choosing this particular asset composition.

Second, while mutual funds issue only one kind of security, ordinary (common) shares, a superfund generally issues more than one kind of instrument and these instruments are different from the regular securities historically available in the market.[16] These two features concerning investment and financing are not entirely independent. The ability to issue a full complement of what we shall call group-state securities is contingent upon the superfund's holdings having a positive value in each state s; moreover, the ability to make short sales (by individuals) unnecessary (to be discussed shortly) requires this value to be substantial in relation to the total market value of all securities for each state.

In Remark 2 (see also Remark 11), we observed that in a frictionless economy the existence of mutual funds and other pure holding companies (each holding 100% of at most one security) has no impact at all on economic welfare, the essential reason being that it does not expand the allocation opportunities faced by investors. The argument in favor of mutual funds, therefore, must rest entirely on their ability to reduce transaction costs and/or their ability to construct a more "suitable" portfolio for the investor. The evidence with respect to the first point is certainly more convincing that the evidence with respect to the second, in principle if not in practice (see, e.g., Jensen [13]).

In contrast, Remark 12 shows that the presence of a superfund improves the economic welfare in a frictionless economy whenever the investors' opportunity set is expanded. In addition, further improvements are achieved as finer and finer breakdowns of the group-states are made (Theorem 3) until in the limit the "ultimate" superfund makes possible the achievement of "maximal" welfare (Remark 14) by achieving, in effect, a complete financial market.

In evaluating the desirability of implementing a superfund, three questions appear most crucial:

(1) What alternatives to the superfund are available and what are their relative merits?

(2) How likely is the superfund to expand the opportunity set faced by investors?

(3) How would the superfund affect investor transaction costs?

It is apparent that these questions involve both theoretical and empirical considerations. We will address each in turn, the first two in this section and the third in Section V.

---

[16] When $K = 1$, the superfund is "equivalent" to a regular mutual fund (see also Remarks 6 and 11).

B. An Alternative

Expansion of the investors' opportunity set may also be accomplished by the creation of securities other than those issued by a superfund. In particular, as shown by Hakansson [10], finer and finer subdivisions of a given firm's securities also improve the economic welfare whenever the rank of the old market structure is increased. Thus, the financing of a firm's expansion by bonds and warrants is better than using bonds alone—again assuming that the first alternative makes possible allocation opportunities not present under the second alternative.

In order to compare the relative merits of supersecurities versus regular security proliferation, we begin by making two key observations. First, supersecurities have positive proceeds a_{js} in only a few states, regular securities in most or in all states. Second, the supply of a supersecurity is in every sense large, while that of a given regular security in a market in which the shares of many firms are traded is clearly small.

Since the optimal holdings in any given security, as a proportion of initial wealth y_i, generally differ substantially among investors, the implication of the second property above is that a security in low supply will in equilibrium be sold by many investors. Since we presently lack the facilities for pure short sales in securities markets, and the absence of pure short-sale opportunities adversely affects welfare, the creation of (low supply) regular securities, *ceteris paribus*, appears less promising than the introduction of supersecurities, in the presence of which short sales, at a minimum, can be sharply reduced (Theorem 2). Turning to the first observation, when the rank of the regular securities market (i.e., of $M1$) is less than n, we saw (following Theorem 1) that the inferiority of $M1$ in relation to a complete financial market ($M2$) is due to the existence of mutually beneficial side bets for which regular securities offer no resolution. As noted, either finer subdivisions of regular securities or the introduction of supersecurities generally make possible at least some of these side bets, thereby improving economic welfare (Theorem 3). Since profitable side-bet opportunities are based on differences in the implicit prices P_{is} of individual states, supersecurities, for which a_{js} is positive for only a few states, appear to offer a more direct, and hence more efficient, means for quickly incorporating the major side-bet opportunities not resolvable within $M1$.

C. Likelihood of Rank Increase

As we have repeatedly stated, neither supersecurities nor subdivisions of regular securities will affect welfare unless they improve the opportunities for final allocation, i.e., unless the rank of $M1$ is increased. We must therefore assess how likely a rank increase is as given sets of group-states and regular securities are further and further subdivided.

With respect to subdivisions of existing securities, it is clearly not easy, at least as a practical matter, to determine whether a proposed set of subdivisions of a given security can be duplicated by already existing securities. In any case, when there are many similar firms in the economy, the likelihood of a rank increase appears more limited; more importantly, the likelihood of a significant welfare improvement in this case seems much more remote. As a practical matter, there are also traditionally severe self-imposed limits on the number of distinct instruments issued by firms. This is true even though in the 1960s considerable ingenuity was applied to the design and marketing of new types of financial instruments.

On the other hand, that a finer breakdown of supersecurities should be accompanied by an increase in rank seems a foregone conclusion. Suppose a new (finer) supersecurity gives the overall market return if that falls between 8 and 10%, inclusive. How could any conceivable combination of real-world regular securities and old supersecurities possibly duplicate that kind of return pattern, combined with, say, a return of 5%, if the market return falls outside the 8–10% range?

D. Options

While the preceding compared some important aspects of supersecurities to regular security proliferation, a similar comparison can be made with respect to options (puts and calls). Options differ from regular securities in that they are created by investors themselves—their very existence, in fact, testifies to the presence of side-bet opportunities not resolvable within the regular security market ($M1$). Schrems [22] and Ross [20] have argued that options also provide an effective means whereby the efficiency of the regular market can be improved. Based on our examination to this point, their effectiveness would seem to fall in between that of regular security proliferation and that of supersecurities. In particular, compared to supersecurities, the supply of options will tend to be lower, they will tend to be attached to "smaller" (individual firm) events, they have positive payoffs for a larger set of basic (relevant) states, are as a group attached to overlapping rather than mutually exclusive states, and (as a result) possibly have a lower chance of increasing the rank of available instruments. In any event, these differences suggest that the degree of welfare improvement achievable with a given number of supersecurities would tend to be greater than that obtainable with the same number of options. Furthermore, as shown by Ross [20], options may be incapable of increasing the rank of the market to n (under heterogeneous probability beliefs), whereas supersecurities always have that capability (Remark 4)—this is true for arbitrary preferences and beliefs. Options are also subject to high transaction costs (see, e.g., Black and Scholes [3]), a characteristic which appears at least partly avoidable in conjunction with supersecurities, as we shall note in Section V.

IV. Taking Cognizance of the Nitty Gritty of Investment Decision Making

A. Which Superfund?

Suppose, then, that we wish to consider the establishment of a superfund. In so doing, two questions immediately arise: (1) How could such a fund in fact be implemented? (2) *Which* superfund should be chosen among all possible such funds? Let us begin by reviewing the situation surrounding the "ultimate" superfund, i.e., one which always achieves a complete financial market by issuing one security for each state s. As we have seen, the strongest argument in favor of a complete financial market rests on the special ability of such a market to achieve a Pareto-efficient allocation of resources among investors. Despite this clear-cut virtue there are, as noted in Section I, at least four important reasons why complete markets have not come into existence: the difficulty of agreeing (a priori) on a set of acceptable time-states, the nontriviality of the subsequent determination of which state actually occurred, "the moral hazard," and the enormity of the number of states, and consequently the number of securities, that apparently would be involved. For example, if 1000 of the regular instruments were capable of yielding one of 10 different proceeds at the end of the period, the number of states n would be greater than 1000^{10}. Clearly, any attempt to grapple with these questions must take into account not only the ability of investors to deal with a huge state-space and extremely small probabilities, but also their *willingness* to do so.

B. Assumption 1

We now make the general supposition, based primarily on armchair observation, that the amount of detail an investor is willing to put up with in making his investment decision is limited. This general premise will be translated into two specific assumptions for the purpose of examining its implications in relation to the superfund.

The first assumption we make is

$$A1 \quad \pi_{is_1}/\pi_{is_2} = \pi_{1s_1}/\pi_{1s_2}, \quad \text{all } s_1, s_2 \text{ such that} \quad W_{s_1} = W_{s_2}, \quad i = 2, \ldots, I$$

By Theorem 4, assumption A1 implies that the Arrow–Debreu securities for all states with an equal supply of such securities can be combined into superstate securities with no effect on investor allocations or welfare. Thus, when A1 holds, the "ultimate" superfund need only issue $N < n$ securities, one for each superstate t, i.e., one for each different possible value of end-of-period total wealth W.

The practical significance of moving from Arrow–Debreu securities to superstate securities should not be overlooked. First, recall that one of the stumbling blocks to implementing a complete financial market has been the difficulty of specifying meaningful state descriptions (how much detail?) and state-spaces S even for single investors, not to mention the difficulties of reaching agreement among *all* investors. This seemingly unsurmountable difficulty has now been eliminated—the relevant states are identified with the different values of *total* end-of-period wealth W.

Second, even with agreement on some complex S, the determination of which state actually occurred might be easier said than done. Suppose, for example, that the earnings of several companies to the end of the period were part of the state description agreed upon. Clearly, one problem is that audited income statements are not available until months after the end of the period. And, as we know, even auditors make mistakes and are challenged, not to mention a host of other reasons for legitimate dispute. In contrast, the value of W can be made available within a few minutes—it is simply the market value of all regular securities at the end of the period—and anyone can quickly verify it if he feels so compelled.

Third, we must consider the "moral hazard." Suppose, as in the previous illustration, the current earnings of some firms were part of the state description s. Then it would not be difficult, at least within a narrow range, for an investor to change the state that actually occurs, by sabotage or even legitimate means. For the investor to (significantly) influence the market value of *all* securities at the end of the period, while not impossible, is clearly a much more difficult task. We shall return to this point shortly.

Finally, the number of possible values N assumed by W, while conceivably quite large, can undoubtedly be expected to be substantially smaller than the number of states contained in any agreed-upon complex set S.

Having observed that the value of A1 is considerable, we must now assess the price we have paid in making it. What A1 says is that the conditional probabilities of each s given t, denoted $\pi_{is|t}$, are the same for all investors. It is important to note that this permits nonhomogeneous assessments for all states, without any restriction at all on the probabilities assigned to superstates. Clearly, then, A1 is much weaker than the assumption of homogeneous probability beliefs contained in most equilibrium models in finance, in particular, the capital asset pricing model, both the one-period version (Sharpe [23], Lintner [15], Mossin [18]) and the continuous-time version of Merton [17].

Ultimately, the realism of A1 is, of course, an empirical matter. But it seems safe to conjecture that if N (the number of distinct values of W) is large, the investor may neither have the time nor the inclination to go beyond an assessment of π_{it}—or, if he did, be willing to rely on the numbers he would thereby obtain.

C. Assumption 2

In the United States, the numbers W_t (the value of all regular securities if superstate t occurs) are in the billions and trillions. We also know that most people are rather uncomfortable in working with large numbers, even if the task is only to attach small numbers (probabilities) to them. A more natural unit than total wealth is the rate of return or the wealth relative R_t (100% plus the rate of return), i.e.,

$$R_t \equiv W_t/Y, \qquad t = 1, \ldots, N$$

where $Y \equiv \sum_{i=1}^{I} y_i$, total investor wealth of the beginning of the period.

Looking at the U.S. stock market since 1925, we find that the realized (annual) values of R_t have fallen in the range (Fisher and Lorie [7])

$$.528 \le R_t \le 2.084 \tag{74}$$

But even with this background, it is, of course, not completely clear what the range of R_t in any given future period is other than that it is quite narrow (such as between 0 and, perhaps, 2).

Before worrying further about how to solve the range problem, let us consider another aspect of R_t (and the estimation of π_{it}). How many people would make a distinction between a return of 8.145 and 8.146%? between 8.1 and 8.2%? between 8 and 9%? My guess is that almost no one would make a distinction in the first case, but almost everyone would in the third one. And after once having had the experience of assessing, or attempting to assess, the probabilities of market returns to the nearest $1/1000$ of 1%, even fewer would do it a second time. Thus, the following assumption is stated with some confidence.

A2 For each interval $\bar{R} \in (0, \infty)$ of length $L(\bar{R})$, there exist numbers $\varepsilon > 0$ and $\bar{r} \in \bar{R}$ such that whenever $L(\bar{R}) \le \varepsilon$, all investors would be willing to substitute the conditional distribution function $F_{\bar{R}}(r)$ for the conditional distribution function $F_{i\bar{R}}(r)$, where

$$F_{i\bar{R}}(r) \equiv \Pr_i\{R_t \le r \,|\, R_t \in \bar{R}\}, \qquad i = 1, \ldots, I$$

$$F_{\bar{R}}(r) \equiv \begin{cases} 0, & \text{if } r < \bar{r} \\ 1, & \text{if } r \ge \bar{r} \end{cases}$$

Clearly, the point $\bar{r}$ may or may not be the midpoint of the interval $\bar{R}$.

It should be emphasized that the meaning of A2 is not that the investor is willing to forego $F_{i\bar{R}}(r)$ for $F_{\bar{R}}(r)$ were $F_{i\bar{R}}(r)$ available: rather, the assertion is that the investor is willing to use $F_{\bar{R}}(r)$ instead of going to the trouble of developing $F_{i\bar{R}}(r)$. Thus, A2 is an attempt to give at least explicit recognition to the costs of performing economic calculations and gathering information prior to making the decision.

D. An Illustration

Casual observation suggests that the interval length for which investors are willing to employ $F_R(r)$ in lieu of $F_{iR}(r)$ is smaller for intervals $\bar{R}$ containing 1 and progressively larger as $\bar{R}$ moves away from the region near 1.

As a purely hypothetical illustration, it is conceivable, on the basis of A1, A2, and (74), that the state-space $\bar{S}$ given in Table I might be agreed upon. Presumably state 121, for example, will be deemed to have occurred if the

Table I

State $\bar{s}$ (No.)	Return on market portfolio	State $\bar{s}$ (No.)	Return on market portfolio
1	−50.0% or less		
2	−49.0%		
3	−48.0%		
		120	14.75%
		121	15.00%
		122	15.5%
40	−11.0%	123	16.0%
41	−10.0%		
42	− 9.5%		
		140	24.5%
		141	25.0%
60	− 0.5%	142	26.0%
61	0.0%	143	27.0%
62	0.25%		
63	0.50%		
64	0.75%	215	99.0%
		216	100.0% or more

market portfolio return was greater than or equal to 14.875% and less than 15.25%, etc. Thus, if the supply of # 121 securities is such that $1 per share can be distributed if the market portfolio return happens to be exactly 15%, then #121 will pay (if it pays at all) from $.9989 to $1.0022 per share, etc.

No hard evidence, of course, is available on the minimum number of securities that would be required for A2 to be satisfied. But it is noteworthy that our example, which achieves a rather high degree of return discrimination, requires the issuance of only 216 securities by the superfund. Clearly, a finer breakdown of returns demands that a larger set of securities be issued. However, recall that before A1 and A2 were invoked, the number of state securities was visualized as being in the neighborhood of 1000^{10}.

E. The Target Partition: S*

For purposes of discussion, we now make the following definition.

Definition 3   A partition $\bar{S} = \{\bar{s}_1, \ldots, \bar{s}_K\}$ of S will be denoted S^* if (i) all investors are willing to substitute $\bar{S}$ for S, (ii) $\bar{S}$ has the smallest K (denoted K^*) of all $\bar{S}$ satisfying (i).

In view of A2, a partition S^* will exist, but need not be unique.

If K^* is small, which it may well be if A1 and A2 are valid, the answer to the question "Which superfund?" seems clear, namely, that superfund which issues securities on the basis of partition S^*. Conceivably, K^* may be in the region from 100 to 1000. As a practical matter, of course, S^* would not be easy to determine. In real life, then, a partition $\bar{S}$ for which (i) is expected to hold for *most* investors might be chosen.

V. Some Implications of S^*

We now examine the implications of establishing a superfund based on partition S^* (which will also be referred to as *the* superfund). In practice, as we have already noted, it may be difficult, of course, to determine S^* so that a partition $\bar{S}$, which provides a complete financial market for a large number of investors, might in fact be selected. In the latter case, the conclusions in this and the following subsections would not necessarily apply to those investors for which $\bar{S}$ is not sufficiently fine to give rise to a complete financial market—but they do apply to all other investors (who are presumably in the majority).

A. Attainable Return Patterns: Examples

It is pointed out in Section III that the strongest argument in favor of the superfund as an alternative to regular security proliferation is its unique ability to expand, in a particularly efficient manner, the return patterns available to the investor. We now illustrate this point by some examples. Suppose that there are 216 supersecurities, corresponding to the superstates shown in Table I, and that their prices p_{s*}, based on a supply of δW_{s*} shares [as opposed to a supply of $\delta W_{\min}$ shares as in (57)], are those in Table II—this gives a "riskless" rate of 7.34% (1/.9316).

Some examples of attainable return patterns are given in Table III. Policy No. 1 would be appropriate for an investor who wished to avoid "all" risk and would be a substitute for a riskless bond of the same maturity. Policy No. 2 might be chosen by an individual who is also very risk-averse but somewhat "optimistic" about the market's chances of going up; an even more "optimistic" investor might choose policy No. 5. A "pessimistic" investor, on the other hand, might select something like policy No. 3. An investor who believes a gain from 10 to 25% in the market is quite likely, but who is also very risk-averse, might invest according to policy No. 6. In any case, it is evident that investors can invest according to their tastes and beliefs in a way which offers unlimited flexibility and requires only a modicum of information processing and verification, compared to what is needed in regular markets: return patterns such as those given in Table III are, at least as a practical matter, simply not available in such markets even when supplemented with numerous options.

Table II

State s^* (No.)	$100p_{s^*}$
1, 2, ..., 41	0.35
42, ..., 60	0.50
61	0.75
62, ..., 120	0.80
121, ..., 141	0.50
142, ..., 165	0.24
166, ..., 216	0.10
$100 \sum_{s^*} p_{s^*} = 93.16$	

Table III

	Return pattern	
No.	Description	Investment policy ($y_i = 10{,}000$)
1	"7.34%" no matter what happens in market	Buy 10,734 shares of #1 through #216
2	"0%" if market goes down or is unchanged, "9.98%" if market goes up	Buy 10,000 shares of #1 through #61, 10,998 shares of #62 through #216
3	"0%" if market goes up, "27.8%" if market goes down or is unchanged	Buy 12,780 shares of #1 through #61, 10,000 shares of #62 through #216
4	"−5%" if market goes down 10% or more, "2%" if market goes down less than 10% or up less than 15%, "29.64%" if market goes up 15% or more	Buy 9500 shares of #1 through #41, 10,200 shares of #42 through #120, 12,964 shares of #121 through #216
5	"−60%" if market goes down or is unchanged, "31.51%" if market goes up	Buy 4000 shares of #1 through #61, 13,151 shares of #62 through #216
6	"13.23%" if market goes up from 10% to 25%, "5%" otherwise	Buy 11,323 shares of #101 through #141, 10,500 shares of all others
7	"256.08%" if market goes up 16%, "6%" otherwise	Buy 35,608 shares of #123, 10,600 shares of all others

B. Short Sales

We now turn to an analysis of the impact on investor transaction costs caused by the presence of the type of new securities we are discussing. Transaction costs will be viewed in a broad sense; thus we will also examine how they are affected by changes in short-sales patterns, borrowing patterns, and the numerosity of securities.

By a direct application of Theorem 2, it follows that no security need be sold short in equilibrium in the presence of a superfund holding a large enough proportion δ of all regular securities outstanding. Even if a smaller δ is chosen, supersecurities need never be sold short and the need for short sales of regular securities would be considerably less than in the absence of a superfund. Since real-world short sales practices, which require a deposit and severely restrict the investment of the proceeds, are distinctly inferior in an economic welfare sense to the pure short sales assumed in Section II, it is clear that the availability of a superfund makes possible a substantial reduction in the "transaction costs" associated with short sales by reducing these costs or entirely eliminating them.

C. Borrowing

Since borrowing is nothing but the short sale of a possibly riskless security, the need for borrowing can also be sharply curtailed or eliminated if a superfund were available. In practice, borrowing investors typically pay a premium over and beyond the rate received by saving investors; furthermore, borrowing is usually restricted by the so-called margin requirement. Both of these phenomena reduce economic welfare among investors compared to what it would otherwise be under *Assumptions* A1 and A2.

To illustrate how borrowing can be avoided in the presence of a superfund based on S^*, assume that investor i wishes to buy z_{i2} shares of the "market portfolio" at price P_2 on margin, borrowing z_{i1} dollars at the *lending* rate (10%) to complete the purchase (thus, $\sum_{s*} p_{s*} = 1/1.10$). The proceeds on each share in state s^* are a_{2s*}, giving him ending wealth $w_i(s^*) = a_{2s*} z_{i2} - 1.10 z_{i1} > 0$, on an investment of $P_2 z_{i2} - z_{i1}$, where, by Eq. (46), $P_2 = \sum_{s*} a_{js*} p_{s*}$. But he can also obtain allocation $w_i(s^*)$ directly, by purchasing $a_{2s*} z_{i2} - 1.10 z_{i1} > 0$ shares of each supersecurity s^*, at the same cost $\sum_{s*} (a_{2s*} z_{i2} - 1.10 z_{i1}) p_{s*} = P_2 z_{i2} - z_{i1}$, i.e., he can replicate a debt position without engaging in any borrowing transaction at all.

In sum, the establishment of a superfund based on S^* makes it possible to eliminate, or at least reduce, certain socially "wasteful" costs such as the costs connected with the approval and monitoring of short sales and margin loans, margin calls, and bankruptcy resulting from investors overextending themselves. In addition, investors will effectively be borrowing at the (risk-free) lending rate of interest, which presumably would be roughly equal to the rate on government securities maturing at the end of the period, a possibility not presently available to most investors.

D. Estimating the Probabilities

In the presence of a superfund based on S^*, investor i must assess the probability vector π_{is*}. The components π_{is*} may be referred to as gross probabilities or macroprobabilities. It is not clear whether investors would be more comfortable estimating such probabilities directly or whether they would prefer building them up from estimates of the likelihood of detailed joint events affecting firms. The latter approach is, of course, enormously more laborious. The first approach is the one used in economic forecasting generally (in favor of the second), and investors may well feel more confident about aggregate estimates based on simple (incomplete) models than such estimates based on a more complex but less "reliable" model. In any case, the superfund permits the investor to bypass the numbers a_{js}—the estimation of which is no simple task—entirely.

E. The Administrative Framework: Iteration Zero

While a detailed discussion of how the superfund might operate in reality is beyond the scope of this chapter, the reader is entitled to some notion of how it might function as a basis for judging its real-world potential. The following possibilities are suggested only as points of departure in initiating a dialog on the subject.

(i)   The superfund would issue supersecurities on an annual (semiannual, triannual?) basis, e.g., at the opening of business each second Monday in January for a period ending at the close of business on Friday preceding the second Monday in January the following year.

(ii)   The composition of each period's "market portfolio" would be announced well in advance and remain fixed for the period. It would consist of a broad cross section of perhaps 2500 of the more actively traded instruments: stocks, bonds, warrants, government securities, whether traded in major, regional, or over-the-counter markets.

(iii)   The value of the superfund at the end of the year would consist of the closing market values of the original instruments, plus dividends and the market value of instruments (or cash) received in exchange in the case of mergers, and from stock splits and stock dividends.

(iv)   Investors holding supersecurities over their whole term would pay no commissions; instead, the cost of floating and operating the superfund would be built into the initial prices.

(v)   During the year, supersecurities would be bought and sold like other securities on a commission basis and would be listed on the major exchanges.

(vi)   As a rule, initial offerings and final redemptions of supersecurities would be paid in cash; in the case of reinvestment from one year to the next, cash exchanged with any investor would be limited to net additions or net withdrawals, if any.

(vii)   When the superfund is expanding its assets prior to the beginning of the year (and, in particular, prior to the beginning of the first year), payments by individual investors for supersecurities could not only be in the form of cash but in the form of regular securities (at least those included in the fund's "market portfolio").

(viii)   Cash and "excess" regular securities received by the superfund in payment for supersecurities would be exchanged (without commission) for "deficit" securities, at previous closing prices, with institutional investors submitting "accept" and "offer" lists. Any remaining "imbalance" in the superfund's holdings would be corrected by open market transactions.

As noted, the above should not be viewed as a concrete proposal but rather as suggestive of how the superfund might operate. It is unclear, for example, whether it would be best to have many small funds, a few large ones, or one very large fund. Small funds would probably be easier to float and would insure competition, but would also entail substantial duplication of effort. One large fund is all that is really needed and may well be readily implementable in countries with a well developed brokerage industry; however, the lack of direct competition may also be a drawback to this approach. Another open question is what the best way to float each set of supersecurities is and how "fine" the state space should be. Simultaneous bidding is clearly one possibility and an ordinary investment-banking underwriting, with the initial prices predetermined, is another.

F. Other Implications

As one might suspect, the impact of a superfund based on S^* would reach well beyond investors (and the securities industry). For the firm, the implications are essentially twofold, touching upon two of its most crucial decisions: capital budgeting and the choice of financing.

Under the usual competitive market assumptions (in essence, that the firm's capital budget is not "big" enough to appreciably affect the prices p_{s*}), the presence of the superfund implies the following (Pareto-efficient) capital budgeting decision rule: Choose that project combination b which maximizes

$$\sum_{s*} v_{s*}(b)p_{s*} \tag{75}$$

where $v_{s*}(b)$ is the net increase in the value of the firm at the end of the current period under project combination b if state $s*$ occurs. The practical significance of this implication should not be overestimated, since the numbers $v_{s*}(b)$ are not easy to come by, especially for long-term projects. But (75) does indicate that the appropriate rule, in the presence of the superfund, is a present value rule (which calls for maximizing the value of the firm) and does pinpoint attention on the critical quantities that are relevant for management to consider.

The essence of the superfund is that it makes possible a "near-ultimate" allocation of resources among investors without having to rely on the allocation possibilities made available by individual firms via their capital structures (which are generally inadequate for the purpose—see Section IIG, especially Remark 8). The implication of this is that the firm's capital structure becomes "less relevant," i.e., that the firm gains little by issuing more than one security. In particular, the issuance of (virtually) risk-free "bonds" can automatically be "transferred" to the superfund without the hampering effects of indenture requirements, etc.

The presence of the superfund is also likely to increase the pressure for abolishment of regulated interest rate maxima on time and savings deposits.[17] The reason for this is that financial institutions accepting (short-term) time deposits will face direct competition from the superfund. Finally, since investors now can avoid borrowing (Section VC), the margin requirement, as an instrument of monetary policy, will lose some of its potency. Other ramifications resulting from implementation of the superfund can also be cited but will, in the interest of space, be left for another occasion.

VI. Nominal Returns versus Deflated Returns

So far, we have implicitly assumed that wealth and return have been expressed in nominal terms. But our analysis would have been equally valid if we had assumed that the constants a_{js}, and hence $w_i(s)$, had been measured in real terms, with the utility functions u_i defined on deflated wealth.

More explicitly, let I_s, where $0 < I_s < \bar{I}$ for some $\bar{I}$, be 1 plus the rate of inflation during the period if state s occurs at the end of the period. Then, using superscript d to denote deflated variables,

$$a_{js}^d = a_{js}/I_s, \qquad w_i^d(s) = w_i(s)/I_s, \qquad s = 1, \ldots, n$$

where $n^d \geq n$, since we may need to subdivide the previous state space S further (call the new state space S^d) in order for the a_{js}^d not to become random variables. All the theorems in Section II now hold as before; in

---

[17] See, e.g., the Hunt Commission Report [12] and Pyle [19].

particular, A1 implies that only aggregate real wealth levels w_s^d need be distinguished by investors. The equilibrium real "riskless" interest rate obtainable via supersecurities will now generally differ substantially from the nominally riskless rate on government securities of comparable maturity. And the relative advantage of the superfund over options, which offer patterns of nominal wealth only, will also be greater than before.

In practice, a broadly based and well-known consumer good type index such as the Consumer Price Index would probably serve as an adequate surrogate for I_s. In any case, the ratio R_t/I_t (where R_t is defined as in Section IVC), rather than R_t alone, now determines which supersecurities pay off at the end of the period.

VII. Multiperiod Extensions

Up to this point we have assumed a single-period model in which all investors have the same horizon. Let us now consider a (Fisherian) multiperiod consumption–investment model with a possibly random horizon. If consumers prefer more to less in each period, are risk-averse, and have infinite marginal utility for a nonnegative level of consumption in each period, then their (possibly conditional) induced utility of wealth functions will satisfy (2) (written somewhat differently) in each period under weak conditions (see, e.g., Fama [6] and Sibley [24].[18] Moreover, the optimal strategy of each investor calls for him to review and (generally) revise his portfolio at the beginning of each period. This implies that (in the absence of exchange friction) all current investments, regardless of the expiration dates of the instruments traded, are made with respect to a horizon which falls at the end of the current period; all information about the future beyond that point is contained in the (currently applicable) induced utility of wealth function(s). As a result, if the decision points of all market participants coincide, a market structure in which single-period Arrow–Debreu securities are issued sequentially as the periods arrive may be equivalent to one in which all maturities of Arrow–Debreu securities are issued at the beginning. The reason for this is twofold: The availability of Arrow–Debreu securities maturing beyond the current period need not change the opportunity set for the current period's investments; their impact may be limited to the currently applicable induced utility of wealth functions, and this impact is based on the *assumption* that such securities will (still) be available in future periods.

This leads us to an important point: The preceding is, of course, true only

---

[18] In particular, all the results in Section II readily extend to the two-period model, with utility functions $U_{is}(c_{i1}, c_{i2})$, $i = 1, \ldots, I$, $s = 1, \ldots, n$, where c_{it} is the ammount of consumption by individual i in period t and s is the state at the beginning of period 2.

if the current-period set of securities is in fact a "complete" set of securities. Whether this is so is determinable by reference to the induced (end-of-period) utility of wealth functions; if these functions depend only on wealth (as they typically do if future return distributions are *perceived* to be independent of previously realized returns and utility functions of consumption are separable), then the superstates given by Theorem 4, identified one period at a time, are adequate if (71) holds. But if the currently applicable utility functions $V[c, (w, \hat{s})]$ depend on an end-of-period state description $(w, \hat{s})$ which goes beyond wealth (w) (see, e.g., Hakansson [9], Rubinstein [21]), then the sequential issuance of securities based on superstates are sufficient to achieve a complete financial market only if the stronger condition

$$\frac{\pi_{is_1} \ \partial V[c, (w, \hat{s}_{i1})]/\partial w}{\pi_{is_2} \ \partial V[c, (w, \hat{s}_{i2})]/\partial w} = \frac{\pi_{1s_1} \ \partial V[c, (w, \hat{s}_{11})]/\partial w}{\pi_{1s_2} \ \partial V[c, (w, \hat{s}_{12})]/\partial w},$$

$$\text{all } s_1, s_2 \in t_k, \quad \text{all } w > b_i, \quad k = 1, \ldots, m, \quad i = 2, \ldots, I \qquad (76)$$

where $s_1 \in \hat{s}_{i1}$, $s_2 \in \hat{s}_{i2}$, all i, holds. However, the concept of a superfund is still viable if (76) is violated, since supersecurities can, in principle, be issued for a state space of unlimited richness; more importantly, since supersecurities apparently cannot be duplicated in the real world, superfunds issuing as few as two securities result in dominating market structures. One of the unanswered questions is the extent to which significant welfare improvements can be obtained by breaking down the supersecurities defined in this paper into even "finer" instruments.

If the investment horizons among investors differ, then it would be necessary for the superfund to issue several maturities, one for each horizon (a somewhat analogous practice occurs in the option market). If A1 or (76) holds for each horizon (whichever is applicable) along with A2, the superfund would again, by sequential issuance of supersecurities applicable to currently relevant investor horizons, achieve all the benefits of a complete financial market. As a practical matter, determining the set of (exactly) relevant terms of supersecurities would not be easy, of course; and multiple-term securities would increase the number of securities in the market.

VIII. Concluding remarks

We have examined the primary implications that would result from the creation of a superfund that would own a substantial portion of the "market portfolio" (say, from 10 to 40%) and (periodically) issue (single-term) securities for a set of prespecified superstates (say, from 100 to 1000). Under assumptions that do not appear unrealistic with respect to preferences, probability beliefs, and the amount of detailed information an investor might be willing to process and develop before making this decision, we found that such a superfund might well provide most of the advantages of a complete financial market for a majority of investors. The main reason for this is that trade in commodities (states) which differ in aggregate (real or nominal) wealth is not presently available even though trade in such commodities is necessary for "market completeness" even under very limited heterogeneity, and is sufficient for "market completeness" when investors exhibit a surprisingly high degree of heterogeneity (Theorem 4). But even when a given superfund does not lead to a complete market, it offers a much more efficient and reliable means of incorporating the major side-bet opportunities left unresolved by conventional financial markets (evidence or the existence of such side-bet opportunities is provided by the market in options) than security proliferation by firms and even the establishment of (more) sizable option markets. Furthermore, the need for actual short sales and margin loans would be sharply reduced, eliminating much of the cost associated with credit approval, collateral requirements, margin account monitoring, margin calls, investor insolvency, etc.; investors will, in effect, be able to make cost-free "pure" short sales and to borrow and lend at the "risk-free" lending rate. Investors who make their portfolio revisions relatively infrequently may also be able to reduce their transaction costs. The main beneficiary would clearly be the small investor, who in the past has been forced to deal with highly disaggregated (and complex) information, limited opportunities for diversification and financing, and high transaction costs (per dollar of investment). While (no-load) mutual funds have made a high degree of diversification available to small investors at something on the order of a pittance, such funds are unable to provide the other advantages of the superfund. And since the superfund would take much of the wind out of the "increase-in-welfare" argument as a reason for security proliferation by firms, the establishment of a superfund might actually reduce the total number of securities traded in the market, compared to what it otherwise would be, over a period of time—with superior welfare results.

Finally, the superfund may be helpful to developing countries in attracting foreign capital, since it makes this possible without giving up domestic control. This in turn may stimulate the development of capital markets in the smaller countries, especially since returns can readily be made available in real terms, i.e., adjusted for inflation (Section VI) and even foreign exchange fluctuations.

References

1. Arrow, K., "The Role of Securities in the Optimal Allocation of Risk-Bearing," *Review of Economic Studies* **31** (1964), 91–96.
2. Arrow, K., "Limited Knowledge and Economic Analysis," *American Economic Review* **64** (1974), 1–10.

3. Black, F., and Scholes, M., "The Valuation of Option Contracts and a Test of Market Efficiency, *Journal of Finance* **27** (1972), 399–417.

4. Cass, D., and Stiglitz, J., "The Structure of Investor Preferences and Asset Returns, and Separability in Portfolio Selection: A Contribution to the Pure Theory of Mutual Funds," *Journal of Economic Theory* **2** (1970), 122–160.

5. Debreu, G., *Theory of Value*, Chapter 7. New York: Wiley.

6. Fama, E., "Multi-period Investment Consumption Decisions," *American Economic Review* **60** (1970), 163–174.

7. Fisher, L., and Lorie, J., "Rates of Return on Investment in Common Stock: The Year-by-Year Record, 1926–65," *Journal of Business* **41** (1968), 291–316.

8. Hakansson, N., "Optimal Investment and Consumption Strategies under Risk for a Class of Utility Functions," *Econometrica* **38** (1970), 587–607.

9. Hakansson, N., "Optimal Entrepreneurial Decisions in a Completely Stochastic Environment," *Management Science: Theory* **17** (1971), 427–449.

10. Hakansson, N., "Ordering Markets and the Capital Structures of Firms, with Illustrations," Finance Working Paper No. 24, Inst. of Business and Economic Res., Univ. of California, Berkeley (1974).

11. Hart, O., "On the Existence of Equilibrium in a Securities Model," *Journal of Economic Theory* **9** (1974), 293–311.

12. Hunt Commission, *The Report of the President's Commission of Financial Structure and Regulation.* Washington, D.C.: US Govt. Printing Office, 1971.

13. Jensen, M., "Risk, the Pricing of Capital Assets, and the Evaluation of Investment Portfolios," *Journal of Business* **42** (1969), 167–247.

14. Koopmans, T., "Is the Theory of Competitive Equilibrium With It?" *American Economic Review,* **44** (1974), 325–329.

15. Lintner, J. "The Valuation of Risk Assets and the Selection of Risk Investment in Stock Portfolios and Capital Budgets," *Review of Economics and Statistics* **20** (1965), 13–37.

16. Merton, R., "Optimum Consumption and Portfolio Rules in a Continuous-Time Model," *Journal of Economic Theory* **3** (1971), 373–413.

17. Merton, R., "An Intertemporal Capital Asset Pricing Model," *Econometrica* **41** (1973), 867–888.

18. Mossin, J., "Equilibrium in a Capital Asset Market," *Econometrica* **34** (1966), 768–783.

19. Pyle, D., "The Losses on Savings Deposits from Interest Rate Regulation," *Bell Journal of Economics and Management Science* **5** (1974), 614–622.

20. Ross, S., "Options and Efficiency," *Quarterly Journal of Economics* **XC** (1976), 75–89.

21. Rubinstein, M., "A Discrete-Time Synthesis of Financial Theory," Parts I and II, Finance Working Papers No. 20 and 21, Institute of Business and Economic Research, Univ. of California, Berkeley (1974).

22. Schrems, E., "The Sufficiency of Existing Financial Instruments for Pareto-Optimal Risk Allocation," Ph.D. thesis, Stanford Univ. (1973).

23. Sharpe, W., "Capital Asset Prices: A Theory of Market Equilibrium Under Conditions of Risk," *Journal of Finance* **19** (1964), 425–442.

24. Sibley, D., "Permanent and Transitory Income Effects in a Model of Optimal Consumption with Wage Income Uncertainty," *Journal of Economic Theory* **11** (1975), 68–82.

25. Stiglitz, J., "On the Optimality of Stock Market Allocation of Investment," *Quarterly Journal of Economics* **86** (1972), 25–60.

Part V

APPLICATIONS OF RISK ANALYSIS

DEFAULT RISK AND THE DEMAND FOR FORWARD EXCHANGE

Michael Adler

Columbia University

Bernard Dumas

E.S.S.E.C., France

I. Introduction

The development of the so-called "modern theory" (MT) of the forward foreign exchange market summarized by Grubel [12] and Stoll [22] purported to offer at least three contributions. First, it established that forward exchange market equilibrium could occur at a forward rate which did not correspond to interest rate parity (IRP). Second, it predicted usefully for forecasting purposes that the equilibrium forward rate would invariably fall in between the IRP forward rate and the expected future spot rate. And third, it supplied a theoretical foundation for government policies of intervention in the forward market which were deemed—given certain assumptions regarding speculators' expectations as to the results of the intervention—to be potentially successful even under market demand conditions that were such as to produce IRP. Our paper aims to investigate and partly to refute these claims. To do so, we employ a two-country model of international investment including transactions in stocks, bonds, and forward contracts, which allows for risks of default. As we shall show, the first

Financial support was provided by the Rockefeller Foundation which, however, bears no responsibility for any opinions expressed herein.

claim survives, but for reasons other than those proposed by the MT; while the second and third do not.

The several deficiencies of the MT stem essentially from its treatment of the forward exchange market as a closed system, isolated from other markets (Stein [20] provides an exception to this rule). The urge to identify the equivalent of demand and supply sides in the market forced many authors (e.g., Sohmen [18] and Grubel [12]), to posit an artificial segmentation of forward market transactions, as between pure arbitrage and pure speculation: arbitrageurs never speculate and vice versa. Because interest arbitrage involves equal and opposite spot and forward transactions, this putative segmentation led to the misleading supposition of a direct quantitative link between the volumes of forward and spot market transactions and an incorrect sense of the predictability of the response of spot, short-term capital flows to monetary policy. Taking the market as isolated and separating it between speculators and arbitrageurs also forced the MT largely to exclude all hedgers, an important group, for whom the linkage necessarily breaks down. But hedgers must be incorporated, as they are below, if forward exchange theory is to be relevant.

Hedgers include all individuals and firms whose net positions in various currencies are accumulated in the course of activities other than pure speculation or arbitrage. They are presumed, probably wrongly, as we shall argue below, to enter the forward markets to cover those positions they consider exposed to exchange risk. While the MT usually lumps importers–exporters with the speculators, portfolio investors cannot be classified one way or the other. Investor-hedgers cannot be treated as pure arbitrageurs because their initial foreign currency positions are not taken solely in response to interest differentials. They are not pure speculators because they are motivated also by potential gains other than the difference between the expected future spot and forward rates. Indeed, hedgers in practice may speculate and do arbitrage as well.

Kenen [14], using a partial equilibrium certainty model of a single international trading firm, was the first to establish the principle that single economic units might normally enter all sides of the market simultaneously. But, aside from Schilling [17], few have chosen to follow his lead.[1] Like Kenen's trading firm, which imports, exports, hedges, and speculates all at once, the investors in our model may undertake transactions simultaneously in several

---

[1] Unlike Kenen, Schilling's nonmathematical discussion of an individual investor also calls attention to the breakdown of the quantity link between the spot and forward markets. The link is not restored by Tsiang's [24] famous device of equating spot speculation with forward speculation plus arbitrage. Tsiang's contribution, however, can be reproduced in both Kenen's model and ours, but this is not required here, since we no longer need to separate forward transactions into pure arbitrage and speculation.

markets. They may trade internationally in goods to an unspecified degree. They will buy internationally diversified portfolios of risky securities. They will borrow and lend at home and abroad by buying or selling bonds which may be risky or riskless. They may speculate in forward exchange contracts and they may undertake interest arbitrage if the opportunity presents itself. Each investor's optimum, from which his demand functions for domestic and foreign risky securities, bonds, and forward exchange contracts are derived in Section II, clearly depends on and affects the conditions leading to equilibrium in the markets for each of the several assets. This simultaneity reveals the fruitlessness of any assertion of a simple connection via arbitrage alone between the volumes of spot and forward transactions. The link is necessarily indirect and will be established by the simultaneous equilibria in the capital and foreign exchange markets.

Our main objective in Sections II and III is to derive an individual's demand function for forward exchange under general uncertainty and in the presence of default risks on foreign exchange contracts and bonds. This analysis clearly reveals that the demand for forward contracts cannot be decomposed linearly into additive component demands for the purposes of arbitrage, speculation, and hedging. The usual MT rendition is therefore demonstrably wrong. The demand for arbitrage which exists only in conjunction with the other two need not involve interest arbitrage at all. Arbitrage will occur between any two linearly dependent sets of risky assets. It will become interest arbitrage only if it is forward contracts and bonds which are stochastically dependent: they are, naturally, when bonds and forward contracts are both riskless. Further, the demand for hedging purposes arises mainly as the result of the availability of forward contracts as an extra risky asset into which the investor may diversify to reduce his total real portfolio risk. Perhaps surprisingly hedging in our model, unlike Kenen's [14] and others, has nothing to do with definitions of the exposure of assets or investment returns to exchange risk. This last point may benefit from further clarification.

At equilibrium with free international trade, it is well known that tradable goods will sell everywhere at spot parity. A version of purchasing power parity will prevail. That is, local goods prices, and exchange rates will always be perfectly coordinated. The real risks which individuals confront are associated with relative price changes which may change their optimal consumption mixes and reduce their expected utilities. Much of the so-called exchange risk disappears in this case as no loss in consumption can ever be suffered merely as a result of an exchange rate change. In such a setting, the scope and usefulness of the forward exchange market is then largely reduced.

In this paper, however, we accept the empirical evidence of shortrun maladjustments of exchange rates to prices (e.g., Gaillot [10]), leaving aside an investigation of the possible causes of such a phenomenon. We take prices and exchange rates both as exogenously determined. Exchange risk therefore has a distinct identity in our formulations.[2] But an investor seeking to maximize the expected utility of his real consumption of a mix of internationally traded goods will not seek to hedge his real future purchasing power by seeking to convert forward all his foreign investment returns and exchange receipts into his own currency—i.e., by covering his exposure. In fact he would do so, as Kenen's firm is assumed to do, only if he desired to consume his own country's goods exclusively.[3] But this desire, if shared by all, would rule out altogether the need for international trade or the motive for foreign investment in the absence of which no foreign exchange market would exist except by fiat.[4] In short, the individual, who in this paper may engage in international trade to an unspecified extent within environmental limits will not hedge by covering exposed assets or income. Rather, he will seek to reduce his real purchasing power risks arising from relative price changes.[5]

With the investor's demand for foreign exchange thus respecified, it is possible to return to the more central concern of confronting, not the MT's assumptions, but rather its predictions. Because the IRP condition is frequently not empirically satisfied, considerable research has been devoted to possible reasons for deviations from parity. Branson [3] attributes departures from IRP to transaction costs which create a band within which deviations can occur. Frenkel and Levitch [9], however, suggest that once the effects of transaction costs are removed, IRP appears to be robust. Other authors largely rely on specific market imperfections for their explanations. Einzig [6], followed by Sohmen [18] and Canterbery [4], argue for institutional constraints on the availability of arbitrage funds which, in the language of the MT, cause the arbitrage net-demand curve for forward contracts to become inelastic with respect to changes in the forward rate. Canterbery further asserts (wrongly, as we shall show) that the presence of hedgers is sufficient to render IRP impossible. Prachowny [16] and Frenkel [8] identify as the culprits capital market imperfections, in the form of borrowing rates

---

[2] We must, therefore, also postulate that the same causes which prevent commodity prices from reaching parity, whatever they may be, also prevent individuals from undertaking instantaneous trade arbitrage, purchasing a good where it is cheap and selling it higher elsewhere. That is, we rule out the possibility of infinite wealth.

[3] The requirement of total conversion of all returns into the home currency, i.e., the implicit assumption of exclusively home-good consumption pervades the forward exchange literature and is not unique to Kenen. However, this reasoning points to a further problem with Kenen's formulation. The arguments of his trader's utility function, defined in terms of mean values and exposure to exchange risk, are inconsistent with the return and risk factors individuals and firms are presumed to respond to in other markets.

[4] We are grateful to Richard Stehle for explaining this argument to us.

[5] A similar point was made by Grauer *et al.* [11].

which rise in an unspecified (and probably unmeasurable) fashion with the volume of arbitrage: Kenen makes a similar assumption. None of these institutional accounts is necessary.

Our explanation of departures of forward rates from IRP is founded, in a manner consistent with recent developments in financial theory, on the existence of risks and the associated costs of default on bonds and especially forward contracts. Others have offered similar suggestions but without rigorous proof. Stoll [23] and Grubel [12] have argued that default risk in arbitrage transactions will make the (hypothetical) pure arbitrage function inelastic. Aliber [2] surmises that probably political risks (i.e., of restrictions on convertibility) are enough to do the trick. Our investor demand model in Section III makes these ideas precise. In the general case, with heterogeneous expectations and default risks on both bonds and forward contracts, IRP will generally not materialize when the forward market is cleared. Even if perfect arbitrage opportunities exist, but between forward contracting and some asset other than bonds, IRP will not prevail; some other parity rate, however, will, and the demand for forward contracts will become indeterminate. In the special case where bonds can be taken as riskless, IRP will prevail both in the presence of convertibility risks on forward contracts (given some additional independence assumptions) and, obviously, in their absence.

It is hard to identify the characteristics of equilibrium in the general case. In Section IV, therefore, we examine equilibrium in the special case where investors everywhere share homogeneous expectations. Even in this relatively arid setting, however, the MT's predictions are not robust. The equilibrium forward rate is not generally a weighted average of the IRP forward rate and the expected future spot rate.[6] And under the conditions which guarantee IRP, successful government intervention in the forward market is impossible.

Section V summarizes and concludes this chapter.

II. The Model and the Optimality Conditions

The creation of a model of international transactions with convertibility risk requires that three features be incorporated in the model:

(1) the existence of several nations;
(2) the risk that convertibility and therefore international payments be

---

[6] It is clear from our equilibrium conditions that it is no longer necessary to distinguish, as Kenen did [14], between "average" or market parity and some "marginal" parity which is internal to the investor's calculus. When market equilibrium is reached, the marginal conditions for every investor's optimum are satisfied. Kenen's problem was that he stopped with his trader's microeconomic problem and did not clear his markets.

suspended when a bond comes due, so that in effect the foreign party must default;

(3)   the comparable risk for forward contracts.

Nations are defined and separated by currency borders. For simplicity, we assume the existence of only two countries. The current spot exchange rate is taken to be 1. The future spot exchange rate is considered random. Rather than the existence of currency borders, it is the randomness of the exchange rate relative to prices which renders the two nations distinguishable, for it introduces a multiplicative risk which investors must take into account in their evaluations and decisions. The future spot rate of exchange is denoted by $\tilde{S}$; $\tilde{S}$ is the number of units of currency 1 per unit of currency 2.

The bonds (whether government or industrial) of each country are subject to a risk of default. The risk differs from country to country; but within a country, all bonds are assumed to have the same risk of default, so that in effect there is only one bond in each country. The risk of default on bonds implies that the amount of payments actually to be discharged by the borrowers is not fully guaranteed. We shall express this fact by considering the rates of interest actually to be paid by the bonds of both countries as random variables $\tilde{r}_1$ and $\tilde{r}_2$. Clearly, these variables are not contractual (or promised) rates and their randomness does *not* purport to represent the fluctuations of contractual rates over time. This is not at all our concern in this chapter.

Finally, a forward exchange market must be organized. Any investor is at liberty to conclude, without restrictions by nationality, agreements for the future exchange of a stipulated amount of foreign currency for his own currency at a stipulated rate F, called the forward rate. Like $\tilde{S}$, F is expressed as the number of units of currency 1 per unit of currency 2. F is not random of course; however, in order to represent the risk of default on forward contracts, which is due to risks of suspension of convertibility, we shall introduce a random variable $\tilde{\varepsilon}$ which takes the value 1 when the total stipulated amount of the transaction is actually executed and takes the value 0 when, for whatever reason, the exchange is not executed at all. Values of $\tilde{\varepsilon}$ between 0 and 1 represent partial default. The random variable $\tilde{\varepsilon}$ actually represents the (random) loss to the investor if his forward contracts default. It is thus a combination of the risk together with the cost of default.

In both cases the convertibility risk is taken to be exogeneous and independent of the decisions made by the various individuals. Therefore, the analytical apparatus here to be presented does not lend itself to the analysis of risks of defaults which result from the financial demise of individuals, as the probability of this default would then vary with the decisions. This is the reason why we have chosen to interpret our default risk as a convertibility risk, for this risk is largely political and little connected with the investors' decisions.

For clarity, we now present all notations in one set of definitions:

Expectations variables

$\tilde{\mathbf{V}}_j$ The future (period 1) payment on a share of stock of country j expressed in currency j; $j = 1, 2$.

$\tilde{r}_j$ Already defined as the rate of interest actually to be paid on bonds.

$\tilde{S}$ Future spot rate of exchange (into currency 1).

$\tilde{\varepsilon}$ Risk times the cost of default on forward contracts.

Decision variables

$\mathbf{x}$ Vector of fractional holdings of country 1 stocks for any investor.

$\mathbf{y}$ Vector of fractional holdings of country 2 stocks.

A,B Amount borrowed in country 1 and 2.

C Amount of currency 2 sold forward.

Market-value variables

F Forward rate of exchange (into currency 1).

$\mathbf{V}_{0j}$ Vector of period 0 country j market values of stocks.

With these notations, the future (period 1) nominal wealth of an individual of any country expressed in units of currency 1 is

$$\tilde{w} = \mathbf{x}'\tilde{\mathbf{V}}_1 - (1 - \tilde{r}_1)A + \tilde{\varepsilon}(F - \tilde{S})C + S[\mathbf{y}'\tilde{\mathbf{V}}_2 - (1 + \tilde{r}_2)B] \qquad (1)$$

and his budget constraint is

$$w_0 + A + B = \mathbf{x}'\mathbf{V}_{01} + \mathbf{y}'\mathbf{V}_{02} + c_0 \qquad (2)$$

where w_0 is the period 0 nominal wealth of the individual, and c_0 the period 0 nominal consumption expenditures by the individual.

The wealth equation adds the domestic wealth, the wealth derived from foreign exchange dealings, and the foreign wealth translated (*not* converted) into currency 1, which serves as a unit of account. The domestic (foreign) wealth is equal to the future value of domestic (foreign) stock holdings minus the discharge of the domestic (foreign) debt.

Nominal wealth, both present and future, is used for real consumption and investment, and the utility function to be maximized in choosing the menu of consumption goods is assumed to be quadratic:

$$\tilde{v} = \mathbf{c}_0'Q\mathbf{c}_0 + \mathbf{q}'\mathbf{c}_0 + \alpha[-\tilde{\mathbf{c}}_1'Q\tilde{\mathbf{c}}_1 + \mathbf{q}'\tilde{\mathbf{c}}_1] \qquad (3)$$

where $\mathbf{c}_0$, $\tilde{\mathbf{c}}_1$ is the vector of real consumption of all goods in periods 0 and 1, Q a positive definite symmetric matrix, $\mathbf{q}$ a vector of positive coefficients, and α the rate of time preference.

The Appendix shows that maximization of (3) with respect to the consumption menu yields the following derived utility function

$$\tilde{v} = -\frac{c_0^2}{\mathbf{p}_0' Q^{-1} \mathbf{p}_0} + \frac{\mathbf{p}_0' Q^{-1} \mathbf{q}}{\mathbf{p}_0' Q^{-1} \mathbf{p}_0} c_0 + \alpha\left(-\frac{\tilde{w}^2}{\tilde{\mathbf{p}}_1' Q^{-1} \tilde{\mathbf{p}}_1} + \frac{\mathbf{p}_1' Q^{-1} \mathbf{q}}{\tilde{\mathbf{p}}_1' Q^{-1} \tilde{\mathbf{p}}_1} \tilde{w}\right) \quad (4)$$

where $\mathbf{p}_0$ and $\tilde{\mathbf{p}}_1$ are the current and future vectors of prices. Although expressed in currency 1, the unit of account, these prices are not necessarily country 1 prices. They are, for each product, the prices to which the investor has access across the world. They might also differ from investor to investor.

It will be convenient to transform (4) into an equivalent objective:

$$\tilde{v} = -c_0^2 + R_0 c_0 + \alpha(-\tilde{w}^2 \tilde{I}^{-1} + \tilde{R}\tilde{w}\tilde{I}^{-1}) \quad (5)$$

where a multiplication by the positive scalar $\mathbf{p}_0' Q^{-1} \mathbf{p}_0$ has been performed and where

$$R_0 = \mathbf{p}_0' Q^{-1} \mathbf{q}, \qquad \tilde{R} = \tilde{\mathbf{p}}_1' Q^{-1} \mathbf{q}, \qquad \tilde{I} = \tilde{\mathbf{p}}_1' Q^{-1} \tilde{\mathbf{p}}_1 / \mathbf{p}_0' Q^{-1} \mathbf{p}_0$$

$\tilde{I}$ is in some sense an inflation index which is not however capable of correcting fully for the change in prices; additional quantities R_0 and $\tilde{R}$ intervene to fully correct for price changes; like Heckerman [13] we could call these "relative price variables." In general, the index $\tilde{I}$ and the variable $\tilde{R}$ are specific to each investor as they contain his own taste parameters; this is not surprising as the same expected price changes affect different people differently depending on their preferences for the various goods. Moreover, as already mentioned, different individuals (of different countries perhaps) may have access to different prices.

In order to avoid absurd results, we *assume* that nominal consumption and nominal wealth will be such that no satiation will ever take place:

$$\partial v/\partial c_0 = R_0 - 2c_0 > 0 \qquad \text{strictly} \quad (6)$$

$$\partial v/\partial w = R - 2w > 0 \qquad \text{strictly} \quad (7)$$

This latter condition is equivalent to an assumption of positive risk aversion:

$$-\frac{\partial^2 v/\partial w^2}{\partial v/\partial w} = \frac{2}{R - 2w} \quad (7a)$$

For compactness, we introduce vector notations:

$$\tilde{\mathbf{V}} = \begin{pmatrix} \tilde{V}_1 \\ S\tilde{V}_2 \\ -(1 + \tilde{r}_1) \\ -\tilde{S}(1 + \tilde{r}_2) \\ \tilde{\varepsilon}(F - \tilde{S}) \end{pmatrix}, \qquad \mathbf{V}_0 = \begin{pmatrix} V_{01} \\ V_{02} \\ -1 \\ -1 \\ 0 \end{pmatrix}, \qquad \mathbf{z} = \begin{pmatrix} x \\ y \\ A \\ B \\ C \end{pmatrix}$$

Then (1) can be rewritten as

$$\tilde{w} = \mathbf{z}'\tilde{\mathbf{V}} \tag{8}$$

and (2) as

$$c_0 = w_0 - \mathbf{z}'\mathbf{V}_0 \tag{9}$$

We substitute (8) and (9) into (5):

$$\tilde{v} = -(w_0 - \mathbf{z}'\mathbf{V}_0)^2 + R_0(w_0 - \mathbf{z}'\mathbf{V}_0) + \alpha[-(\mathbf{z}'\tilde{\mathbf{V}})^2\tilde{I}^{-1} + \tilde{R}\tilde{I}^{-1}\mathbf{z}'\tilde{\mathbf{V}}] \tag{10}$$

Taking the derivative of $E(\tilde{v})$ with respect to $\mathbf{z}$, we obtain the first-order condition:

$$-[-2(w_0 - z'\mathbf{V}_0) + R_0]\mathbf{V}_0 + \alpha E[(-2\mathbf{z}'\tilde{\mathbf{V}} + \tilde{\mathbf{R}})\tilde{I}^{-1}\tilde{\mathbf{V}}] = \mathbf{0} \tag{11}$$

Before proceeding to solve these equations, we pause to analyze the second-order conditions. The quadratic terms in $E(\tilde{v})$ are

$$-(\mathbf{z}'\mathbf{V}_0)^2 - \alpha E[(\mathbf{z}'\tilde{\mathbf{V}})^2\tilde{I}^{-1}]$$

Since this quantity is nonpositive, we are assured that the solution of Eq. (11) could never be a minimum of $E(\tilde{v})$. Rather, the solution of Eq. (11) when it is unique is the strict global maximum; and, if it is not unique, then it is because $E(\tilde{v})$ admits of several maxima. This latter circumstance occurs when the elements of $\tilde{\mathbf{V}}$ are linearly dependent across states of nature $(\mathbf{z}'\tilde{\mathbf{V}} = 0$ for some $\mathbf{z} \neq \mathbf{0})$ *and* the prices $\mathbf{V}_0$ happen to satisfy the same linear relationship $(\mathbf{z}'\mathbf{V}_0 = 0)$ as the elements of $\tilde{\mathbf{V}}$; Eq. (11) then admits of an infinitely large number of solutions, which are all maxima of $E(\tilde{v})$.

We might note in passing some cases where the elements of $\tilde{\mathbf{V}}$ are linearly dependent and where, therefore, for some prices the decisions are indeterminate. One such circumstance is the case where riskless interest arbitrage is possible: r_1 nonstochastic, r_2 nonstochastic, and $\varepsilon = 1$.

Then,

$$\mathbf{z} = \begin{pmatrix} 0 \\ 0 \\ F(1 + r_2)/(1 + r_1) \\ -1 \\ (1 + r_2) \end{pmatrix}$$

satisfies $\mathbf{z}'\tilde{\mathbf{V}} = 0$ for all states of nature. This case however will generally be ruled out by convertibility risk, since from the standpoint of any individual the foreign bonds and the forward contracts entail default risk. A second case of linear dependence occurs when there is free trade (with the resulting spot parity of prices), and two firms, one in country 1, the other in country 2, produce the same product. If we further assume that these firms have nonstochastic shares of the time-1 world market[7] and distribute the proceeds of their time-1 sales to their stockholders, then one element of $\tilde{\mathbf{V}}_1$ will be proportional to one element of $\tilde{S}\tilde{\mathbf{V}}_2$.

III. The Demand Schedules

The optimality condition (11) can be rewritten as

$$-2[\mathbf{V}_0\mathbf{V}_0' + \alpha E(\tilde{\mathbf{V}}\tilde{I}^{-1}\tilde{\mathbf{V}}')]\mathbf{z} = (-2w_0 + R_0)\mathbf{V}_0 - \alpha E(\tilde{R}\tilde{I}^{-1}\tilde{\mathbf{V}}) \quad (12)$$

Whenever the elements of $\tilde{\mathbf{V}}$ are linearly independent across states of nature, the matrix on the left-hand side of (12) is positive definite and one can obtain a general expression for the demand schedules:

$$\mathbf{z} = \tfrac{1}{2}[(1/\alpha)\mathbf{V}_0\mathbf{V}_0' + E(\tilde{\mathbf{V}}\tilde{I}^{-1}\tilde{\mathbf{V}}')]^{-1}[E(\tilde{R}\tilde{I}^{-1}\tilde{\mathbf{V}}) - (1/\alpha)(-2w_0 + R_0)\mathbf{V}_0]$$

However, we are mostly interested in the variation of the demand schedule for forward contracts C, the last element of $\mathbf{z}$. For this purpose, we partition all vectors and matrices, defining

$$\tilde{\mathbf{V}}^* = \begin{pmatrix} \tilde{\mathbf{V}}_1 \\ \tilde{S}\tilde{\mathbf{V}}_2 \\ -(1+\tilde{r}_1) \\ -\tilde{S}(1+\tilde{r}_2) \end{pmatrix}, \qquad \mathbf{V}_0^* = \begin{pmatrix} \mathbf{V}_{01} \\ \mathbf{V}_{02} \\ -1 \\ -1 \end{pmatrix}, \qquad \mathbf{z}^* = \begin{pmatrix} x \\ y \\ A \\ B \end{pmatrix}$$

and

$$G = (1/\alpha)\mathbf{V}_0^*\mathbf{V}^{*\prime} + E(\tilde{\mathbf{V}}^*\tilde{I}^{-1}\tilde{\mathbf{V}}^{*\prime})$$

so that the matrix on the left-hand side of (12) can now be written as

$$\alpha \left[\begin{array}{c|c} G & E[\tilde{\varepsilon}(F - \tilde{S})\tilde{I}^{-1}\tilde{\mathbf{V}}^*] \\ \hline E[\tilde{\varepsilon}(F - \tilde{S})\tilde{I}^{-1}\tilde{\mathbf{V}}^*] & E[\tilde{\varepsilon}^2(F - \tilde{S})^2\tilde{I}^{-1}] \end{array} \right] \quad (13)$$

and Eq. (12) can be decomposed into

$$-2\{G\mathbf{z}^* + E[\tilde{\varepsilon}(F - \tilde{S})\tilde{I}^{-1}\tilde{\mathbf{V}}^*]C\} = (1/\alpha)(-2w_0 + R_0)\mathbf{V}_0^* - E(\tilde{R}\tilde{I}^{-1}\tilde{\mathbf{V}}^*) \quad (12a)$$

$$-2\{E[\tilde{\varepsilon}(F - \tilde{S})\tilde{I}^{-1}\tilde{\mathbf{V}}^*]\mathbf{z}^* + E[\tilde{\varepsilon}^2(F - \tilde{S})^2\tilde{I}^{-1}]C\} = -E[\tilde{R}\tilde{I}^{-1}\tilde{\varepsilon}(F - \tilde{S})] \quad (12b)$$

---

[7] A paper by Dumas [5] shows that market shares are not stochastic if and only if the production functions exhibit no input-elasticity uncertainty.

Hence, we get the optimal $\mathbf{z}^*$ (stocks and bonds holdings) and the optimal forward contracting:

$$\mathbf{z}^* = \tfrac{1}{2}G^{-1}\{E(\tilde{R}\tilde{I}^{-1}\tilde{\mathbf{V}}^*) - (1/\alpha)(-2w_0 + R_0)\mathbf{V}_0$$
$$- 2E[\tilde{\varepsilon}(F - \tilde{S})\tilde{I}^{-1}\tilde{\mathbf{V}}^*]C\} \tag{14a}$$

$$C = \frac{1}{2}\frac{E[(R - 2\tilde{\mathbf{V}}^{*\prime}\mathbf{z}^*)\tilde{I}^{-1}\tilde{\varepsilon}(F - \tilde{S})]}{E[\tilde{\varepsilon}^2(F - \tilde{S})^2\tilde{I}^{-1}]} \tag{14b}$$

under the assumption that the elements of $\tilde{\mathbf{V}}^*$ (the reduced vector) are linearly independent, so that G is positive definite and nonsingular. We observe that the investment-borrowing decision $\mathbf{z}^*$ depends on the forward contracting decision C and vice versa. If we call $\mathbf{z}_0^*$ the value of the optimal investment and borrowing which would prevail in the absence of a forward market $(C = 0)$, we can rewrite (14a) as

$$\mathbf{z}^* = \mathbf{z}_0^* - G^{-1}E[\tilde{\varepsilon}(F - \tilde{S})\tilde{I}^{-1}\tilde{\mathbf{V}}^*]C$$

Substituting this equation into (14b) yields

$$C = \frac{1}{2}\frac{E[(\tilde{R} - 2\tilde{\mathbf{V}}^{*\prime}\mathbf{z}_0^*)\tilde{I}^{-1}\tilde{\varepsilon}(F - \tilde{S})]}{D} + \frac{N}{D}C \tag{15a}$$

$$= \frac{1}{2}\frac{E[\tilde{R}\tilde{I}^{-1}\tilde{\varepsilon}(F - \tilde{S})]}{D} - \frac{E[\tilde{\varepsilon}(F - \tilde{S})\tilde{I}^{-1}\tilde{\mathbf{V}}^{*\prime}]\mathbf{z}_0^*}{D} + \frac{N}{D}C \tag{15b}$$

where

$$N = E[\tilde{\varepsilon}(F - \tilde{S})\tilde{I}^{-1}\tilde{\mathbf{V}}^{*\prime}]G^{-1}E[\tilde{\varepsilon}(F - \tilde{S})\tilde{I}^{-1}\tilde{\mathbf{V}}^*]$$
$$D = E[\tilde{\varepsilon}^2(F - \tilde{S})^2\tilde{I}^{-1}]$$

As this is the point in the derivation where the anatomy of the demand schedule is clearest, it may be useful to hold off the final steps in order to elucidate the various motives which push individuals to contract forward for currencies.

The first term in (15b) represents the demand for forward contracts which would exist if no alternative instruments (stocks or bonds) were available for investment $(\mathbf{z}^* = 0)$; therefore, it is essentially a demand which is motivated by the relative levels of the forward and spot rates—we shall call it the "speculative demand." The incentive for such a demand is the spread between $E(\tilde{R}\tilde{I}^{-1}\tilde{\varepsilon})F$ and $E(\tilde{R}\tilde{I}^{-1}\tilde{\varepsilon}\tilde{S})$; the deterrent (in the denominator) which is common to all three terms is a combination of the exchange risk and the convertibility risk of forward contracts, since the appearance of squared terms implies the presence of variances and covariances.

The second term in (15b) represents a demand which is connected with the individual's portfolio investment and borrowing and which could perhaps be called "hedging demand." Hedging here is tantamount to diversification which the investor will undertake to reduce his real risks. This label should, therefore, not be identified with the one used by Grubel [12], for instance. The structure of this demand in this and the traditional analysis differ markedly. To illustrate, we note that C, which represents, as we recall, the demand for the forward conversion of currency 2 into currency 1—a nonsymmetric variable indeed—is influenced similarly (i.e., with the same signs) by investment in country 1 or in country 2, and by borrowing in country 1 or in country 2. This indicates that the purpose of this "hedging" demand is *not*, as it was in the traditional analysis, to prepare the ground for the riskless conversion of the bulk of (i.e., the expected value of) the investor's foreign income into his home currency (cf. Solnik [19]); rather, the forward contracts are themselves risky securities. By diversifying into these securities, the forward contracting which we observe here is intended *to reduce the variability* of the purchasing power value of the investor's future income, wherever it may originate from. This forward contracting, that is, is not undertaken for the sake of conversion but as a means—quite exactly—of hedging against or diversifying away purchasing power risk. This analysis can be confirmed by the examination of the optimality conditions (12a) and (12b). In (12b), which is the equation for the optimal forward contracting, the left-hand side, which is the derivative of the square term in the utility function and which captures variance risk, is seen to contain $\mathbf{z}^*$, while the right-hand side, which is the derivative of the expected-wealth term, is seen to not contain it. Further, on the right-hand side of (12a), we note that the expected returns, expressed in currency 1, $E(\tilde{R}\tilde{I}^{-1}\tilde{\mathbf{V}}^*)$ are computed without regard to the forward rate F. This shows that these expected returns are *not* evaluated "on a covered basis," as they would be if they were converted by means of forward contracts.

Finally, the third term in (15b), which makes C a function of itself, is the result of the two-way interaction between the forward contracting decision and the investment–borrowing decision. Since we have assumed that the elements of $\tilde{\mathbf{V}}^*$ are linearly independent—which implies that G and therefore G^{-1} are positive definite—it is clear that $N > 0$; moreover, $D > 0$ on inspection. Hence the coefficient of C in this third term is positive. We further prove that when $\tilde{\varepsilon}(F - \tilde{S})$ is linearly independent of $\tilde{\mathbf{V}}^*$, this coefficient is strictly less than 1. When that is the case, (13) is positive definite, so that its determinant, which—by a theorem on partitioned matrices—happens to be $|G|(D - N)$, is strictly positive. But since $|G| > 0$, it follows that $D > N$ and $N/D < 1$. If, however, $\tilde{\varepsilon}(F - \tilde{S})$ were linearly dependent on $\tilde{\mathbf{V}}^*$, then it will be apparent from what follows that for some value of F which we shall denote F_p, the coefficient of C in (15) is equal to 1, and the variable C cancels from the equation so that the demand for forward contracts becomes indeterminate. This occurs, of course, whenever forward contracting and some other financial instruments, or combination thereof, are perfect substitutes. We therefore suggest calling this last term of (15) the "arbitrage demand."

Assuming that $\tilde{\varepsilon}(F - \tilde{S})$ is linearly independent of $\tilde{\mathbf{V}}^*$, or, if they are dependent, that $F \neq F_p$, we solve (15), getting

$$C = \tfrac{1}{2}E[(\tilde{R} - 2\tilde{\mathbf{V}}^{*\prime}\mathbf{z}_0^*)\tilde{I}^{-1}\tilde{\varepsilon}(F - \tilde{S})]/\Delta_a \tag{16}$$

or

$$C = C_s + C_h \tag{17}$$

where

$$C_s = \tfrac{1}{2}E[\tilde{R}\tilde{I}^{-1}\tilde{\varepsilon}(F - \tilde{S})]/\Delta_a$$

$$C_h = -E[\tilde{\varepsilon}(F - \tilde{S})\tilde{I}^{-1}\tilde{\mathbf{V}}^*]\mathbf{z}_0^*/\Delta_a$$

$$\Delta_a = E[\tilde{\varepsilon}^2(F - \tilde{S})^2\tilde{I}^{-1}] - E[\tilde{\varepsilon}(F - \tilde{S})\tilde{I}^{-1}\tilde{\mathbf{V}}^{*\prime}]G^{-1}E[\tilde{\varepsilon}(F - \tilde{S})\tilde{I}^{-1}\tilde{\mathbf{V}}^*]$$

$= D - N$, or the difference between the denominator and the numerator of the coefficient of the "arbitrage demand" in (15).

Clearly, it is not possible to decompose the total demand into the sum of three terms corresponding to the three motives of speculation, hedging, and arbitrage. Rather, the arbitrage motive acts as a multiplier of the other two. Specifically, since $0 < \Delta_a < D$, it amplifies the hedging and speculative terms, in comparison with what they were in the formulation of Eq. (15).

A. The Demand Function for Forward Exchange without Perfect Arbitrage Opportunities

We now study the variations of C as a function of F, under the assumption that $\tilde{\varepsilon}(F - \tilde{S})$ is linearly independent of $\tilde{\mathbf{V}}^*$ (i.e., absence of perfect arbitrage opportunities). As a prelude to the study of this case, we remark that any function of the type

$$C = (aF + b)/(cF^2 + dF + e)$$

where $cF^2 + dF + e > 0$ for all F, has the graph drawn in Fig. 1 when $a > 0$, and a graph roughly symmetric to Fig. 1 where $a < 0$.

Consider first the speculative demand C_s. We have

$$a = \tfrac{1}{2}E[\tilde{R}\tilde{I}^{-1}\tilde{\varepsilon}] > 0$$

so that, when there are no perfect arbitrage opportunities, the graph of this demand is *as in Fig.* 1. The slope is positive at the intercept, which is

$$F_s = \frac{E[\tilde{R}\tilde{I}^{-1}\tilde{\varepsilon}\tilde{S}]}{E[\tilde{R}\tilde{I}^{-1}\tilde{\varepsilon}]} > 0$$

$$= E(\tilde{S}) + \frac{\text{cov}[\tilde{S}, \tilde{R}\tilde{I}^{-1}\tilde{\varepsilon}]}{E[\tilde{R}\tilde{I}^{-1}\tilde{\varepsilon}]}$$

Next, for the hedging demand,

$$a = -E[\tilde{\varepsilon}\tilde{I}^{-1}\tilde{\mathbf{V}}^{*\prime}]\mathbf{z}_0^*$$

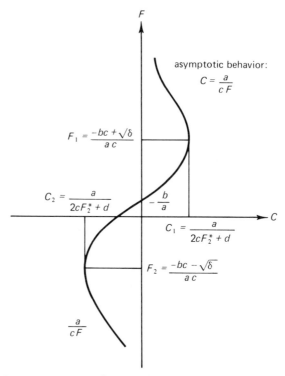

Fig. 1. The graph of $C = (aF + b)/(cF^2 + dF + e)$ when $a > 0$ and $cF^2 + dF + e > 0$ for all F. $\delta = (bc)^2 + (ae - bd)ac > 0$.

There is no foolproof way to ascertain the size of this quantity. If, however, we make the rather inocuous assumption that, in the absence of a forward market, the investor would nevertheless have managed to have a positive period-one nominal wealth in practically all states of nature, then generally, $\tilde{\mathbf{V}}^{*\prime}\mathbf{z}_0^* > 0$ and therefore $a < 0$. We conclude that the hedging demand usually has a graph symmetric to Fig. 1, which is down-sloping at its intercept:

$$F_h = \frac{E[\tilde{\varepsilon}\tilde{S}\tilde{I}^{-1}\tilde{V}^{*\prime}]z_0^*}{E[\tilde{\varepsilon}\tilde{I}^{-1}\tilde{V}^{*\prime}]z_0^*} = E(\tilde{S}) + \frac{\mathrm{cov}[\tilde{S}, \tilde{\varepsilon}\tilde{I}^{-1}\tilde{V}^{*\prime}]z_0^*}{E[\tilde{\varepsilon}\tilde{I}^{-1}\tilde{V}^{*\prime}]z_0^*}$$

No excessive faith should, however, be placed in this result, for two reasons. First, obviously the wealth $\tilde{V}^{*\prime}z_0^*$, although positive in most states of nature, might be so when $\tilde{\varepsilon}\tilde{I}^{-1}$ is small (high inflation, large default on forward contracts) and might instead be negative when $\tilde{\varepsilon}\tilde{I}^{-1}$ is large; but it is hard to imagine systematic reasons why this should be so. The second reason is more important: the a coefficient of the hedging demand carries a negative sign largely because [see Eq. (16)] the marginal utility is $\tilde{R} - 2\tilde{V}^{\prime}z$, a fact which, by Eq. (7a), causes the risk aversion to increase with wealth. As we know, this is a flaw of the quadratic utility function. For a well-behaved utility function, we should perhaps not expect the hedging demand to be down-sloping. More than likely, however, for other utility functions it might not be possible to decompose the demand into the sum of two terms—speculative and hedging terms—so that the question would not arise.

Finally, consider the total demand as given by (16). Condition (7), which sets the limits of acceptability of the quadratic utility function, implies

$$\tilde{R} - 2\tilde{V}^{\prime}\mathbf{z} > 0$$

Let us therefore assume that the available returns do not drive the investor to violate condition (7). Further, if we assume that, in the absence of the forward market, the condition would still be satisfied, $R - 2\tilde{V}^{*\prime}z_0^* > 0$. Then, we conclude that for the overall demand schedule,

$$a = \tfrac{1}{2}E[(\tilde{R} - 2\tilde{V}^{*\prime}z_0^*)\tilde{I}^{-1}\tilde{\varepsilon}] > 0$$

This implies that Fig. 1 is usually the graph applicable to the total demand for forward contracts and that the slope at the intercept is

$$F_t = \frac{E[(\tilde{R} - 2\tilde{V}^{*\prime}z_0^*)I^{-1}\tilde{\varepsilon}\tilde{S}]}{E[(\tilde{R} - \tilde{V}^{*\prime}z_0^*)\tilde{I}^{-1}\tilde{\varepsilon}]} > 0$$

$$= E(\tilde{S}) + \frac{\mathrm{cov}[\tilde{S}, (\tilde{R} - 2\tilde{V}^{*\prime}z_0^*)\tilde{I}^{-1}\tilde{\varepsilon}]}{E[(\tilde{R} - 2\tilde{V}^{*\prime}z_0^*)\tilde{I}^{-1}\tilde{\varepsilon}]}$$

is positive. This implies that the positive slope of the speculative demand has been able to override the negative slope of the hedging schedule. We have represented the combined picture corresponding to this most usual case in Fig. 2.

B. The Demand Function for Foreign Exchange with Perfect Arbitrage Opportunities

Consider now the case where there exist perfect arbitrage opportunities. We already know that for $F = F_p$, the demand becomes indeterminate, a fact which we have represented by the horizontal line in Fig. 3. When $F \neq F_p$, the demand is still given by (16), but this function reduces to a hyperbolic one because F_p is then a root of both the denominator and the

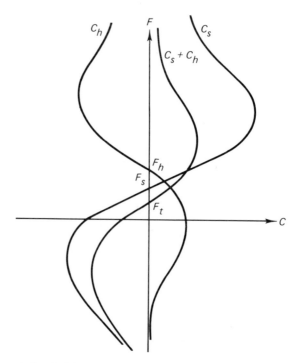

Fig. 2. The speculative, hedging, and overall demand schedules when there are no perfect arbitrage opportunities.

numerator of (16). To see this, let us write that perfect arbitrage opportunities exist; this means that there exists a vector such that

$$\tilde{\varepsilon}(F - \tilde{S}) = \gamma'\tilde{V}* \tag{18}$$

where γ is a linear function of F. Substitute (18) into the denominator Δ_a of (16) to get

$$\Delta_a = \gamma'H\gamma - \gamma'HG^{-1}H\gamma$$

where H stands for $E(\tilde{V}*\tilde{I}^{-1}\tilde{V}*')$. But, by the definition of G and the binomial inverse theorem of matrix theory, we have

$$G^{-1} = H^{-1} - \frac{H^{-1}V_0^*V_0^{*\prime}H^{-1}}{\alpha + V_0^{*\prime}H^{-1}V_0^*}$$

so that

$$\Delta_a = \gamma'H\gamma - \gamma'HH^{-1}H\gamma + \frac{\gamma'V_0^*V_0^{*\prime}\gamma}{\alpha + V_0^{*\prime}H^{-1}V_0^*}$$

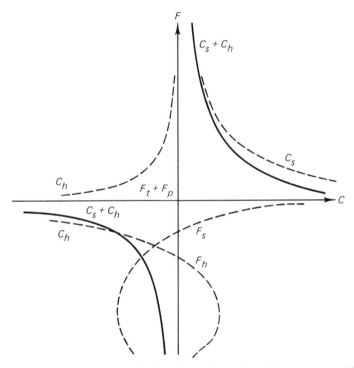

Fig. 3. The demand schedules when there exist perfect arbitrage opportunities.

Hence $\Delta_a = 0$ is equivalent to

$$\gamma'(F)V_0^* = 0 \tag{19}$$

which, not surprisingly, is the equation to be solved to get F_p. It expresses that F_p must be at parity with the prices of the securities to which forward contracting is equivalent. Now, for the numerator of (16); substitution of (18) gives

$$\text{numerator of } (16) = \tfrac{1}{2}\gamma'E(\tilde{R}\tilde{I}^{-1}\tilde{V}^*) - 2Hz_0^*$$

But then, by (12a) (with $C = 0$), z_0^* satisfies

$$E(\tilde{R}\tilde{I}^{-1}\tilde{V}^*) - 2Gz_0^* = (1/\alpha)(-2w_0 + R_0)V_0^*$$

or

$$E(\tilde{R}\tilde{I}^{-1}\tilde{V}^*) - 2Hz_0^* = (1/\alpha)(-2w_0 + R_0)V_0^* + (2/\alpha)V_0^*V_0^{*\prime}z_0^*$$

Hence

$$\text{numerator of (16)} = \tfrac{1}{2}\gamma'V_0^*[(1/\alpha)(-2w_0 + R_0) + (2/\alpha)V_0^{*\prime}z_0^*]$$

As the bracketed term has no reason to be zero, this implies that the root of the numerator is the solution of

$$\gamma'V_0^* = 0$$

Since γ is a linear function of F, the solution of the above is unique and equal to F_p.

As a result, (16) can be written in the form

$$C = (a/c)[(F - F_p)/(F - F_p)^2] = (a/c)[1/(F - F_p)]$$

or a rectangular hyperbolic function of F, which we have drawn as a solid line in Fig. 3. The reader might be surprised to find that for $F \neq F_p$, in the presence of perfect arbitrage opportunities, the demand for forward contracts is finite (except when F approaches F_p). It would seem that the investor is foregoing an opportunity to reach infinite wealth. But, with a quadratic utility function, the investor is not interested in infinite wealth; as a matter of fact, he dreads infinite positive wealth as much as infinite negative wealth. The hyperbola drawn in Fig. 3 corresponds to the peak utility level ever reachable by means of arbitrage when $F \neq F_p$. Not surprisingly, when the spread $(F - F_p)$ is small, it takes a larger amount of forward contracting to get the investor to his optimal wealth level, than it does when the spread is large.

It might be revealing of the impact of the arbitrage motive on the other demands to draw the speculative and hedging demand curves separately in the case where there exists an arbitrage opportunity. One possible configuration is shown as dotted lines on Fig. 3. One sees how the arbitrage motive has blown out the two demands at $F = F_p$, much like it did amplify them—without driving them to infinity—in the case where no *perfect* arbitrage was possible.

C. Demand for Forward Exchange in a Special Case

A special situation of some interest in view of what follows is one in which one assumes

(1) $\tilde{r}_1 = r_1$, nonstochastic,

(2) $\tilde{r}_2 = r_2$, nonstochastic,

(3) $\tilde{\varepsilon}$ random, but independent of both $\tilde{S}$ and $(\tilde{R} - 2\tilde{V}^{*\prime}\mathbf{z}_0^*)\tilde{I}^{-1}$

Here interest rates and bonds are risk-free in both countries. But this is clearly not a case which generally includes perfect forward arbitrage opportunities, for $\tilde{\varepsilon}$ is random. Such opportunities would exist if also either (a) we had $\tilde{\varepsilon} = 1$ and nonrandom (see Section II) or (b) risky forward contracting, $\tilde{\varepsilon}(F - S)$, were (coincidentally) perfectly correlated with investing in some other asset (Section III.B). In both these instances (the first being a special case of the second), $F = F_p$ and the demand for forward contracts as a function of the forward exchange rate is indeterminate.

In the more general case, i.e., in the presence of both default risks on bonds and of convertibility risks together with the associated costs of default on forward contracts, C is a single-valued function of F over the relevant range for each investor. C will be equal to zero for some value of F. But if investors have different inflation indices and taste parameters, the value of F for which $C = 0$ will generally differ from one individual to the next. This implies that interest parity will be produced only by coincidence as investors' demands for forward contracts are aggregated and the forward market is cleared.

What makes the situation at hand interesting is that the three assumptions above guarantee that $C = 0$ for everybody, regardless of differences in tastes and inflation indices, at the single value of $F = (1 + r_1)/(1 + r_2)$. Consequently, IRP will prevail at equilibrium in this case, despite the existence of the risks and costs of default on forward contracts. Clearly, writers are wrong to argue that such risks alone will eliminate IRP (cf. Aliber [2]).

That $C = 0$ for $F = F_p = (1 + r_1)/(1 + r_2)$ can be demonstrated simply. Specifically we seek to show that this value of F will make the numerator of (16) zero, while its denominator remains nonzero. To benefit from the derivations of the previous section, let us pick, for convenience, the vector $\gamma' = [0, 0, -F/(1 + r_1), 1/(1 + r_2)]$. Clearly,

$$\gamma'\tilde{V}^* = F - \tilde{S} \qquad (20)$$

and, at the interest-rate-parity value F_p,

$$\gamma'V_0^* = 0$$

Substituting (20) into (16), and using Eq. (12a) as before, we obtain

$$C = [E(\tilde{\varepsilon})/2\Delta_a][(1/\alpha)(-2w_0 + R_0) + (2/\alpha)V_0^{*\prime}\mathbf{z}_0^*]\gamma'V_0^*$$

Since $\gamma'V_0^* = 0$ makes the numerator zero, we conclude that $C = 0$ for $F = F_p$, provided only that $\Delta_a \neq 0$. But this is true, since, by substituting (20),

$$\Delta_a = \text{var}(\tilde{\varepsilon})\gamma'H\gamma + [E(\tilde{\varepsilon})]^2(\gamma'V_0^*)^2/(\alpha + V_0^{*\prime}H^{-1}V_0^*) \neq 0 \quad \text{Q.E.D.}$$

IV. Equilibrium with Homogeneous Expectations

Having made sure earlier that the solutions of (11) will always be bona fide maxima of $E(\tilde{v})$, we can proceed to make further use of that equation. In this section, we derive from (11) equilibrium pricing relationships, in a special case.

Specifically, we decompose (11) into its components:

$$-[-2(w_0 - \mathbf{z}'\mathbf{V}_0) + R_0]\mathbf{V}_{01} + \alpha E[(-2\mathbf{z}'\tilde{\mathbf{V}} + \tilde{R})\tilde{I}^{-1}\tilde{\mathbf{V}}_1] = \mathbf{0} \qquad (11a)$$

$$-[-2(w_0 - \mathbf{z}'\mathbf{V}_0) + R_0]\mathbf{V}_{02} + \alpha E[(-2\mathbf{z}'\tilde{\mathbf{V}} + \tilde{R})\tilde{I}^{-1}\tilde{S}\tilde{\mathbf{V}}_2] = \mathbf{0} \qquad (11b)$$

$$[-2(w_0 - \mathbf{z}'\mathbf{V}_0) + R_0] - \alpha E[(-2\mathbf{z}'\tilde{\mathbf{V}} + \tilde{R})\tilde{I}^{-1}(1 + \tilde{r}_1)] = 0 \qquad (11c)$$

$$[-2(w_0 - \mathbf{z}'\mathbf{V}_0) + R_0] - \alpha E[(-2\mathbf{z}'\tilde{\mathbf{V}} + \tilde{R})\tilde{I}^{-1}\tilde{S}(1 + \tilde{r}_2)] = 0 \qquad (11d)$$

$$\alpha E[(-2\mathbf{z}'\tilde{\mathbf{V}} + \tilde{R})\tilde{I}^{-1}\tilde{\varepsilon}(F - \tilde{S})] = 0 \qquad (11e)$$

Then we multiply (11c) by $\mathbf{V}_{01}$ and add it to (11a), multiply (11d) by $\mathbf{V}_{02}$ and add it to (11b), subtract (11c) from (11d), and finally repeat (11e), obtaining, respectively,

$$E\{(-2\mathbf{z}'\tilde{\mathbf{V}} + \tilde{R})\tilde{I}^{-1}[\tilde{\mathbf{V}}_1 - (1 + \tilde{r}_1)\mathbf{V}_{01}]\} = \mathbf{0} \qquad (20a)$$

$$E\{(-2\mathbf{z}'\tilde{\mathbf{V}} + \tilde{R})\tilde{I}^{-1}\tilde{S}[\tilde{\mathbf{V}}_2 - (1 + \tilde{r}_2)\mathbf{V}_{02}]\} = \mathbf{0} \qquad (20b)$$

$$E\{(-2\mathbf{z}'\tilde{\mathbf{V}} + \tilde{R})\tilde{I}^{-1}[1 + \tilde{r}_1 - \tilde{S}(1 + \tilde{r}_2)]\} = 0 \qquad (20c)$$

$$E[(-2\mathbf{z}'\tilde{\mathbf{V}} + \tilde{R})\tilde{I}^{-1}\tilde{\varepsilon}(F - \tilde{S})] = 0 \qquad (20d)$$

Equations (20a–d) do not lend themselves readily to solution for equilibrium in the general case. Few analytical points emerge beyond the existence of complex interdependencies among key variables. Numerical solution procedures using estimates of key parameters could doubtlessly be employed to unravel the knots for explorations of policy-related issues. One thing is obvious: Interest rate parity is not an equilibrium solution for the forward rate in the general case. This is clearly seen as follows. Noting that Eq. (16) emerged from (11a–e), we can sum (16) across investors, and set $\sum_k C_k = 0$ to clear the forward market alone. Then,

$$F = \frac{\sum_k\{E[(\tilde{R}_k - 2\tilde{\mathbf{V}}^{*\prime}\mathbf{z}_{0k}^*)\tilde{I}^{-1}\tilde{\varepsilon}\tilde{S}]/\Delta_{ak}(F)\}}{\sum_k\{E[(\tilde{R}_k - 2\tilde{\mathbf{V}}_k^{*\prime}\mathbf{z}_{0k}^*)\tilde{I}^{-1}\tilde{\varepsilon}]/\Delta_{ak}(F)\}}$$

and $F = (1 + r_1)/(1 + r_2)$ is not a solution.

Nevertheless, some insights can be obtained from examining equilibrium in a special instance. A most relevant case, in view of the literature on capital asset pricing on the one hand and the forward exchange market on the other, is that in which expectations are assumed to be homogeneous. Despite their empirical convenience, homogeneous expectations are theoretically a troublesome enough proposition in a one-country setting. It is immediately apparent that they are more problematic when applied internationally. This constitutes a warning to future investigators who may be tempted blithely to assume homogeneous expectations as a convenient prelude to empirical tests.

The requisite homogeneity assumptions are as follows:

(a) Investors everywhere have equal or proportional inflation indices, $\tilde{I}^{-1}$, in all states of nature.

This can perhaps be justified by the very strong double assumption that

(a1) commodity prices everywhere are the same *and*
(a2) individuals have the same matrix Q of taste parameters.

(b) Individuals have generally different relative price variables, $\tilde{R}$. We note from (7a) that maintaining diversity in $\tilde{R}$ guarantees diversity in risk aversions.

(c) Investors everywhere share identical expectations of future payoffs, $\tilde{V}$.

For this assumption to be consistent with our initial definitions of default risks as exogenous convertibility risks, homogeneity of beliefs regarding $\tilde{V}$ requires, for extraneous reasons, that

(c1) $\tilde{r}_1 = r_1$, nonstochastic,
(c2) $\tilde{r}_2 = r_2$, nonstochastic,
(c3) $\tilde{\varepsilon} \leq 1$, stochastic or nonstochastic.

The essential reason for these extra requirements is that homogeneity of expectations about $\tilde{V}$ requires in turn homogeneity of perception of all default risks due to suspension of convertibility. For these to be exogenous, in the sense that they are independent of individuals' decisions, they must be imposed from the outside and apply equally to all investors regardless of nationality. But, a (capricious) government-imposed suspension of convertibility will tend to affect perceptions of default risks on bonds differently than those on forward contracts. By merely suspending foreign exchange trading, the authorities cannot force individuals to default equally on all their obligations. They may still honor their debts in their own currency and necessarily will default only on those debts, the servicing of which requires conversion. Expectations of default risk on bonds therefore necessarily remain heterogeneous when the risk itself is exogenous. The same suspension of convertibility, however, can be consistent with homogeneously perceived risks of default on forward contracts. The government can prevent everyone from honoring his forward exchange contractual obligations. All that is required is that the suspension affect equally all transactions, not only between residents and foreigners, but also, separately, among foreigners and among residents. If the foreign exchange market is closed, no one can trade or settle off the market or go to another market abroad. In short, for expectations of $\tilde{V}$ to be homogeneous, bonds must be assumed to be default-risk-free in the face of convertibility risks if the inconsistency is to be avoided.

Using these three assumptions, we can sum Eqs. (20a–d) over the individuals and apply the equilibrium conditions:

$$\sum_k \mathbf{z}_k = \begin{pmatrix} 1 \\ 1 \\ 0 \\ 0 \\ 0 \end{pmatrix} = \mathbf{e} \tag{21}$$

where $\mathbf{e}$ is a vector containing a 1 in all locations corresponding to stock securities, thus expressing the conditions that all stocks must be held, and zeros in the positions for borrowing and forward contracting to express the fact that there is a zero net supply of securities when these markets are cleared. The result of summing (20) is, after solution for the price variables, all denominated in terms of country 1's currency:

$$V_{01} = \frac{1}{1+r_1} \frac{E(\tilde{M}\tilde{V}_1)}{E(\tilde{M})} = \frac{1}{1+r_1} \left[E(\tilde{V}_1) + \frac{\text{cov}(\tilde{V}_1, \tilde{M})}{E(\tilde{M})} \right] \tag{22a}$$

$$V_{02} = \frac{1}{1+r_2} \frac{E(\tilde{M}\tilde{S}\tilde{V}_2)}{E(\tilde{M}\tilde{S})} = \frac{1}{1+r_1} \left[E(\tilde{S}\tilde{V}_2) + \frac{\text{cov}(\tilde{S}\tilde{V}_2, \tilde{M})}{E(\tilde{M})} \right] \tag{22b}$$

$$1 = \frac{(1+r_2)}{(1+r_1)} \frac{E(\tilde{M}\tilde{S})}{E(\tilde{M})} = \frac{1+r_2}{1+r_1} \left[E(\tilde{S}) + \frac{\text{cov}(\tilde{S}, \tilde{M})}{E(\tilde{M})} \right] \tag{22c}$$

$$F = \frac{E(\tilde{M}\tilde{S}\tilde{\varepsilon})}{E(\tilde{M}\tilde{\varepsilon})} = E(\tilde{S}) + \frac{\text{cov}(\tilde{S}, \tilde{M}\tilde{\varepsilon})}{E(\tilde{M}\tilde{\varepsilon})} \tag{22d}$$

where $\tilde{M} = (\sum_k \tilde{R}_k - 2\mathbf{e}'\tilde{V})\tilde{I}^{-1}$, a "real" market index.

The structure of these equations makes their interpretation clear: (22a) and (22b) are the equilibrium valuation equations for stocks; (22c) gives the international structure of interest rates; and (22d) expresses the forward exchange rate. Some features of this simultaneous equilibrium system are worth noting.

The valuation equations for stocks, (22a) and (22b), have a form analogous to the well-known capital asset pricing model (CAPM) for purely domestic securities. Unlike most renditions, however, they are expressed in real, not nominal terms. The "international market price of risk" may be identified with $1/E(\tilde{M})$. Typically, one would expect the covariance terms to be negative. They would clearly be negative if, as is assumed in most early versions of the domestic CAPM, relative prices were taken as fixed, and investors, therefore, shared identical and constant relative price variables R_k. In these circumstances, the relevant covariance would be between the values of stocks, denominated in currency 1, with the international market portfolio similarly valued, which would be held by all investors. Stochastic relative prices, however, make $\tilde{M}$ generally different from a simple index of the international market. The international market portfolio will not necessarily be held by all investors everywhere. However, it is not our purpose, and it is impossible on the basis of (22a) and (22b) alone, either to specify differences in investors' optimal portfolios by nationality or to explore the circumstances which might make the covariance terms positive.

On the basis of (22c), nominal national interest rates will generally be unequal. The spread is due to the difference, if any, between the expected future and current spot rates and the covariance between the former and the general index $\tilde{M}$. There is no reason to suppose that this covariance is invariably positive or negative.

Turning now to the forward exchange rate, our focus in this paper, (22d) reveals, as others have found [11, 19], that F is generally a biased estimator of $E(\tilde{S})$. Whether F will be above or below $E(\tilde{S})$ will depend on the sign of $\text{cov}(\tilde{S}, \tilde{M}\tilde{\varepsilon})/E(\tilde{M}\tilde{\varepsilon})$. F will still be a biased estimate of $E(\tilde{S})$ if $\tilde{\varepsilon}$ is nonstochastic or if, following the assumptions of Section III.C, $\tilde{\varepsilon}$ is taken as stochastic but also independent of both $\tilde{M}$ and $\tilde{S}$, i.e., when the $\tilde{\varepsilon}$ cancels in (22d) and F is independent of the risk of default on forward contracts. But, given these extra assumptions, one can combine (22c) and (22d), producing: $F = (1 + r_1)/(1 + r_2)$. IRP prevails at equilibrium in these special cases. When $\tilde{\varepsilon}$ is random but independent of $\tilde{M}$ and $\tilde{S}$, IRP occurs at an equilibrium value of $C = 0$ (Section III.C). But when $\tilde{\varepsilon}$ is nonrandom, IRP exists while the equilibrium value of C is indeterminate (Section III.B). Homogeneity of expectations alone without additional independence assumptions does not guarantee IRP.

As an empirical matter, as we reported in the introduction, IRP is not produced in actual forward markets. In the absence of transaction costs which can account for deviations from IRP, one of the major contributions of the traditional theory was that it could be used to interpret actual rate patterns in real-world forward markets. Specifically, that theory predicts that

$$E(\tilde{S}) \gtreqless F_t \quad \text{as} \quad F_t \gtreqless F_p \quad \text{or, in other words,} \quad E(\tilde{S}) \gtreqless F_t \gtreqless F_p$$

where F_t and F_p represent the observed (equilibrium) and IRP forward rates, respectively. The final question we address is whether and under what conditions this prediction holds true in our more general model.

For this purpose, it is most convenient to depart from the market equilibrium context and to appeal directly to the conditions (11a–c) for the individual's optimum, from which his demand curves for forward exchange were earlier derived. As in Section III.C, let r_1 and r_2 be nonstochastic. By way of contrast and extension, let us relax the assumption that $\tilde{\varepsilon}$ is independent of $\tilde{S}$ and the composite variable $(\tilde{R} - \tilde{V}^{*\prime}\mathbf{z}_0^{*})\tilde{I}^{-1}$, denoted henceforth by $\tilde{m}$, so that IRP will not result at equilibrium. This new situation is clearly consistent with the existence of homogeneous expectations. If, in addition, investors were also to share identical relative-price parameters $\tilde{R}$, their risk aversions and, therefore, all demand curves would be identical. With this extra homogeneity assumption, the results obtained below for a single investor would hold, also, when individual demands are aggregated.

As in Section III.A, we may rewrite the individual's equilibrium price for forward contracts, i.e., the forward rate for which $C = 0$, as

$$F_t = [E(\tilde{S}\tilde{m}\tilde{\varepsilon})/E(\tilde{m}\tilde{\varepsilon})] = E(\tilde{S}) + [\mathrm{cov}(\tilde{S}, \tilde{m}\tilde{\varepsilon})/E(\tilde{m}\tilde{\varepsilon})] \tag{23}$$

Turning next to, and equating, Eqs. (11c) and (11d), clearly $E[\tilde{m}(1 + \tilde{r}_1)] = E[\tilde{m}\tilde{S}(1 + \tilde{r}_2)]$.

When r_1 and r_2 are nonstochastic, as assumed above,

$$F_p = (1 + r_1)/(1 + r_2) = E(\tilde{m}\tilde{S})/E(\tilde{m}) = E(\tilde{S}) + [\mathrm{cov}(\tilde{S}, \tilde{m})/E(\tilde{m})] \tag{24}$$

Equations (23) and (24) express F_t and F_p each as a function of $E(S)$. Clearly, $F_t \gtrless E(\tilde{S})$ as $\mathrm{cov}(\tilde{S}, \tilde{m}\tilde{\varepsilon}) \gtrless 0$ and $F_p \gtrless E(\tilde{S})$ as $\mathrm{cov}(\tilde{S}, \tilde{m}) \gtrless 0$. We note in passing that for every individual neither F_p nor F_t will be an unbiased estimate of $E(\tilde{S})$ unless $\tilde{S}$ is independent of $\tilde{m}$ and $\tilde{\varepsilon}$, despite the nonrandomness of r_1 and r_2. This conclusion holds true at equilibrium, even if expectations are homogeneous.

Rewriting (23) and (24), respectively,

$$F_t = [E(\tilde{\varepsilon})E(\tilde{m}\tilde{S}) + \mathrm{cov}(\tilde{\varepsilon}, \tilde{m}\tilde{S})]/E(\tilde{m}\tilde{\varepsilon})$$

$$E(\tilde{m}\tilde{S}) = E(\tilde{m})F_p$$

we may relate F_t and F_p to each other:

$$F_t = [E(\tilde{\varepsilon})E(\tilde{m})F_p + \mathrm{cov}(\tilde{\varepsilon}, \tilde{m}\tilde{S})]/[E(\tilde{m})E(\tilde{\varepsilon}) + \mathrm{cov}(\tilde{m}, \tilde{\varepsilon})] \tag{25}$$

Subtracting F_p from both sides of (25), we obtain

$$F_t - F_p = K/E(\tilde{m}\tilde{\varepsilon})$$

where

$$K = \mathrm{cov}(\tilde{\varepsilon}, \tilde{m}\tilde{S}) - \mathrm{cov}(\tilde{m}, \tilde{\varepsilon})\left[E(S) - \frac{\mathrm{cov}(\tilde{S}, \tilde{m})}{E(\tilde{m})}\right] \tag{26}$$

Obviously, $F_t - F_p \gtreqless 0$ as $K \gtreqless 0$. Using (23) and (24) and the condition contained in (26), we can proceed to tabulate the six possible relationships among F_t, F_p, and $E(S)$, as shown in Table I.

Of the six possible cases in Table I, only two, those emphasized by heavy outlines, correspond to the patterns predicted by the traditional model according to which either $E(\tilde{S}) \le F_t \le F_p$, or $E(\tilde{S}) \ge F_t \ge F_p$. However, the

Table I

Six Possible Relationships Among F_p, F_t, and $E(S)$

		$\mathrm{cov}(\tilde{S}, \tilde{m})$	
		< 0	> 0
$\mathrm{cov}(\tilde{S}, \tilde{m}\tilde{\varepsilon}) > 0$	$K > 0$	$F_p < E(\tilde{S})$ $F_t > E(\tilde{S})$ $F_t > F_p$	$F_p > E(\tilde{S})$ $F_t > E(\tilde{S})$ $F_t > F_p$
	$K < 0$	Impossible	$F_p > E(\tilde{S})$ $F_t > E(S)$ $F_t < F_p$
$\mathrm{cov}(\tilde{S}, \tilde{m}\tilde{\varepsilon}) < 0$	$K > 0$	$F_p < E(S)$ $F_t < E(\tilde{S})$ $F_t > F_p$	Impossible
	$K < 0$	$F_p < E(\tilde{S})$ $F_t < E(\tilde{S})$ $F_t < F_p$	$F_p > E(\tilde{S})$ $F_t < E(\tilde{S})$ $F_t < F_p$

four "nontraditional" cases in Table I reveal that $E(\tilde{S})$ might fall between F_p and F_t or, also, on the side of both F_t and F_p opposite to the one predicted by the traditional theory. In short, the traditional theory represents a very special case. Since there is little reason a priori to specify the signs of $\mathrm{cov}(\tilde{S}, \tilde{m}\tilde{\varepsilon})$, $\mathrm{cov}(\tilde{S}, \tilde{m})$, and K, we do not hazard even the speculation that the pattern predicted by the traditional model is more likely than the rest. It may be, but the question is an empirical matter.[8]

[8] Some further indication of the validity of the traditional model's prediction would be available if one could assume that $\tilde{\varepsilon}$, $\tilde{m}$, and $\tilde{S}$ are all normally distributed and correlated (which, strictly speaking, is impossible given the limits on the variation of $\tilde{\varepsilon}$). With normality (cf. Stevens [21], p. 1241)

$$\mathrm{cov}(\tilde{\varepsilon}, \tilde{m}\tilde{S}) = E(\tilde{S}) \, \mathrm{cov}(\tilde{\varepsilon}, \tilde{m}) + E(\tilde{m}) \, \mathrm{cov}(\tilde{\varepsilon}, \tilde{S})$$

Equation (25) can then be rewritten as

V. Summary and Concluding Remarks

This paper has examined under uncertainty the demand for forward exchange contracts determined, not in isolation as has largely been the case hitherto, but rather simultaneously with the real demands for domestic and foreign stocks and bonds. Our model incorporates explicitly, rather than vaguely as have others, the probability of default risks and their associated costs mainly on forward contracts, but also, in the general case, on bonds. As a consequence, our results vary substantially from those of the traditional, so-called modern theory (MT) of foreign exchange. Some of these should be reemphasized.

It is generally not possible to separate the demand for forward contracts neatly into distinct demands for the purposes of speculation, hedging, and arbitrage. Thus, traditional graphical renditions of the MT which exhibit separate demand curves for arbitrageurs and speculators (wrongly lumping hedgers with the latter) are generally misleading.

Our model reveals for each investor the existence of a speculative demand which responds to be sure to the spread between the forward and expected future spot rates. But we also observe a demand for hedging, a motive not usually distinguished in the MT, *essentially for the purpose of portfolio diversification*. The forward-exchange contracting decision is thus linked inseparably to the investment and borrowing decisions. But it is specifically not undertaken for the purpose of guaranteeing the currency 1 value of the returns of risky assets denominated in currency 2—these returns are not evaluated on a covered basis. Rather, the objective of hedging by diversifying into risky forward contracts is to reduce the real, purchasing-power value of the investor's future returns, wherever they may arise. Finally, in a radical contradiction of the traditional formulation, our model makes clear that an "arbitrage function" does not exist separately. The arbitrage demand for forward contracts cannot be added to the speculative and hedging demands. Rather, the arbitrage motive operates multiplicatively, amplifying the other two. Therefore, since the same individual may simultaneously speculate and hedge, his arbitrage demand for forward contracts cannot be rendered in-

---

$$F_t = \frac{E(\tilde{m})E(\tilde{\varepsilon})F_p + E(\tilde{S})\,\mathrm{cov}(\tilde{m}, \tilde{\varepsilon})}{E(\tilde{m})E(\tilde{\varepsilon}) + \mathrm{cov}(\tilde{m}, \tilde{\varepsilon})} + \frac{E(\tilde{m})\,\mathrm{cov}(\tilde{\varepsilon}, \tilde{S})}{E(\tilde{m}\tilde{\varepsilon})} \qquad (25')$$

Equation (25') reveals that F_t will be a simple weighted average of F_p and $E(\tilde{S})$, and will fall between them, only if, in addition, $\mathrm{cov}(\tilde{\varepsilon}, \tilde{S}) = 0$ and $\mathrm{cov}(\tilde{m}, \tilde{\varepsilon}) > 0$. Note, however, that if $\tilde{S}$ is independent not only of $\tilde{\varepsilon}$ but also of $\tilde{m}$, $F_t = E(\tilde{S}) = F_p$. Although no equilibrium is being assumed, we obtain the relationship $F_t = F_p$ in this case for the reason that any discrepancy between the two would cause the investor's borrowing decisions to become infinite.

dependently. The notion of separating speculators, arbitrageurs, and hedgers is nonsense.

In fact, it may be unlikely that true arbitrage opportunities will be available in the general case. The existence of such opportunities requires that the returns to forward contracting be linearly and, therefore, stochastically dependent on the returns to some other (portfolio of) risky assets. In other words, arbitrage is possible when the combined convertibility and exchange risks on forward contracts are equal to the (per unit) risks of some (portfolio of) risky securities. The difficulties with identifying empirically and *ex ante*, assets which are equivalently risky in this sense should be manifest. But if such opportunities do exist, each investor's demand for forward contracts will become indeterminate at some parity forward rate F_P, which may or may not be set at interest rate parity. F_p will be equal to the IRP forward rate if it is bonds which are perfect substitutes for forward contracts. And then, forward contracts as a market instrument are redundant.

In practice, perfect arbitrage opportunities may exist temporarily in such settings as the interbank dealer market, where in the short-term and under "normal" conditions, the risks of default on inter-bank borrowing and of suspension of convertibility could be presumed to be absent. One would then expect IRP to be observed in that market.[9] But if this market were not freely accessible to all, IRP might not prevail elsewhere or in general, even though there did exist one kind of lending which was exactly equivalent to forward contracting.

In the general case, indeed, there is no reason to expect IRP or any other predictable forward exchange rate, to materialize at equilibrium. The expression for F_t shows it to depend on information regarding both investors' marginal utilities and their heterogeneous expectations as to security returns, default risks, price-level changes, and exchange rate variations. Could such variables be observed or estimated, however, simulations of equilibrium by numerical methods could be performed.

To obtain analytical results which could be contrasted with those of the MT, we therefore undertook to investigate forward market equilibrium when expectations were assumed to be homogeneous. This assumption, it will be recalled, is problematic in the international setting. *Inter alia*, it necessitates that real bonds be presumed riskless, since in the presence of convertibility risks, risky bonds cannot be regarded as equally risky by all investors regardless of nationality when all default risks are exogenous.

Given homogeneous expectations, however, we were able to clear all markets simultaneously and solve for equilibrium, internationally priced stock

---

[9] In fact, IRP rates are used as quotes in the dealer market in normal times, between "good names."

values, the international structure of interest rates, and the equilibrium forward exchange rate. The latter will be a biased estimate of the expected future spot rate unless the future spot exchange rate $\tilde{S}$ is stochastically independent of both convertibility risks $\tilde{\varepsilon}$ and the international market index $\tilde{M}$ measured in real terms. And IRP will be produced at equilibrium if only the convertibility risks, in turn, are independent of both $\tilde{S}$ and $\tilde{M}$.

Further examination of the case with homogeneous expectations brings out two important implications which are relevant in practice. The first is that the MT's predictions regarding the relationship among the expected spot, forward, and interest parity exchange rates will be correct only under the special circumstances set forth in Table I. That is, the MT itself represents only a very special case. The second is that under those conditions which make bonds and forward contracts perfect substitutes and which therefore also produce IRP, *it is impossible for the government successfully to affect the volume of short-term capital flows by intervening in the forward exchange market.* In this case, the forward exchange trading decisions are indeterminate for everyone and so, of course, is the equilibrium volume of forward contracting. The MT allows the speculative demand for foreign exchange, by intersecting the inelastic arbitrage schedule, to determine the equilibrium volume of transactions and, therefore, implies that by "counterspeculation" the government can affect this volume along with the reverse arbitrage capital flows. But when forward contracting is an arbitrary decision and forward contracts a redundant security, it is obviously impossible to specify or predict how much of them will be traded. Fortunately, our theory bears this out.

Our results and remarks are subject to but a few caveats. The major one is that our analysis is subject to the limitations of the quadratic utility function. Unfortunately, in a two- or multiperiod setting, other utility functions produce optimality conditions which cannot be solved for the demand for forward contracts. Equally, it is incorrect to assume normality in connection with convertibility risks. Numerical solutions, were they to be obtained for other utility functions, would reveal different curvature but similar shapes for the demand functions portrayed in Figs. 1–3.

Finally, we must emphasize that ours is not a full general equilibrium model. Present and future spot exchange rates, relative prices, domestic and foreign interest rates, as well as all default risks are taken as exogenous. These assumptions, which will be relaxed in future research, prevent us in the meantime from analyzing the causes of exchange risk or from offering further policy recommendations. Previous attempts (e.g., Feldstein [7]) at linking expectations of the future spot rate with the current forward rate, were naturally inconclusive, since they postulated the link *ex nihilo.* What is needed is a set of expectations of future spot exchange rates and other variables, derived from the analysis of future market equilibria.

Appendix. Consumption Choices With Quadratic Utility

Given a cardinal quadratic utility function in many commodities,

$$u = -\mathbf{c}'Q\mathbf{c} + \mathbf{q}'\mathbf{c}$$

where Q is a positive definite symmetric matrix and $\mathbf{q}$ is a vector of positive coefficients, and a budget constraint.

$$\mathbf{c}'\mathbf{p} = w$$

where w is current nominal wealth used for current consumption and $\mathbf{p}$ is a vector of prices; the Lagrangean is

$$L = \mathbf{c}'Q\mathbf{c} + \mathbf{q}'\mathbf{c} - \lambda[\mathbf{c}'\mathbf{p} - w]$$

so that the optimality conditions are

$$-2Q\mathbf{c} + \mathbf{q} = \lambda\mathbf{p}$$

The optimal consumption package is then

$$\mathbf{c} = \tfrac{1}{2}Q^{-1}[\mathbf{q} - \lambda\mathbf{p}]$$

Substituting in the budget constraint

$$\tfrac{1}{2}\mathbf{p}'Q^{-1}[\mathbf{q} - \lambda\mathbf{p}] = w$$

one obtains λ:

$$\lambda = (\tfrac{1}{2}\mathbf{p}'Q^{-1}\mathbf{q} - w)/\tfrac{1}{2}\mathbf{p}'Q^{-1}\mathbf{p}$$

The optimal consumption after substitution is, therefore,

$$\mathbf{c} = \tfrac{1}{2}Q^{-1}\left[\mathbf{q} - \frac{\tfrac{1}{2}\mathbf{p}'Q^{-1}\mathbf{q} - w}{\tfrac{1}{2}\mathbf{p}'Q^{-1}\mathbf{p}}\mathbf{p}\right]$$

The resulting utility level is

$$u = \int^{w}\lambda\,dw = -\frac{w^2}{\mathbf{p}'Q^{-1}\mathbf{p}} + \frac{\mathbf{p}'Q^{-1}\mathbf{q}}{\mathbf{p}'Q^{-1}\mathbf{p}}w$$

These consumption choices would take place at each point in time, provided only that the current wealth is given. Let us therefore consider a two-period utility function:

$$\tilde{v} = -\mathbf{c}_0'Q\mathbf{c}_0 + \mathbf{q}'\mathbf{c}_0 + \alpha[-\tilde{\mathbf{c}}_1 Q\tilde{\mathbf{c}}_1 + \mathbf{q}'\tilde{\mathbf{c}}_1]$$

where future consumption $\tilde{\mathbf{c}}_1$ is not known certainly. Substituting each period's optimal consumption decision, the derived utility function of current total nominal consumption (c_0, a scalar) and future nominal wealth (w) is

$$\tilde{v} = -\frac{c_0^2}{\mathbf{p}_0' Q^{-1} \mathbf{p}_0} + \frac{\mathbf{p}_0' Q^{-1} \mathbf{q}}{\mathbf{p}_0' Q^{-1} \mathbf{p}_0} c_0 + \alpha \left[-\frac{\tilde{w}^2}{\tilde{\mathbf{p}}_1 Q^{-1} \tilde{\mathbf{p}}_1} + \frac{\tilde{\mathbf{p}}_1' Q^{-1} \mathbf{q}}{\tilde{\mathbf{p}}_1 Q^{-1} \tilde{\mathbf{p}}_1} \tilde{w} \right]$$

where the future wealth is to be fully consumed in the second period, and where $\mathbf{p}_0$ is the vector of current prices while $\tilde{\mathbf{p}}_1$ is the random vector of future prices.

References

1. Adler, M., and Dumas, B., "Optimal International Acquisitions," *Journal of Finance* (March 1975), 1–19.
2. Aliber, R. Z., "The Interest Rate Parity Theorem: A Reinterpretation," *Journal of Political Economy* **81**, No. 6 (November/December 1973).
3. Branson, W. H., "The Minimum Covered Interest Differential Needed for International Arbitrage Activity," *Journal of Political Economy* **77**, No. 6 (November/December 1969), 1028–1035.
4. Canterbery, E. R., "Foreign Exchange, Capital Flows and Monetary Policy," Princeton Studies in International Finance Section, Department of Economics, Princeton Univ., Princeton, New Jersey (1965).
5. Dumas, B., "International Trade and Investment under Production and Monetary Uncertainty," Working Paper, Columbia Univ. (June 1975).
6. Einzig, P. A., *A Dynamic Theory of Forward Exchange*. New York: Macmillan, 1961.
7. Feldstein, M. S., "Uncertainty and Forward Exchange Speculation," *The Review of Economics and Statistics* **50**, No. 2 (May 1968), 182–192.
8. Frenkel, J. A., "Elasticities and the Interest Parity Theory," *Journal of Political Economy* **81**, No. 3 (May/June 1973), 741–747.
9. Frenkel, J. A., and Levitch, R. M., "Covered Interest Arbitrage: Unexploited Profits?" *Journal of Political Economy* (April 1975).
10. Gaillot, H. J., "Purchasing-Power Parity as an Explanation of Long-Term Changes in Exchange Rates," *Journal of Money, Credit and Banking* (April 1970).
11. Grauer, F., Litzenberger, R. H., and Stehle, R., "Sharing Rules and Equilibrium in an International Capital Market under Uncertainty," Research Paper No. 245, Graduate School of Business, Stanford Univ. (February 1975).
12. Grubel, H. G., *Forward Exchange, Speculation and the International Flow of Capital*. Stanford, California: Stanford Univ. Press, 1966.
13. Heckerman, D., "On the Effects of Exchange Risk," *Journal of International Economics* **3**, No. 3 (November 1973), 379–388.
14. Kenen, P. B., "Trade, Speculation and the Forward Exchange Rate," *Trade Growth and the Balance of Payments* (R. E. Baldwin *et al.*, ed.), pp. 143–169. Chicago, Illinois: Rand-McNally, 1965.
15. Keynes, J. M., *A Tract on Monetary Reform*. New York: Macmillan, 1923.
16. Prachowny, M. F., "A Note on Interest Parity and the Supply of Arbitrage Funds," *Journal of Political Economy* **78**, No. 3 (May/June 1970), 540–545.
17. Schilling, D., "Forward Exchange and Currency Position," *The Journal of Finance* **24**, No. 5 (December 1969), 875–886.
18. Sohmen, E., *Flexible Exchange Rates*. Chicago, Illinois: Univ. of Chicago Press, 1969.

19. Solnik, B. H., "Equilibrium in an International Capital Market," *Journal of Economic Theory* (April 1974).
20. Stein, J. L., "The Nature and Efficiency of the Foreign Exchange Market," Essays in International Finance, No. 40, Princeton Univ. (1962).
21. Stevens, G. V. G., "Two Problems in Portfolio Analysis: Conditional and Multiplicative Random Variables," *Journal of Financial and Quantitative Analysis* (December 1971), 1234–1250.
22. Stoll, H. R., "An Empirical Study of the Forward Exchange Market Under Fixed and Flexible Exchange Rate Systems," *Canadian Journal of Economics* **1**, No. 1 (February 1968), 55–78.
23. Stoll, H. R., "Causes of Deviation from Interest Rate Parity," *Journal of Money, Credit and Banking* **4**, No. 1 (February 1972), 113–117.
24. Tsiang, S. C., "The Theory of Forward Exchange and the Effects of Government Intervention in the Forward Exchange Market," *IMF Staff Papers* (April 1959), 75–106.

OPTIMAL COUPON RATE, TAXES, AND COLLUSION BETWEEN BORROWER AND LENDER

Fred D. Arditti   *Yoram C. Peles*

University of Florida   *The Hebrew University*

The objectives of this chapter are (1) to determine the optimal coupon payment for a firm striving to minimize post-tax payments to bondholders, and (2) to demonstrate that the actions of the firm acting to minimize its post-tax debt payment, in the face of potential bondbuyers who act in their own self-interest as wealth-maximizers, result in a market issue price that is identical to that obtained if both firm and buyers were to collude in selecting a coupon rate that would minimize *the sum* of tax payments of the coalition's participants.

I. Assumptions

The analysis is restricted to single-period bonds and is initially conducted in a deterministic system under two different tax systems. This is covered in Section II. In Section III, the certainty assumption is dropped and the effects of possible bankruptcy on optimal coupon rate are investigated when investors are risk neutral.

In essence, the problem is studied in the environment of the Canadian tax

The authors wish to thank Haim Levy and Marshall Sarnat for helpful comments.

laws. The coupon payment by the firm is deductible as a normal business expense, saving the firm that portion equal to the corporate tax rate; the recipient of the coupon income is taxed at the personal rate. With regard to the discount, if any, on the bond.

> Under paragraph 20(1)(f) all or a portion of the bond discount paid in the year . . . on interest-bearing obligations issued after June 18, 1971 are deductible (by the corporation). The deduction may be claimed for the whole of the discount . . . if (a) the obligation was issued for at least 97 percent of its face value, and (b) the actual yield does not exceed 4/3 of the interest rate shown to be payable on the outstanding balance at the time the payment was made. In any other case, only one-half of the lesser of the amount paid and the amount by which the lesser of the principal amount and amounts paid in the year or any preceding year exceeds the amount for which the obligation was issued is deductible [2, pp. 4768–4769].

Prior to June 18, 1971 a borrower who issued bonds at a discount could not deduct all or part of the discount as interest [2, p. 4769].

With respect to the bondbuyer,

> Under the present Act such amounts [discounts] . . . are taxable to lenders at capital gains rates (2, p. 4769].

Prior to June 18, 1971, the gain to the lender attributed to the discount was not taxed, i.e., the tax rate on such capital gains was zero [2, p. 4769].

While our analysis is in concert with the Canadian case, there exist other major economies whose tax treatment of bond payments closely approximate that of Canada; consequently, this study provides some insight into the coupon rate problem for these countries. For example, in France the corporation is permitted to deduct the full coupon payment, but only 12% of the discount, while the bondholder pays the personal rate on the coupon, but a flat 12% on the capital gain resulting from any discount (see [6, pp. 493–494, 498]). In Japan the corporation treats the coupon and full discount as deductible interest, while the individual pays a 15% tax on appreciation due to the discount (see [3, pp. 27, 62]). As you will see, our model (Sections II.A, II.B, and III) precisely describes the Japanese tax systems, since it treats bondbuyers as homogeneous with respect to tax brackets.[1] Although the above

---

[1] The United States Tax Code does not differentiate between coupon payments and the issue discount; therefore, both are fully deductible by the corporation as interest and taxable at the personal rate to the bondholder (see McCarthy *et al.* [4], p. 524). However, discussions with security brokers and accountants inform us that information as to whether the bond was issued at a discount is not passed on to the buyer or seller. Thus, the original buyer may immediately sell his bond to another who, upon maturity, reports the appreciation due to the discount as the capital gain income. Therefore, we cautiously add that in practice the analysis of this paper might well apply to the U.S.

indicates that our model is descriptive of the tax systems of various countries, each having a different currency, in the subsequent analysis we shall simply use the dollar as the unit of currency.

II. The Analysis Under Certainty

A. *The Optimal Coupon Payment for the Present Canadian Tax Law*

The problem we wish to solve may be stated as follows: The firm has decided on the amount of debt to raise, in our case $1000; the issued bonds mature in one year, at which time the firm must pay the bondholders the coupon on each bond plus each bond's face value. We assume that the firm pays nothing during this period of time, and that both the firm and its bondholders believe that interest and face value will be paid with certainty, i.e., the probability of default is zero. Given these assumptions, the firm's objective is to find that bond coupon that will minimize its end-of-period post-tax payment to bondholders.

Now the goal of every security holder is to obtain the highest after-tax receipts. If the firm offers a bond that carried a coupon of C dollars, we assume prospective investors are willing to pay $1000 for that bond, i.e., they are willing to pay its face value.[2] In this event, their after-tax receipts when the bond matures will amount to $C(1 - t_i) + 1000$, where t_i denotes the personal tax rate on ordinary income. On the other hand, if the firm sets the coupon payment at C_d, then these same investors would be willing to pay an amount P for each bond, such that their post-tax receipts under this alternative will amount to $C(1 - t_i) + 1000$. Since the firm wishes to raise $1000, and since each bond that carries a coupon of C_d will sell for P dollars, the firm must issue $1000/P$ bonds. Consequently, investors will set a P such that the after-tax receipts that emanate from an initial investment of $1000 in bonds that carry a coupon of C_d and which amount to

$$[C_d(1 - t_i) + 10^3 - t_g(10^3 - P)]10^3/P$$

where t_g is the tax rate on long-term capital gains income, will be equal to $C(1 - t_i) + 1000$.

Formally, we choose to characterize the firm's decision problem as a choice between two alternatives: It may issue bonds at par, in which case its end-of-period after-tax payments amount to $C(1 - t) + (10^3)$, where t symbolizes the corporate tax rate, or it may issue bonds that carry a coupon of C_d and result in end-of-period after-tax payments of $[C_d(1 - t) - t(10^3 - P) + 10^3]10^3/P$—recall that $10^3/P$ denotes the number of bonds ori-

---

[2] The C value set is such that $C/1000$ will equal the market interest rate, which in turn is determined by investors trying to maximize the utility of their consumption flows over time.

ginally issued in order to raise the necessary $1000. Because the federal government considers as interest the sum of the coupon payment plus amortized discount on the bond. In this case, $10^3 - P$, the tax deductability of interest payments results in savings of $t(C_d + (10^3 - P))10^3/P$ to the corporation, and is so indicated in the bracketed term that represents the per bond after-tax payment of the corporation. The firm will select that C_d that maximizes the difference between the costs of these two alternatives. This is equivalent to searching for that coupon C_d that *minimizes* the post-tax payments that must be made in order to raise $1000 at the period's beginning. The mathematical statement of the firm's problem follows.

$$\text{maximize} \quad L = \max\{[C(1 - t) + 10^3]$$

$$- \{[C_d(1 - t) - t(10^3 - P) + 10^3]10^3/P\}\} \quad (1)$$

$$\text{subject to} \quad C(1 - t_i) + 10^3$$

$$= [C_d(1 - t_i) + 10^3 - t_g(10^3 - P)]10^3/P \quad (2)$$

$$C_d \geq 0, \, P > 0 \quad (3)$$

We now seek to determine the optimal coupon rate by solving the problem stated in (1)–(3), given the existing tax structure in which the capital gains tax rates are less than the personal tax rates.

$$\max L = \max\{(C + 10^3)(1 - t) - (10^3/P)[(1 - t)(C_d + 10^3)]\} \quad (1a)$$

Similarly (2) can be written as

$$10^3/P = [C(1 - t_i) + 10^3(1 - t_g)]/[C_d(1 - t_i) + 10^3(1 - t_g)] \quad (2a)$$

The substitution of (2a) into (1a) yields

$$\max L = \max\left\{(C + 10^3)(1 - t)\right.$$

$$\left. - \left[\frac{C(1 - t_i) + 10^3(1 - t_g)}{C_d(1 - t_i) + 10^3(1 - t_g)}\right](1 - t)(C_d + 10^3)\right\} \quad (1b)$$

The firm must determine the C_d that maximizes the expression for L in Eq. (1b) and satisfies the inequality constraints stated in (3)—$C_d \geq 0$ and $P > 0$.

Taking the derivative of (1b) with respect to C_d, we obtain

$$\frac{dL}{dC_d} = +\frac{[C(1 - t_i) + 10^3(1 - t_g)]}{[C_d(1 - t_i) + 10^3(1 - t_g)]^2}\{(1 - t_i)(1 - t)(C_d + 10^3)$$

$$- [C_d(1 - t_i) + 10^3(1 - t_g)](1 - t)\} \quad (4)$$

or

$$\frac{dL}{dC_d} = - \frac{C(1 - t_i) + 10^3(1 - t_g)}{[C_d(1 - t_i) + 10^3(1 - t_g)]^2} \, 10^3(1 - t)(t_i - t_g) < 0 \qquad (5)$$

if $t_i > t_g$. We find that the derivative of L with respect to C_d is negative throughout the range of admissible C_d values. Consequently, L attains its maximum at $C_d = 0$. Substitution of $C_d = 0$ into (2a) shows that the corresponding P satisfies the feasibility conditions of (3). Note that the optimum coupon value of zero turns out to be independent of the corporate tax rate t, and depends only on the fact that $t_g < t_i$.[3]

B. Collusion between Firm and Bondholder

Let us now consider a somewhat different problem in regard to the coupon payment. Suppose the firm and bondholder form a coalition, the purpose of which is to select a coupon rate that will minimize the coalition's total tax payments resulting from the issuance of $1000 worth of bonds. Then, the coalition's objective is to choose a C_d which satisfies the following mathematical statement.

$$\text{minimize } M = \min\{[t_i C_d - t(C_d + 10^3 - P) + t_g(10^3 - P)]10^3/P\} \qquad (6)$$

subject to the market forces that determine bond price, given by (2) or (2a), and the additional conditions imposed by (3).

---

[3] In passing, three points should be made. First, one cannot deduce the optimal coupon size by merely focusing on the objective function, for while lowering C_d reduces the after-tax payment to be made by the firm on each bond issued, namely $[C_d(1 - t) - t(10^3 - P) + 10^3]$, a reduction in C_d induces a fall in P [see (2)] which forces the firm to issue more bonds in order to raise $1000—the number of bonds being $10^3/P$.

Second, one should not be misled into thinking that because the objective function includes the term $-t(10^3 - P)$ the corporate tax bill will be unaffected by a change in C_d, since corporate tax savings (dissavings) of $-t \, \Delta C_d$ will be offset by dissavings (savings) of $+t \, \Delta P$. The savings, $-t \, \Delta C_d$, will only be canceled by the dissavings, $+t \, \Delta P$, if $\Delta P = \Delta C_d$. However, the constraint (2) may give a ΔP to ΔC_d relation different from $\Delta P = \Delta C_d$.

Third, strictly speaking, if $C_d = 0$ and C is somewhat greater than 30, then the model of this section (II.A) must be altered to allow for the fact that a discount greater than 97% will result in the issued bonds, and, therefore, only one-half of this amount is deductible by the firm as interest expense against its corporate income [see condition (a) of paragraph 20(1)(f) of the Canadian tax law, reproduced on the first page of this text]. It would be easy enough to work out this case in addition to the main one already analyzed in Section II.A. However, from the model based on the law preceding June 18, 1971 and the corresponding analysis presented in Section II.C, the reader will see that this "greater than 97% discount case" is intermediate between the two polar cases studied in Sections II.A and II.C, the solutions of which provide the implications of the intermediate case.

The substitution of (2a) into (6) yields

$$\min M = \min\Big\{[(t_i - t)C_d - 10^3(t - t_g)]$$

$$\times \left[\frac{C(1 - t_i) + 10^3(1 - t_g)}{C_d(1 - t_i) + 10^3(1 - t_g)}\right] + 10^3(t - t_g)\Big\} \qquad (6a)$$

The optimal value of C_d is again found by inspecting the derivative of M with respect to C_d. The derivative is given by,

$$\frac{dM}{dC_d} = \frac{C(1 - t_i) + 10^3(1 - t_g)}{[C_d(1 - t_i) + 10^3(1 - t_g)]^2} \{(t_i - t)[C_d(1 - t_i) + 10^3(1 - t_g)]$$

$$- [(t_i - t)C_d - 10^3(t - t_g)](1 - t_i)\} \qquad (7)$$

The sign of which is determined by

$$(t_i - t)(1 - t_g) + (t - t_g)(1 - t_i) \qquad (8)$$

or

$$(t_i - t_g)(1 - t) > 0 \qquad \text{if} \quad t_i > t_g \qquad (9)$$

Thus, given $t_i > t_g$, the tax payment of the coalition is minimized when $C_d = 0$.

Now one can see that the firm's problem of selecting a coupon rate that minimizes the firm's after-tax payments to bondholders is equivalent to the problem faced by a coalition of firm and bondholders who unite against the tax authorities. In the primary problem that we treated, firm and bondholders act independently, each one trying to maximize his own wealth. Yet we obtain a result identical to the collusion solution. The reason for this similarity in solutions lies in the market mechanism determining price, given by Eq. (2). Any action taken by one party to increase his share of post-tax receipts is confronted by a counteraction by the other party in order to prevent his wealth from being decreased. The only action supported by both parties are those lowering tax payments, since this will increase the amount left to be distributed among both parties.

C. The Tax System Prior to June 18, 1971

Only the coupon payment is tax deductible against corporate income. The amortization of the bond discount is not considered an interest payment by the tax authorities and therefore not tax deductible by the corporation against business income. Given this alteration, the objective function of a firm wishing to minimize after-tax payments to bondholders becomes

$$\text{maximize } R = \max\{(1 - t)C + 10^3 - [C_d(1 - t) + 10^3]10^3/P\} \quad (10)$$

subject to constraints (2) or (2a) and (3). Upon substituting (2a) for $10^3/P$ in (10), we obtain for R,

$$R = (1 - t)C + 10^3 - [C_d(1 - t) + 10^3]$$
$$\times [(1 - t_i)C + (1 - t_g)10^3]/[(1 - t_i)C_d + (1 - t_g)10^3] \quad (11)$$

To solve the problem we study the derivative of (11), bearing in mind that an acceptable solution must satisfy (3). The derivative of (11) with respect to C_d is

$$\frac{dR}{dC_d} = -(1 - t)\frac{(1 - t_i)C + (1 - t_g)10^3}{(1 - t_i)C_d + (1 - t_g)10^3}$$
$$+ \frac{(1 - t_i)[(1 - t)C_d + 10^3][(1 - t_i)C + (1 - t_g)10^3]}{[(1 - t_i)C_d + (1 - t_g)10^3]^2} \quad (12)$$

The sign of (12) is determined by

$$-(1 - t)[(1 - t_i)C_d + (1 - t_g)10^3] + (1 - t_i)[(1 - t)C_d + 10^3] \quad (13)$$

So dR/dC_d will be positive, zero, or negative, depending upon whether

$$(1 - t_i) \gtreqless (1 - t_g)(1 - t) \quad (14)$$

Therefore, if $(1 - t_i) > (1 - t_g)(1 - t)$, then the firm should issue bonds that command a premium, while if $(1 - t_i) < (1 - t_g)(1 - t)$, then the optimal coupon is zero.

Now let us investigate the optimal coupon rate if the firm and bondholders enter into a coalition designed to minimize total tax payments under this tax system. The objective function becomes

$$\text{minimize } S = \min\{[(t_i - t)C_d + t_g(10^3 - P)]10^3/P\} \quad (15)$$

subject to constraints (2) and (3).
Substituting (2a) for $10^3/P$ gives

$$S = [(t_i - t)C_d + t_g10^3][C(1 - t_i) + 10^3(1 - t_g)]/[C_d(1 - t_i) + 10^3(1 - t_g)]$$
$$- 10^3t_g \quad (16)$$

Taking the derivative with respect to C_d gives

$$\frac{dS}{dC_d} = (t_i - t)\left[\frac{C(1 - t_i) + 10^3(1 - t_g)}{C_d(1 - t_i) + 10^3(1 - t_g)}\right] - \frac{[C(1 - t_i) + 10^3(1 - t_g)]}{[C_d(1 - t_i) + 10^3(1 - t_g)]^2}$$

$$\times (1 - t_i)[(t_i - t)C_d + t_g 10^3] \tag{17}$$

Upon simplification, we find that the sign of dS/dC_d is determined by the following condition

$$(1 - t_g)(t_i - t) - t_g(1 - t_i) \gtreqless 0 \tag{18}$$

which can be written as

$$(1 - t_g)(1 - t) - (1 - t_i) \gtreqless 0 \tag{19}$$

Again we obtain the result that the firm and bondholders acting against each other, in order to maximize their respective post-tax wealth, are brought into collusion against the tax authorities through the market mechanism that determines security price—although, under this alternative tax system the functional relationship between the optimal coupon rate and the tax variables is different than the relationship derived in Section II.B.

C. Consideration of Bankruptcy

We now extend the analysis of Sections II.A and II.B to uncertainty by admitting the possibility of bankruptcy. Bankruptcy must be preceded by insolvency, which means that the firm is unable to meet cash obligations as they come due or because claims on the firm exceed the value of its assets. When a business is insolvent, its creditors must decide whether they will gain more by forcing the firm's liquidation or by allowing the firm to continue its operations after some reorganization. Bankruptcy is the name given to the legal procedure carried out by the courts under which the firm is liquidated and the proceeds are distributed among its creditors.

Let us consider the possibility of bankruptcy in light of our model. Suppose the amount that the firm has available at the end of the period (after the inclusion of all corporate tax savings) to distribute to bondholders is denoted by X, a variable that obeys a given probability distribution. If X falls short of the interest and principal on the debt, then we assume that the firm is forced into bankruptcy, and X less the costs incurred during the bankruptcy accrues to bondholders.

To simplify our analysis, we assume that bondholders consider the possibility of two states with respect to the repayment of their loan; either the principal and interest will be paid in full or bankruptcy will result, in which case the bondholder receives nothing. In other words, we consider the extreme cases of X greater than or equal to the coupon, plus face value of the debt and X less than the amount owed on the bonds outstanding. If the latter occurs, bankruptcy follows, which in turn implies that after all other claims and legal costs are satisfied nothing remains for the bondholder.

The preceding discussion and the additional assumption of risk-neutrality on the part of investors transforms the price-determining constraint into[4]

$$[1 - F(C + 10^3)][(1 - t_i)C + 10^3] + [F(C + 10^3)] \cdot t_g 10^3$$

$$= \left[1 - F\left(C_d \frac{10^3}{P} + \frac{10^6}{P} \right) \right] \left[(1 - t_i)C_d \frac{10^3}{P} + \frac{10^6}{P} - t_g\left(\frac{10^6}{P} - 10^3 \right) \right]$$

$$+ \left[F\left(C_d \frac{10^3}{P} + \frac{10^6}{P} \right) \right] t_g 10^3 \tag{20}$$

where $F(C + 10^3) = \text{probability}(X < C + 10^3)$, the probability of bankruptcy if the firm issues bonds at par, hereafter denoted by F_1, and $F(C_d(10^3/P) + (10^6/P)) = \text{probability}(X < C_d 10^3/P + 10^6/P)$, the probability of bankruptcy if firm issues bonds carrying a coupon equal to C_d, hereafter denoted by F_2. Note that if bankruptcy occurs, the bondholder receives only the tax saving due to the loss of his original investment; the amount of these savings being $t_g 10^3$. The constraint given by Eq. (20) may be rearranged to give

$$10^3/P = (1 - F_1)[C(1 - t_i) + 10^3(1 - t_g)]/(1 - F_2)[C_d(1 - t_i) + 10^3(1 - t_g)]$$
$$\tag{21}$$

Now let us consider what the firm's objective function should be when the possibility of bankruptcy is introduced into the system. In answering this question, we underline two obvious but important points. First, the firm can only increase shareholder wealth while it remains alive and, therefore, it should try to minimize the probability of bankruptcy. Second, while it is a "going concern" the firm would like to minimize after-tax payments to bondholders.

With these twin objectives in mind, we take another look at Eq. (1), or equivalently, (1a), which describes the firm's goal under certainty; namely, the minimization of after-tax payments to bondholders. Therefore,

$$\text{maximize } L = \max\{(C + 10^3)(1 - t) - (10^3/P)[(1 - t)(C_d + 10^3)]\} \tag{1a}$$

satisfies our second objective, the "going concern" goal. Now, what about

---

[4] The C value set is an amount such that $C/1000$ provides security investors with that expected rate of return which will maximize their expected utility of consumption flows over time, given that they must now part with \$1000 and taking into consideration the probability of not being paid.

Eq. (1a) with respect to the first objective mentioned above, the minimization of bankruptcy? Clearly, (1a) is maximized when $(C_d + 10^3)10^3/P$ is minimized. But selecting a C_d value that minimizes $(C_d + 10^3)10^3/P$ is equivalent to minimizing $F([C_d + 10^3]10^3/P)$, since F is monotonically increasing. Therefore, we see that the objective function used in the certainty case [(1) or (1a)] remains the relevant objective function in the uncertainty case.[5]

To find the optimal C_d value, we substitute (21) into (1a) to obtain

$$L = (C + 10^3)(1 - t) - (C_d + 10^3)(1 - t)$$
$$\times \frac{(1 - F_1)[C(1 - t_i) + 10^3(1 - t_g)]}{(1 - F_2)[C_d(1 - t_i) + 10^3(1 - t_g)]} \quad (22)$$

and then take the derivative of (22) with respect to C_d, which gives

$$\frac{dL}{dC_d} = -(1 - t)\frac{(1 - F_1)[C(1 - t_i) + 10^3(1 - t_g)]}{(1 - F_2)[C_d(1 - t_i) + 10^3(1 - t_g)]}$$
$$+ \frac{(C_d + 10^3)(1 - t)(1 - F_1)[C(1 - t_i) + 10^3(1 - t_g)]}{[(1 - F_2)[C_d(1 - t_i) + 10^3(1 - t_g)]]^2}$$
$$\cdot (1 - F_2)(1 - t_i) - F_2'[C_d(1 - t_i) + 10^3(1 - t_g)] \quad (23)$$

where

$$F_2' = (d/dC_d)F([C_d + 10^3]10^3/P)$$

The sign of (23) is determined by

$$-1 + \frac{(C_d + 10^3)\{(1 - F_2)(1 - t_i) - F_2' \cdot [C_d(1 - t_i) + 10^3(1 - t_g)]\}}{(1 - F_2)[C_d(1 - t_i) + 10^3(1 - t_g)]} \quad (24)$$

or

$$-1 + \frac{(C_d + 10^3)(1 - t_i)}{C_d(1 - t_i) + 10^3(1 - t_g)} - \frac{F_2'}{(1 - F_2)} \quad (24a)$$

Now,

$$(C_d + 10^3)(1 - t_i)/[C_d(1 - t_i) + 10^3(1 - t_g)] \le 1 \qquad \text{iff} \quad t_i \ge t_g$$

---

[5] This same objective function would result if we assumed that the firm is more optimistic with respect to solvency than are bondholders. For a compelling argument in favor of such an assumption, see Alchian and Demsetz [1, p. 789, footnote 14]. In our particular case, it would be necessary to assume that while bondholders see some chance of bankruptcy, the firm sees none.

Furthermore, we claim that $F'_2 \geq 0$ at the optimal point. To prove this, we assume that $F'_2 < 0$ and find a contradiction. We know that the probability of bankruptcy F_2 varies directly with $(C_d + 10^3)10^3/P$; thus $F'_2 < 0$ implies that if we raise C_d, then $(C_d + 10^3)10^3/P$ decreases. But from Eq. (1a) we know that if we are at the optimum, then $(C_d + 10^3)10^3/P \leq C + 10^3$, for we are at the point of minimum payments to bondholders. Therefore, the assumption of $F'_2 < 0$ at the optimum leads to a contradiction, since if $F'_2 < 0$, then payments to bondholders could be further reduced by increasing C_d.[6]

The conclusion of the above analysis is that the sign of (23) is negative for $t_i > t_g$. Hence the optimum is given by $C_d = 0$, the same result obtained in our certain world (see Section II.A).

III. Collusion under Uncertainty

Is the solution of the previous section identical to that which would arise from a coalition of firm and bondholder in an effort to reduce the total of their taxes?

To answer this question, we must first recognize that in the uncertainty case the coalition will not only wish to minimize their total tax bill while the firm remains solvent, but it also wishes to avoid bankruptcy. Recognition of the goal of avoiding bankruptcy follows from the basic assumption that both firm and bondholder are wealth maximizers. Therefore, while tax savings amount to $t_g 10^3$ if bankruptcy occurs, bankruptcy forces losses in wealth to the coalition totaling $10^3(1 - t_g)$ plus after-tax interest income to bondholders and equity investment and post-tax earnings to the firm (shareholders). Naturally, the losses exceed the savings.

Now we know, from the certainty collusion problem studied in Section II.B, that the coupon payment that minimizes the coalition's tax payments while the firm is a "going concern" is $C_d = 0$. Furthermore, from the uncertainty analysis in Section III.A, we know that a coupon rate of zero minimizes the probability of firm bankruptcy. Consequently, we find in our study of the optimal coupon rate under uncertainty that firm and bondholder, working through the price mechanism, behave as if they are in collusion to maximize the firm's chances of survival, while minimizing the total of their tax payments during the firm's existence.

---

[6] If $t_i = t_g$, then $F'_2 = 0$. The reader can prove it by the same reasoning used in the above paragraphs.

IV. Summary and Concluding Remarks

The main findings are:

(1)   The optimal coupon rate is determined by the taxes levied on the firm and the bondholder. Under the existing tax system, the firm's after-tax payments to bondholders are a minimum when the coupon payment is set equal to zero. Altering the tax system may change the optimum, but taxes still play the key role. When we look at an alternative tax system, the optimal coupon payment remains a corner solution—if it pays to issue bonds that command a premium, then the higher the coupon rate the better; if it is desirable to issue bonds that sell at a discount, then the coupon should be set equal to zero.

(2)   The very same optimal solution—a coupon rate of zero—is obtained for a coalition formed by firm and bondholders against the tax authorities. That is, the solution reached by the firm minimizing payments to bondholders while bondholders in turn act to minimize their wealth is identical to that which minimizes total tax payments by the above coalition. While in our primary problem the firm and bondholder each works in his own interest against the other party, the market mechanism that determines bond price produces the collusion-type solution. The market sets up a coalition between participants in the firm against the outer world. When the certainty assumption is relaxed and the possibility of bankruptcy considered, the above conclusions remain valid, given that investors are risk-neutral.

While we assumed risk-neutrality in our analysis, the results of this analysis seem to hold for risk averters, i.e., individuals with decreasing marginal utility. The reason is the coupon, $C_d = 0$, that minimizes the firm's after-tax payments while it is solvent, also minimizes the probability of bankruptcy. But if individuals who are risk-neutral favor such a solution, then risk averters will be no less desirous of this coupon rate, since it is the utility loss arising from bankruptcy that weighs heavily in the risk averter's expected utility calculation.

We do find that a great deal of corporate debt carries a zero coupon rate, e.g., banker's acceptances and commercial paper. However, we also observe firms issuing bonds with a positive coupon rate. How can this be explained in light of our analysis? First, given that a bond's duration exceeds one year, its rate of return fluctuations will be lower the higher the coupon rate it carries. Second, the tax authorities may set a lower limit on coupon payments. Finally, the firm may believe that its potential bondholders consist of tax-free institutions, e.g., pension funds, or tax paying individuals who can gain the advantage of the capital gains minus personal tax differential by selling the bond prior to the date of coupon payment, thus realizing the accrued interest as a capital gain (bond washing).

References

1. Alchian, A. A., and Demsetz, H., " Production, Information Costs, and Economic Organization," *American Economic Review* (December 1972).
2. "Canadian Tax Report," CCH Canadian Limited, Don Mills, Ontario (October 1974).
3. "A Digest of Principal Taxes: Japan," Ernst and Ernst, New York (September 1968).
4. McCarthy, C., Mann, B., Abbin, B., Gregory, W., and Lindgren, J., *The Federal Income Tax: Its Sources and Applications.* Englewood Cliffs, New Jersey: Prentice-Hall, 1968.
5. Telser, L. G., *Competition, Collusion, and Game Theory.* New York: Macmillan, 1971.
6. *World Tax Series: Taxation in France,* Harvard Law School, Commerce Clearing House, Chicago, Illinois, 1966.

AN OPTIMAL SCREENING POLICY FOR
R & D PROJECTS

Arie Melnik and Moshe A. Pollatschek

Technion—Israel Institute of Technology

I. Introduction

Our aim is to present a method suitable for the purpose of screening a large volume of research and development (R & D) projects. In order to accomplish this objective, we develop a method which uses stage approach for project screening. Our proposed procedure is applicable to a company, or a government agency, which faces the problem of screening a large number of projects. In principle, this method is also suitable for other screening problems (such as screening load applications, candidates for a job, etc.). Usually the screening process involves two types of policy decision: selection policy and budget policy. We shall focus on the selection problem and develop a systematic screening formula which is based on sequential analysis.[1]

This is a revised version of a paper presented at the NCRD Conference on Decision Making Under Uncertainty, March 1975.

[1] A discussion of R & D budget policy can be found in Albala [1], Kamien and Schwartz [9], and Rosen and Souder [11]. For a detailed discussion of the allocation of R & D expenditures, the use of quantitative methods and various selection criteria see Cetron *et al.* [3], Kamien and Schwartz [10], and Baker and Freeland [2]. These sources contain also an extensive bibliography on the use of quantitative models in the selection and development of R & D projects.

In our model, the R & D process is viewed as consisting of a number of stages. After each stage, the projects are examined and a decision is made on whether to continue or discontinue their development. As each project advances through the R & D stages, the magnitude of the required development resources increases. Therefore, it is important to make an appropriate (optimal) screening at the end of each stage in order to minimize overall R & D costs for a given number of projects or, alternatively, to maximize the number of successful projects to a total cost constraint.

The rigorous treatment of R & D problems started with the application of programming techniques to improve the selection of R & D project portfolios.[2] It continued with a dynamic, multistage analysis of individual projects. In this work, we do not concentrate on individual projects. Instead, our method is concerned with establishing a criterion for screening projects when cost parameters (assumed to be known) are taken explicitly into account. In the face of increasing costs, our objective is to identify the most promising R & D projects and allocate funds for their further development. In other words, we wish to develop a policy in order to answer the question of how many projects to approve at the end of each stage. Our decision variable is defined in terms of the proportion of projects which pass on from one R & D stage to another. Thus, we are interested in the proportion of projects which survive the entire R & D process and go on to commercial production.

Section II contains a description of the R & D process and a definition of the variables used in the subsequent analysis. We consider a population of project ideas which enter the R & D path. This population contains good projects whose (expected) present value is expected to be positive and projects whose expected net present value is negative. Our selection problem is defined as maximizing the number of good projects, given a fixed budget. In Section III we define a measure of screening performance and discuss its mathematical properties. Our model is specified in Section IV where we also derive an optimal selection policy for a case in which there is no budget constraint. In Section V we derive the optimal selection policy for the case of fixed budget. This policy is shown to be directly related to the overall budget, to the development costs per project at each stage, and to the number of projects under consideration.

---

[2] A typical example of the programming approach can be found in Charnes and Stedry [4]. For summary and analysis see Gear *et al.* [6]. For models which explicitly take into account the multistage nature of R & D projects see Gear and Lockett [7, 8]. They make use of a decision-free format to describe individual projects and then select an optimal subset of branches.

II. The R & D Process

The R & D process can be viewed as consisting of a number of stages. After each stage, projects are examined and a decision is made on whether to continue or discontinue their development. A schematic view of the process is presented in Fig. 1. The figure refers to four stages but since, conceptually, a larger number of stages may be considered, the model is developed for any number of stages.

Stage No.   1   2   3   4

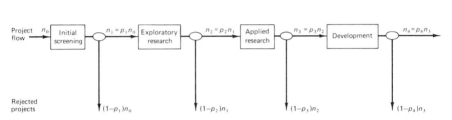

Fig. 1. R & D stages.

In Fig. 1, four typical stages of the R & D process are shown. We begin with the *initial screening* stage. To this stage, new project ideas are entered. Conceptually, every R & D project starts with an idea whose technical and commercial value is hardly known. In the initial screening stage, preliminary commercial and technological studies are made (e.g., surveys of the literature) in order to determine if a project is worthy of further development. In stage 2, *exploratory research* is conducted. This stage includes the definition of the new process or product (or their improvement), technological design and quantifications of the process' parameters. If the product is approved in principle, it goes on to stage 3 for *applied research*. In this stage, a detailed development of the product is carried out, including determination of its engineering design. The fourth stage includes detailed *development* work. This work consists of a pilot project supplemented with detailed engineering and marketing studies. At this stage, the design of the production plant is also considered and its investment costs as well as operating costs are measured. If a favorable decision is accepted after this stage, the product will go into commercial production.

Viewing the schematic R & D process in general, the circles after each stage i denote decision points. After a given stage is completed, a proportion p_i of the available projects is determined by the decision maker. This proportion $(0 < p_i < 1)$ represents the most promising portion of the projects which passed the preceding stage. If we denote n_i as the number of projects which enter stage $i + 1$ of the R & D process, then $n_i = p_i n_{i-1}$. Given that n_{i-1} projects have gone through stage i and given p_i, the remaining $(1 - p_i)n_{i-1}$ projects are discontinued at the ith decision point.

In Fig. 1, n_0 denotes the number of product ideas with which we start. After each stage some of them will advance to the next stage and some will be discontinued. After the fourth (and final) R & D stage, $n_4 = p_4 n_3$ projects will go into post-R & D production. Given n_0, the number of projects which survive the entire R & D process depends on p_i $(i = 1, 2, \ldots, k)$, which is, in turn, determined by the decision maker (after each stage is completed). In this work we are interested in formulating an optimal screening policy. In terms of Fig. 1, we wish to determine an optimal p $(i = 1, 2, \ldots, k)$.

By and large, each of the four stages depicted in Fig. 1 represents a fairly defined part of the entire R & D process. At each stage, investment costs of amount c_i are assessed against each project. For simplicity, we assume that each project costs the same as every other project which goes through stage i. As we progress from one stage to another, increased investment is required. Thus, in general, we expect $c_1 < c_2 < \cdots < c_k$ when k stages are considered.[3] This information in itself is not sufficient to determine the relative magnitude of the total cost of each R & D stage, because the number of projects reaching say, stage 4, has been greatly reduced by the mortality of projects in previous stages.

To facilitate the exposition, we assume that all projects passing through the R & D process are homogeneous by stage. By this we mean that each project costs the same as all the other projects which are processed with it in stage i. Eventually, a project may turn out to be a "good" project (in the sense that in the final analysis its net present value is positive) or a "bad" project [i.e., associated with a negative net present value (npv)]. Again, for the sake of simplicity, we assume that all the good projects are homogeneous in the sense of possessing the same net present value for each stage. The same assumption applies to the group of bad projects. This simplifying assumption permits us to ignore the ranking of all the projects (by their present value) at this stage and to focus instead on selecting those projects whose expected npv is positive.

Assume now that n_0 project ideas enter the first stage. Some of them will turn out in the end to be good projects ($npv > 0$) and others will prove to be bad ($npv < 0$). At each stage, the decision maker attempts to sort out the good projects from the bad ones. The precision of the selection depends on the amount of information available at the appropriate stage. In the first

---

[3] On the other hand, each subsequent stage decreases the degree of uncertainty with reference to its commercial success.

stages it is usually very difficult to sort out the good projects which should be further developed. Later on, as a project is developed, the quality of the data used to gauge its technical and commercial feasibility increases and it becomes easier to differentiate between good and bad projects. Therefore, we may conclude that the precision of the selection improves as we approach the final stages of the process. Another way to improve the selection is to invest more in each stage of the process. Our ability to differentiate between good and bad projects at stage i should be better (other things being equal) the higher the c_i (the research cost per projects at that stage).

Clearly, the selection of projects along the R & D sequential path can be improved by investing more in research and development. Basically, the problem is how to allocate resources along the R & D path (and determine p_i) in order to maximize the *npv* of the entire operation; that is, to maximize the sum (of *npv*) profits resulting from successful projects, and losses resulting from a production of bad projects and R & D expenses. This optimizing behavior is discussed in Section IV. In many cases, however—and this applies to government agencies as well as firms—the overall R & D budget is given as $\bar{C}$. In such cases the firm is interested in minimizing resources lost (in investment) in unsuccessful projects. This is the problem which we consider in Section V. There we analyze what would be $p_1, p_2, \ldots, p_k$ (and the allocation of resources among development stages) in order to maximize the number of good projects (i.e., net profit) when the R & D budget is given.[4]

III. A Definition of Screening Performance

Let g_i be the number of good projects whose net present value, after stage i, is expected to be positive; and g_0 be the number of good projects at the beginning of the entire R & D process. Since n_i is the total number of projects at stage i, by definition $g_i \leq n_i$.[5] Since the objective of the decision maker is to pass on the good projects (and reject the bad projects), his performance measure may be defined as $y_i = g_i/g_{i-1}$. If all the good projects emanating from stage $i - 1$ (that is, g_{i-1}) were identified at the time and managed to pass stage i successfully, then $g_i = g_{i-1}$, and $y_i = 1$. On the other hand if none of the good projects are passed at the stage, then $y = 0$. In general, $0 \leq y_i \leq 1$.

---

[4] We may define it as "how to reject the bad projects at the earliest possible stage and approve all the good projects in all the stages."

[5] Note that the total population of projects at each stage is n_i. This population is composed of g_i good projects and $(n_i - g_i)$ bad projects. The ideal situation occurs when $n_i = g_i$. In this situation none of the projects considered has a negative expected *npv*.

In the preceding section it was noted that the ability to identify desired projects depends on the amount invested at each stage. Therefore, y_i is a monotonously increasing function of c_i and p_i. The more we invest in examining each project at stage i (i.e., the higher the c_i) and the higher the proportion of projects which pass the stage, the higher is y_i.[6] If no investment is made at stage i such that $c_i = 0$, we cannot expect to select a large proportion of good projects. The selection without the particular information gained due to the investment in stage i is basically a pure random process, and in such a case we expect the same ratio among good projects as between bad projects.[7] Symbolically,

$$y_i = g_i/g_{i-1} = p_i \tag{1}$$

Another extreme is when unlimited funds are invested in each stage. In this case $c_i \to \infty$ and we expect that this extremely large investment will enable the decision maker to reject only bad projects and to pass only good projects. This case is expressed as

$$y_i = \frac{g_i}{g_{i-1}} = \begin{cases} (n_{i-1}/g_{i-1})p_i & \text{if } 0 \le p_i \le g_{i-1}/n_{i-1} \\ 1 & \text{if } 1 \ge p_i \ge g_{i-1}/n_{i-1} \end{cases} \tag{2}$$

Ordinarily, we expect an investment of amount $0 < c_i < \infty$ in each R & D stage. The resulting function $y_i = f_{c_i}(p_i)$, indexed by c_i, should therefore lie between Eqs. (1) and (2). Its nature is illustrated in Fig. 2. Equation (1) is given by the line AD and Eq. (2) is described by the broken line ABD. When an amount of $c_i^* > 0$ is invested in each project at stage i, a concave line is obtained and, as the amount increases to $c_i^{**} > c_i^*$, the line becomes closer to the line of Eq. (2).

The function $f_{c_i}(p_i)$ fulfills the following requirements (dropping the subscript):

(i) $f_c(p)$ is a continuous function of p
(ii) $f_c(0) = 0$
(iii) $f_c(1) = 1$
(iv) $f_c'(p) > 0$ for $0 \le p \le 1$ and $0 \le c < \infty$ (provided $f_c'(p)$ exists)
(v) $f_c''(p) \le 0$ for $0 \le p \le 1$ and $0 \le c < \infty$ (provided $f_c''(p)$ exists)
(vi) $\min[1, (n_{i-1}/g_{i-1})p] > f_c(p) > p$ for $0 \le p \le 1$ and $0 < c < \infty$
(vii) $0 < c^* < c^{**} < \infty \Rightarrow f_{c*}(p) < f_{c**}(p)$

---

[6] This argument has an intuitive appeal. Note that as the entire population of projects increases, at each stage, the number of good projects increases. Therefore, y_i should be an increasing function of p_i. In addition, given p_i, we expect that additional investment in each stage of the R & D process will improve the ability to identify good projects.

[7] When $c_i = 0$, $(g_i/n_i)/(g_{i-1}/n_{i-1}) = 1$ and, therefore, $y_i = g_i/g_{i-1} = n_i/n_{i-1} = p_i$ which is stated as Eq. (1).

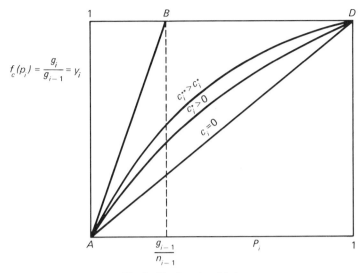

Fig. 2. The function $f_{c_i}(p_i)$.

(viii) $\lim\limits_{c \to 0} f_c(p) = p$

(ix) $\lim\limits_{c \to \infty} f_c(p) = \begin{cases} (n_{i-1}/g_{i-1})p & \text{if } 0 \le p \le g_{i-1}/n_{i-1} \\ 1 & \text{if } 1 \ge p \ge g_{i-1}/n_{i-1} \end{cases}$

Requirement (i) asserts the nature of the relationship between y_i and p_i. Specifically, no sudden improvement in y [or $f_c(p)$] is expected when an infinitesimal change occurs in p. Requirements (ii) and (iii) imply that if no project is admitted to the stage, then no good project is admitted, and that if the entire project population enters the ith stage, then all the good projects enter as well. According to (iv), $f_c(p)$ is an increasing function of p. As the proportion of total projects (that pass to the next stage) increases, so does the proportion of good projects. In (v) we specify that $f_c(p)$ is a concave function of p. The implication of this requirement, in terms of our analysis, is that as p increases, the corresponding rate of change of y decreases. If the selection process is at work, we should expect that most of the good projects are chosen first. Therefore, as we move on the p axis to the right, fewer good projects are left. Thus, at larger p values we shall pass more bad projects (compared to lower p values), and this phenomenon is expressed as requirement (v). Combining requirements (iv) and (v), we may state that while y increases with p, it does so at a declining rate. This statement implies "decreasing marginal returns" of y in terms of p.

Requirement (vi) indicates that $f_c(p)$ should be constrained by the triangle *ABD* (Fig. 2). Requirement (vii) is merely a compact statement of the notion that the bigger the investment in a R & D stage, the better is the quality of the selection of projects. In terms of Fig. 2 it says that the line associated with c_i^{**} should be higher in comparison to the line associated with c_i^*. Requirements (viii) and (ix) tells us that at the limits, when $c \to 0$ or ∞, $f_c(p)$ approaches Eq. (1) or (2), respectively.

By requirements (i), (ii), and (iv), the inverse of $f_c(p)$ exists (except for the extreme case when $c \to \infty$). If we denote this inverse as $h_c(y)$, then

$$p = h_c(y) \Leftrightarrow y = f_c(p)$$

The inverse function fulfills nine requirements parallel to the requirements fulfilled by $f_c(p)$. [The requirements of the inverse $h_c(y)$ are listed in the Appendix in the same order as requirements (i)–(ix).] In our case, it is mathematically more convenient to employ the inverse.

There are many functional relationships between p and y which fulfill the above requirements. One such function is

$$p = h_c(y) = (1 - \lambda_c)y^{\beta_c} + \lambda_c y, \tag{3}$$

where λ_c and β_c are two parameters such that $g_{i-1}/n_{i-1} \le \lambda_c \le 1$, and $\beta_c \ge 1$. Equation (3) is introduced here as an example of a (possible) specific relationship between p and y. We may observe that (3) satisfies requirements (i)–(vi), while (vii) is satisfied if β_c is an increasing function of c and λ_c is a decreasing function of c. Requirement (viii) is obtained if $\lim_{c \to 0} \lambda_c = 1$ and $\lim_{c \to 0} \beta_c = 1$, and condition (ix) obtains if $\lim_{c \to \infty} \lambda_c = g_{i-1}/n_{i-1}$ and $\lim_{c \to \infty} \beta = \infty$. The entire set of conditions is fulfilled for (3) if we assume (for the sake of illustration) that λ_c and β_c are defined by

$$\lambda_c = \frac{[1 + \mu(g_{i-1}/n_{i-1})c]}{(1 + \mu c)}, \qquad \beta_c = 1 + \alpha c \tag{4}$$

for some parameters $\alpha > 0$ and $\mu > 0$.

IV. The Model

We define V_i as the discounted value (if any) of the income of a project which is sold to others before the R & D is completed, for stages $i = 1, 2, \ldots, k$. By and large, bad projects are not expected to generate positive income for the unit engaged in R & D, and we do not expect it to sell good projects, so in most cases we expect V_i to be zero. However, occasionally it may be possible to sell a bad project to an interested party for a positive sum. We also define W to be the net discounted present value of a good project which goes into production and $\bar{W}$ as the present value of the loss generated by a bad project. We further let $F_i(n_{i-1}, g_{i-1})$, $i = 1, 2, \ldots, k$ be the maximum of the net present value of all the projects considered just before stage i, and it is a function of the number of projects, their distribution (good versus bad), and the magnitude of V, W, and $\bar{W}$. Thus, we include in F_i all the profits, losses, and R & D expenses which occur from stage i to (and including) the production stage.

Assume now that we are just before the stage of commercial investment implementation. That is to say, all k R & D stages have been passed. The total value of all the projects which passed through the final (kth) stage of development and which are about to enter commercial production is $F_{k+1}(n_k, g_k)$. This is the sum of (positive) income generated by good projects and (negative) expenditures caused by bad projects. More succinctly,

$$F_{k+1}(n_k, g_k) = Wg_k - \bar{W}(n_k - g_k) = (W + \bar{W})g_k - (\bar{W})n_k \qquad (5)$$

where g_k is the number of good projects which passed the k stages of the R & D process and $(n_k - g_k)$ is the corresponding number of bad projects.

Consider now the final R & D stage. This is the last stage before the research and development process is completed. We are about to enter the kth stage and the decision maker at that point wishes to maximize the value of total project population. The function to be maximized is

$$F_k(n_{k-1}, g_{k-1})$$
$$= \max_{1 \geq p_k \geq 0} \left[-c_k n_{k-1} + (1 - p_k)n_{k-1} V_k + F_{k+1}(p_k n_{k-1}, y_k g_{k-1}) \right] \quad (6)$$

The first term within the brackets stands for the development cost of stage k and the second term is the value of the projects that were sold to others. The third term in the maximand is the left-hand side of (5), written in the notations of stage k (rather than $k + 1$). Since the function relating y to p is single valued (Appendix), we can use $h_k(\cdot)$, instead of $f_k(\cdot)$, in which case (6) becomes

$$F_k(n_{k-1}, g_{k-1}) = \max_{0 \leq y_k \leq 1} \{ -c_k n_{k-1} + [1 - h_k(y_k)]n_{k-1} V_k$$
$$+ F_{k+1}[h_k(y_k)n_{k-1}, y_k g_{k-1}] \} \qquad (7)$$

Equation (6) or (7) holds not only for the kth stage, but also for stages $i = 1, 2, \ldots, k - 1$ with the appropriate change of notation. The maximum benefit from R & D is achieved upon maximization of $F_1(n_0, g_0)$. If we select the good projects before the first stage, net income from both R & D and production is maximized.

When (3) replaces $h_k(\cdot)$ and (5) is substituted for F_{k+1} in (7), the maximand is analytic and concave in y. Its derivative with respect to y is

$$g_{k-1}(W + \bar{W}) - n_{k-1}(V_k + \bar{W})[\lambda_c + (1 - \lambda_c)\beta_c y^{\beta_c - 1}] \tag{8}$$

From (8) we obtain the optimal y for stage k, y_k^*:

$$y_k^* = \begin{cases} \bar{y}_i & \text{if} & 0 \leq \bar{y} \leq 1 \\ 0 & \text{if} & \bar{y} < 0 \\ 1 & \text{if} & \bar{y} > 1 \end{cases} \tag{9}$$

where

$$\bar{y}_k = \left[\frac{\{[g_{k-1}(W + \bar{W})/n_{k-1}(V_k + \bar{W})] - \lambda_c\}}{\beta_c(1 - \lambda_c)} \right]^{1/(\beta_c - 1)}$$

Recalling the definition of y_i [Eq. (1)], it seems appropriate to note that $y_k^* = 1$ is an extreme case where all the good projects that entered stage $k - 1$ are also admitted to stage k. The other extreme is $y_k^* = 0$, in which none of the successful projects that entered stage $k - 1$ is approved for further R & D in stage k. Both extremes are unrealistic in practical situations. This conclusion can be obtained by investigating $\bar{y}$. By the definition of $\bar{y}_k$ and the fact that $\lambda_c < 1$, $\beta_c > 0$, and $y_k > 0$,

$$n_{k-1} V_k < g_{k-1} W - (n_{k-1} - g_{k-1})\bar{W} \tag{10}$$

This equation states that by selling projects in the middle of the R & D process, we expect to gain less than what could be obtained by further development, and eventually production, of the projects in hand.[8] This situation is always assumed to hold, hence $\bar{y}_k > 0$.

A similar line of reasoning may be applied to the other extreme case. If $\bar{y}_k = 1$, it means that too much money is spent on research at stage k. The maximal effort in stage k which is worthwhile yields the equality

$$\beta_c = \frac{[g_{k-1}(W + \bar{W})/n_{k-1}(V_c + \bar{W})] - \lambda_c}{(1 - \lambda_c)} \tag{11}$$

which is obtained by equaling $\bar{y}$ [in (9)] to one. If β_c, V_c, and λ_c are known functions of c, this yields an equation in c.

We therefore conclude that in any practical case $0 < \bar{y}_k < 1$, the optimal solutions is obtained according to the upper line on the right hand side of (9). The stages preceding k are computed by recursions in the typical manner

---

[8] If the reverse of (10) were to obtain, there is no point in continuing the R & D process and the firm might just as well discontinue its R & D operation.

of dynamic programming. One can maximize (6) or (7) when k is replaced by the proper index of the relevant stage. Obtaining the optimal solution becomes more complicated for stages prior to k, and we do not derive it here. We wish, however, to make the following comments about its derivation:

(a) It should be noted that the maximand, in each step, is a concave function. This follows from the fact that $h_i(\cdot)$ in convex and $F_{k+1}(\cdot, \cdot)$ is linear.

(b) For any given stage, $F_i(n_{i-1}, g_{i-1})$ is analytical if $0 \le \bar{y} \le 1$ and $\beta_c > 1$.[9] This follows from the fact that $F_{k-1}(\cdot, \cdot)$ and $h_i(\cdot)$ are analytical for each i, and y_i^* is also analytical.

(c) From the two observations above, it is clear that y_i^* is found by differentiating the maximand at each stage i and equating it to 0. The derivative is well defined by (b).

V. Optimization with Fixed Budget

Thus far we have dealt with optimizing the screening projects without a budget constraint [Eq. (9)]. We turn now to consider this optimization procedure when the overall budget is given. As before, there are k stages of research and development. If a project passes all k stages, it goes into commercial production, which is defined as stage $k + 1$. We shall assume that the firm allocates a fixed amount $\bar{C}$ for the development and production of a new product. This sum should in turn be allocated for the production and for the various R & D stages. Each product that goes into production (defined as stage $k + 1$) costs c_{k+1}, while the cost of R & D is c_i for each project which goes through stage i.

In order to obtain explicit results, we shall assume

$$f_c(p_i) = p_i^{\beta_c} \tag{12}$$

where $0 < \beta_c \le 1$. In terms of Fig. 2, when $\beta_c = 1$ we are on the straight line AD, and as β_c gets smaller it corresponds to increasingly curved lines lying above AD.[10] Given (12), the process begins, as before, with an inflow of n_0 (g_0 of which are good) projects to the first stage. We wish to maximize g_k, which is the number of good projects (i.e., with a positive present value) that

---

[9] $\bar{y}_i$ is the value for which the left derivative of the maximand (with respect to y) is nonnegative and the right derivative is nonpositive.

[10] Admittedly, Eq. (12) does not satisfy requirements (vi) and (ix). Nevertheless, for a wide range in the triangle ABD it may represent a good approximation to real-life situations, especially if g_{i-1}/n_{i-1} is small.

go into commercial production. Given n_0 and $\bar{C}$, our problem can be stated as:

$$\text{maximize} \quad g_k$$

$$\text{subject to} \quad n_0 c_1 + n_1 c_2 + \cdots + n_{k-1} c_k + n_k c_{k+1} \leq \bar{C} \qquad (13)$$

$$n_i = p_i n_{i-1}, \qquad i = 1, 2, \ldots, k \qquad (14)$$

$$g_i = g_{i-1} p_i \qquad (15)$$

each term on the left-hand side of (13) represents the total cost of a specific stage (which is the cost per project times the number of projects passing through the stage). Equation (14) defines the number of projects entering stage i. Equation (15) defines g_i, where the expression for $f_i(p_i)$ is substituted from (12), and $0 \leq p_i \leq 1$.

In order to bring the optimization problem to a more convenient form, we substitute (14) for the n_i terms in (13). We further substitute (15) to the maximand g_k and multiply it by $n_0^{\beta_1}/g_0$. Our optimization problem is now restated as:

$$\text{maximize} \quad (n_0^{\beta_1}/g_0)g_1(g_2/g_1)(g_3/g_2) \cdots (g_k/g_{k-1})$$

$$= (n_0 p_1)^{\beta_1} p_2^{\beta_2} p_3^{\beta_3} \cdots p_k^{\beta_k} \qquad (16)$$

$$\text{subject to} \quad a_1(n_0 p_1) + a_2(n_0 p_1)p_2$$

$$+ \cdots + a_k(n_0 p_1)p_2 \cdots p_k \leq 1 \qquad (17)$$

where $a_i = c_{i+1}/(\bar{C} - n_0 c_1)$, $i = 1, 2, \ldots, k$, and $n_0 p_1 > 0$, $1 \geq p_i > 0$, $i = 2, 3, \ldots, k$.

Defining now $x_1 = n_0 p_1$, $x_i = p_i x_{i-1}$, $i = 2, 3, \ldots, k$; we have the following geometric programming problem (see Duffin *et al.* [5], pp. 78–81)

$$\text{minimize} \quad x_i^{-\alpha_1} x_2^{-\alpha_2} \cdots x_k^{-\alpha_k} \qquad (18)$$

$$\text{subject to} \quad a_1 x_1 + a_2 x_2 + \cdots + a_k x_k \leq 1, \; x_i > 0$$

$$\text{for each } i \qquad (19)$$

$$\text{and} \qquad x_1 \geq x_2 \geq \cdots \geq x_k > 0 \qquad (20)$$

where $\alpha_i = \beta_i - \beta_{i+1}$, $i = 1, 2, \ldots, k - 1$ and $\alpha_k = \beta_k$. The constraint of (19) is straightforward, and the requirement in (20) follows from the requirement $1 \geq p > 0$. If (20) is not considered, the dual variables, δ_0 [corresponding to (18)] and δ_i [corresponding to the ith term of (19)], should then satisfy: $\delta_0 = 1$ and $\delta_i - \alpha_i \delta_0 = 0$. The solution for the dual is

$$\delta_i = \alpha_i = \beta_i - \beta_{i+1}, \qquad i = 1, 2, \ldots, k$$

In order to obtain a geometric programming solution, β_i must fulfill

$$\beta_1 \geq \beta_2 \geq \cdots \geq \beta_k \geq 0 \qquad (21)$$

According to the theory of geometric programming,

$$a_i x_i = \delta_i \Big/ \sum_{i=1}^{k} \delta_i = \alpha_i \Big/ \sum \alpha_i = (\beta_i - \beta_{i+1})/\beta_1, \qquad i = 1, 2, \ldots, k$$

At the optimum

$$x_i = \frac{\beta_i - \beta_{i+1}}{a_i \beta_1} = \frac{(\bar{C} - n_0 c_1)(\beta_i - \beta_{i+1})}{c_{i+1} \beta_1}$$

from which we get (upon making appropriate substitutions)

$$p_1 = [(\bar{C} - n_0 c_1)(\beta_1 - \beta_2)]/n_0 c_2 \beta_1 \qquad (22)$$

which should be smaller than 1, and

$$p_i = [(\beta_i - \beta_{i+1})/(\beta_{i-1} - \beta_i)](c_i/c_{i+1}) \qquad (23)$$

The p_i values in (22) and (23) are the optimal p levels. These are the selection ratios at each stage when the overall R & D and production budget is given. Note that if β_i decreases by a decreasing rate, then the first term in the right-hand side of (23) is smaller than 1. The second term in that equation is also smaller than 1 because $c_{i+1} > c_i$ (the cost per project per stage increases as we move to more advanced stages in the R & D process). Therefore, p_i is smaller than 1 and positive (which is the case in almost any situation),[11] if some plausible assumptions are made.

The optimal policy then is to choose the control variable p_1, for the first R & D stage. Having completed this first stage, subsequent optimal values of p (for the stages following stage 1) are found by (23). If (22) is not smaller than 1, and the optimal decision variable is $p_1 = 1$, then the second p becomes the first meaningful p in the sense that it fulfills $p_2 \leq 1$, and the subsequent analysis is as before.[12] When n_0, $\bar{C}$, and c_i are given, an optimal decision requires an empirical estimate (or a preconceived knowledge) of the value of β.

Appendix.   The Inverse of $f_c(p)$

As noted in the text, by requirements (i), (ii), and (iv), the inverse of $f_c(p)$ exists except in the case when $c \to \infty$. The purpose of this Appendix is to list

[11] Note also that (20) is assured if $p_i \leq 1$.
[12] Note that when $p_1 = 1$ is optimal, $p_2 = (\bar{C} - n_0 c_1 - n_0 c_2)(\beta_2 - \beta_3)/n_0 c_3 \beta_2 \leq 1$ replaces (22).

the nine requirements which the inverse fulfills. The requirements fulfilled by the inverse, $p = h_c(y)$, are listed in the same order as the nine requirements which appear for $y = f_c(p)$ in the text. They are:

(I) $h_c(y)$ is a continuous function of y for $c < \infty$

(II) $h_c(0) = 0$

(III) $h_c(1) = 1$

(IV) $h'_c(y) > 0$ [that is, $h_c(y)$ is an increasing function] for $0 \leq y \leq 1$, and $0 \leq c < \infty$

(V) $h''_c(y) \geq 0$ [that is, $h_c(y)$ is convex] for $0 \leq y \leq 1$ and $0 \leq c < \infty$

(VI) $y > h_c(y) > (g_{i-k}/n_{i-1})$ for $0 \leq y \leq 1$ and $0 < c < \infty$

(VII) $0 < c^* < c^{**} < \infty \Rightarrow h_{c*}(y) > h_{c**}(y)$

(VIII) $\lim\limits_{c \to 0} h^c(y) = y$

(IX) $\lim\limits_{c \to \infty} h_c(y) = \begin{cases} (g_{i-1}/n_{i-1})y & \text{if} \quad 0 \leq y < 1 \\ 1 & \text{if} \qquad y = 1 \end{cases}$

These requirements are equivalent to requirements (i)–(ix) which refer to the function $f_c(p)$.

References

1. Albala, A., "Stage Approach for Developing Budgeting Policy for R & D Projects," *OR, Statistics & Economic Mimeograph Series*, No. 144, Industrial & Management Eng., Israel Institute of Technology (January 1974).

2. Baker, N., and Freeland, J., "Recent Advances in R & D Benefit Measurement and Project Selection Methods," *Management Science* **21**, No. 10 (June 1975), 1164–1175.

3. Cetron, M. J., Martino, J., and Roepcke, L., "The Selection of R & D Program Content— Survey of Quantitative Methods," *IEEE Transaction on Engineering Management* **EM-14**, No. 1 (March 1967), 4–13.

4. Charnes, A., and Stedry, A. C., "A Change-Constrained Model for Real-Time Control in R & D Management," *Management Science* **12**, No. 8 (August 1966), B353–B362.

5. Duffin, R. J., Peterson, E. L., and Zener, C., *Geometric Programming*. New York: Wiley, 1967.

6. Gear, A. E., Lockett, A. G., and Pearson, A. W.: "An Analysis of Some Portfolio Selection Models for R & D," *IEEE Transactions on Engineering Management* **EM-18**, No. 2 (May 1971), 66–77.

7. Gear, A. E., and Lockett, A. G.: "A Dynamic Model of Some Multi-Stage Aspects of R & D Portfolios," *IEEE Transactions on Engineering Management* **EM-20**, No. 1 (February 1973a), 22–25.

8. Gear, A. E., and Lockett, A. G., "Representation and Analysis of Multi-Stage Problems in R & D," *Management Science* **15**, No. 8 (April 173b), 947–959.

9. Kamien, M. I., and Schwartz, N. L., "Expenditure Patterns for Risky R & D Projects," *Journal of Applied Probability* **8** (March 1971), 60–73.

10. Kamien, M. I., and Schwartz, N. L.: "Market Structure and Innovation: A Survey," *Journal of Economic Literature* **13**, No. 1 (March 1975), 1–37.

11. Rosen, E. M., and Souder, W. E.: "A Method for Allocating R & D Expenditures," *IEEE Transactions on Engineering Management* **EM-12**, No. 3 (September 1965), 87–93.

OPTIMAL INVESTMENT AND FINANCING PATTERNS UNDER ALTERNATIVE METHODS OF REGULATION

Edwin J. Elton and Martin J. Gruber

New York University

Introduction

Consideration of the intertemporal interdependencies of economic decisions has recently come to play an increasingly important role in the economic literature. One area where an intertemporal structure is especially important is in constructing a generalized model of firm valuation, financing, and investment. The purpose of this chapter is to construct such a model for a firm subject to regulation. We shall examine both the case where the regulatory constraint is continuously enforced and the case where there is a regulatory lag.

The framework adopted is that of a dynamic set of continuous time activities. Modigliani and Miller's [17, 18] definition of the value of stockholder wealth is assumed to hold at each moment in time. Investment opportunities are taken as exogenously determined. Given a criterion of maximizing the wealth of initial stockholders and given a generalized investment schedule, we derive optimal rates of capital accumulation, rates of earnings growth, and time paths of dividends, external equity, and additions to debt.

Differences in the optimum time path of these variables will be examined for the unregulated firm, the firm where the regulatory constraint is continuously enforced, and the firm with a lag in the enforcement of the constraint. In addition, we shall discuss the effect of these differences on the efficiency of the allocation of resources.

I. The Basic Structure

In order to analyze this problem, we must first define some symbols.

$S(t)$ market value of common equity at time t.

$s_n(t)$ the dollar amount of new floatation of common stock occurring at time t. New common stock is assumed to be issued ex-dividend.[1]

i interest rate on debt. It is assumed constant over time.

$b_N(t)$ dollar value of bonds issued at time t.

$K(t)$ book value of equity at time t.

$B(t)$ dollar value of bonds outstanding at time t.

ρ rate of return of equity holders of an all equity firm in a particular risk class.

$k(t)$ rate of return to equity holders at time t. When debt equals zero, $k(t) = \rho$.

$D(t)$ total dividends paid at time t.

τ corporate income tax rate.

$X^{\tau}(t)$ total earnings of the firm at time t net of economic depreciation, after tax, and before interest. X^{τ} thus includes the tax advantage of debt.

$r(I)$ average rate of return on new investment of amount I. $r(I)$ is defined after tax, but before interest. It thus incorporates any tax advantages associated with new debt.

$r_m(I)$ marginal rate of return on investment I.

r^* average rate of return when an optimum amount of new investment is undertaken by the regulated firm.

r' average rate of return when an optimum amount of new investment is undertaken by a nonregulated firm.

R the rate of return the firm is allowed to earn on its book value. R is defined in terms of after tax, before interest, earnings (X^{τ}).

In the rest of the paper we shall drop the time subscript except where it might lead to confusion and dots will be used to indicate derivatives (i.e., $\dot{S}$ is the change in S with respect to time).

---

[1] $s_N(t)$ and $b_N(t)$ are really rates of new security floatation in the continuous time formulation of the problem.

In order to derive a model that maximizes stockholder wealth, we need a valuation equation. In this chapter we shall use[2]

$$S(t) = [1/1 + k(t)][D(t) + S(t + 1) - s_N(t)]$$

where $k(t)$ is a function of $B(t)$ and $S(t)$. In continuous time

$$\dot{S} = kS - D + s_N \tag{1}$$

This equation is the standard valuation equation used in most of the economic literature. For example, it is the one used by Miller and Modigliani [17]. The behavioral assumption underlying it is that future policies of the firm are fully anticipated and capitalized.[3] Integration of Eq. (1) yields

$$S(0) = \int_0^\infty [D(w) - s_N(w)] \exp\left[-\int_0^w k(u)\, du\right] dw$$

where w and u are variables of integration. Notice that if k is a constant over time, the above equation becomes

$$S(0) = \int_0^\infty [D(w) - s_N(w)] e^{-kw}\, dw$$

Thus Eq. (1) is the differential equation underlying a valuation equation which equates the wealth of the current stockholders $S(0)$ with the present value of future dividends to the current stockholders. This valuation equation has been shown to be equivalent to valuation equations utilizing earnings and cash flows.[4]

Modigliani and Miller [18], under the assumption of perfect capital markets have shown that arbitrage will cause the single period after tax yield on common stocks to be[5]

$$\rho + (1 - \tau)(\rho - i)(B/S)$$

Elton and Gruber [8] have shown that this relationship is equally as valid for the firm subject to regulation. In the continuous time framework, this ex-

---

[2] Miller and Modigliani [17], Eq. (3). This is a standard valuation equation used in most analyses. A recent example is by Krouse [15]. Krouse's equation is identical, except that he allows the issuance of stock at other than market prices.

[3] For example, this implies that new investments at time zero do not lead to a readjustment of the value of the firm at time 1, since the value of this investment is already fully reflected in the current price.

[4] See Miller and Modigliani [17].

[5] A number, of alternative proofs of this are available. Hamada [11] and Hirshleifer [12] are two examples.

pression will still represent the after tax yield at any point in time, so the expression for after tax yield can be written as

$$k(t) = \rho + (1 - \tau)(\rho - i)(B(t)/S(t)) \tag{2}$$

where the after tax yield on equity at time t is seen to depend on the market value of debt and equity at time t.[6] Modigliani and Miller have shown that Eq. (2) implies that the firm should add as much debt as possible. Modigliani and Miller have argued that the firm was prevented from adding an unlimited amount of debt by institutional constraints on its debt-to-equity ratio. For regulated firms it is probably most reasonable to assume that the debt constraint is formulated in terms of the book value of the ratio of debt to equity.[7] In equation form this is

$$\theta \geq B(t)/K(t) \tag{3}$$

In order to analyze the firm policies, we must develop expressions to link firm decision variables with the parameters of the valuation equation. Dividends are determined by equating sources and uses. The firm is assumed to have three sources of funds: earinings, new equity, and new debt.[8] These funds can be used to pay interest, invest, and pay dividends. In an optimal feasible solution, the sources must equal the uses, or[9]

$$X^\tau + s_N + b_N = D + I + iB$$

Rearranging to solve for D yields

$$D = X^\tau + s_N + b_N - I - iB \tag{4}$$

While s_N, b_N, D, and I can be set at each point independent of what occurred at other times, B and X^τ are accumulations of previous decisions. We need expressions to show how they change at each point in time. The change in B is easy to state. The change in B is simply equal to the new debt, or

$$\dot{B} = b_N \tag{5}$$

---

[6] The assumption is being made that the basic level of interest rates and required yield on stock (under any given debt to equity ratio) are constant over time.

[7] In testimony on capital structure most attention seems to be given to measures of debt and equity in book terms. For an explanation of the effects of alternative formulations of the debt constraint for unregulated firms, see Elton et al. [10].

[8] Economic and real depreciation are assumed to be equal so that depreciation does not enter into this relationship.

[9] A feasible solution requires only that sources exceed uses. Inspection easily shows that surplus funds are nonoptimal, since their use (for example, as dividends) increases the objective function. Thus, cash is nonoptimal and the inequality can be stated as an equality.

Two equations will be used to express the change in earnings. Both incorporate assumptions concerning regulatory behavior. While there is no unique description of the regulatory process that fits all regulatory agencies at all points in time, there are some widely accepted principles.[10] It is generally accepted that the regulatory commission sets prices so that the firm's earnings are equal to an allowed rate of return on the rate base. The allowed rate of return is defined in terms of after tax, but before interest, earnings (X^τ). Thus, it incorporates the effect of debt on taxes.[11] The rate base is the book value of debt plus equity. We shall examine two variations of this basic model: one assuming the earnings constraint is continually enforced and one assuming it is enforced with a lag. If the regulatory constraint is continuously enforced, then the firm can never earn more than this allowed rate of return. It is easy to show that if $R < r'$, it is never optimum for the firm to earn less.[12]

Consequently, if regulation is continually enforced, then at each point in time the firm will earn R on its book value. A change in earnings can only take place if there has been a change in the book value of the firm and, in fact, the change in earnings must be equal to R times the change in book value. If regulation is continually enforced, then

$$\dot{X}^\tau = R(\dot{K} + b_N) \qquad \text{and} \qquad X^\tau = R(K + B) \tag{6}$$

Under this definition of regulation, the firm is free to select any group of investments it chooses as long as the average rate of return on the investments accepted is no larger than R. Now at any moment in time a firm will have an upper limit on the amount of investment it can take at some rate R.[13] Let us define the maximum amount of investment available at an average rate of R as I_{max}. Then the firm is constrained by

$$I \leq I_{max} \tag{7}$$

---

[10] Myers [20] provides an excellent description of the state of regulation.

[11] This definition of regulation has important implications for the effect of debt on earnings for the regulated firm. While earnings before interest and taxes are unchanged by an unregulated firm's financing mix, earnings before interest, but after taxes, are unchanged for the regulated firm. See Elton and Gruber [8] and Myers [20] for further discussion of this point.

[12] To earn less it must accept projects below the cost of funds, which lowers stockholder wealth. If $R > r'$, the firm's optimum course is to behave like a nonregulated firm. Hence, we will limit the discussion of this model of regulation to cases where $R < r'$. This point will be discussed in detail in Section II.

[13] If the regulations operate so as to guarantee the firm a rate of return R, then the firm should take an infinite amount of investment. We are assuming that while the regulator will lower prices so that the firm earns no more than R, it will not allow the firm to raise prices if the firm invests at a rate below R.

Another possible form of behavior by the regulatory agency is when the constraint on the rate of return on book value is enforced with some lag. Each period, the regulator adjusts earnings by some proportion of the difference between actual earnings and the allowed earnings on book value.[14] If C is the adjustment factor, earnings are adjusted by

$$C[R(K + B) - X^\tau]$$

Earnings can also change through new investment. The change in earnings due to new investment is assumed to be equal to the product of new investment (I) and the rate of return $r(I)$. The only restrictions placed on the return function is that it is a continuous decreasing function in I. This assumption is consistent with projects being ranked in order of decreasing return. Note that when there is regulatory lag, there is no reason to limit the amount of investment available, since it is no longer profitable for the firm to take all investments. Combining the change in earnings due to regulatory behavior and the change due to new investment, we have for the case of regulatory lag

$$\dot{X}^\tau = C[R(K + B) - X^\tau] + r(I)I \tag{8}$$

In stating an equation for $\dot{X}$ we have added a new variable (whose value is also an accumulation of past decisions), the book value of common equity K. Book value of common equity changes by the amount of new investment, less any associated debt financing. In equation form this is

$$\dot{K} = I - b_N \tag{9}$$

The optimal behavior of a firm over time can now be studied as a control problem with states S, K, and B, and controls s_n, b_n, and I. The objective function is[15]

$$\max S(0)$$

As discussed above, the equations governing the system are

Differential equations

$$\dot{S} = kS - D + s_N \tag{1}$$

[14] Other forms of regulatory lag are possible. The most common alternative assumption is that the adjustment is enforced periodically. This has intuitive appeal. However, its disadvantage is that it leads to model forms which are intractable except for very special cases (see Klevorick [13]).

[15] The objective function should really include an adjustment for changes in initial debt (see Elton *et al.* [10]). However, it can be shown that it is optimum for the firm to operate at the maximum debt equity ratio. In this case, no initial adjustment is necessary. Since we can ignore any initial adjustment with no loss in generality, and since it simplifies the exposition, we shall do so in this paper.

$$\dot{B} = b_N \tag{5}$$

$$\dot{K} = I - b_N \tag{9}$$

Equalities

$$k = \rho + (1 - \tau)(\rho - i)(B/S) \tag{2}$$

$$D = X^\tau + s_N + b_N - I - iB \tag{4}$$

The following debt equity constraint

$$\theta K - B \geq 0 \quad \text{(book constraint)} \tag{3}$$

One of the following regulatory constraints

$$X^\tau = R(K + B) \quad \text{(continuous enforcement)} \tag{6}$$

$$\dot{X}^\tau = C[R(K + B) - X^\tau] + r(I)I \quad \text{(regulatory lag)} \tag{9}$$

With continuous enforcement

$$I \leq I_{\max} \tag{7}$$

Initially, we shall add two further constraints: that dividends are nonnegative $(D \geq 0)$ and that new equity sales are nonnegative $(s_N \geq 0)$. Later these constraints will be shown to be redundant and will be dropped.

This formulation simply clarifies the problem as finding the time sequence of investment, new equity financing, and new debt financing, which maximizes the wealth of initial stockholders, given the regulatory constraint, the financing constraint, and the inability to pay negative dividends. The optimum time path of investments and sources of funds is to be jointly determined over time.

II. Analysis When Regulation Is Continuously Enforced

Initially we shall examine the optimal firm behavior when regulation is continuously enforced. The problem is solved using the maximum principle of Pontryagin et al. [21] and Mangasarian [16]. They proved that the necessary conditions of the maximum principle are also sufficient whenever the problem is convex. Clearly Mangasarian's results hold in our problem, and his formulation of the Maximum Principle is used below.

Let us construct the Lagrangian function.

$$L(t) = \psi_S(t)[k(t)S(t) - D(t) + s_N(t)] + \psi_B(t)b_N(t) + \psi_K(t)[I(t) - b_N(t)]$$
$$+ \gamma_1(t)D(t) + \gamma_2(t)s_N(t) + \gamma_3(t)[I_{\max} - I(t)] + \lambda(t)[\theta K(t) - B(t)] \tag{10}$$

ψ_S, ψ_B, and ψ_K are the adjoined variables associated with the differential Eqs. (1), (5), and (9), respectively. The values of the adjoined variables at time t can be interpreted as the values of the associated state variables at time t. Thus, $\psi_S(t)$ and $\psi_B(t)$ give the value (cost) of equity and debt at time t, respectively, and $\psi_K(t)$ gives the value of an additional dollar of book equity at time t. These values are determined in terms of the objective function (i.e., in terms of the wealth of initial shareholders). $\gamma_1(t)$, $\gamma_2(t)$, $\gamma_3(t)$, and $\lambda(t)$ are the dual variables associated with the constraints.

By the maximum principle for an optimal solution:

(1)   The adjoined variables should behave according to the following differential equations: $\dot{\psi}_S = -\partial L/\partial S$; $\dot{\psi}_B = -\partial L/\partial B$; $\dot{\psi}_K = -\partial L/\partial K$.

(2)   The transversality conditions (see Arrow and Kurz [1], pp. 45–51) imply that: $\psi_S(\infty) = 0$, $\psi_B(\infty) = 0$, and $\psi_K(\infty) = 0$.

(3)   Since at every moment of time, the Lagrangian function must be maximized with respect to the control variables $\partial L/\partial s_N = \partial L/\partial b_N = \partial L/\partial I = 0$.

(4)   In addition, $\lambda(t) \geq 0$ and $\lambda(t)[\theta K(t) - B(t)] = 0$.

These conditions are used in the appendix to derive the optimal solution. The properties of this solution allow us to determine the optimum valuation, investment, and financing of the firm. The initial value of the firm and the value of stockholder wealth in the continuous enforcement case is given by

$$S(0) = \frac{X^{\tau}(0)}{\rho} + \frac{(R - N)I}{\rho^2} + \frac{(\rho - i)\theta\tau}{\rho}K(0) - \theta K(0) \tag{11}$$

$$V(0) = S(0) + B(0) = \frac{X^{\tau}(0)}{\rho} + \frac{(R - N)I}{\rho^2} + \frac{(\rho - i)\tau\theta}{\rho}K(0) \tag{12}$$

where $X^{\tau}(0) = R[K(0) + B(0)] = R[K(0)(1 + \theta)]$.

The value of the firm is a function of the initial earnings, the allowed rate of return, the investment opportunities facing the firm, the institutional constraint on debt funds, and the tax savings on the firm's initial debt. Dividend policy is irrelevant, though the value of the firm was stated as the present value of all future dividends.

A. The Effect of R on Investment Behavior

The effect of the allowed rate of return R on the value of the firm and the firm's investment behavior can now be analyzed. Examining Eq. (A11) shows that as long as R exceeds the cost of funds, γ_3 is positive. A positive γ_3 implies that for a given R, the firm maximizes stockholder wealth by accepting the maximum amount of investment available at the rate R.[16] The reason for this can easily be seen from the valuation Eq. (11) and (12). As long as $R > N$, then $[(R - N)I]/\rho^2$ is positive, and for a given R, stockholder wealth is maximized by making I as large as possible ($I = I_{max}$). When $R = N$, the constraint on the maximum amount of investment is no longer binding and $\gamma_3 = 0$. An examination of Eqs. (11) and (12) shows that when R is equal to N, the terms containing I cancel out and neither the value of the firm nor the value of stockholder wealth is effected by the amount of investment taken. Regulation then has a disastrous side effect in that there is no incentive for the firm to take efficient investments.[17] If R is set below N, then from Eqs. (11) and (12) it is easy to see that the value of the firm is maximized by accepting no new investment. Thus, optimal investment behavior implies taking the maximum amount of investments available at the rate R if $R > N$ implies that the amount of investment is a matter of indifference if $R = N$ and implies no investment if $R < N$.

In order to see which investments are undertaken by the firm when $R > N$, let us examine the investment schedule. We shall assume that the investment schedule consists of projects ranked from best to worst by rate of return. Such an investment schedule is depicted in Fig. 1. Figure 1 shows the marginal rate of return $r_m(I)$ that can be earned as a function of I.

Since for any R we want to accept the maximum amount of investment, investments should be accepted along the investment schedule (from high return to lower return) until the average rate of return on the bundle of investments equals R. Equivalently, a value of I equal to I_{max} should be found so that

$$R = \frac{1}{I_{max}} \int_0^{I_{max}} r_m(I)\, dI$$

Differentiating by parts and applying Liebnetz's rule

$$\frac{dR}{dI_{max}} = \frac{1}{I_{max}} \left[-\frac{1}{I_{max}} \int_0^{I_{max}} r_m(I)\, dI + r_m(I_{max}) \right]$$

$$= \frac{1}{I_{max}} [-R + r_m(I_{max})] \tag{13}$$

Since the average rate of return is higher than the cutoff rate, $dR/dI_{max} < 0$

---

[16] An assumption underlying the Lagrangian was that it was optimal for the firm to operate at the R set by the regulators. Shortly, however, we shall see that this is true only if $R \leq r'$. The basic model and results are not applicable for $R > r'$.

[17] This is a common result of the Averch–Johnson literature. It is interesting, since $R = N$ has often been defined as the most effective form of regulation.

New Equity
Financing

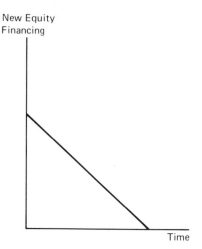

Time

Fig. 1. New equity financing over time.

and $dI_{max}/dR < 0$. Therefore, the amount of investment which can be accepted by the firm goes up as R is decreased.

If R is set equal to the average rate of return, the firm would earn in the absence of regulation, then the regulated firm would accept the same investments as the unregulated firm and regulation would have no effect.[18] As shown by Elton *et al.* [10], this involves accepting all investments yielding greater than the cost of funds. As R is lowered, more and more investments are accepted. As shown in Fig. 1, more investments imply a lower marginal rate of return. Thus, as R is lowered, the regulated firm accepts projects farther and farther below the cost of funds. As regulations become more effective in constraining profit, it also leads to a misallocation of resources in the form of an inefficiently heavy use of capital.

Since lowering R when R is less than r' implies acceptance of projects below the cost of funds, and since we are assuming that regulators do not increase prices, then there is no incentive for the firm with $R < r'$ not to operate at the maximum rate R. If $R > r'$, this is no longer true. Since $R = r'$ implies accepting all projects with return larger than the cost of funds, and since $\partial I_{max}/\partial R < 0$, then operating at the rate R where $R > r'$ implies rejecting projects yielding more than the cost of funds. However, an examination of the valuation equation shows that this is not optimal. Rather, it is optimal to accept all projects earning more than the cost of funds. Thus, if $R > r'$, the

---

[18] The unregulated firm also has an incentive to take the maximum amount of investments available at any average rate of return greater than the cost of capital. See Elton *et al.* [10].

regulated firm operates so as to earn r' on its investments, and thus acts as an unregulated firm.[19]

B. *The Financing Pattern of the Regulated Firm*

Having examined the investment behavior of the regulated firm, it remains to examine the implications of regulation for the optimal pattern of financing. In this section we shall restrict our discussion to the firm where $r' > R > N$. If $R > r'$, the firm acts as an unregulated firm, and this has already been analyzed in Elton *et al.* [10]. If $r' < N$, no investments would be accepted, and so no new financing would be undertaken.

As shown in the Appendix, it is always optimal for the firm to operate at the maximum debt/equity ratio. Furthermore, dividend policy is a matter of indifference. The fact that the value of stockholder wealth is unaffected by dividend policy does not imply that new equity is also a matter of indifference. As shown in the Appendix, the minimum new equity financing is

$$s_N(t) = \max\left\{0, \left[-C - \left(R - i\frac{\theta}{1+\theta}\right)It_{\max}\right]\right\} \tag{14}$$

where $C = R(1 + \theta)K(0) - I_{\max}/(1 + \theta) - i\theta K(0)$.

Assume for a moment that the second term is binding and, therefore, the minimum new equity financing is positive. In this case, the minimum amount of new equity will change at the rate

$$\frac{\partial s_N(t)}{\partial t} = -\left(R - i\frac{\theta}{i+\theta}\right)I_{\max} \tag{15}$$

Any level above this minimum level leaves the value of the firm unchanged. θ is greater than zero, thus $\theta/(1 + \theta)$ is less than 1. Since without loss of generality, R can be assumed to be larger than i, the minimum new equity financing declines with time until it is zero. The amount of new debt the firm will sell is easy to derive from Eqs. (5), (9), and (3):

$$b_N = \dot{K} = \theta(I_{\max} - b_N), \qquad b_N = I_{\max}\frac{\theta}{1+\theta} > 0 \tag{16}$$

Before leaving this section it remains to examine how the financing pattern changes with a change in the regulatory rate R. The change in the value of the firm over time can be seen from Eq. (12)

$$\dot{V} = \frac{RI_{\max}}{\rho}, \qquad \frac{\partial \dot{V}}{\partial R} = \left(I_{\max} + R\frac{\partial I_{\max}}{\partial R}\right)\frac{1}{\rho}$$

---

[19] An implication of this is that investment by the firm at an average rate of return less than the regulated rate is an indication of either ineffective regulation or nonoptimal management behavior.

The sign of $(I_{\max} + R\,\partial I_{\max}/\partial R)$ is easy to determine. From Eq. (13)

$$\frac{\partial I_{\max}}{\partial R} = \frac{I_{\max}}{-R + r_m(I_{\max})}$$

Therefore $I_{\max} + R\,\partial I_{\max}/\partial R$ is equal to

$$I_{\max} + \frac{RI_{\max}}{-R + r_m(I_{\max})}$$

Rearranging, we obtain

$$I_{\max}\left[1 + \frac{1}{-1 + r_m(I_{\max})/R}\right]$$

Since $r_m(I_{\max})/R$ is a number between zero and one, this expression is negative. Thus, an increase in R leads to a smaller increase in the value of the firm over time.

In order to examine the effect of the allowed rate of return on new equity financing, we must first examine its effect on the initial level of new equity financing and then on the rate of change of new equity financing over time. From Eq. (14)

$$\frac{\partial s_N(0)}{\partial R} = -\frac{\partial C}{\partial R} = -(1 + \theta_2)K(0) + \frac{1}{1 + \theta}\frac{\partial I_{\max}}{\partial R}$$

Since both terms on the right-hand side of this expression are negative, the higher the allowed rate of return, the lower will be the initial level of new equity financing.

From Eq. (15), the rate of change in the minimum new equity financing over time with changes in the allowable rate of return is

$$\frac{\partial(\partial s_N/\partial t)}{\partial R} = -\left(I_{\max} + R\frac{\partial I_{\max}}{\partial R} - i\frac{\theta}{1 + \theta}\frac{\partial I_{\max}}{\partial R}\right)$$

Using Eq. (13), the derivative is equal to

$$-I_{\max}\left[1 + \frac{\{R - i[\theta/(1 + \theta)]\}}{-R + r_m(I_{\max})}\right] \quad \text{or} \quad -I_{\max}\left[1 + \frac{R - i[\theta/(1 + \theta)]}{R - r_m(I_{\max})}\right]$$

The sign of the derivative thus depends on the magnitude of $i[\theta/(1 + \theta)]$ and $r(I_{\max}) \cdot [\theta/(1 + \theta)]$ is a number less than one. Since the firm should be able to invest an unlimited amount of funds at prevailing interest rates, $r_m(I_{\max}) \geq i$ and $r_m(I_{\max}) > i[\theta/(1 + \theta)]$. Thus, the derivative is positive and an increase in R decreases the speed with which minimum new equity financing declines to zero.

Finally, using Eq. (16), a change in the amount of debt due to a change in the regulated rate of return is

$$\partial b_N/\partial R = [\theta/(1 + \theta)](\partial I/\partial R)$$

Since $\partial I/\partial R$ is negative, the higher the regulated rate, the lower the amount of new debt the firm will sell.

Having analyzed the optimum financing, investment, and valuation for a firm subject to continuous regulation, we shall now examine the effect of introducing a lag into the regulating process.

III. Analysis with Regulatory Lag

With regulatory lag, the Lagrangian function becomes

$$L(t) = \psi_s(t)[k(t)S(t) - D(t) + s_N(t)] + \psi_B(t)b_N(t) + \psi_K(t)[I(t) - b_N(t)]$$
$$+ \psi_X(t)\{CR[K(t) + B(t)] - CX(t) + r(I)I(t)\} + \gamma_1(t)D(t) + \gamma_2 s_N(t)$$
$$+ \lambda(t)[\theta K(t) - B(t)] \tag{17}$$

In the appendix, we use the maximum principle to obtain values for the adjoined variables and conditions for the solution to be at the optimum.

A. The Appropriate Cutoff Rate for New Investment

From (A16), (A21), (A23), and (A24) we can derive a cutoff rate for new investment. Substituting (A21), (A23), and (A24) in (A19) and simplifying, we have

$$r_m(I) = N + C[(N - R)/\rho] \tag{18}$$

where $N = \rho - \tau(\rho - i)[\theta/(1 + \theta)]$. N is the rate of return security holders would expect to receive in the absence of regulation.[20] In the unregulated case, all investments with a post-tax, pre-interest yield higher than N increase the value of the firm, while those with a yield below N decrease the value of the firm. Hence, in the unregulated case, N is the firm's marginal cost of capital.[21] The introduction of regulation with a lag changes the cutoff rate by $C[(N - R)/\rho]$. Most descriptions of the regulatory process describe

[20] This is the same value that Modigliani and Miller [18] found for the after-tax earnings yield in their single period analysis of the unregulated firm. It is also identical to the rate found by Elton *et al.* [10] in their continuous time model of the unregulated firm. To compare the yield *m* of that paper with N of this paper, one must convert the definition of cash flows used in [10] to those used in this paper.

[21] This is not the expression Modigliani and Miller call the cutoff rate (see footnote 16 of [18]). Rather, it is the expression they call the after-tax earnings yield. The minimum return a project must earn for it to increase the value of the firm depends on how the cash flows are calculated (after tax, after interest charges, after tax advantage of debt, etc.). In [18] Modigliani and Miller use the cutoff rate to refer to the minimum rate of return that must be earned before the flows associated with debt financing. Hence, the term they call the cutoff rate is not N. This should not disturb the reader, since when cash flows are defined as they are in this paper, Modigliani and Miller's after-tax yield becomes the appropriate cutoff rate for new investment and this is identical to our term N.

R (the allowable rate of return) as being set above the firm's cost of capital. If $R > N$, then from Eq. (18) the marginal cutoff rate for new investment should lie below the firm's cost of capital.

If $R > N$, changes in the regulatory parameters have the following effects. An increase in R leads to more projects being accepted at rates farther and farther below the cost of capital. The greater the lag (the smaller is C), the closer the cutoff rate is to the cutoff rate for the unregulated firm.

If $R = N$, then the cutoff rates for the regulated firm and unregulated firm are identical. Unlike the static case (see Baumol and Klevorick [3]) or the case of continuous enforcement, investment policy is not a matter of complete indifference. Rather, the firm accepts all projects with a yield higher than its cost of capital (those projects that are economically justified), and rejects those with a yield below its cost of capital. The length of the regulatory lag has no effect on which projects are accepted.

If $R < N$, the cutoff rate for the regulated firm is above the cutoff rate for the unregulated firm. Once again, an increase in R leads to more projects being accepted, and the greater the lag, the closer the cutoff rate for the regulated firm approaches that of the unregulated firm.

Consequently, the only situation in which the firm's investment policy leads to an appropriate allocation from the point of view of the economy as a whole is when the regulated rate of return is equal to the cost of funds. In all other cases, optimum firm behavior calls for accepting projects that yield below the cost of funds or rejecting projects that yield above the cost of funds, and hence leads to a misallocation of resources. The reader should note that the introduction of a lag in the regulatory process has created a regulatory rate for which optimal firm behavior leads to an efficient allocation of resources. As we have seen earlier, when the regulatory process is binding at all times (continuous enforcement), resources will always be misallocated. Misallocation of resources is often discussed in terms of capital labor ratios. The same sort of effect is present in this model. To see this, we first must discuss the schedule of all investments facing the firm.

There are two possible explanations for an investment schedule that has projects yielding above N. First, high yield investment could simply reflect increases in the demand for the firm's product over time. Second, demand could remain constant and the presence of high yield investments could be reflecting changing technology. For most firms it is probably a combination of these reasons. However, it is instructive to assume for a moment that the investment schedule and high yield investments are only a result of changing technology, and that demand is constant through time.

In this case, the investment schedule can be properly viewed as resulting from the change in costs due to changes in the production function. Projects yielding more than the cost of funds are investments which save sufficient labor costs that their present value at the cost of funds is positive. Investments yielding less than the cost of funds are projects that save less in labor costs and whose present value is negative. For the firm to be at the optimum point on its production function, it should take all investments yielding more than the cost of funds, and reject all projects yielding less. Any other decision involves an incorrect capital–labor trade-off. Much of the regulatory literature deals with the efficiency of the capital–labor choice of regulated firms (the so-called Averich–Johnson conclusion). As just discussed, if $R = N$ and demand is held constant, the firm subject to regulatory lag would operate at an efficient point on its production schedule. However, if $R > N$, then the firm would use too much capital and if $R < N$, it would use too little. Thus, holding demand constant, the resolution of the argument concerning whether regulated firms have too much capital depends on the assumption concerning the relationship between R and N.

B. Regulation and Price Changes

The fact that optimum firm behavior can call for the selection of projects yielding less than the cost of funds does not imply that the regulatory agency is continually adjusting prices upward, so the firm can still obtain its allowed rate of return. To examine what price adjustments are made, we have to derive an equilibrium expression for $\dot{X}^\tau$. Examining Eq. (8) for $t = 0$ shows that

$$\dot{X}^\tau = CR[K(0) + B(0)] - CX^\tau(0) + r^*I \qquad (19)$$

and, for $t = 1$,

$$\dot{X}^\tau = CR[K(1) + B(1)] - CX^\tau(1) + r^*I$$
$$= CR[K(0) + B(0)] - CX^\tau(0) + CR(\dot{K} + \dot{B}) - CX^\tau + r^*I$$

In equilibrium these are equal. Equating these equations and rearranging yields

$$C\dot{X}^\tau = CR(\dot{K} + \dot{B}) \qquad \text{or} \qquad \dot{X}^\tau = RI \qquad \text{for} \quad C \neq 0$$

Substituting back into Eq. (19), we have

$$RI = C\{R[K(t) + B(t)] - X^\tau(t)\} + r^*I \qquad (20)$$

If RI is greater than r^*I, prices are continually being increased. If RI is smaller than r^*I, prices are continually being decreased.

We know from Eq. (18) that if $R = N$, then the cutoff rate for new investment is equal to N and r^* is greater than R. Thus, if R is set equal to the firm's cost of capital, prices will be continuously decreased over time. Now, if $R < N$, the cutoff rate for new investment from Eq. (18) goes up, and r^* is still larger than R, so prices will continue to be decreased over time for any $R \leq N$. However, as R is increased above N, the cutoff rate for new investment is lowered and eventually a value of R is reached for which $R > r^*$, and prices will have to be continuously increased over time. Let us define $\bar{r}$ as that value of r^* for which prices will not be lowered or raised over time. While we cannot set a value for $\bar{r}$ in the absence of a specific investment schedule, we can define a range within which it must lie. We have already seen that $\bar{r} > N$. We can now show that $\bar{r} < r'$. If R were equal to r', then for r^* to be equal to R, the cutoff rate for new investment would have to equal N. But, from Eq. (18) the cutoff rate is lower than N, since R is higher than N. Thus, $r^* < R$ and prices must be lowered over time; therefore, we know that $N < \bar{r} < r'$.

Investment in projects yielding more than the cost of funds creates an economic profit. This profit can be distributed in part to stockholders in the form of increased dividends and in part to consumers in the form of lower prices. To see how the potential benefits are split, let us examine earnings at time t. We know that

$$RI = CR[k(t) + B(t)] - CX^{\tau}(t) + r^*I$$

Rearranging and solving for $X(t)$ yields

$$X^{\tau}(t) = [(r^* - R)/C] + R[K(t) + B(t)]$$

Thus, earnings at time t are composed of two terms. The first term is the difference in earnings from the allowed rate of return because of regulatory lag. The second term is the allowed earnings. If there had been no regulation and the firm had continuously had investment opportunities of I at an average rate of r^*, then the firm's earnings would be $r^*[K(t) + B(t)]$. The difference between these two is the amount of the benefit from new investment that has been passed on to consumers in the form of lower prices. It is

$$\{(r^* - R)[K(t) + B(t)] - [(r^* - R)I/C]\}$$

As before, $r^* > R$ is a necessary condition for new investments to result in lower prices for consumers.[22]

In addition, consumers are being hurt because of investment below the cost of funds. The gain to consumers would be higher if the firm did not take projects below the cost of funds.

C. Regulation and Stockholder Wealth

In order to examine the effect of regulation on stockholder wealth, we must examine the valuation equation. In the Appendix, we derive the market

---

[22] The assumption being made is that $K(t) + B(t) > I/C$.

value of the firm [Eq. (A25)]. It is

$$S(0) + B(0) = \frac{X^\tau(0)}{\rho} + \frac{(R - N)I}{\rho^2} + \frac{\tau(\rho - i)}{\rho} B(0)$$

New investment also effects $X^\tau(0)$. From Eq. (8), we have

$$X^\tau(0) = (r^* - R)I/C + R[K(0) + B(0)]$$

Substituting this into the valuation equation yields

$$S(0) + B(0) = \frac{(r^* - R)I}{C\rho} + \frac{R[K(0) + B(0)]}{\rho} + \frac{(R - N)I}{\rho^2} + \frac{\tau(\rho - i)}{\rho} B(0) \quad (21)$$

This is identical to the valuation equation for the regulated firm with continuous enforcement except for the term $(r^* - R)I/C\rho$.

In the previous section we showed that the only value of R which leads to
the same investments by the firm subject to a lag and the firm with no lag is
$R = \bar{r}$. If $R = \bar{r}$, then $R = r^*$ and $(r^* - R)I/C\rho = 0$. Thus, if $R = \bar{r}$, the two
methods of regulation lead to the same value of of the firm. At all other
values of R, a different investment strategy is optimum. However, the firm
subject to a lag could select the same investments as the firm with no lag. As
just shown, such a choice leads to the same valuation. It does not make the
same choice only if an alternative is more profitable. Thus, if $R \neq \bar{r}$ the firm
subject to regulatory lag has a higher valuation than the firm subject to
continuous enforcement.

In order to compare this equation to the valuation equation for the unregulated firm presented in (10), we must change the definition of earnings
and return on new investment. When we make these changes, the valuation
equations are identical except for the term representing the benefit from new
investment.[23] In the regulated case, this term is $(R - N)I/\rho^2$. The term
representing the benefit from new investment for the unregulated firm is
$(r' - N)I'/\rho^2$.

No definitive statement can be made about the value of the unregulated
firm in relation to the value of the firm with regulatory lag, since the $X^\tau(0)$ is

---

[23] In particular, if r' is the average rate of return on new investment when the tax advantage
of debt is ignored and $X^{\tau'}(t)$ is the earnings after tax, but before the tax advantage of debt, then
$RI = r'I + itB(0)$ and $X^\tau(0) = X^{\tau'}(0) + itB(0)$. With these substitutions, the equation in the text
becomes

$$S(0) + B(0) = [X^{\tau'}(0)/\rho] + [(r' - m)I/\rho^2] + \tau B(0)$$

which is identical to the valuation equation for the unregulated case as shown in Elton *et al.*
[10].

a function of regulation and need not be the same. However, the relation can be specified for two cases. The first is the case where $X^{\tau}(0)$ is the same for the two firms (perhaps because regulation was just imposed). In this case, if the allowed rate of return is lower (higher) than the average rate of return on new investment for the unregulated firm, the value of the firm with regulatory lag is lower (higher).[24]

If investment always occurred at the same rate of return, then we could again compare the value of the regulated and unregulated firm. In this case, $X^{\tau}(0) = (r^* - R)I/C + R[K(0) + B(0)]$ for the firm subject to regulatory lag, and $X^{\tau}(0) = r'[K(0) + B(0)]$ for the unregulated firm. Since we expect the allowed regulatory rate of return to be set lower than the rate of return which a firm would earn in the absence of regulation, the regulated firm should have a lower value.[25]

D. The Effect of a Change in Regulatory Parameter on Firm Value

In this section we shall examine what happens to firm value when a regulatory agency changes one of the regulatory parameters. We start by examining the effect of a change in the allowed rate of return on the earnings of the firm. We initially assume that the firm does not change the investments it undertakes because of a change in R. If the allowed rate of return were not changed, then from Eq. (8),

$$\dot{X}^{\tau}(t) = C\{R[K(t) + B(t)] - X^{\tau}(t)\} + r^*I$$

---

[24] Note that this is not identical to the condition where consumers receive lower prices. If $r' > R > r^x$, consumers will have prices being increased and yet the wealth of the stockholders in the regulated firm is lower. This occurs because some new investment is below the cost of funds.

[25] The terms that are different are

$$\frac{(r^x - R)I}{C\rho} + \frac{R[K(0) + B(0)]}{\rho} + \frac{(R - N)I}{\rho^2}$$

for the regulated firm, and

$$\frac{r'[K(0) + B(0)]}{\rho} + \frac{(r' - N)I}{\rho^2}$$

for the unregulated firm. If $R > N$, then $r' > r^x$. By inspection, if $C > \rho$ and $r' \geq R \geq r^x$, then the value of the firm with regulatory lag is lower. However, if $R > r' > r^x$ (an unusual event), and the second and third terms of the expression for the regulated firm shown above are sufficiently larger than the first term, then the regulated firm has a higher value. If $N > R$, then the third term for the regulated firm is negative. Except for infinitesimal C, the regulated firm has a lower value.

Now, if we let $\dot{X}'$ represent the change in earnings subsequent to a change in the allowable rate of return by an amount Δ, then

$$X^{\tau\prime}(0) = C\{(R + \Delta)[K(0) + B(0)] - X^\tau(0)\} + r^*I = \dot{X}^\tau(0) + C\,\Delta[K(0)+B(0)]$$

$$X^{\tau\prime}(1) = C\{(R + \Delta)[K(1) + B(1)] - X^\tau(1) - C\,\Delta[K(0) + B(0)]\} + r^*I$$

$$= \dot{X}^\tau(1) + C\,\Delta[K(1) + B(1)] - C^2\,\Delta[K(0) + B(0)]$$

In general

$$X^{\tau\prime}(t) = \dot{X}^\tau(t) + C\,\Delta[K(t) + B(t)] - C^2\,\Delta[K(t-1) + B(t-1)]$$

$$+ C^3\,\Delta[K(t-2) + B(t-2)] - C^4\,\Delta[K(t-3) + B(t-3)] + \cdots$$

Since C is a number less than one, and $K(n) + B(n) \geq K(n-1) + B(n-1)$ for any n, $\dot{X}^{\tau\prime}(t)$ is larger than $\dot{X}^\tau(t)$ for any value of t. Thus, if the level of investments is left unchanged, all future earnings of the firm are increased by an increase in R. Now, since the firm has the option of leaving the level of investment the same, any change in the level of investment can only lead to a further increase in earnings and, hence, a further increase in the value of the firm. Consequently, an increase in the allowed rate of return must increase the value of the regulated firm.[26]

Now assume C is increased for a firm in equilibrium by an amount Δ. Once again we shall ignore changes in the investment policy.

$$\dot{X}^{\tau\prime}(0) = (C + \Delta)\{R[K(0) + B(0)] - X^\tau(0)\} + r^*I$$

$$= \dot{X}^\tau(0) + \Delta\{R[K(0) + B(0)] - X^\tau(0)\}$$

$$\dot{X}^{\tau\prime}(1) = (C + \Delta)\{R[K(1) + B(1)] - X^{\tau\prime}(1)\} + r^*I$$

$$= (C + \Delta)(R[K(1) + B(1)] - X^\tau(1)$$

$$- \Delta\{R[K(0) + B(0)] - X^\tau(0)\}) + r^*I$$

$$= \dot{X}^\tau(1) + \Delta\{R[K(1) + B(1)] - X^\tau(1)\}$$

$$- (C + \Delta)\,\Delta\{R[K(0) + B(0)] - X^\tau(0)\}$$

$$\dot{X}^{\tau\prime}(t) = \dot{X}^\tau(t) + \Delta\{R[K(t) + B(t)] - X^\tau(t)\}$$

$$- (C + \Delta)\,\Delta\{R[K(t-1) + B(t-1)] - X^\tau(t-1)\}$$

$$+ (C + \Delta)^2\,\Delta\{R[K(t-2) + B(t-2)] - X^\tau(t-2)\} \cdots$$

---

[26] We have not shown the converse. Examining $\dot{X}^\tau$ for a decrease in R shows that a decrease in R lowers earnings. However, changes in the optimum investment stream would have the opposite effect.

Since $C + \Delta$ is a number less than 1, $\dot{X}^{\tau'}(t)$ will be larger (smaller) than $\dot{X}^{\tau}(t)$ when $R[K(t) + B(t)]$ is larger (smaller) than $X^{\tau}(t)$. From previous analysis we know that $R[K(t) + B(t)] > X^{\tau}(t)$ implies that the regulations raise prices over time. Thus, if prices are being raised over time $R > r^*$, an increase in C raises earnings. On the other hand, if $R < r^*$ an increase in C lowers earnings.

Now let us introduce the effect of changing investment due to a change in the regulatory lag. We know that since the firm has the option of keeping investment unchanged, any change in investment must result in an increase in both earnings and the value of the firm. Because of this influence we can only make definitive statements about the effect of changing C on the value of the firm when the changes that take place in the absence of investment changes are positive. Thus, we can see that if $R > r^*$, an increase in C raises the value of the firm, while if $R < r^*$, a decrease in C raises the value of the firm. This result is intuitively appealing, for it implies that if the regulatory commission is lowering prices over time, the value of the firm is maximized by the largest regulatory lag. If it is raising prices, the value is maximized by the smallest regulatory lag. Having examined the effect of regulation on investment and the value of the firm, it remains to examine how regulation effects new financing.

E. New Financing and Regulation

As shown in the Appendix, the debt equity constraint is always binding. This is the same result found in the unregulated case and the case of continuous enforcement of the regulatory constraint. In the Appendix, we also show that dividend policy is irrelevant. However, this does not imply that new equity financing is irrelevant. The minimum new equity financing as given by equation (A24) is

$$s_N \geq \max\left[0, \left(-X^{\tau}(0) + \frac{I}{1 + \theta} + i\theta K(0)\right) - \left(RI - \frac{i\theta I}{1 + \theta}\right)t\right]$$

If the second term in the above equation is larger than zero, then new equity financing changes linearly over time by

$$\partial s_N(t)/\partial t = -I[R - i(\theta/1 + \theta)]$$

Since without loss of generality we can assume that the allowable rate of return is at least as high as the interest rate, the above expression is negative and new equity rates decrease linearly over time.

The effect of changes in regulatory parameters on the rate of new equity sales can now be determined:

$$\frac{\partial[\partial s_N(t)/\partial t]}{\partial R} = -I - R\frac{\partial I}{\partial R} + i\frac{\theta}{1+\theta}\frac{\partial I}{\partial R}$$

Since $\partial I/\partial R$ is greater than zero [from Eq. (18)] and R is greater than i, this derivative is negative. Thus, increases in the allowable rate of return lead to decreases in the rate of new equity sales over time.

In order to determine the effect of changes on the speed of regulatory adjustment on new equity sales, examine

$$\frac{\partial[\partial s_N(t)/\partial t]}{\partial C} = -R\frac{\partial I}{\partial C} + i\frac{\theta}{1+\theta}\frac{\partial I}{\partial C}$$

The change in investment with increases in C, $\partial I/\partial C$, is negative if $N > R$, is zero if $N = R$, and positive if $R > N$. Therefore, if $N > R$, the rate of change in new equity sales is increased with increases in C; if $N = R$, it is unchanged, and if $N < R$, it is decreased.

Now let us examine the effect of changes in regulatory parameters on new debt financing. We have already seen that the amount of new debt that will be sold at any instant in time is given by

$$b_N = I\theta/(1+\theta)$$

The change in new debt financing with a change in R is

$$\frac{\partial b_N}{\partial R} = \frac{\theta}{1+\theta}\frac{\partial I}{\partial R}$$

Since $\partial I/\partial R$ is positive, an increase in the allowed rate of return will result in an increase in new debt financing.

The change in new debt financing with a change in C is given by

$$\frac{\partial b_N}{\partial C} = \frac{\theta}{1+\theta}\frac{\partial I}{\partial C}$$

If $R > N$, then this derivative is positive and an increase in C leads to an increase in new debt financing. If $N = R$, then the derivative is zero and changes in C do not effect the new debt financing. Finally, if $N > R$, then the derivative is negative and an increase in C results in less new debt financing.

As a last step, we shall examine the change in the growth of the firm over time with changes in the regulatory parameters. From Eq. (A25), the change in the market value of the firm over time is

$$\dot{V} = \frac{RI}{\rho} + \frac{\tau(\rho - i)}{\rho}I\frac{\theta}{1+\theta}$$

The change in the value of the firm with a change in the allowed rate of return is

$$\frac{\partial \dot{V}}{\partial R} = \frac{I}{\rho} + \frac{R\, \partial I/\partial R}{\rho} + \frac{\tau(\rho - 1)}{\rho}\, \frac{\theta}{1 + \theta}\, \frac{\partial I}{\partial R}$$

Since $\partial I/\partial R$ is positive, the rate of change in the value of the firm will increase with increases in the allowed rate of return.

The change in the value of the firm with a change in C is

$$\frac{\partial \dot{V}}{\partial C} = \frac{R}{\rho}\, \frac{\partial I}{\partial C} + \frac{\tau(\rho - i)}{\rho}\, \frac{\theta}{1 + \theta}\, \frac{\partial I}{\partial R}$$

Thus, if $R > N$, an increase in C (a decrease in regulatory lag) increases the rate of change in the value of the firm, while if $R = N$, a change in C leaves the value of the firm unchanged, and finally, if $R < N$, a decrease in C (an increase in regulatory lag) increases the rate of change in the level of the firm.

IV. Conclusion

We have explored the implications of both instantaneous regulation and regulation with a lag on the time path of the optimum investment financing and valuation of the firm. In addition, the effect of changes in regulatory parameters on optimum firm behavior have been explored in great detail. Rather than review all the analytical expressions derived in the body of this chapter, to relate optimum firm behavior to the parameters of the regulatory process, let us just reiterate one of the important policy implications of our paper. Under continuous regulation there is no way that regulators can force a firm to allocate resources efficiently other than setting the regulatory rate equal to that which the firm would earn in the absence of regulation (in fact opting out of the regulatory business). However, the introduction of a lag into the regulatory process allows regulators considerable more flexibility in controlling the behavior of a regulated firm. In this case, setting the allowable rate of return equal to a firm's cost of capital results in the acceptance of all "efficient" projects by the firm. Furthermore, by combining changes in the regulatory rate with lags of different sizes, the regulatory agency can obtain alternative trade-offs between expansion of services (more investment) and the acceptance of efficient investments, as well as alternative allocation of the gains from efficient investment between shareholders and customers of the regulated firm. While the establishment of optimum levels for these trade-offs is beyond the scope of this paper, the analytical models presented herein should guide the regulators in setting a policy to obtain those goals which they deem desirable.

Appendix

A. Derivations for Regulation with Continuous Enforcement

Equation (10) represents the appropriate formulation of the Lagrangian for this problem. Applying the maximum principle, the following conditions should be satisfied at the optimum for all $t \in [0, \infty]$

$$\partial L/\partial s_N = \gamma_1 + \gamma_2 = 0 \tag{A1}$$

$$\partial L/\partial b_N = -\psi_S + \psi_B - \psi_K + \gamma_1 = 0 \tag{A2}$$

$$\partial L/\partial I = \psi_S + \psi_K - \gamma_1 - \gamma_3 = 0 \tag{A3}$$

where

$$\dot{\psi}_S = -\partial L/\partial S = -\rho \psi_S \tag{A4}$$

$$\dot{\psi}_B = -\partial L/\partial B = -[(1-\tau)\rho + i\tau]\psi_S + \lambda - (R-i)\gamma_1 + R\psi_S \tag{A5}$$

$$\dot{\psi}_K = -\partial L/\partial K = R\psi_S - R\gamma_1 - \theta\lambda \tag{A6}$$

Since γ_1 and γ_2 are nonnegative, (A1) implies that $\gamma_1 = \gamma_2 = 0$ and thus the nonnegativity constraints on dividends and new equity sales are redundant and γ_1 and γ_2 can be eliminated from the equations. Notice that $\dot{\psi}_B$ and $\dot{\psi}_K$ are functions of λ.

To proceed further with our analysis, it is necessary to get an explicit solution for λ. From (A2), we know that $-\dot{\psi}_S + \dot{\psi}_B - \dot{\psi}_K = 0$ for all t. Substituting from (A4), (A5), and (A6), we obtain

$$\rho\psi_S - (1-\tau)\rho\psi_S - i\tau\psi_S + R\psi_S + \lambda - R\psi_S + \theta\lambda$$

Solving for λ, we get

$$\lambda = [-\tau(\rho - i)/(1 + \theta)]\psi_S \tag{A7}$$

Substituting for λ in Eqs. (A4), (A5), and (A6) and solving the differential equations, using the transversality conditions, yields

$$\psi_S = -e^{-\rho t} \tag{A8}$$

$$\psi_B = \left[\frac{R-N}{\rho}\right] e^{-\rho t} \tag{A9}$$

$$\psi_K = \left[\frac{R}{\rho} + \frac{\tau(\rho - i)[\theta/(1 + \theta)]}{\rho}\right] e^{-\rho t} \tag{A10}$$

$$\gamma_3 = \frac{R-N}{\rho} e^{-\rho t} \tag{A11}$$

Next we derive the value of the firm and the value of the common stock. From Eq. (1), we know that

$$\dot{S} = kS - D + s_N$$

Substituting in Eq. (2) for k and in Eq. (4) for D, we have

$$\dot{S} = \rho S + (1 - \tau)\rho B + i\tau B - X^\tau - b_N + I$$

Since ψ_S is negative, λ is always positive and the debt equity constraint is binding in every period. Thus, $\theta K = B$, $b_N = I\theta/(1 + \theta)$ and $\dot{K} = I/(1 + \theta)$. Substituting these expressions and Eq. (6) into the above equation yields

$$\dot{S} = \rho S + [(1 - \tau)\rho + i\tau]\theta \left[K(0) + \frac{I}{1 + \theta} t \right] - R(K + B) - \frac{\theta I}{1 + \theta} + I$$

But $R[K(t) + B(t)]$ is equal to beginning earnings $R[K(0) + B(0)]$, plus the change in earnings due to new investment $[R(\dot{K} + b_N) = RI]$ times the number of periods of investment. Simplifying and substituting for $R(K + B)$ yields

$$\dot{S} = \rho S + [(1 - \tau)\rho + i\tau]\theta \left[K(0) + \frac{I}{1 + \theta} t \right] - X^\tau(0) - RIt + \frac{I}{1 + \theta}$$

Solving the differential equation yields

$$S(0) + B(0) = \frac{X^\tau(0)}{\rho} + \frac{(R - N)I}{\rho^2} + \frac{\tau(\rho - i)}{\rho} B(0) \tag{A12}$$

The minimum amount of new equity is also easy to derive. New equity financing must be sufficient to guarantee a nonnegative dividend. Since $\gamma_1 = 0$, additional new equity financing has no effect on the objective function. Thus, S_N must be sufficient for the following to be an equality.

$$D = R(K + B) + s_N + b_N - I - iB$$

Therefore

$$S_N \geq \max[0, -R(K + B) - b_N + I + iB]$$

However

$$-R(K + B) - b_N + I + iB = R[K(0) + B(0)] - R(\dot{K} + \dot{B})t - b_N + I$$

$$+ i\theta[K(0) + \dot{K}t]$$

Substituting $\theta I/(1 + \theta)$ for b_N, $I/(1 + \theta)$ for $\dot{K}$ and rearranging and simplifying yields

$$s_N \geq \max \left[0, \left\{ -R[K(0) + B(0)] + \frac{I}{(1 + \theta)} + i\theta K(0) \right\} - \left(RI - \frac{i\theta I}{1 + \theta} \right) t \right]$$
(A13)

B. *Analysis with Regulatory Lag*

The Lagrangian is now given by Eq. (17). As before, substituting for D and applying the maximum principle, we get

$$\frac{\partial L}{\partial s_N} = \gamma_1 + \gamma_2 = 0 \tag{A14}$$

$$\frac{\partial L}{\partial b_N} = -\psi_S + \psi_B - \psi_K + \gamma_1 = 0 \tag{A15}$$

$$\frac{\partial L}{\partial I} = \psi_S + \psi_K + \{r(I) + I\,[\partial r(I)/\partial I]\}\psi_X = 0 \tag{A16}$$

$$\dot{\psi}_S = -\partial L/\partial S = -\rho\psi_S \tag{A17}$$

$$\dot{\psi}_B = -\partial L/\partial B = -[(1 - \tau)\rho + i\tau]\psi_S + \lambda + i\gamma_1 - CR\psi_X \tag{A18}$$

$$\dot{\psi}_X = -\partial L/\partial X = \psi_S + C\psi_X - \gamma_1 \tag{A19}$$

$$\dot{\psi}_K = -\partial L/\partial K = -CR\psi_X - \theta\lambda \tag{A20}$$

As before, since γ_1 and γ_2 must be nonnegative, (A14) implies that $\gamma_1 = \gamma_2 = 0$, the nonnegativity constraints are redundant and γ_1 and γ_2 can be eliminated from all equations. Again to solve for λ, we notice that since (A15) holds for all t, then $-\dot{\psi}_S + \dot{\psi}_B - \dot{\psi}_K = 0$. Substituting from (A17), (A18), and (A20) yields

$$\lambda = [-\tau(\rho - i)/(1 + \theta)]\psi_S$$

Substituting for λ in the differential Eqs. (A17), (A18), (A19), and (A20), and using the appropriate transversality conditions as before with the additional conditions that $\psi_K(\infty) = 0$, yields

$$\psi_S = -e^{-\rho t} \tag{A21}$$

$$\psi_B = [-1 + CR/(\rho + C)\rho]e^{-\rho t} \tag{A22}$$

$$\psi_X = [1/(\rho + C)]e^{-\rho t} \tag{A23}$$

$$\psi_K = \left[\frac{CR}{\rho(\rho + C)} + \frac{\theta\tau(\rho - i)}{\rho(1 + \theta)} \right] e^{-\rho t} \tag{A24}$$

Next we derive the value of the firm. We know that

$$\dot{S} = kS - D + s_N$$

Substituting in Eq. (2) for k and in Eq. (4) for D and simplifying, we have

$$\dot{S} = \rho S + (1 - \tau)\rho B + i\tau B - X^\tau - b_N + I$$

Since ψ_S is negative, λ is always positive and the debt equity constant is binding in every period. Thus, as before, $\theta K = B$, $b_N = \theta I/(1 + \theta)$, and $\dot{K} = I/(1 + \theta)$. Utilizing these equations, we have

$$\dot{S} = \rho S + [(1 - \tau)\rho + i\tau]\theta \left[K(0) + \frac{I}{1 + \theta} t \right] - X^\tau(0) - \dot{X}t - \frac{\theta I}{1 + \theta} + I$$

As discussed in the text, $\dot{X}^\tau = RI$. Utilizing this and solving the differential equation, we have

$$S(0) + B(0) = \frac{X^\tau(0)}{\rho} + \frac{(R - N)I}{\rho^2} + \frac{\tau(\rho - i)}{\rho} B(0) \qquad (A25)$$

The minimum amount of new equity must be sufficient to guarantee a nonnegative dividend. Since $\gamma_1 = 0$, any additional new equity financing leaves the objective function unaffected. Therefore

$$s_N(t) \geq \max(0, -X^\tau - b_N + I + iB) \qquad (A26)$$

Substituting $I/(1 + \theta)$ for $\dot{K}$, $\theta I/(1 + \theta)$ for b_N, and RI for $\dot{X}^\tau$ and simplifying yields

$$s_N(t) \geq \max \left[0, \left\{ \left[-X^\tau(0) + \frac{I}{1 + \theta} + i\theta K(0) \right] - \left(RI - \frac{i\theta I}{1 + \theta} \right) t \right\} \right] \qquad (A27)$$

References

1. Arrow, K., and Kurz, M., *Public Investment, the Rate of Return, and Optimal Fiscal Policy.* Baltimore, Maryland: Johns Hopkins Press, 1970.
2. Bailey, E., and Coleman, R., "The Effect of Lagged Regulation in an Averch–Johnson Model," *Bell Journal of Economics and Management Science* **2**, No. 1 (Spring, 1971), 278–293.
3. Baumol, W. J., and Klevorick, A., "Input Choices and Rate of Return Regulation: An Overview of the Discussion," *Bell Journal of Economics and Management Science* **1**, No. 2 (Autumn 1972), 544–568.
4. Davis, B. E., and Sparrow, F. T., "Valuation Models in Regulation," *Bell Journal of Economics and Management Science* **3**, No. 2 (Autumn 1972), 544–568.
5. Davis, E. G., "Investment and Rate of Return for the Regulated Firm," *Bell Journal of Economics and Management Science* **1**, No. 1 (Autumn 1970), 245–270.
6. Davis, E. G., "A Dynamic Model of the Regulated Firm with a Price Adjustment Mechanism," *Bell Journal of Economics and Management Science* **4**, No. 1 (Spring 1973), 270–283.

7. Dorfman, R., "An Economic Interpretation of Optimal Capital Theory," *American Economic Review* **59**, No. 5 (December 1969), 817–831.

8. Elton, E. J., and Gruber, M. J., "Valuation and the Cost of Capital for Regulated Industries," *Journal of Finance* (June 1971).

9. Elton, E. J., and Gruber, M. J., "Valuation and the Cost of Capital for Regulated Industries—Further Results," *Journal of Finance* (December 1973).

10. Elton, E. J., Gruber, M. J., and Lieber, Z., "The Optimal Investment, Financing, and Valuation of the Firm: An Intertemporal Analysis," unpublished manuscript.

11. Hamada, R., "Portfolio Analysis Market Equilibrium and Corporate Finance," *Journal of Finance* **24**, No. 1 (March 1969), 13–31.

12. Hirschlaefer, J., "Investment Decisions under Uncertainty: Choice Theoretic Approaches," *Quarterly Journal of Econojics* **79** (November 1965), 509–536.

13. Klevorick, A., "The Behavior of a Firm Subject to Stochastic Regulatory Review," *Bell Journal of Economics and Management Science* **4**, No. 1 (Spring 1973), 57–89.

14. Krouse, C., "Optimal Financing and Capital Structure Programs for the Firm," *Journal of Finance*, Vol. XXVIII (June, 1958), 1057–1071.

15. Krouse, C., "On the Theory of Optimal Investment Dividends and Growth in the Firm," *American Economic Review* **43**, No. 3 (June 1973).

16. Mangasarian, O. L., "Sufficient Conditions for the Optimal Control of Nonlinear Systems," *SIAM Journal of Control* **IV** (1966), 139–152.

17. Miller, M., and Modigliani, F., "Dividend Policy Growth and the Valuation of Shares," *Journal of Business* **34** (October 1961), 411–433.

18. Modigliani, F., and Miller, M. "Corporate Income Taxes and the Cost of Capital: A Correction," *American Economic Review* **53** (June 1963), 433–443.

19. Modigliani, F., and Miller, M., "The Cost of Capital Corporation Finance and the Theory of Investments," *American Economic Review* **48** (June 1958), 261–297.

20. Myers, S., "A Simple Model of Firm Behavior Under Regulation and Uncertainty," *Bell Journal of Economics and Management Science* **4**, No. 1 (Spring 1973), 304–316.

21. Pontryagin, L. S., Boltyanskii, V. G., Gamkrelidze, R. V., and Mishchenko, E. F., *The Mathematical Theory of Optimal Processes*. New York: Wiley and Sons, 1962.

AUTHOR INDEX

Numbers in parentheses are reference numbers and indicate that an author's work is referred to although his name is not cited in the text. Numbers in italics show the page on which the complete reference is listed.

SUBJECT INDEX

A
B 7
C 8
D 9
E 0
F 1
G 2
H 3
I 4
J 5